The Home-Baking Cookbook

Written & Illustrated by Natalie G. Sylvester

Grosset & Dunlap
A Filmways Company
Publishers · New York

Copyright © 1973 by Natalie G. Sylvester
All rights reserved
Published simultaneously in Canada
Library of Congress Catalog Card
          Number: 73-7494
ISBN: 0-448-02208-7
1978 Printing
Printed in the United States of America

Contents

Cookies	7
Squares	55
Pies	101
Yeast Breads	197
Quick Breads	247
Index	295

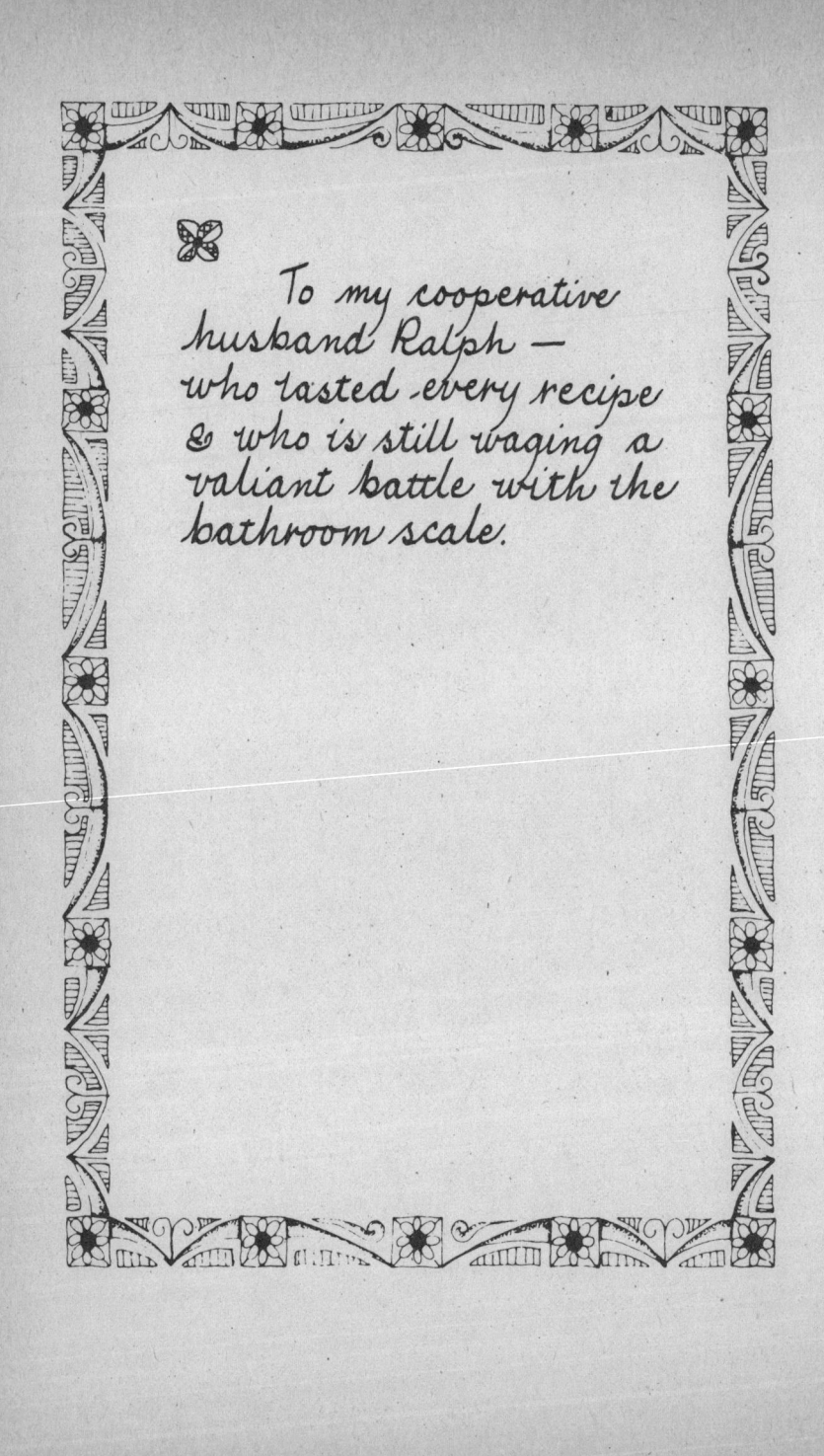

To my cooperative
husband Ralph —
who tasted every recipe
& who is still waging a
valiant battle with the
bathroom scale.

Acknowledgment

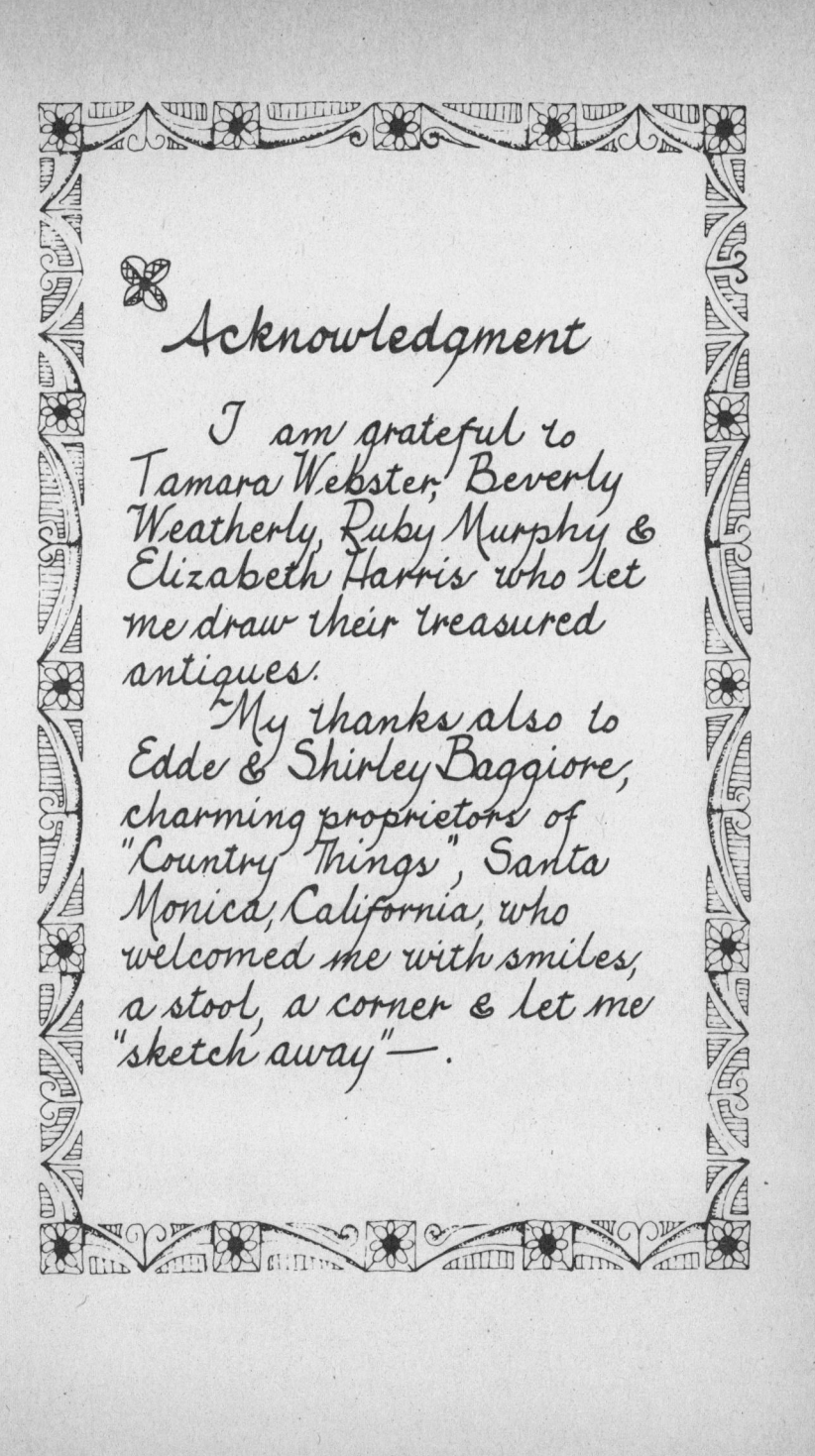

I am grateful to Tamara Webster, Beverly Weatherly, Ruby Murphy & Elizabeth Harris who let me draw their treasured antiques.

My thanks also to Edde & Shirley Baggiore, charming proprietors of "Country Things", Santa Monica, California, who welcomed me with smiles, a stool, a corner & let me "sketch away"—.

Anise Drops

3 eggs (be sure they are at room temp.)
1 cup + 2 Tblsp. sugar
1¾ cups flour
½ tsp. baking powder
½ tsp. salt
1 tsp. anise extract

Beat eggs until fluffy. Add sugar gradually & beating constantly. Beat for 20 minutes. Sift flour, baking powder & salt. Add to egg mixture. Beat 3 minutes more. Add anise extract. Drop by teaspoonfuls on well-greased & floured cookie sheets. Let stand overnight to dry. Bake at 325° about 10 minutes - until cream color but not brown. Makes 90 cookies, 1½" in diameter.

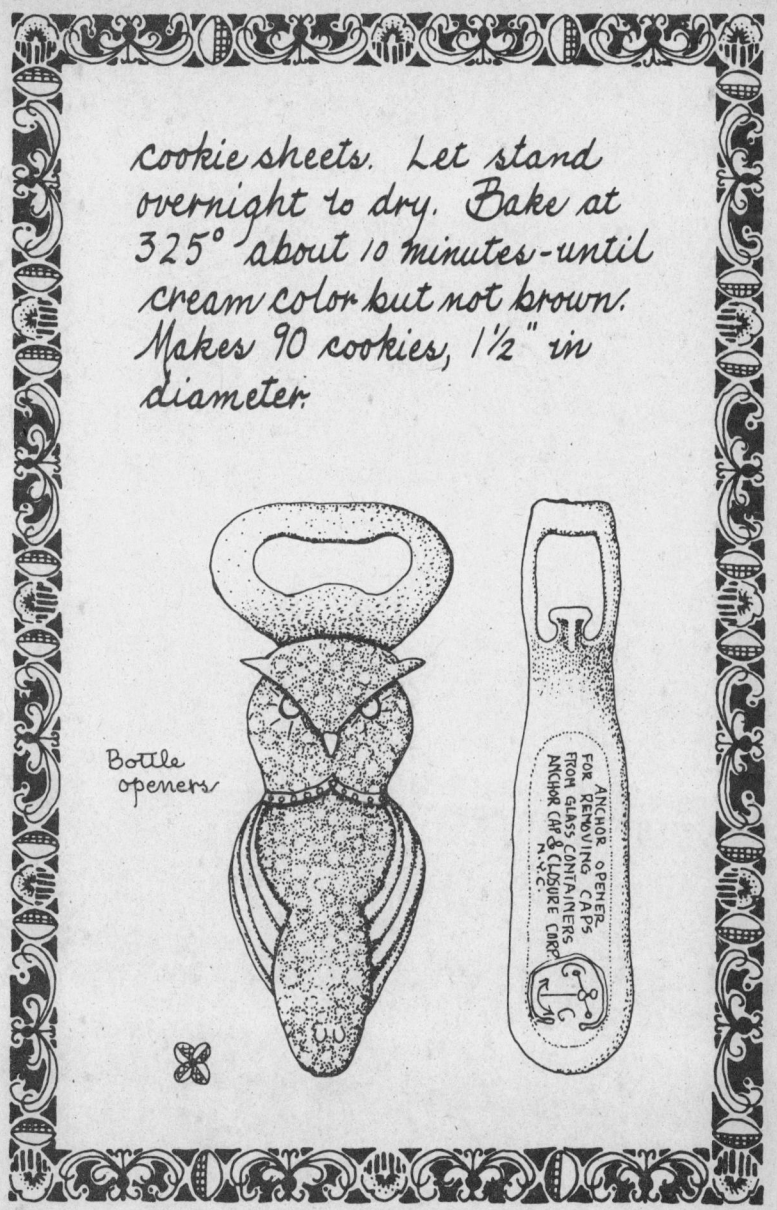

Bottle openers

Butter Nut Cookies

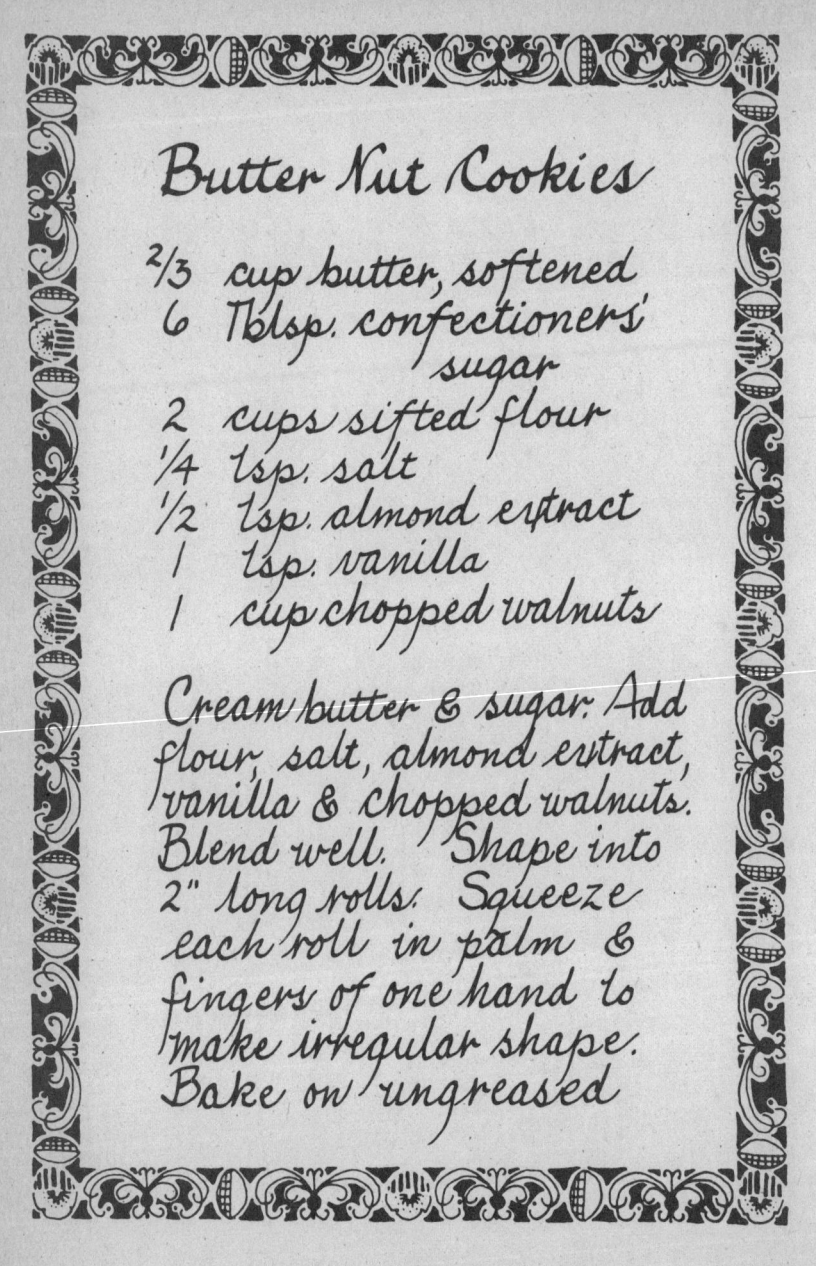

2/3 cup butter, softened
6 Tblsp. confectioners' sugar
2 cups sifted flour
1/4 tsp. salt
1/2 tsp. almond extract
1 tsp. vanilla
1 cup chopped walnuts

Cream butter & sugar. Add flour, salt, almond extract, vanilla & chopped walnuts. Blend well. Shape into 2" long rolls. Squeeze each roll in palm & fingers of one hand to make irregular shape. Bake on ungreased cookie sheet in a 350° oven, about 15 minutes. Makes about 3½ dozen.

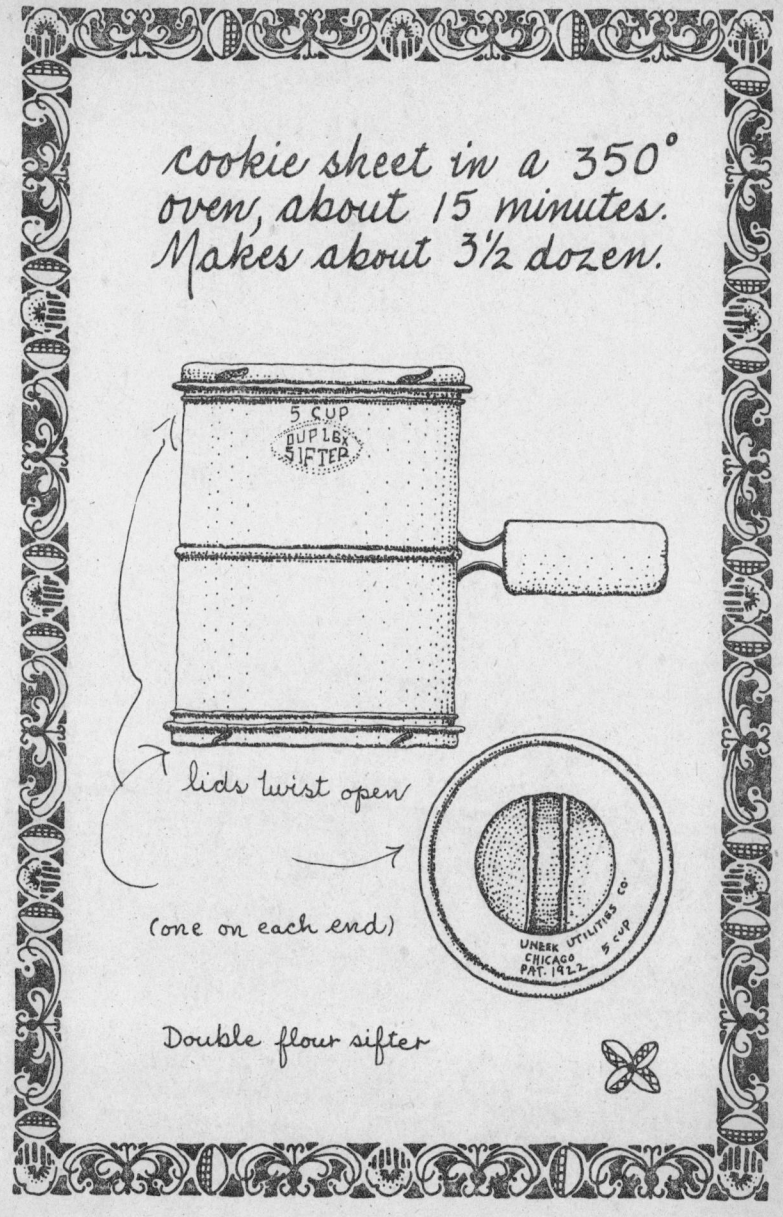

lids twist open
(one on each end)

Double flour sifter

Caraway Cookies

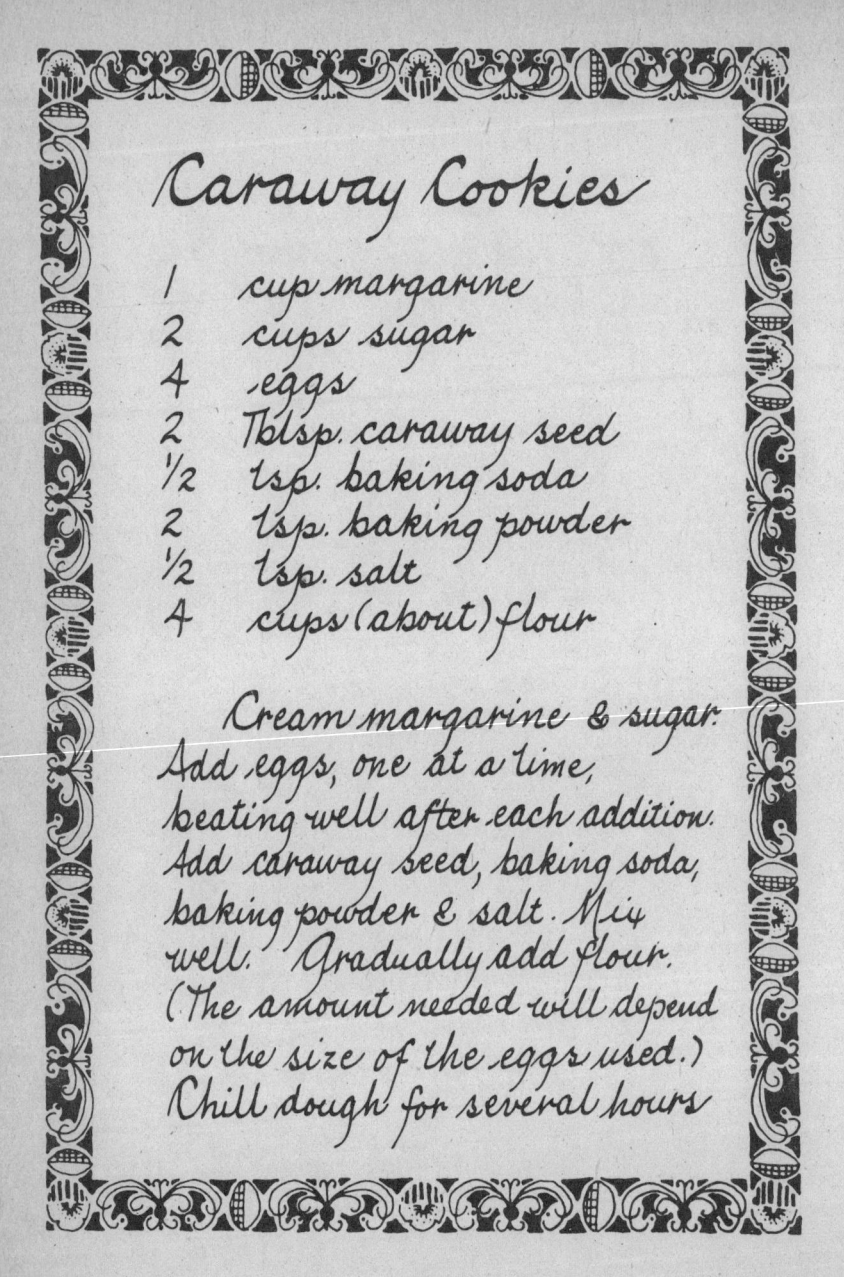

1 cup margarine
2 cups sugar
4 eggs
2 Tblsp. caraway seed
½ tsp. baking soda
2 tsp. baking powder
½ tsp. salt
4 cups (about) flour

Cream margarine & sugar. Add eggs, one at a time, beating well after each addition. Add caraway seed, baking soda, baking powder & salt. Mix well. Gradually add flour. (The amount needed will depend on the size of the eggs used.) Chill dough for several hours

in refrigerator. Roll out on floured board to 1/8" thickness. Cut with cookie cutter. Place on greased cookie sheet. Bake at 375° about 10 min.
              Makes 6 dozen.

Wire egg basket

Carrot Cookies

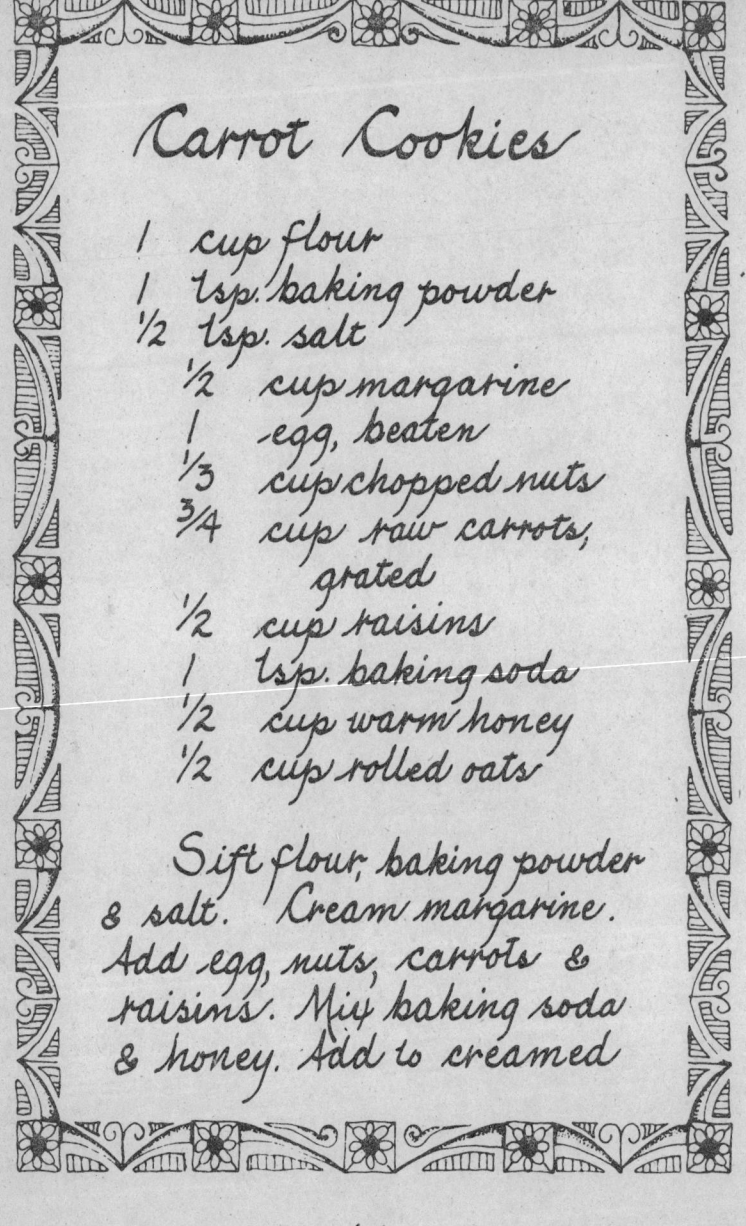

- 1 cup flour
- 1 tsp. baking powder
- ½ tsp. salt
- ½ cup margarine
- 1 egg, beaten
- ⅓ cup chopped nuts
- ¾ cup raw carrots, grated
- ½ cup raisins
- 1 tsp. baking soda
- ½ cup warm honey
- ½ cup rolled oats

Sift flour, baking powder & salt. Cream margarine. Add egg, nuts, carrots & raisins. Mix baking soda & honey. Add to creamed

mixture. Add sifted dry ingredients & rolled oats. Mix until well blended. Drop by teaspoonfuls on greased cookie sheet. Bake at 350° for 12-15 min.   Makes 6 doz.
✤ This is a very rich cookie, so make bite-size.

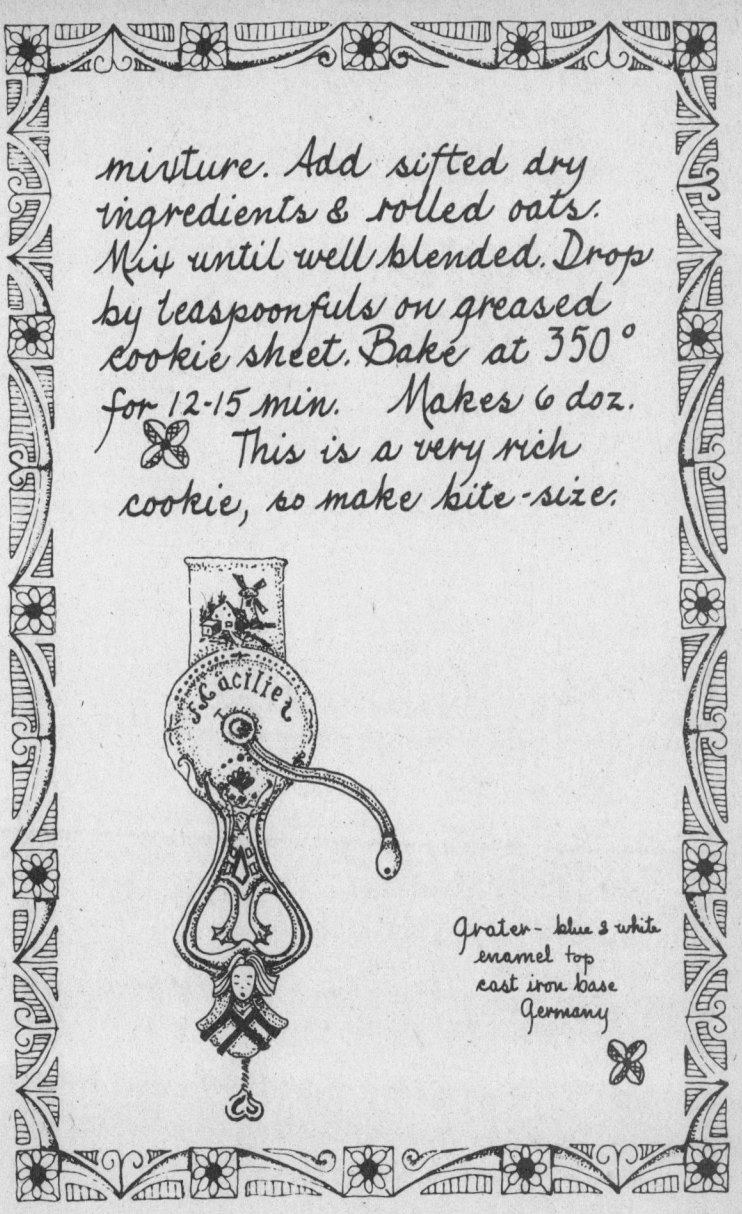

Grater- blue & white enamel top cast iron base Germany

Cherry Cookies

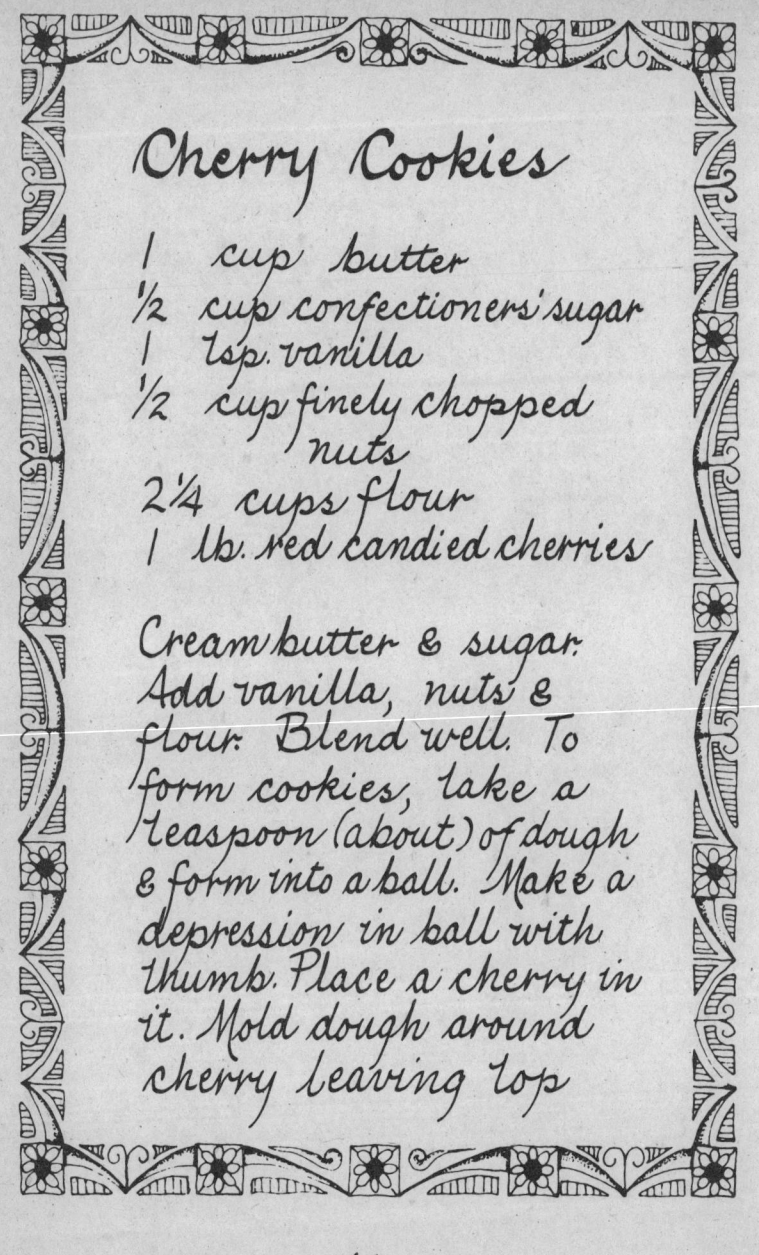

1 cup butter
½ cup confectioners' sugar
1 tsp. vanilla
½ cup finely chopped nuts
2¼ cups flour
1 lb. red candied cherries

Cream butter & sugar. Add vanilla, nuts & flour. Blend well. To form cookies, take a Teaspoon (about) of dough & form into a ball. Make a depression in ball with thumb. Place a cherry in it. Mold dough around cherry leaving top exposed. Place on ungreased cookie sheet. If dough is too soft to handle, chill for 1 hour in refrigerator. Bake at 350° for 15-20 minutes. Makes 6 dozen.

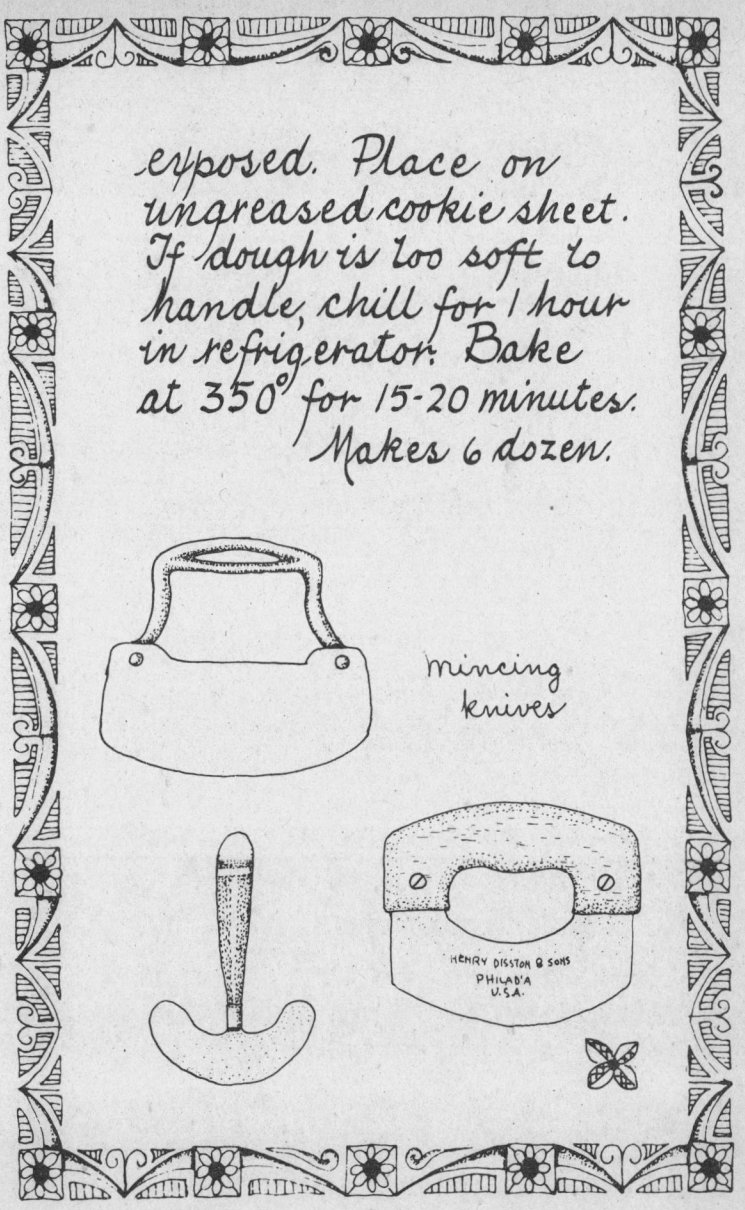

mincing knives

Chocolate Wafers

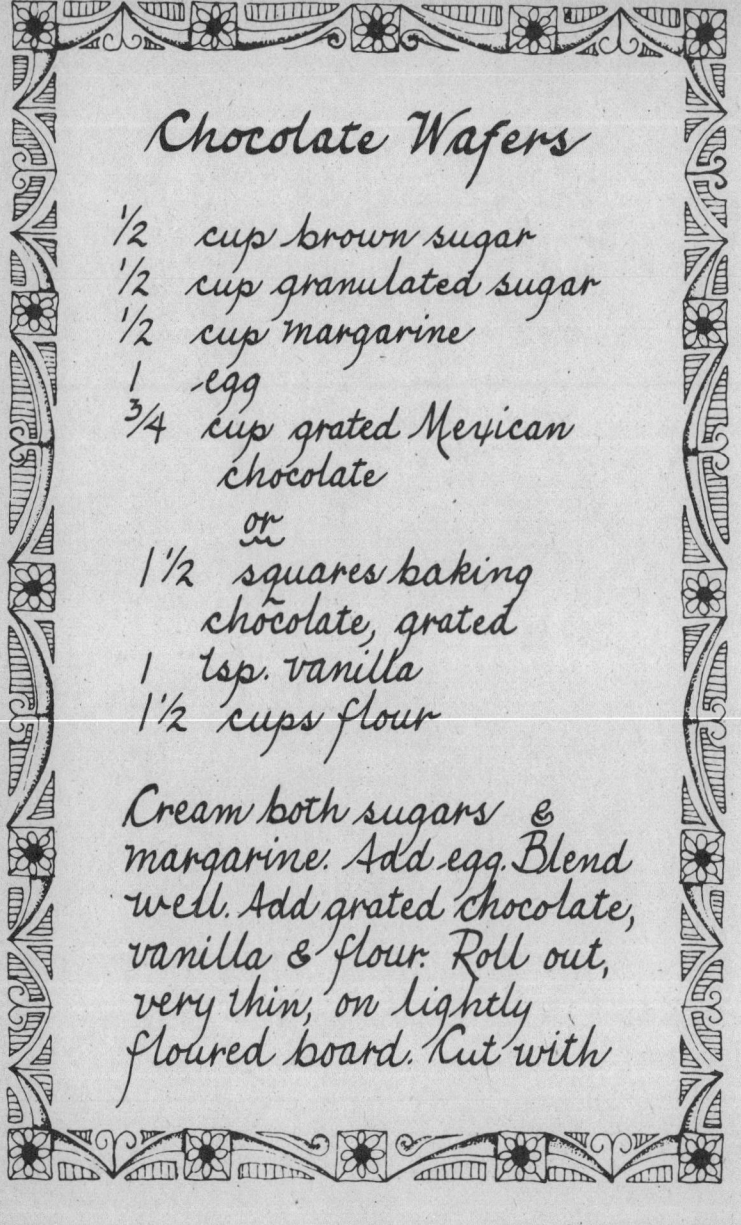

½ cup brown sugar
½ cup granulated sugar
½ cup margarine
1 egg
¾ cup grated Mexican chocolate

or

1½ squares baking chocolate, grated
1 tsp. vanilla
1½ cups flour

Cream both sugars & margarine. Add egg. Blend well. Add grated chocolate, vanilla & flour. Roll out very thin, on lightly floured board. Cut with

cookie cutter. Place on ungreased cookie sheet. Bake at 400° about 5 to 7 minutes. These cookies will stay crisp if stored in an airtight container.
        Makes 4 dozen.

Coffee mill metal ← drawer

Date Rolls

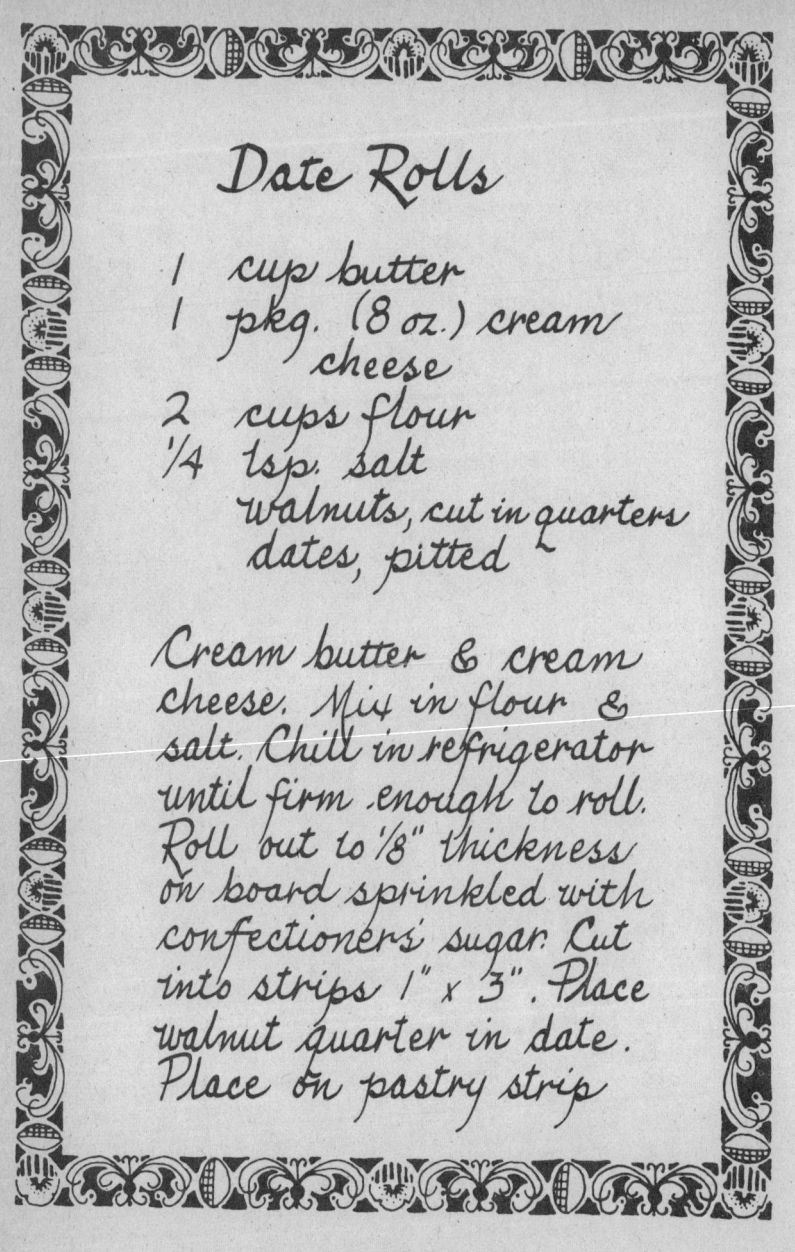

1 cup butter
1 pkg. (8 oz.) cream cheese
2 cups flour
¼ tsp. salt
    walnuts, cut in quarters
    dates, pitted

Cream butter & cream cheese. Mix in flour & salt. Chill in refrigerator until firm enough to roll. Roll out to ⅛" thickness on board sprinkled with confectioners' sugar. Cut into strips 1" x 3". Place walnut quarter in date. Place on pastry strip

& roll up. Place overlap side down on ungreased cookie sheet. Bake at 375° about 15 minutes.

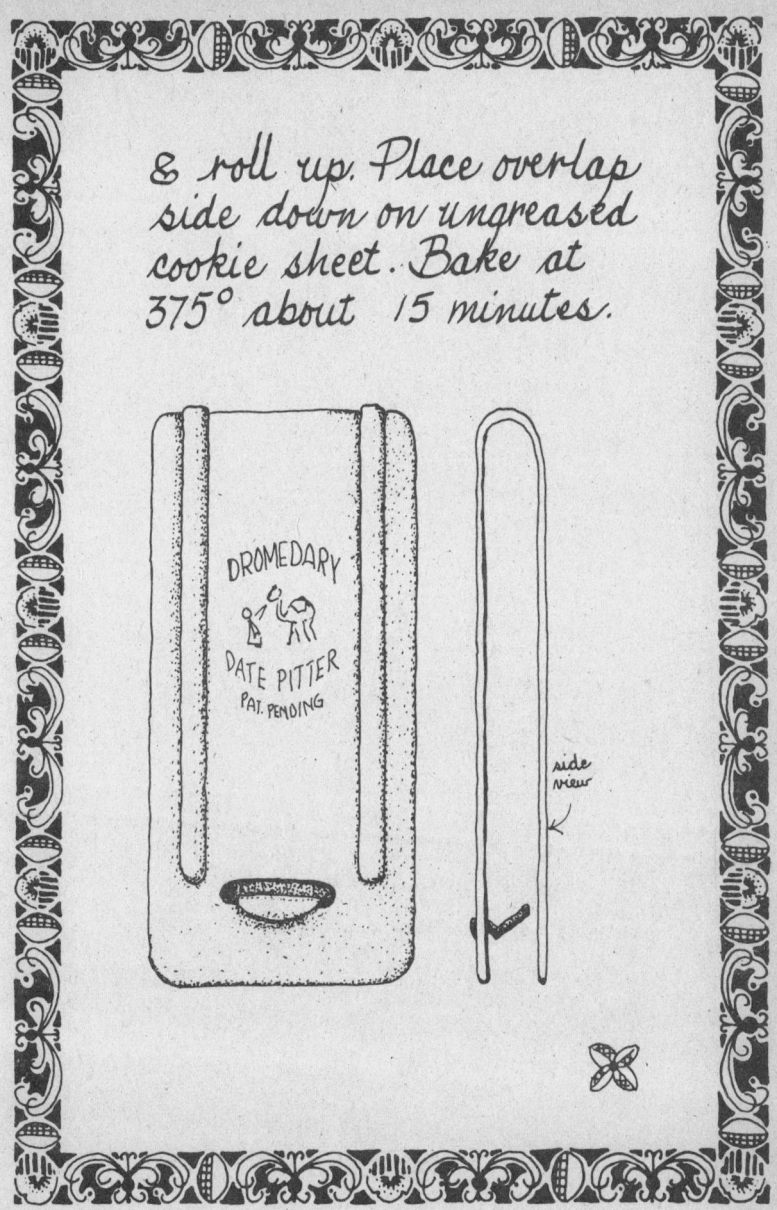

English Cookies

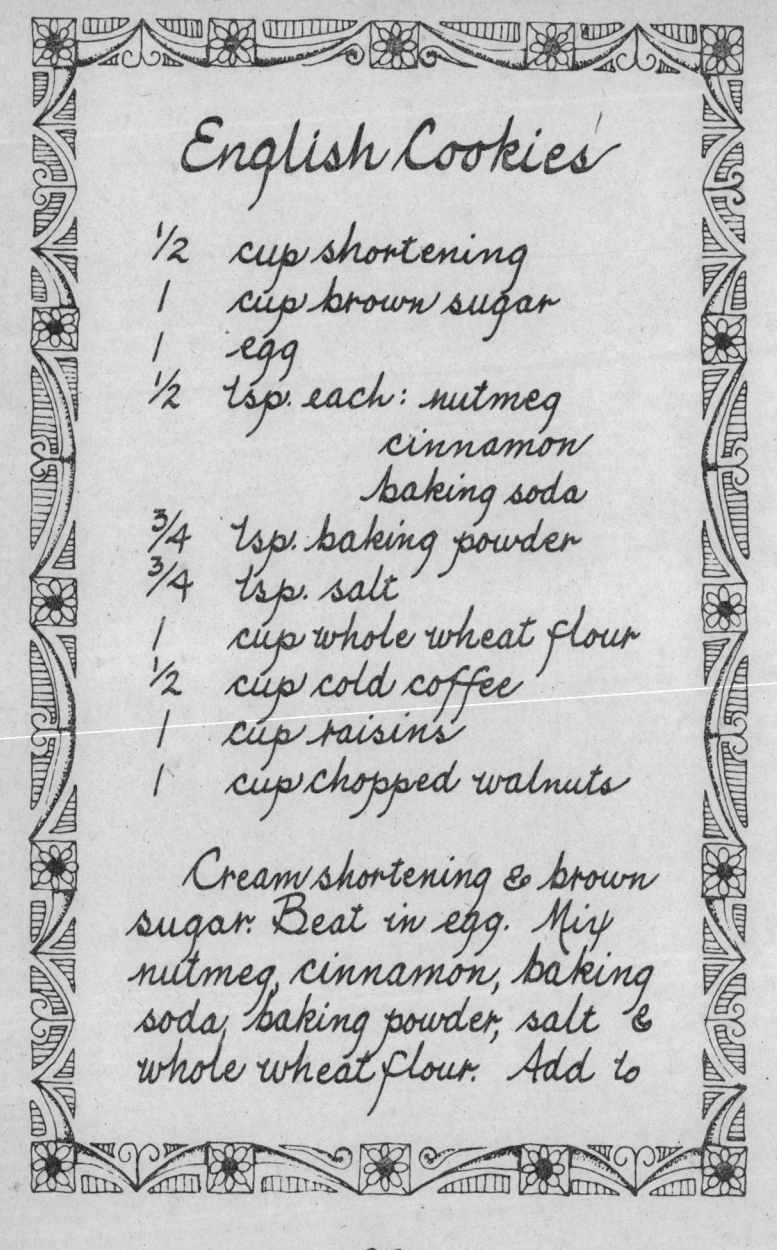

- ½ cup shortening
- 1 cup brown sugar
- 1 egg
- ½ tsp. each: nutmeg
  cinnamon
  baking soda
- ¾ tsp. baking powder
- ¾ tsp. salt
- 1 cup whole wheat flour
- ½ cup cold coffee
- 1 cup raisins
- 1 cup chopped walnuts

Cream shortening & brown sugar. Beat in egg. Mix nutmeg, cinnamon, baking soda, baking powder, salt & whole wheat flour. Add to

first mixture alternately with coffee. Add raisins & chopped walnuts. Drop by teaspoonfuls on greased cookie sheet. Bake at 375° for 10-15 minutes.
   Makes 3 dozen.

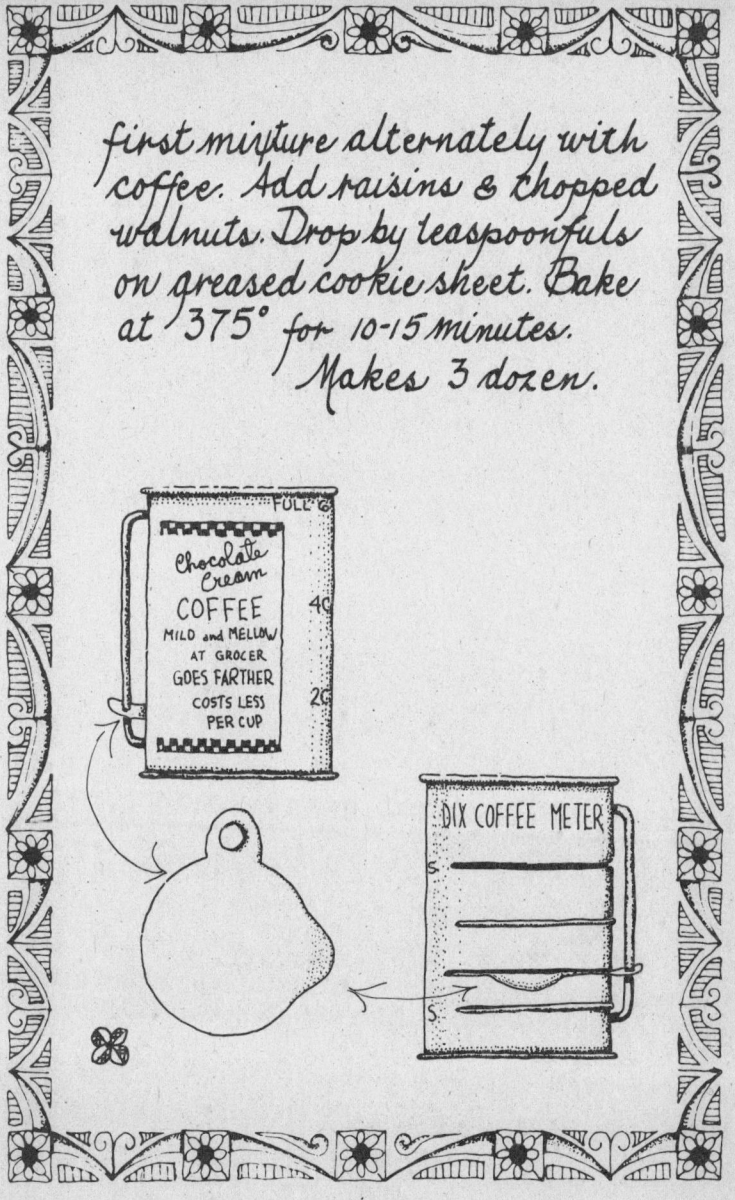

Figaroons

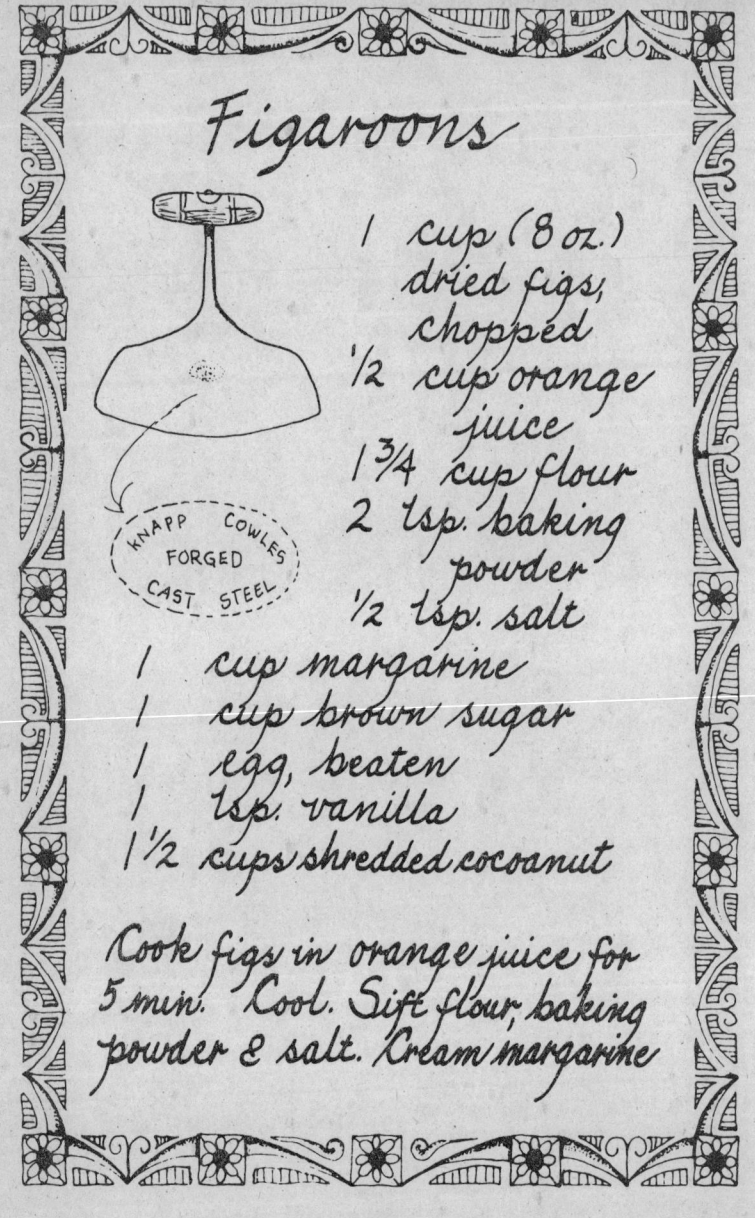

KNAPP COWLES FORGED CAST STEEL

1 cup (8 oz.) dried figs, chopped
½ cup orange juice
1¾ cup flour
2 tsp. baking powder
½ tsp. salt
1 cup margarine
1 cup brown sugar
1 egg, beaten
1 tsp. vanilla
1½ cups shredded cocoanut

Cook figs in orange juice for 5 min. Cool. Sift flour, baking powder & salt. Cream margarine

& brown sugar. Add egg, vanilla & cooked figs. Add sifted ingredients. Blend well. Drop by teaspoonfuls into cocoanut. Form into balls. Place on greased cookie sheet. Bake at 375° for 12-15 min.

Makes 5 dozen.

❈ These cookies are also good rolled in graham cracker crumbs instead of cocoanut.

Mincing knives
back
front

Ginger Snaps

- ½ cup margarine
- ½ cup brown sugar
- ½ cup molasses
- 2 Tblsp. vinegar
- 1 tsp. baking soda
- 2 cups flour
- 1 tsp. salt
- 1 tsp. cinnamon
- ½ tsp. cloves
- 1 Tblsp. ginger

Melt margarine. Add sugar & molasses. Add vinegar & baking soda. Stir until mixture foams. Sift flour, salt, cinnamon, cloves & ginger. Add to first mixture & mix well.

Roll out on floured board to 1/8" thickness. Cut with cookie cutter. Place on greased cookie sheet. Bake at 400° for about 8 minutes.
 Makes 4 dozen.

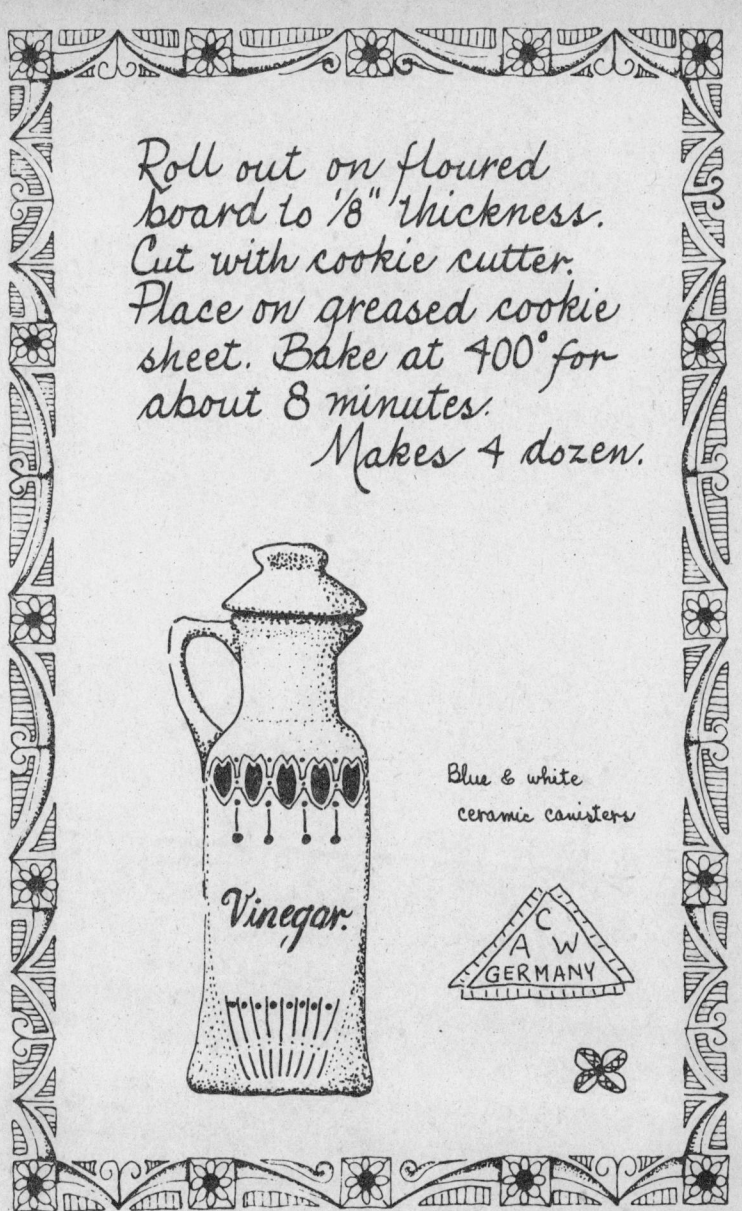

Blue & white ceramic canisters

Gumdrop Cookies

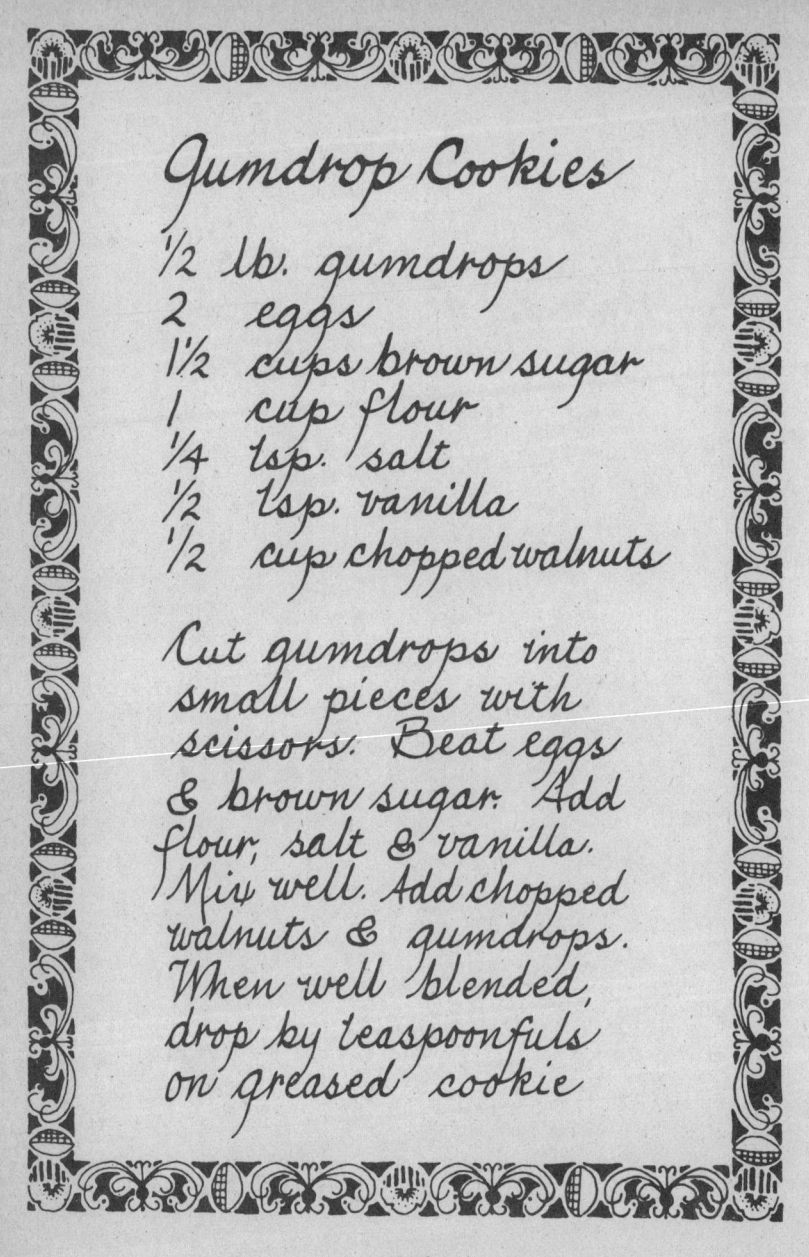

½ lb. gumdrops
2 eggs
1½ cups brown sugar
1 cup flour
¼ tsp. salt
½ tsp. vanilla
½ cup chopped walnuts

Cut gumdrops into small pieces with scissors. Beat eggs & brown sugar. Add flour, salt & vanilla. Mix well. Add chopped walnuts & gumdrops. When well blended, drop by teaspoonfuls on greased cookie sheet. Bake in a 375° oven about 12-15 min. Makes 4 dozen.

Indurated fibre ware salt box

Hermits

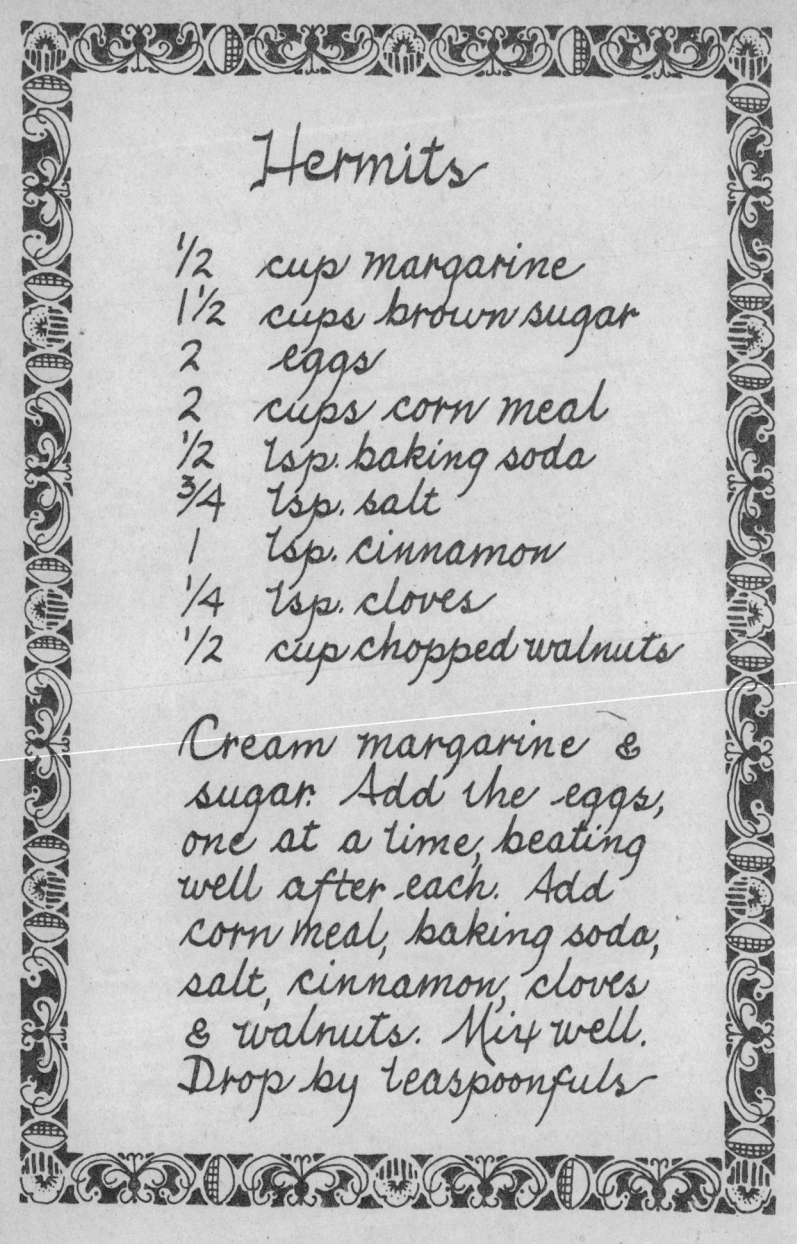

½ cup margarine
1½ cups brown sugar
2 eggs
2 cups corn meal
½ tsp. baking soda
¾ tsp. salt
1 tsp. cinnamon
¼ tsp. cloves
½ cup chopped walnuts

Cream margarine & sugar. Add the eggs, one at a time, beating well after each. Add corn meal, baking soda, salt, cinnamon, cloves & walnuts. Mix well. Drop by teaspoonfuls on greased cookie sheet. Bake at 375° about 12 to 15 minutes. Makes 4 dozen.

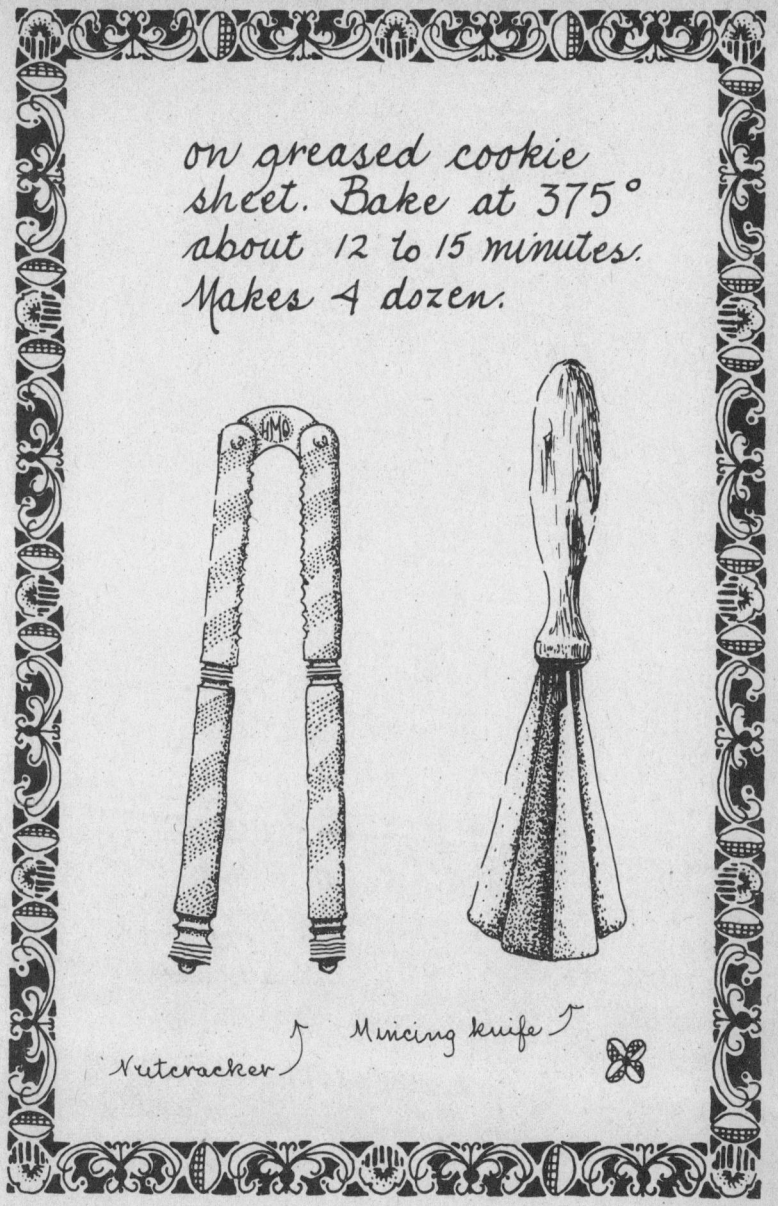

Nutcracker   Mincing knife

Licorice Cookies

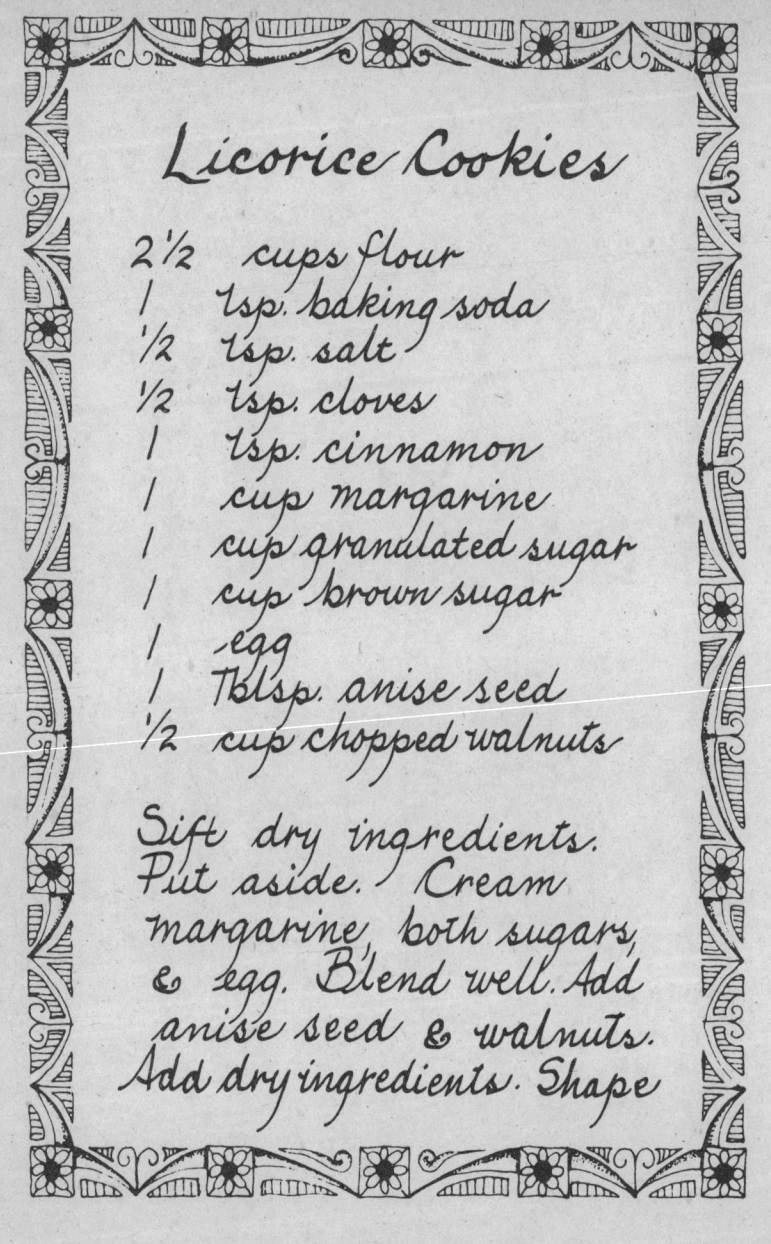

2½ cups flour
1 tsp. baking soda
½ tsp. salt
½ tsp. cloves
1 tsp. cinnamon
1 cup margarine
1 cup granulated sugar
1 cup brown sugar
1 egg
1 Tblsp. anise seed
½ cup chopped walnuts

Sift dry ingredients. Put aside. Cream margarine, both sugars, & egg. Blend well. Add anise seed & walnuts. Add dry ingredients. Shape

into two 12" long rolls. Place in waxed paper & refrigerate overnight. Slice thin. Place on ungreased cookie sheet. Bake at 375° 12-15 min.
  Makes 6 dozen.

2 burner lamp stove

Mock Macaroons

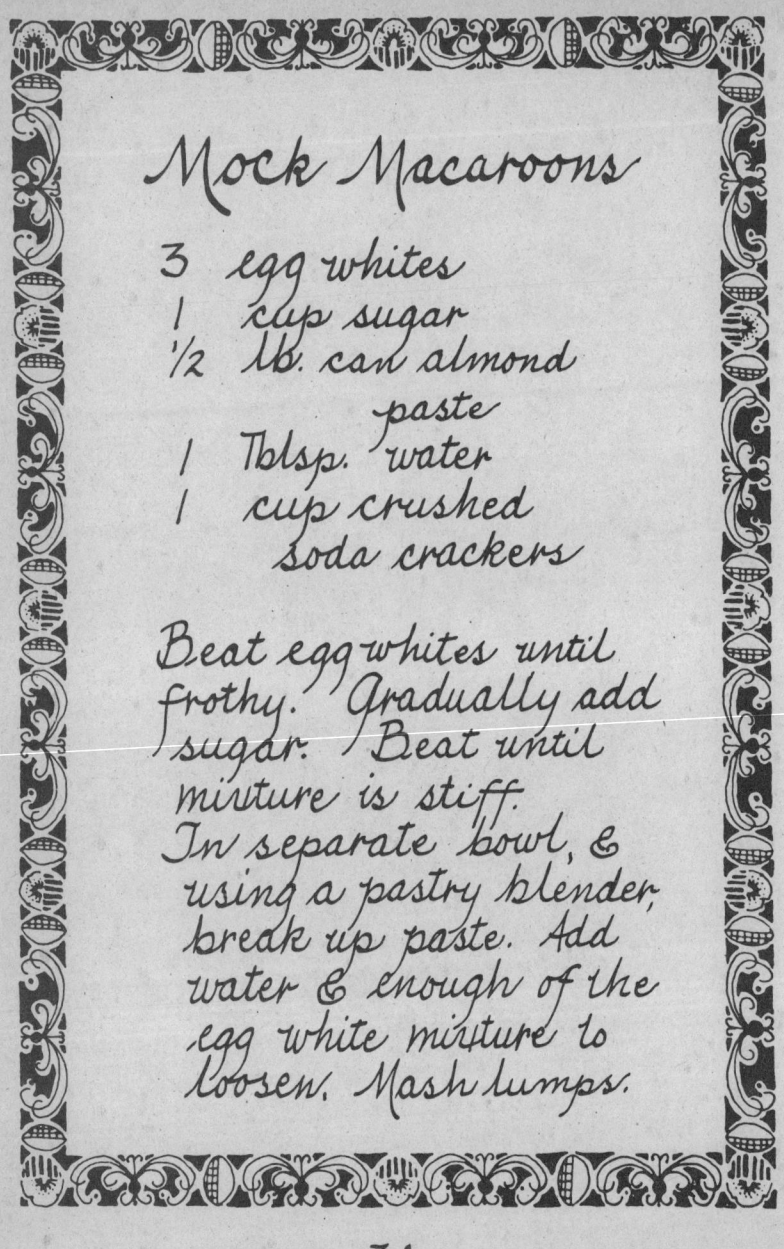

3 egg whites
1 cup sugar
½ lb. can almond paste
1 Tblsp. water
1 cup crushed soda crackers

Beat egg whites until frothy. Gradually add sugar. Beat until mixture is stiff. In separate bowl, & using a pastry blender, break up paste. Add water & enough of the egg white mixture to loosen. Mash lumps.

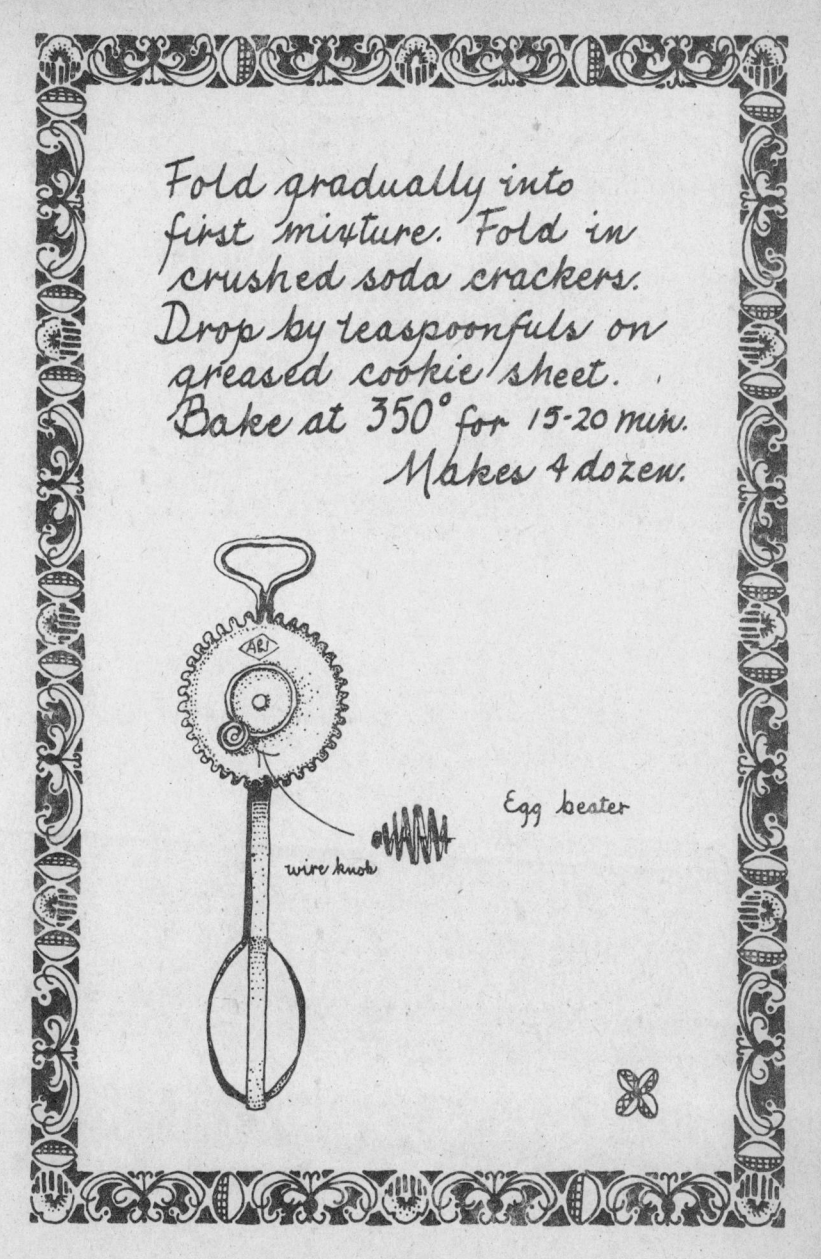

Fold gradually into first mixture. Fold in crushed soda crackers. Drop by teaspoonfuls on greased cookie sheet. Bake at 350° for 15-20 min. Makes 4 dozen.

Egg beater

wire knob

Peanut Butter Balls

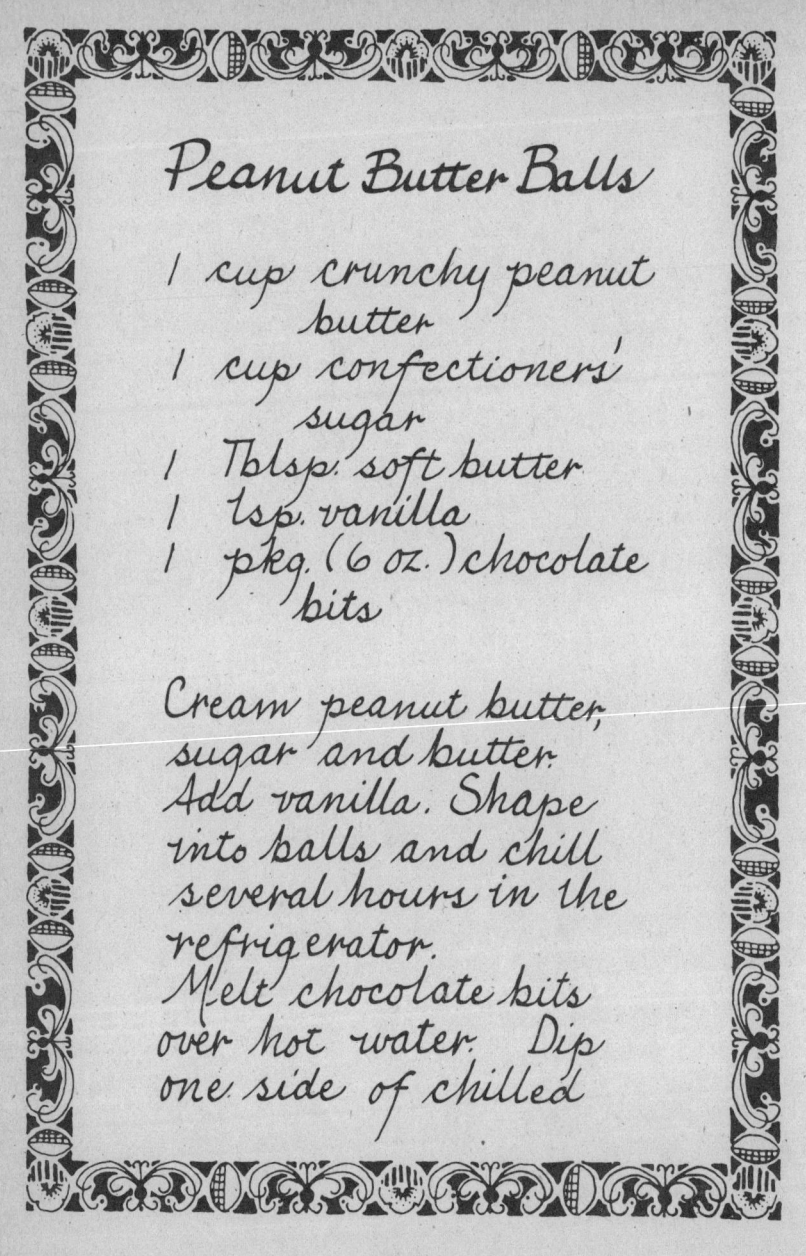

1 cup crunchy peanut butter
1 cup confectioners' sugar
1 Tblsp. soft butter
1 tsp. vanilla
1 pkg. (6 oz.) chocolate bits

Cream peanut butter, sugar and butter. Add vanilla. Shape into balls and chill several hours in the refrigerator. Melt chocolate bits over hot water. Dip one side of chilled

ball in melted chocolate.
Place on waxed paper
and return to refrigerator
until ready to serve.
Makes about 4 dozen.
These cookies will keep
indefinitely if refrigerated.

Brass scale

Peanut Butter Dots

½ cup margarine
1 cup sugar
½ cup peanut butter
1 egg
2 Tblsp. milk
1¼ cups flour
½ tsp. salt
½ tsp. baking soda
1 pkg. (6 oz.) chocolate bits

Cream margarine & sugar until light. Add peanut butter, egg & milk. Mix well. Sift flour, salt & baking soda. Add gradually to creamed mixture. Add chocolate bits. Drop by teaspoonfuls (these are very rich cookies so make them small) on ungreased cookie sheet. Bake in a 375° oven, about 8-10 minutes. Makes 5 dozen.

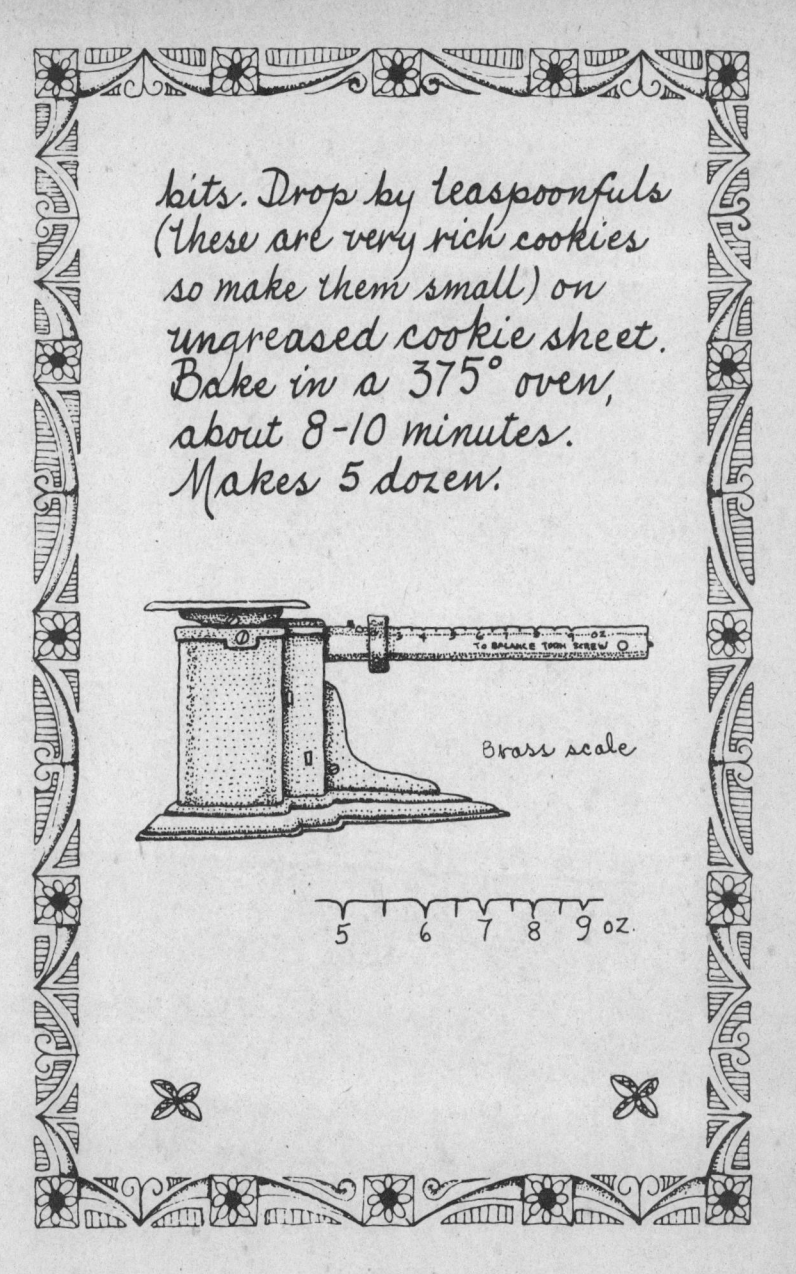

Brass scale

Persimmon Cookies

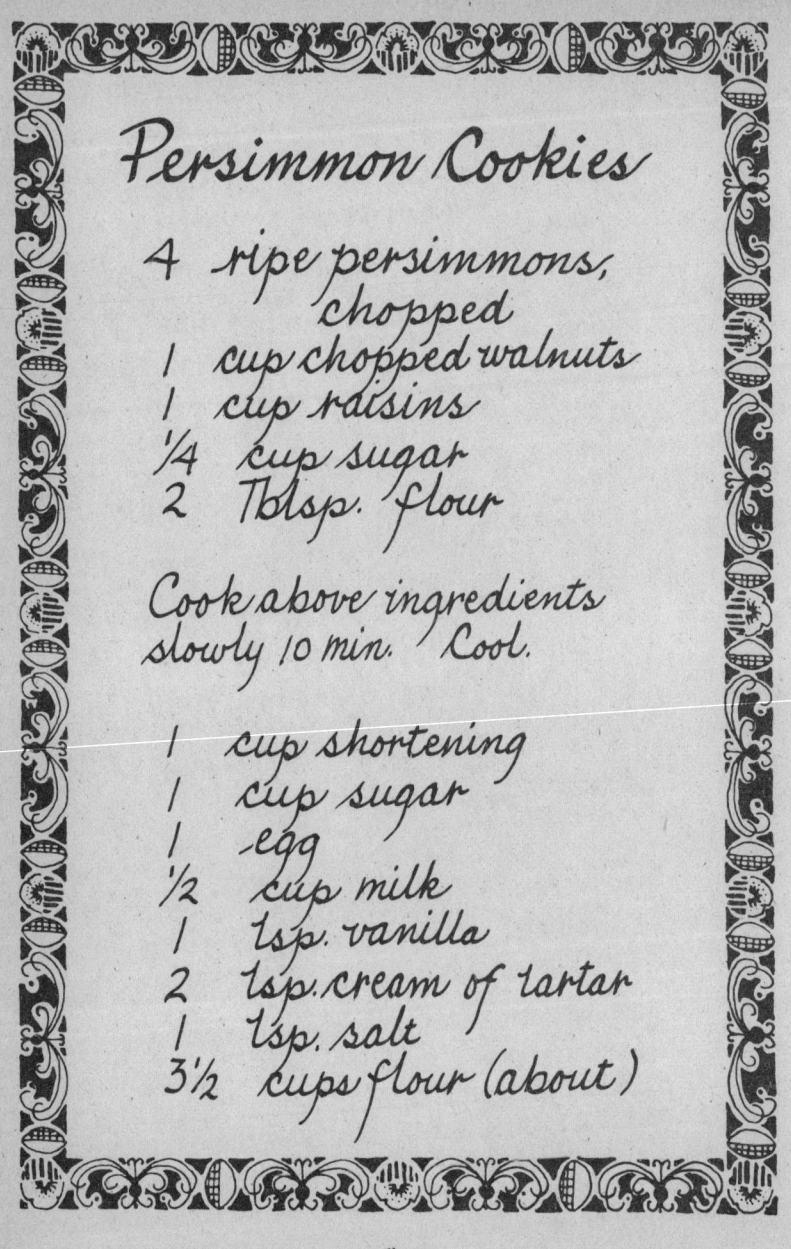

4 ripe persimmons, chopped
1 cup chopped walnuts
1 cup raisins
¼ cup sugar
2 Tblsp. flour

Cook above ingredients slowly 10 min. Cool.

1 cup shortening
1 cup sugar
1 egg
½ cup milk
1 tsp. vanilla
2 tsp. cream of tartar
1 tsp. salt
3½ cups flour (about)

Cream shortening & sugar. Add egg, milk, vanilla, cream of tartar, salt & flour. Blend well. Roll out on floured board. Cut in rounds, about 2½" diameter. Put scant tsp. filling on each round. Fold in half. Crimp edge with fork to seal. Bake at 350° for 12-15 minutes.

Wire basket

Pineapple Cookies

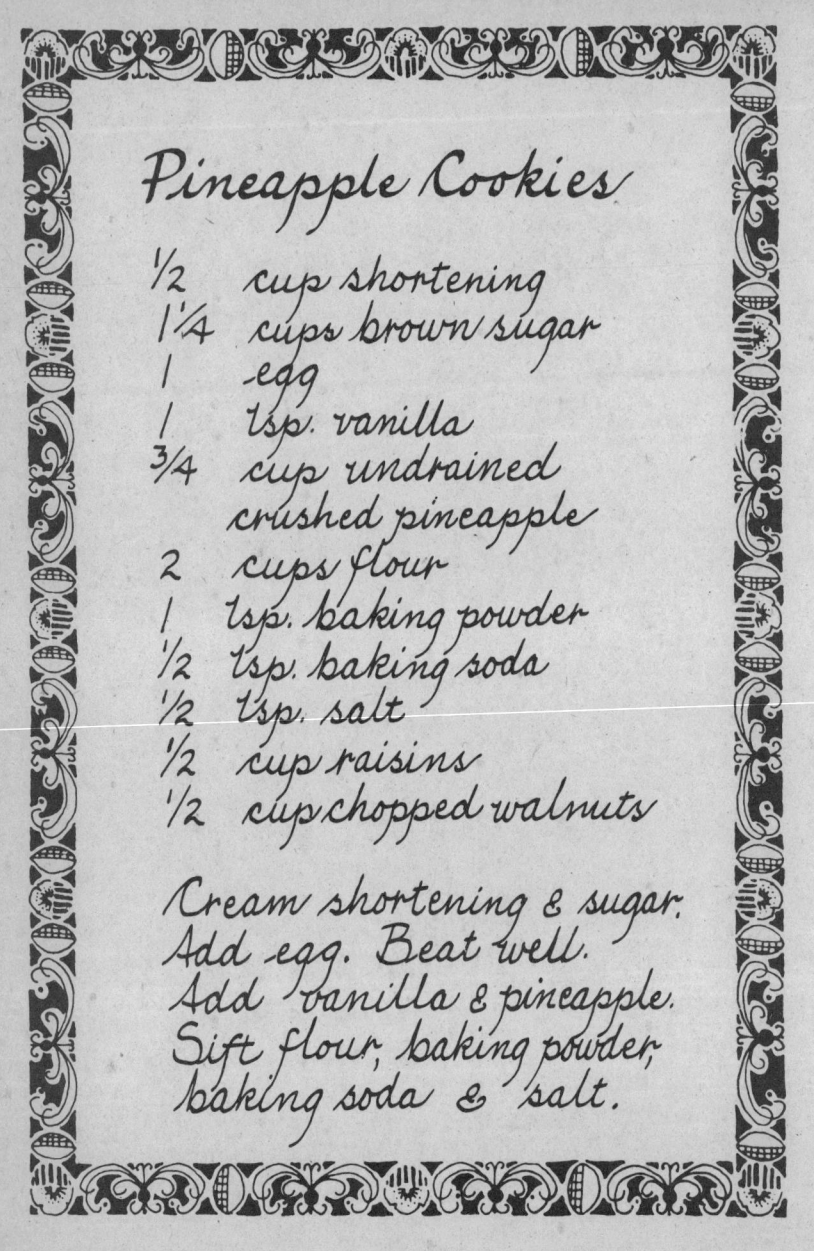

½ cup shortening
1¼ cups brown sugar
1 egg
1 tsp. vanilla
¾ cup undrained crushed pineapple
2 cups flour
1 tsp. baking powder
½ tsp. baking soda
½ tsp. salt
½ cup raisins
½ cup chopped walnuts

Cream shortening & sugar. Add egg. Beat well. Add vanilla & pineapple. Sift flour, baking powder, baking soda & salt.

Add to the creamed mixture. Add raisins & walnuts. Drop by teaspoonfuls on greased cookie sheet. Bake at 375° about 12-15 min. Makes 4 dozen.

MADE IN JAPAN

Tea pot

white porcelain - blue design

Pumpkin Cookies

2½ cups flour
2 tsp. baking powder
½ tsp. baking soda
½ tsp. nutmeg
½ tsp. cinnamon
½ tsp. salt
¼ tsp. ginger
¼ tsp. cloves
1 cup granulated sugar
½ cup brown sugar
½ cup margarine
2 eggs, beaten
1½ cups canned pumpkin
1 cup raisins
1 cup chopped walnuts

Sift dry ingredients. Cream sugars & margarine. Add

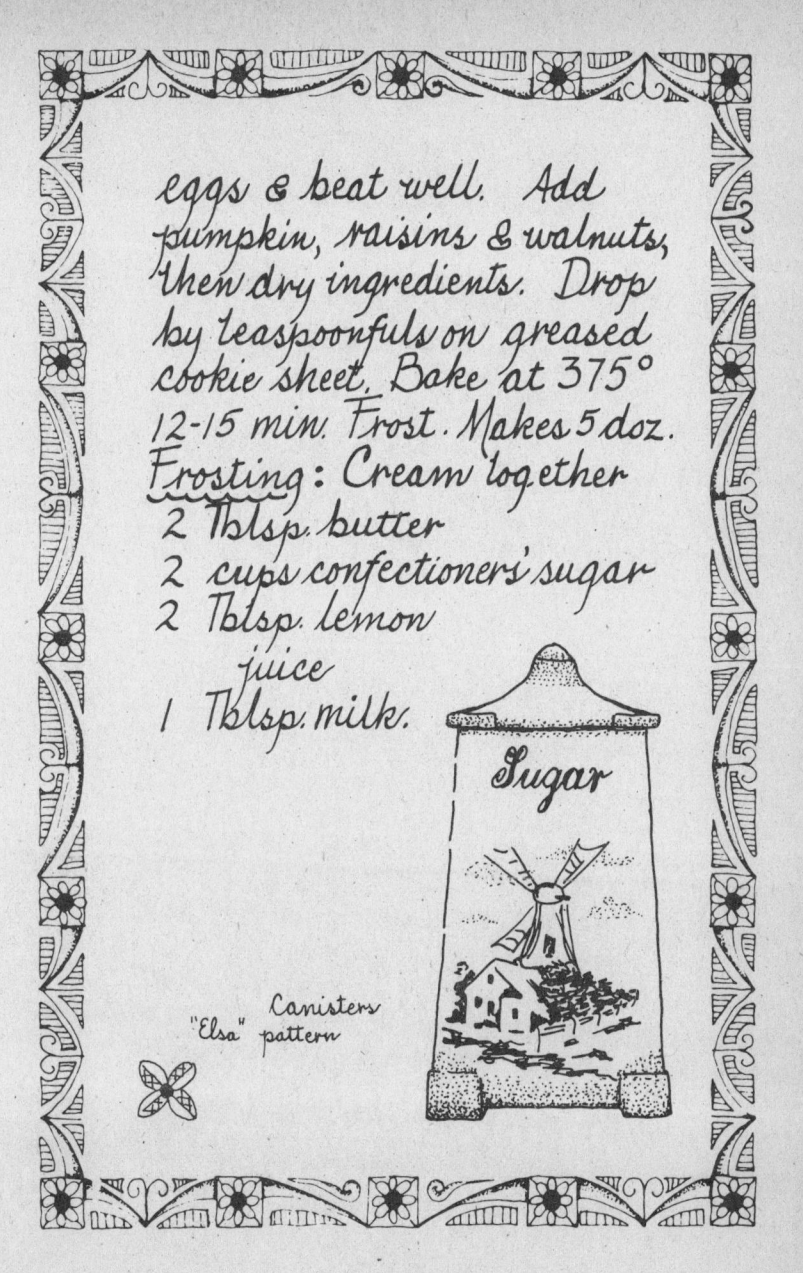

eggs & beat well. Add pumpkin, raisins & walnuts, then dry ingredients. Drop by teaspoonfuls on greased cookie sheet. Bake at 375° 12-15 min. Frost. Makes 5 doz.

Frosting: Cream together
- 2 Tblsp. butter
- 2 cups confectioners' sugar
- 2 Tblsp. lemon juice
- 1 Tblsp. milk.

Canisters "Elsa" pattern

Sesame Seed Cookies

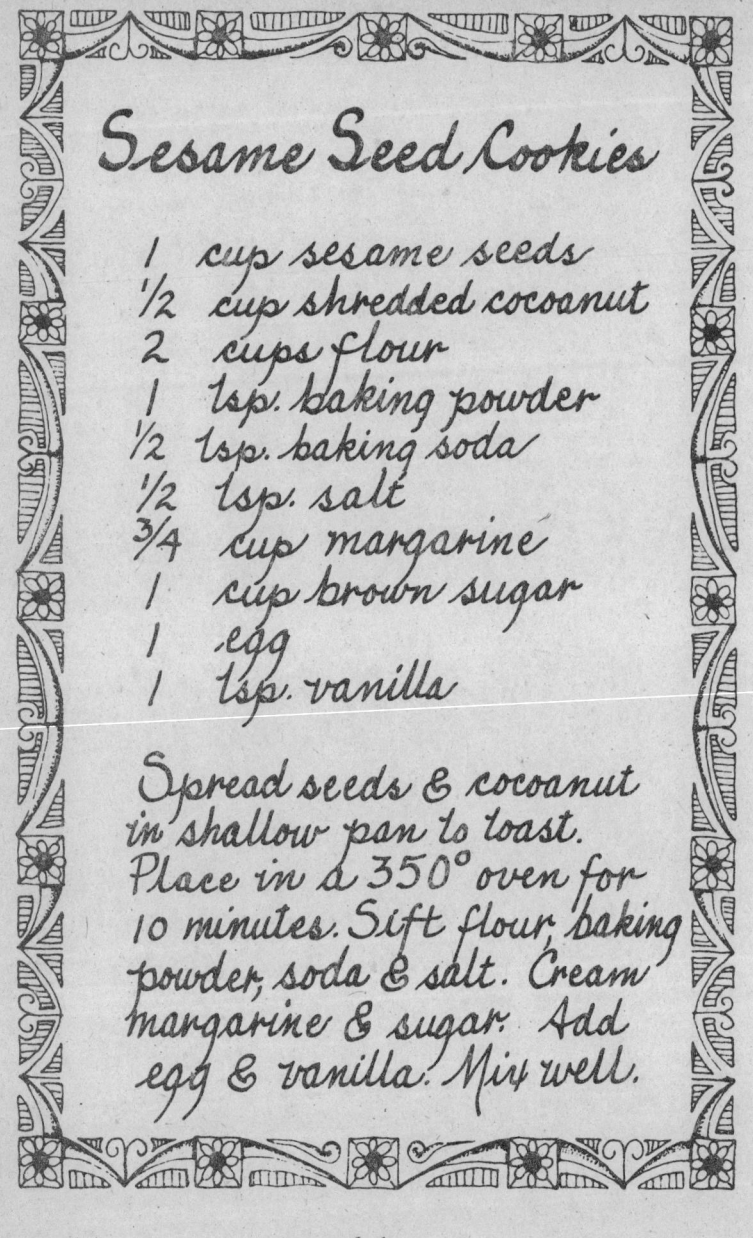

1 cup sesame seeds
1/2 cup shredded cocoanut
2 cups flour
1 tsp. baking powder
1/2 tsp. baking soda
1/2 tsp. salt
3/4 cup margarine
1 cup brown sugar
1 egg
1 tsp. vanilla

Spread seeds & cocoanut in shallow pan to toast. Place in a 350° oven for 10 minutes. Sift flour, baking powder, soda & salt. Cream margarine & sugar. Add egg & vanilla. Mix well.

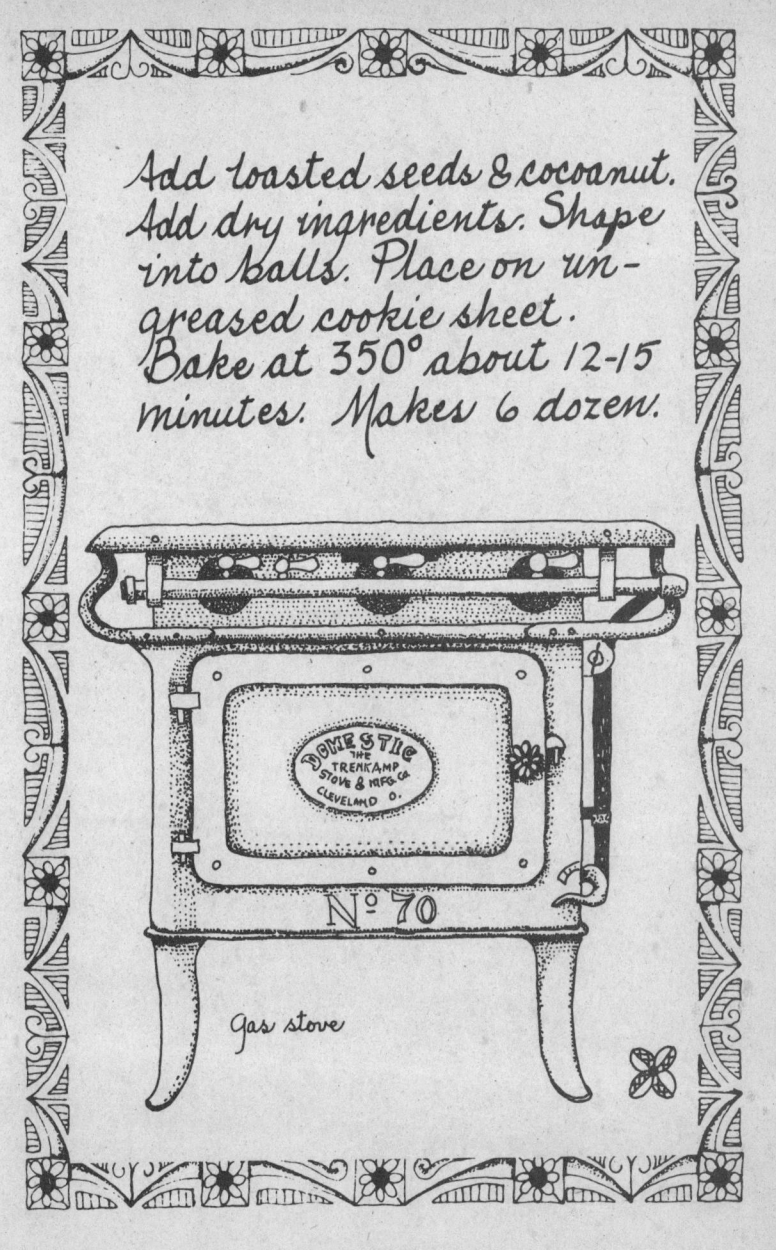

Add toasted seeds & cocoanut.
Add dry ingredients. Shape
into balls. Place on un-
greased cookie sheet.
Bake at 350° about 12-15
minutes. Makes 6 dozen.

gas stove

Skillet Cookies

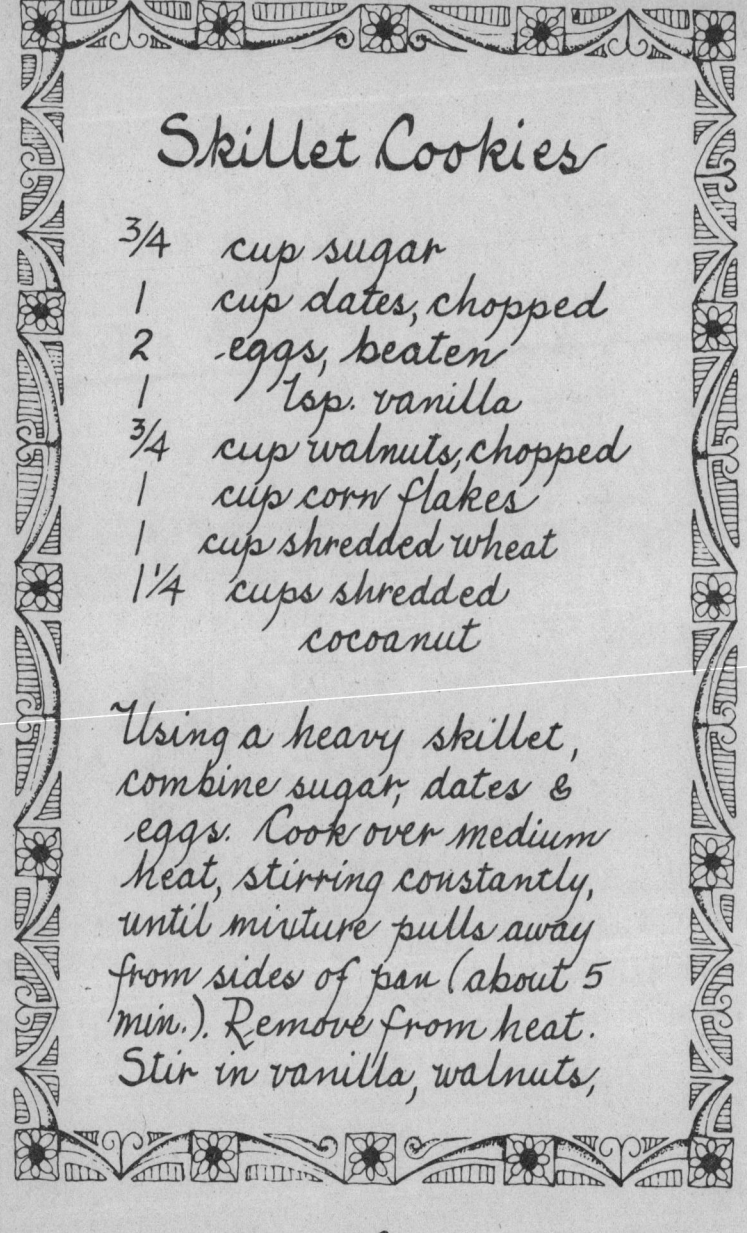

3/4	cup sugar
1	cup dates, chopped
2	eggs, beaten
1	tsp. vanilla
3/4	cup walnuts, chopped
1	cup corn flakes
1	cup shredded wheat
1 1/4	cups shredded cocoanut

Using a heavy skillet, combine sugar, dates & eggs. Cook over medium heat, stirring constantly, until mixture pulls away from sides of pan (about 5 min.). Remove from heat. Stir in vanilla, walnuts,

& corn flakes. Crumble shredded wheat & add to mixture. Cool slightly. Moisten hands in cold water. Take spoonfuls of dough & shape with hands into rounds. Roll in cocoanut. Chill. Store in refrigerator.

Makes 2 doz.

Blue & white enamelware skillet

side

Tropical Cookies

4 tsp. butter
2 sq. baking chocolate
2 Tbtsp. milk
1 egg
1 cup honey
1 tsp. lemon juice
1 cup flour
1 cup corn meal
2½ tsp. baking powder
½ tsp. salt

Melt butter & chocolate together. Cool. Add milk, egg, honey & lemon juice. Mix well. In separate bowl combine flour, corn meal, baking powder & salt. Add gradually to

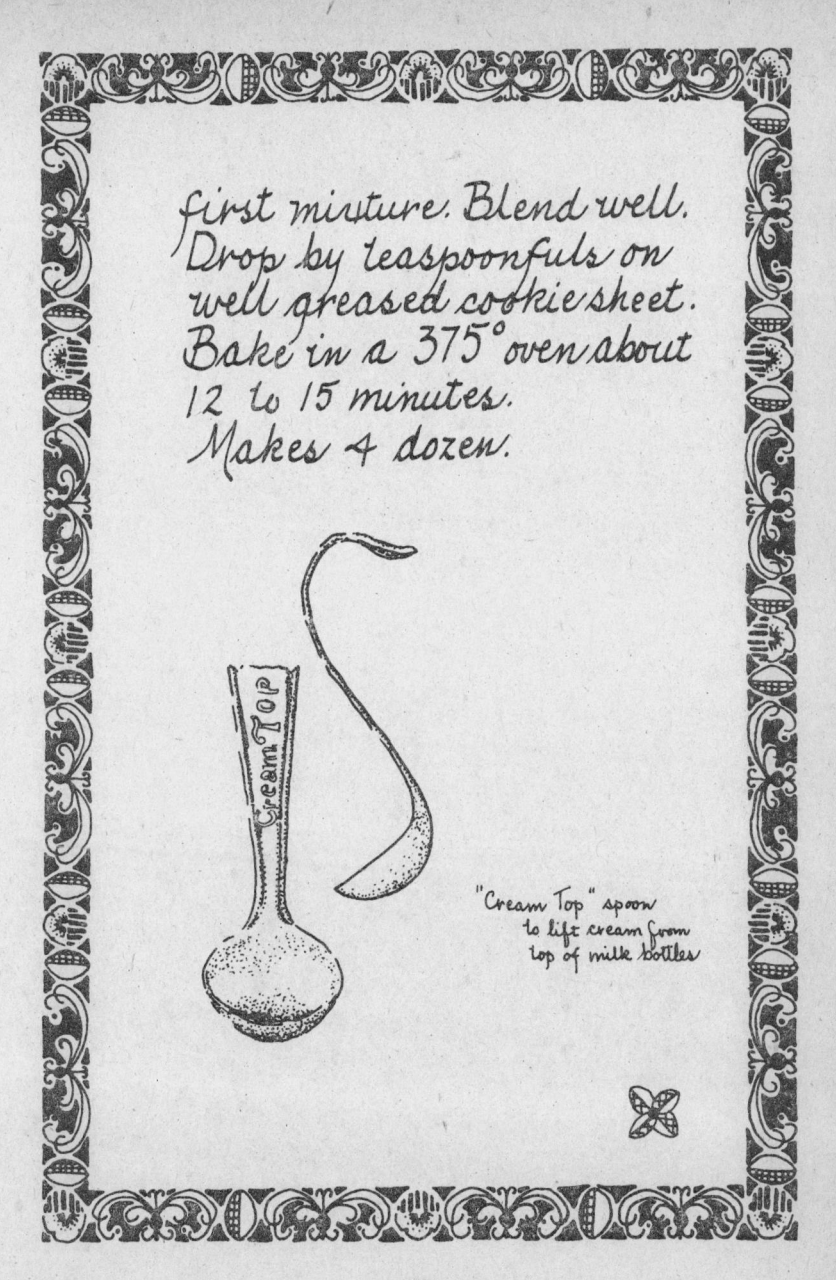

first mixture. Blend well.
Drop by teaspoonfuls on
well greased cookie sheet.
Bake in a 375° oven about
12 to 15 minutes.
Makes 4 dozen.

"Cream Top" spoon
to lift cream from
top of milk bottles

Wheat Germ Cookies

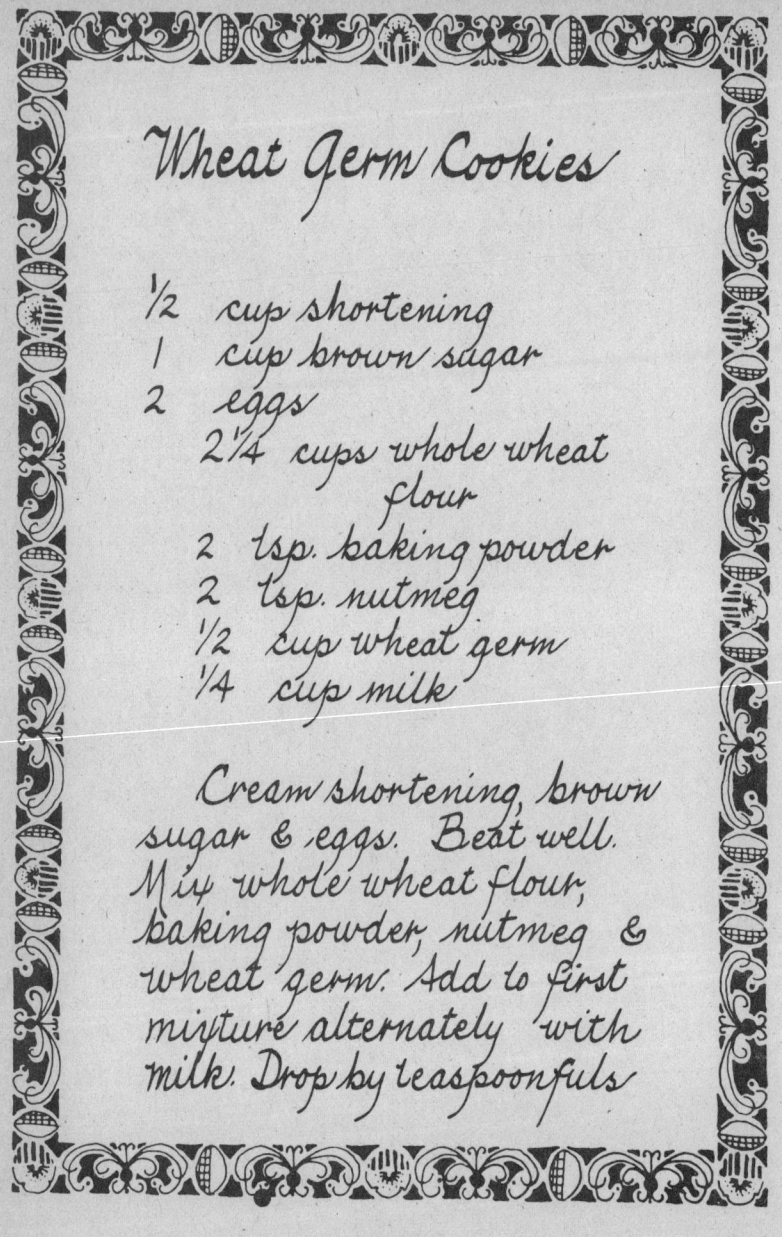

½ cup shortening
1 cup brown sugar
2 eggs
2¼ cups whole wheat flour
2 tsp. baking powder
2 tsp. nutmeg
½ cup wheat germ
¼ cup milk

Cream shortening, brown sugar & eggs. Beat well. Mix whole wheat flour, baking powder, nutmeg & wheat germ. Add to first mixture alternately with milk. Drop by teaspoonfuls

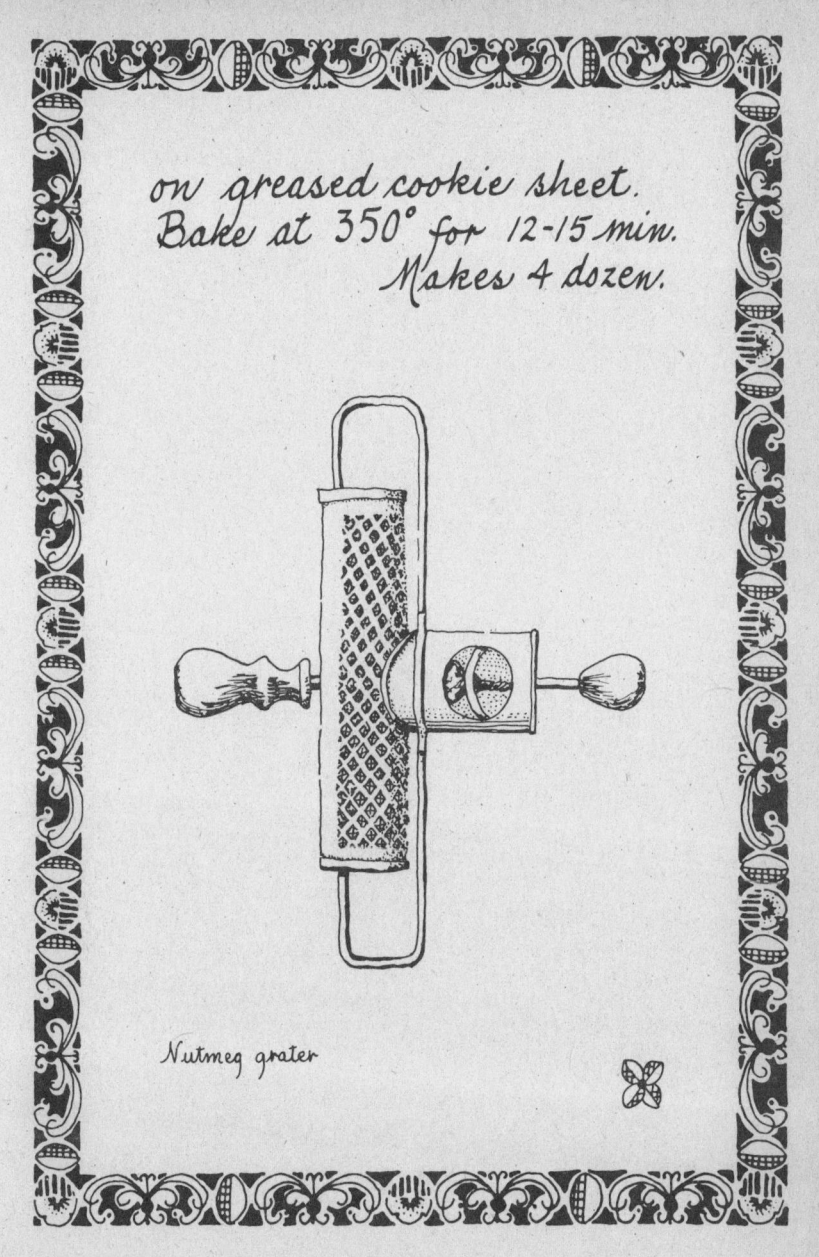

on greased cookie sheet.
Bake at 350° for 12-15 min.
Makes 4 dozen.

Nutmeg grater

Squares

Apple Squares

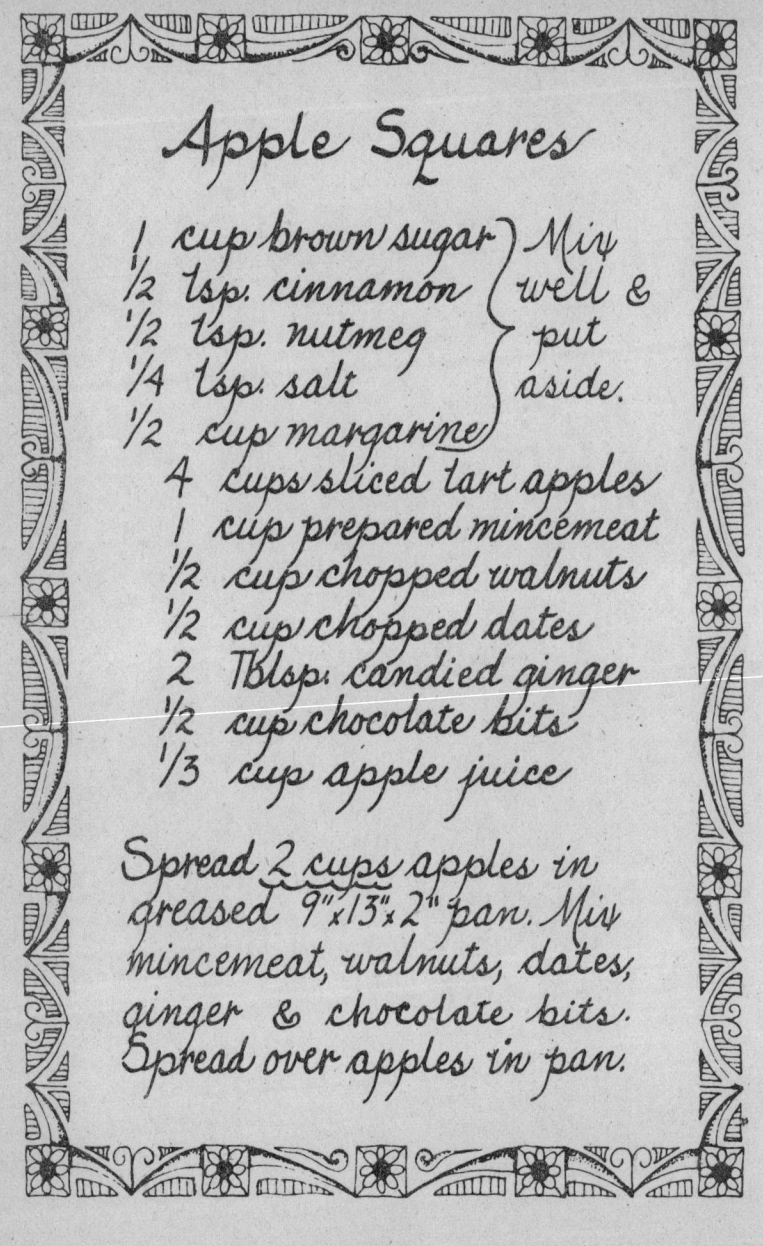

1 cup brown sugar ⎫
½ tsp. cinnamon   ⎬ Mix well & put aside.
½ tsp. nutmeg   ⎪
¼ tsp. salt   ⎭
½ cup margarine
4 cups sliced tart apples
1 cup prepared mincemeat
½ cup chopped walnuts
½ cup chopped dates
2 Tblsp. candied ginger
½ cup chocolate bits
⅓ cup apple juice

Spread 2 cups apples in greased 9"x13"x2" pan. Mix mincemeat, walnuts, dates, ginger & chocolate bits. Spread over apples in pan.

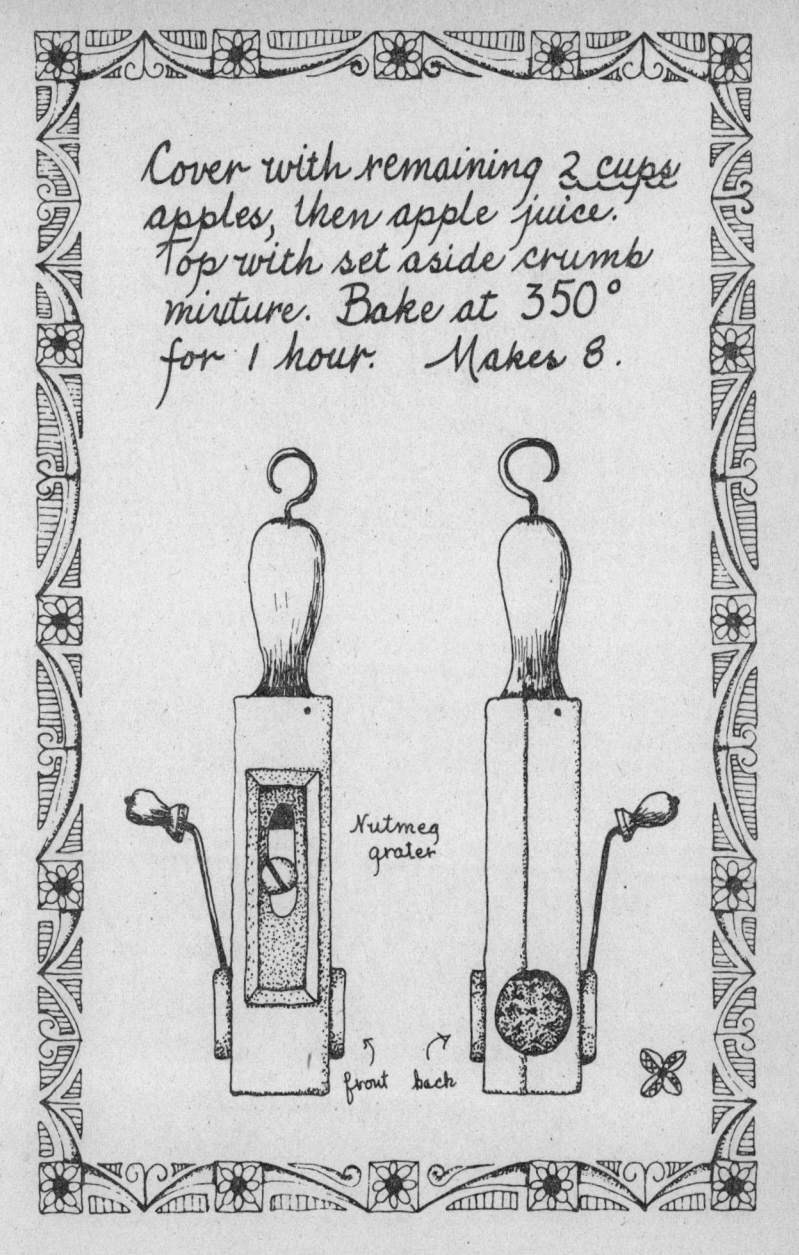

Cover with remaining 2 cups apples, then apple juice. Top with set aside crumb mixture. Bake at 350° for 1 hour.   Makes 8.

Nutmeg grater

front back

Apricot Squares

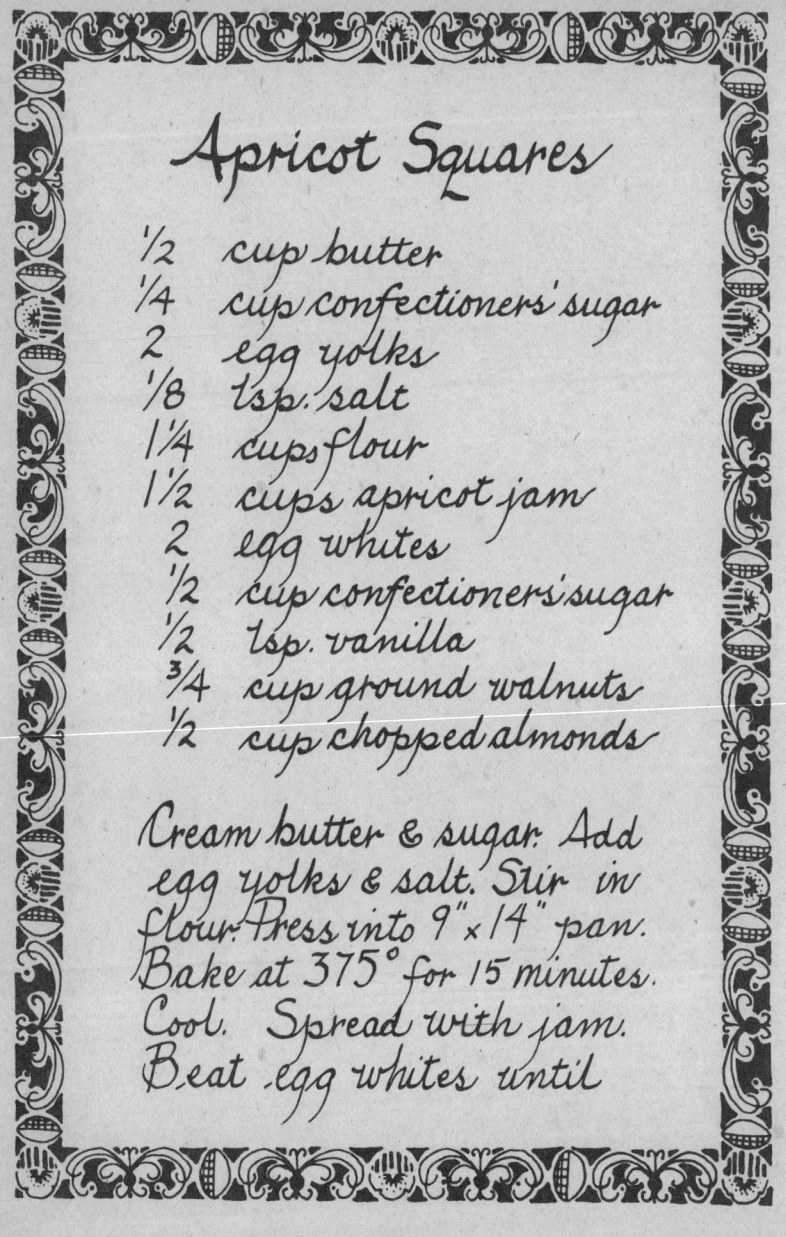

½ cup butter
¼ cup confectioners' sugar
2 egg yolks
⅛ tsp. salt
1¼ cups flour
1½ cups apricot jam
2 egg whites
½ cup confectioners' sugar
½ tsp. vanilla
¾ cup ground walnuts
½ cup chopped almonds

Cream butter & sugar. Add egg yolks & salt. Stir in flour. Press into 9" x 14" pan. Bake at 375° for 15 minutes. Cool. Spread with jam. Beat egg whites until stiff. Gradually add sugar. Beat until very stiff. Fold in vanilla & walnuts. Spread over jam. Sprinkle with almonds. Bake at 425° 10 minutes — or until brown. Makes 28.

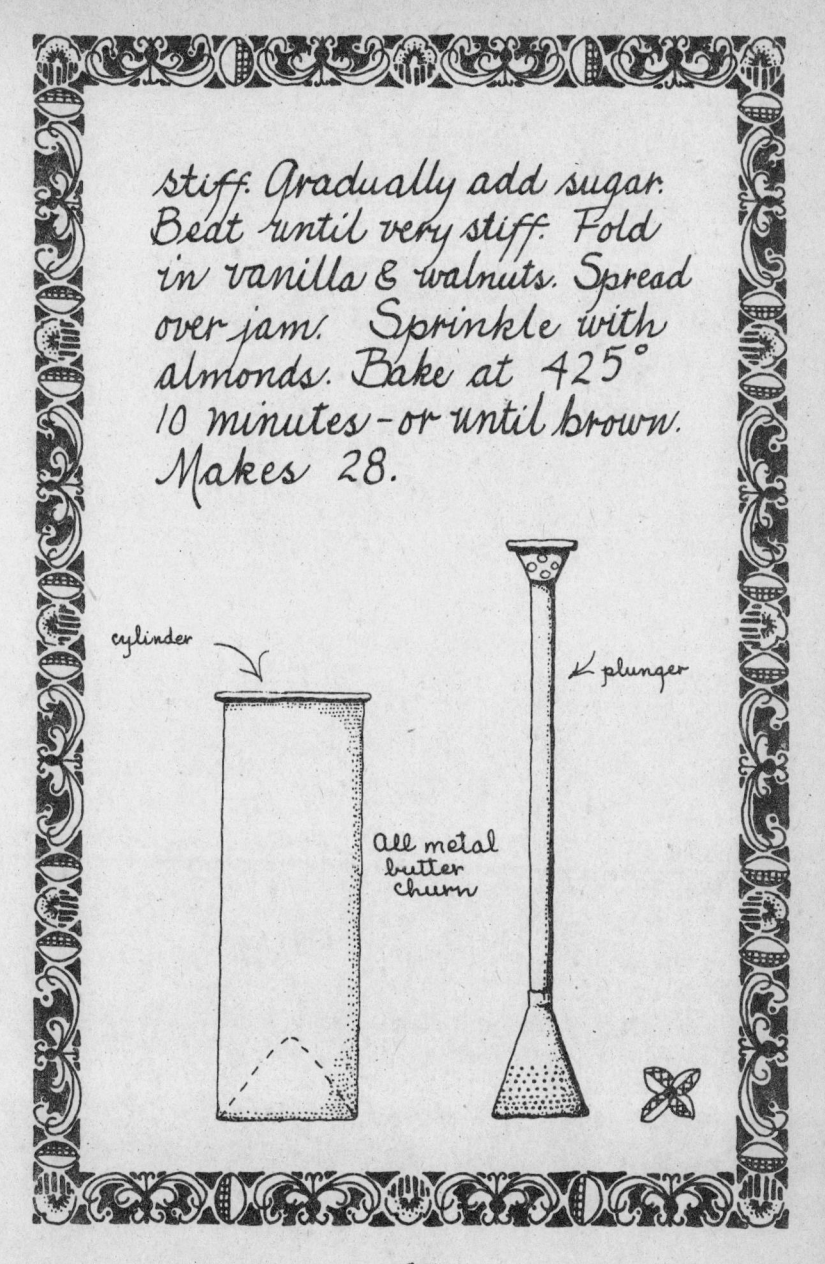

cylinder

All metal butter churn

plunger

Brownie Squares

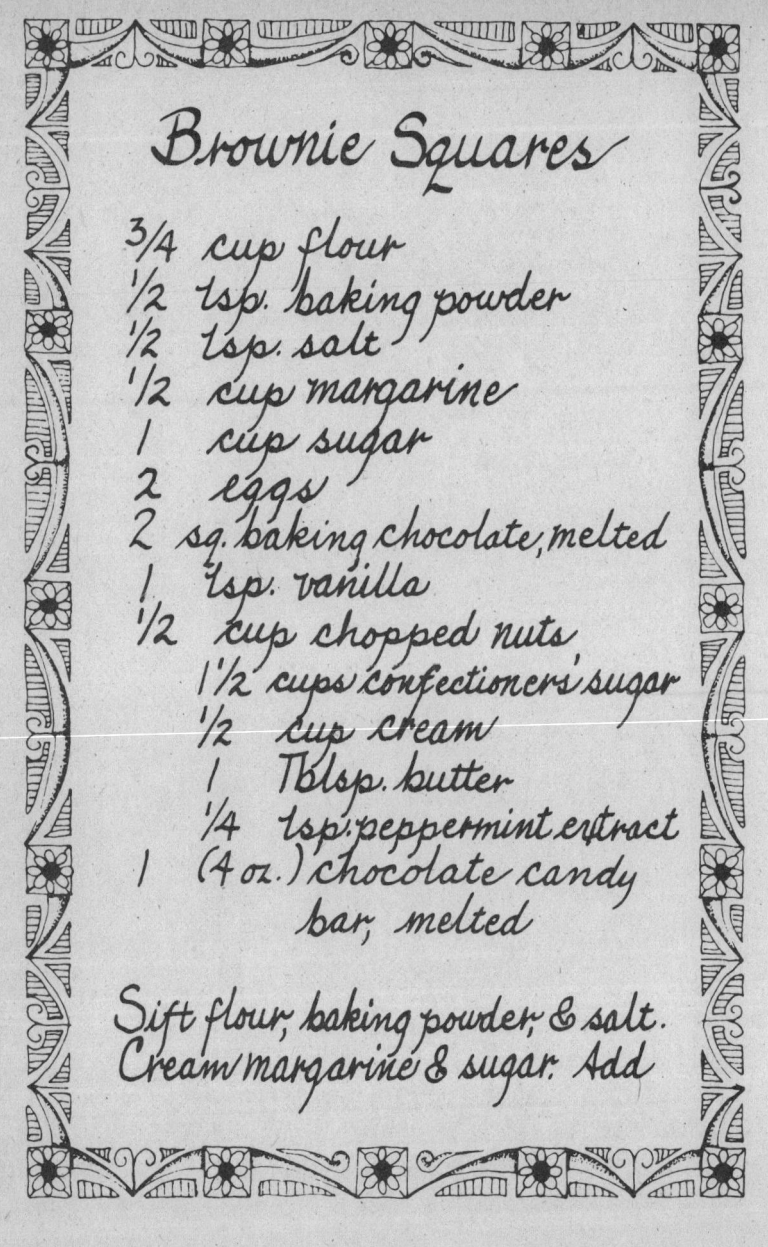

3/4 cup flour
1/2 tsp. baking powder
1/2 tsp. salt
1/2 cup margarine
1 cup sugar
2 eggs
2 sq. baking chocolate, melted
1 tsp. vanilla
1/2 cup chopped nuts
   1 1/2 cups confectioners' sugar
   1/2 cup cream
   1 Tblsp. butter
   1/4 tsp. peppermint extract
   1 (4 oz.) chocolate candy bar, melted

Sift flour, baking powder, & salt. Cream margarine & sugar. Add

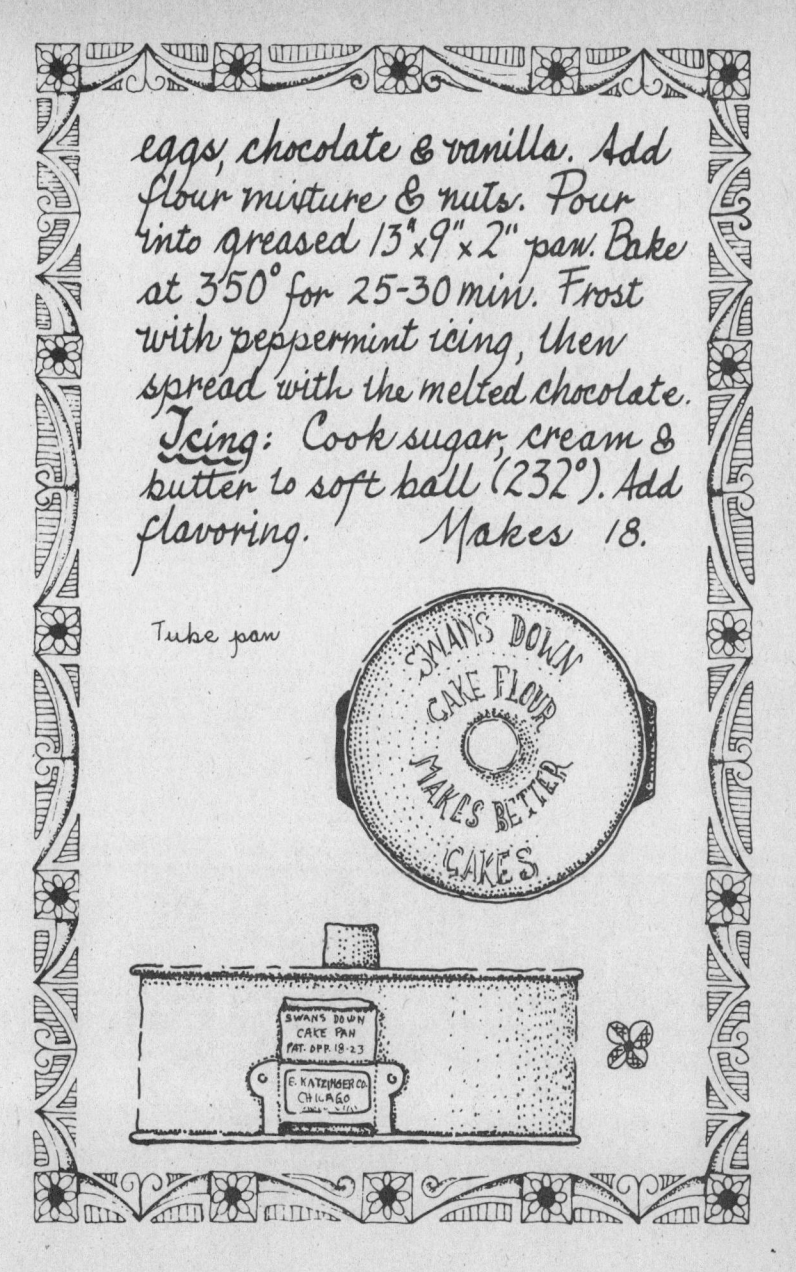

eggs, chocolate & vanilla. Add flour mixture & nuts. Pour into greased 13"x 9"x 2" pan. Bake at 350° for 25-30 min. Frost with peppermint icing, then spread with the melted chocolate.
  <u>Icing</u>: Cook sugar, cream & butter to soft ball (232°). Add flavoring.   Makes 18.

Tube pan

Butterscotch Squares

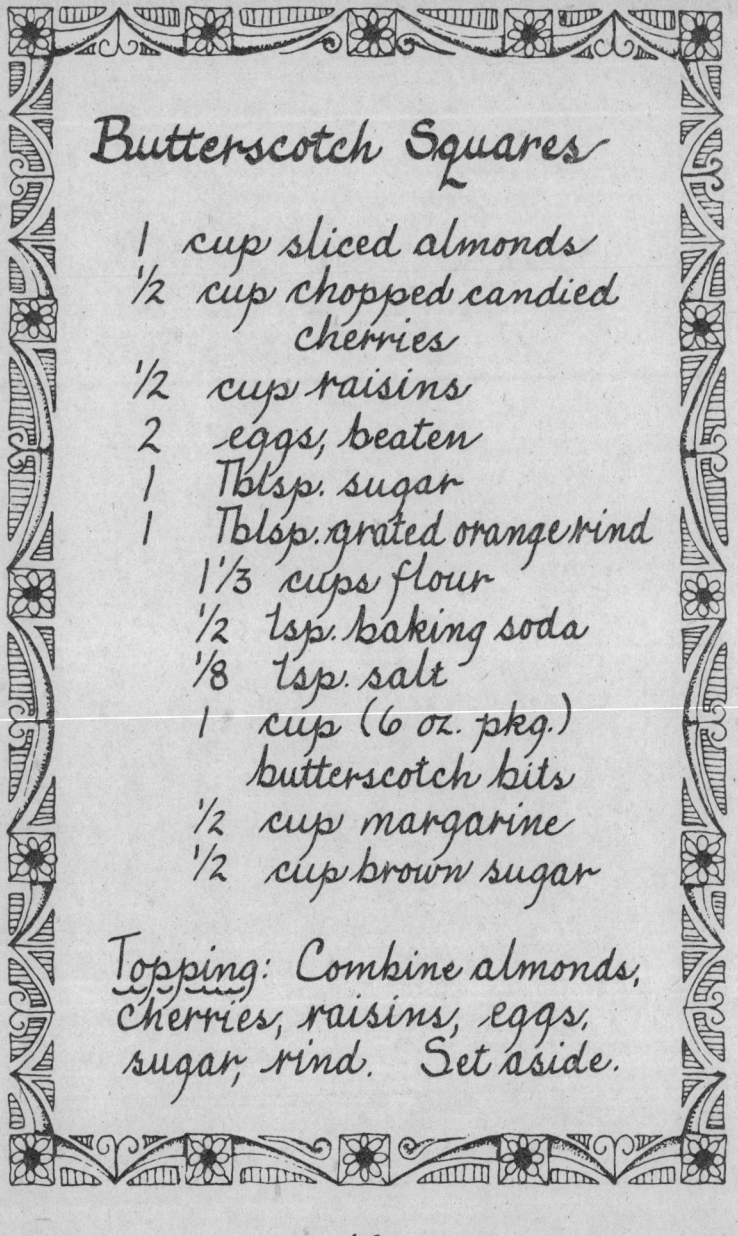

1 cup sliced almonds
½ cup chopped candied cherries
½ cup raisins
2 eggs, beaten
1 Tblsp. sugar
1 Tblsp. grated orange rind
1⅓ cups flour
½ tsp. baking soda
⅛ tsp. salt
1 cup (6 oz. pkg.) butterscotch bits
½ cup margarine
½ cup brown sugar

Topping: Combine almonds, cherries, raisins, eggs, sugar, rind. Set aside.

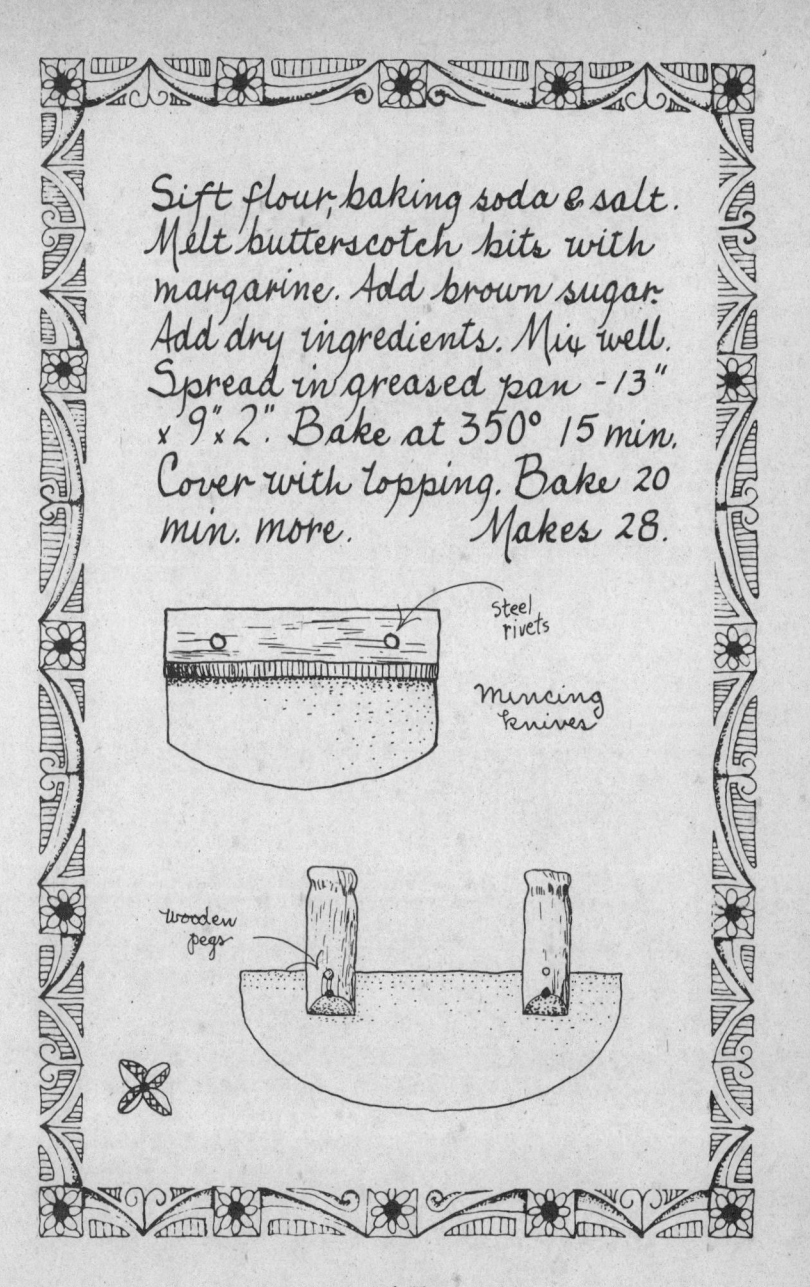

Sift flour, baking soda & salt. Melt butterscotch bits with margarine. Add brown sugar. Add dry ingredients. Mix well. Spread in greased pan - 13" x 9" x 2". Bake at 350° 15 min. Cover with topping. Bake 20 min. more. Makes 28.

steel rivets

mincing knives

wooden pegs

California Squares

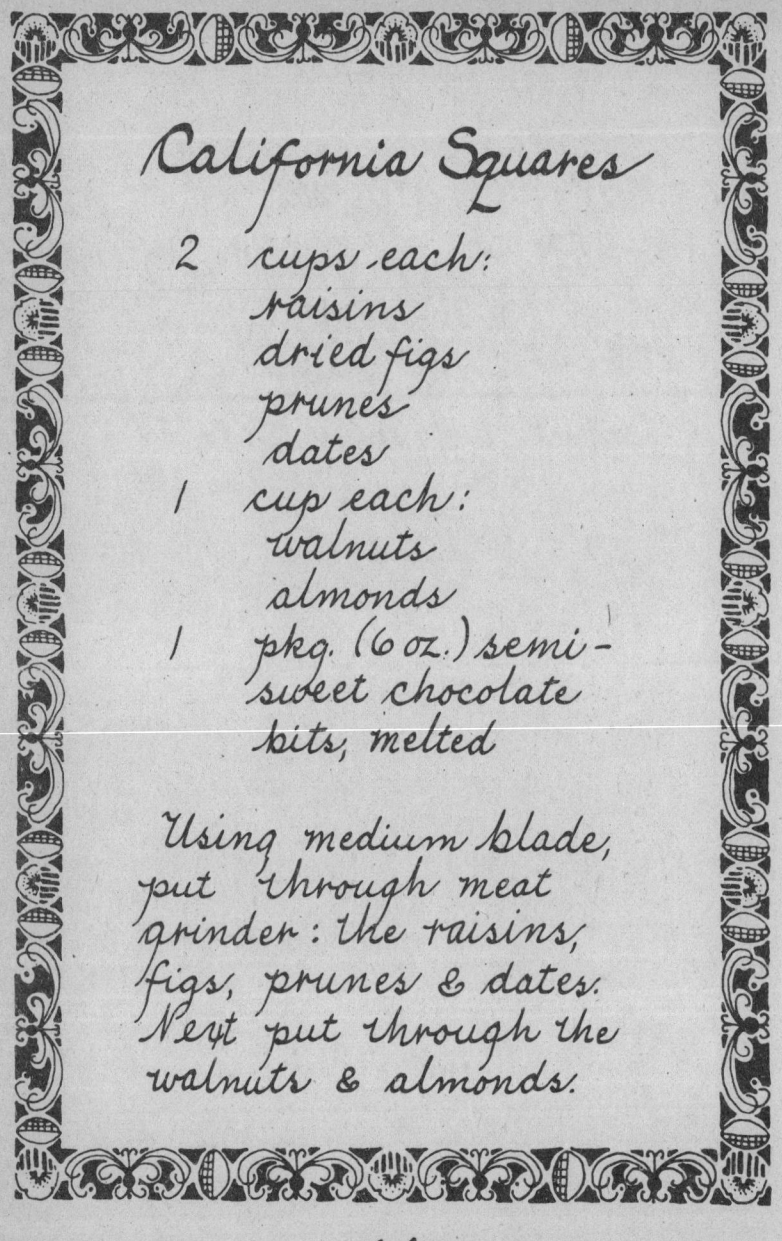

2 cups each:
    raisins
    dried figs
    prunes
    dates
1 cup each:
    walnuts
    almonds
1 pkg. (6 oz.) semi-sweet chocolate bits, melted

Using medium blade, put through meat grinder: the raisins, figs, prunes & dates. Next put through the walnuts & almonds.

Blend well. Press into buttered 13" x 9" x 2" pans. Spread melted chocolate over top. Cut into squares. Store in a cool place. Makes 40.

label → BREVETTO "VELOX" 24 1599

Coffee roaster tin & brass

Cereal Squares

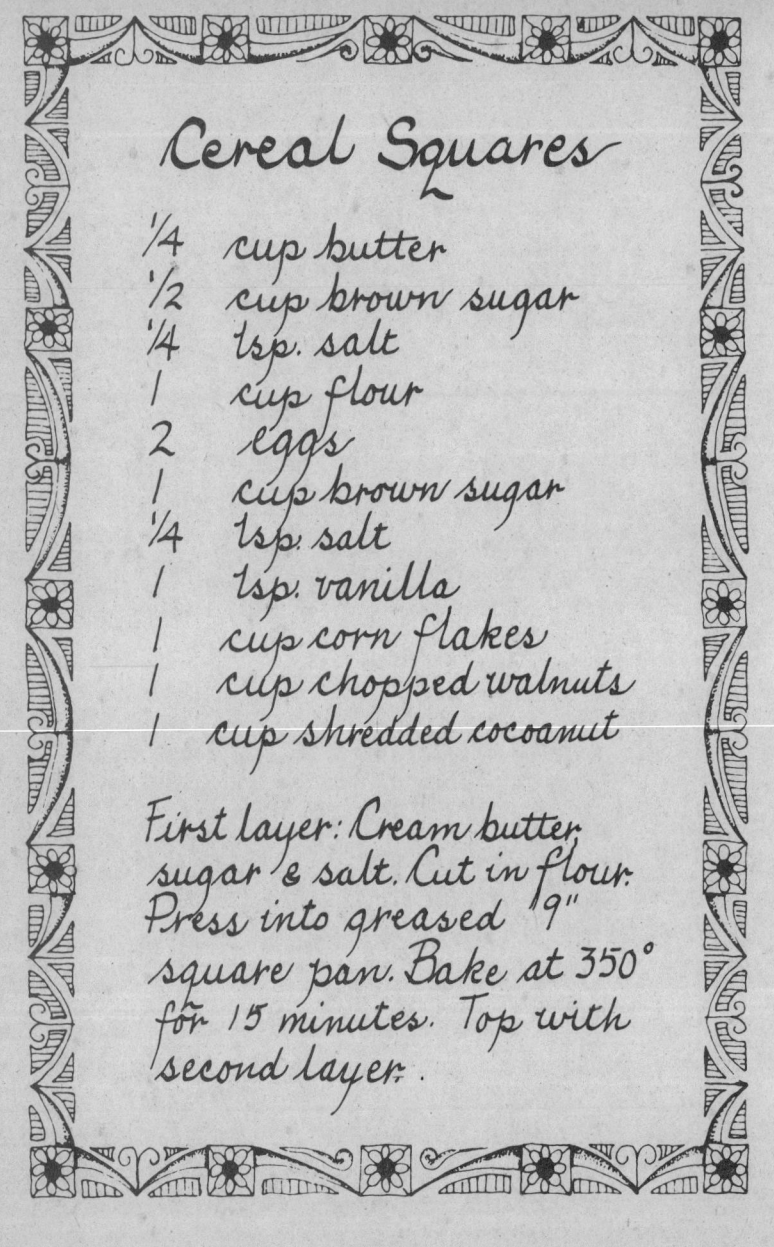

1/4	cup butter
1/2	cup brown sugar
1/4	tsp. salt
1	cup flour
2	eggs
1	cup brown sugar
1/4	tsp. salt
1	tsp. vanilla
1	cup corn flakes
1	cup chopped walnuts
1	cup shredded cocoanut

First layer: Cream butter, sugar & salt. Cut in flour. Press into greased 9" square pan. Bake at 350° for 15 minutes. Top with second layer.

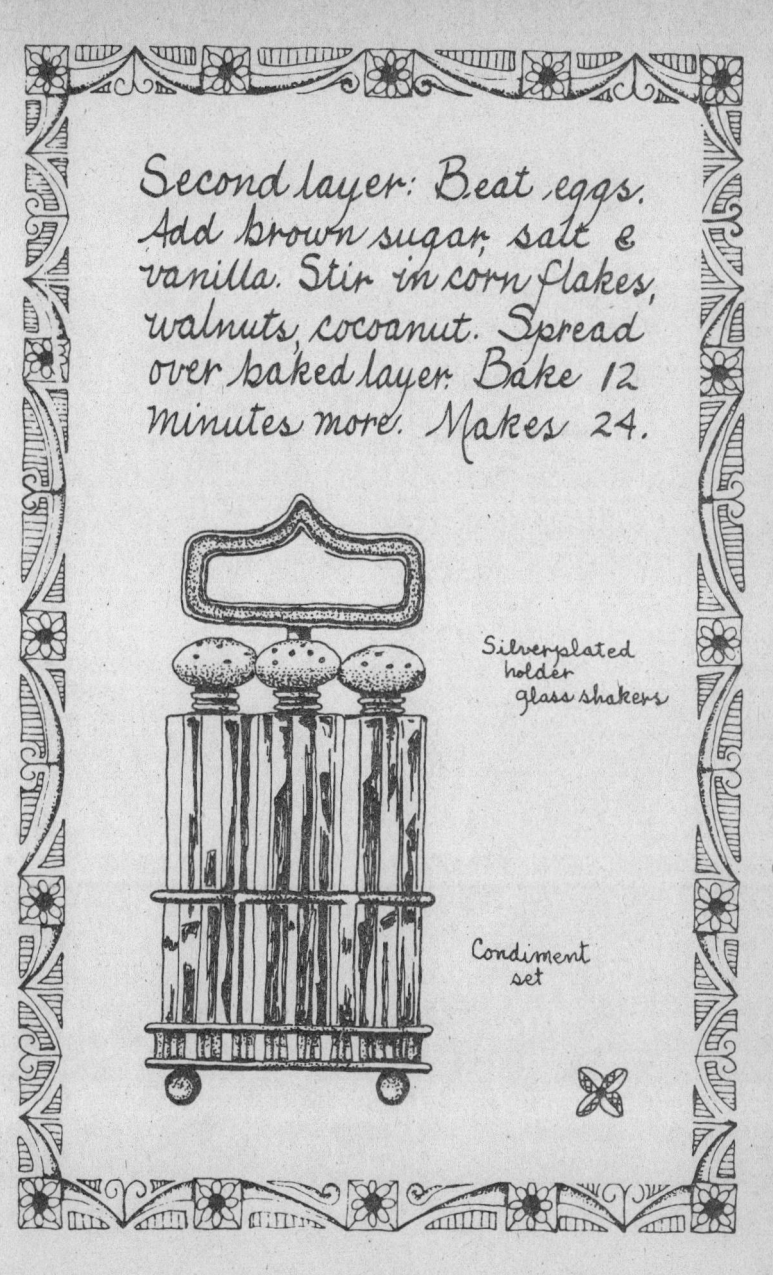

Second layer: Beat eggs. Add brown sugar, salt & vanilla. Stir in corn flakes, walnuts, cocoanut. Spread over baked layer. Bake 12 minutes more. Makes 24.

Silverplated holder glass shakers

Condiment set

Cheese Squares

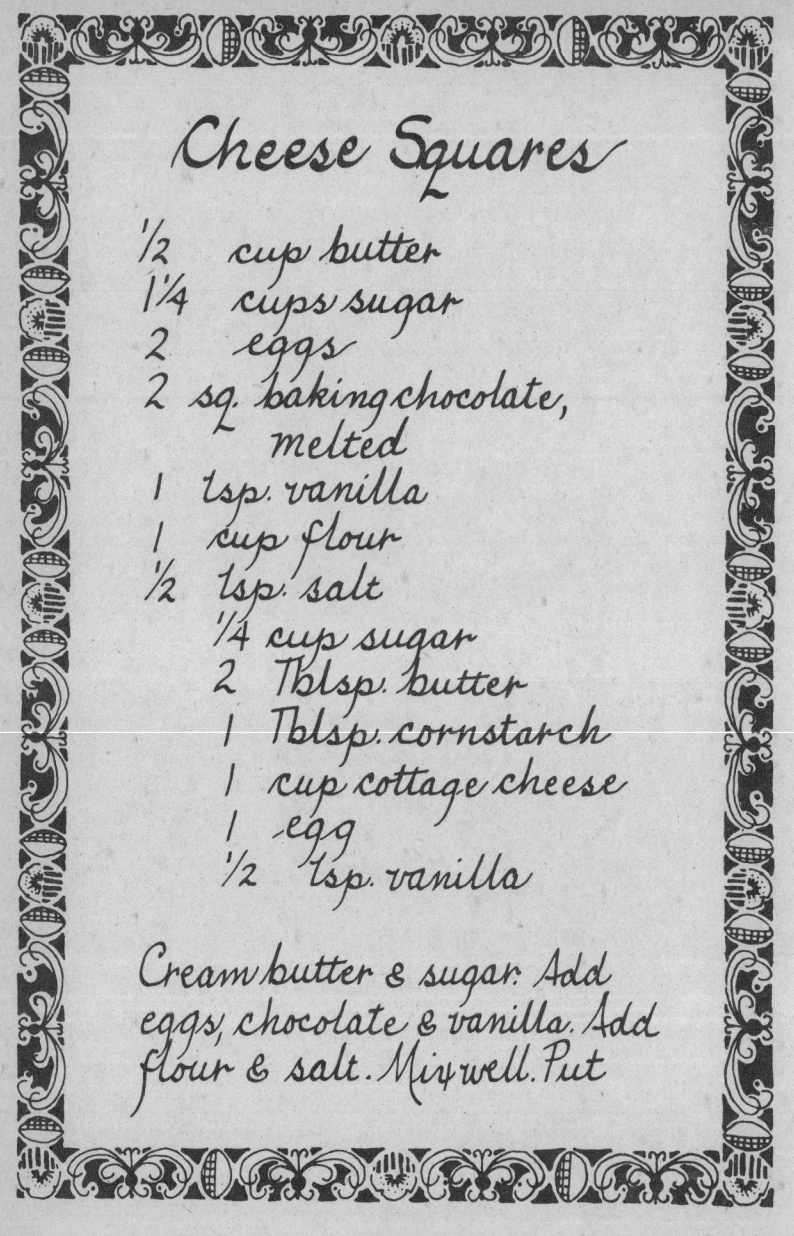

½ cup butter
1¼ cups sugar
2 eggs
2 sq. baking chocolate, melted
1 tsp. vanilla
1 cup flour
½ tsp. salt
¼ cup sugar
2 Tblsp. butter
1 Tblsp. cornstarch
1 cup cottage cheese
1 egg
½ tsp. vanilla

Cream butter & sugar. Add eggs, chocolate & vanilla. Add flour & salt. Mix well. Put aside. Cream sugar & butter. Add cornstarch, cheese, egg & vanilla. Blend well. Spread ½ the first mixture in greased 8" sq. pan. Pour cheese mixture on top. Pour rest of first mixture on cheese. Bake at 375° for 45 min.　　　Makes 2 dozen.

white cedar butter churn

Cherry Squares

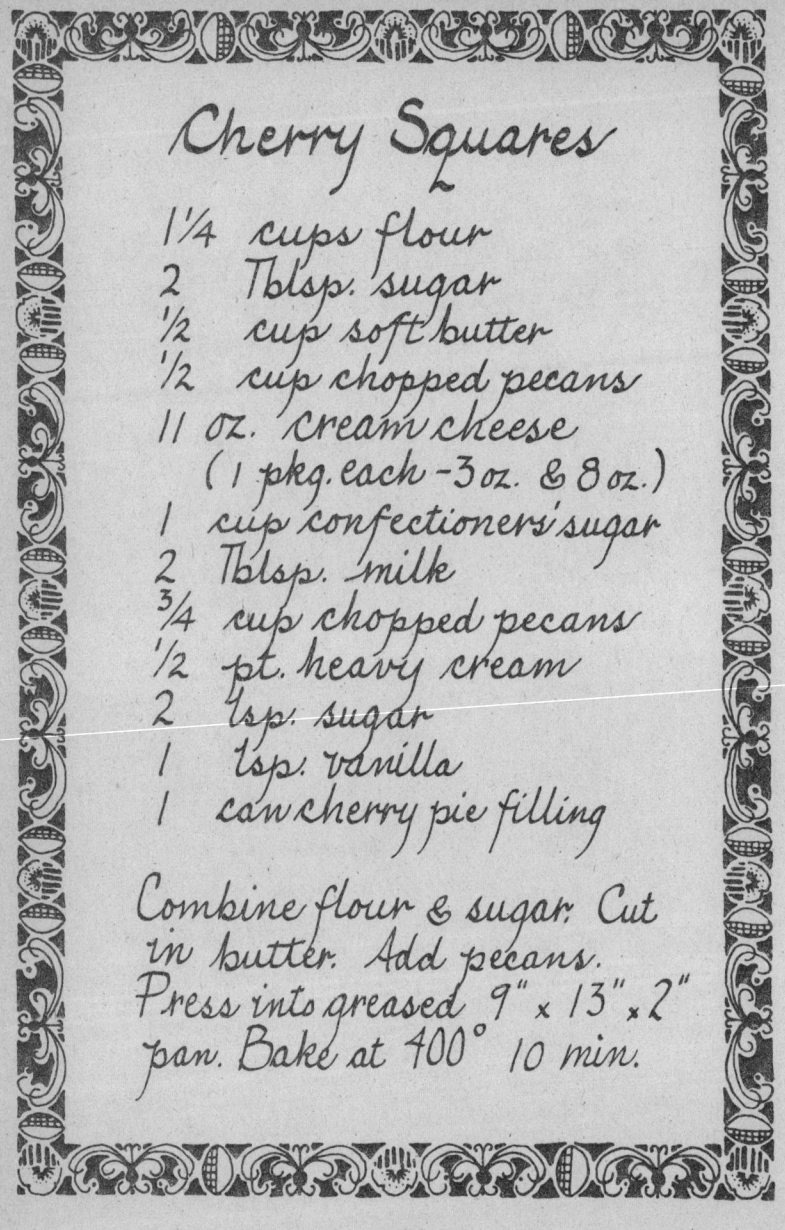

1¼ cups flour
2 Tblsp. sugar
½ cup soft butter
½ cup chopped pecans
11 oz. cream cheese
 (1 pkg. each - 3 oz. & 8 oz.)
1 cup confectioners' sugar
2 Tblsp. milk
¾ cup chopped pecans
½ pt. heavy cream
2 tsp. sugar
1 tsp. vanilla
1 can cherry pie filling

Combine flour & sugar. Cut in butter. Add pecans. Press into greased 9" x 13" x 2" pan. Bake at 400° 10 min.

Cool. Mix cheese, sugar & milk. Spread on top of mixture in pan. Sprinkle with pecans. Whip cream. Add sugar & vanilla. Spread on mixture. Top with cherry pie filling. Chill 8 hours.
   Makes 12.

Turkey red table cover

Chewer's Squares

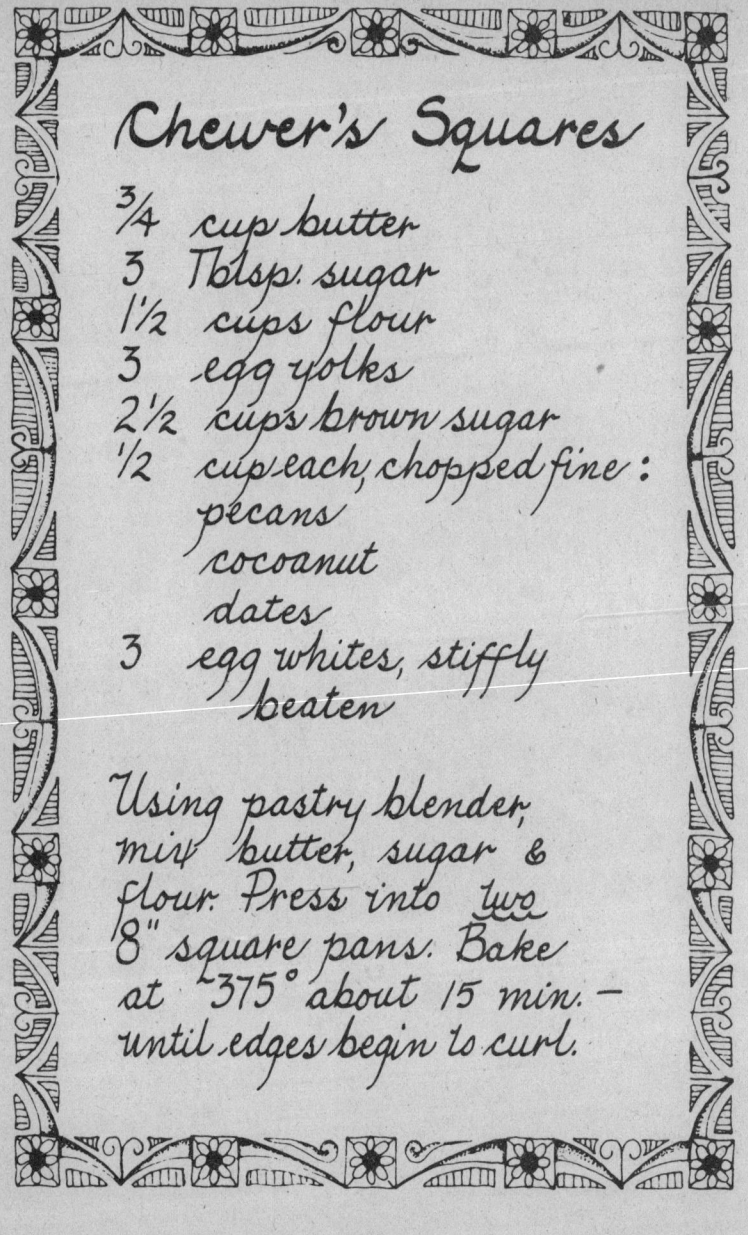

3/4 cup butter
3 Tblsp. sugar
1½ cups flour
3 egg yolks
2½ cups brown sugar
½ cup each, chopped fine:
   pecans
   cocoanut
   dates
3 egg whites, stiffly beaten

Using pastry blender, mix butter, sugar & flour. Press into two 8" square pans. Bake at 375° about 15 min.— until edges begin to curl.

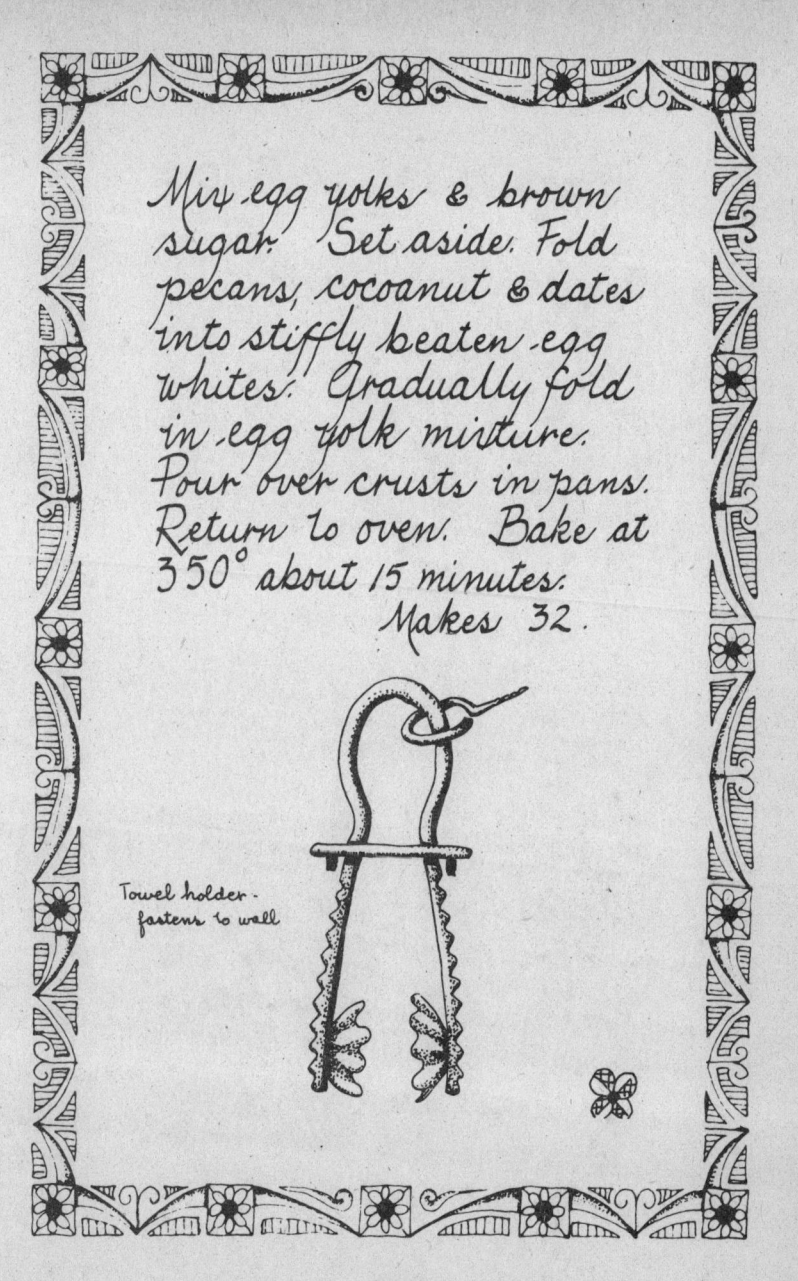

Mix egg yolks & brown sugar. Set aside. Fold pecans, cocoanut & dates into stiffly beaten egg whites. Gradually fold in egg yolk mixture. Pour over crusts in pans. Return to oven. Bake at 350° about 15 minutes.
    Makes 32.

Towel holder - fastens to wall

Chocolate Mint Squares

½ cup margarine, melted
1 cup sugar
2 eggs, beaten
2 squares baking chocolate, melted
½ tsp. peppermint extract
½ cup flour
½ cup chopped almonds

Mix margarine & sugar. Beat in eggs until mixture is light. Add chocolate & peppermint extract. Add flour, then almonds. Blend well. Pour into well-greased

13" x 9" x 2" pan. Bake at 350° about 20-30 minutes. Cool. Cut into squares. Makes 48.

Match holder
tin
sandpaper center

Cocoanut Squares

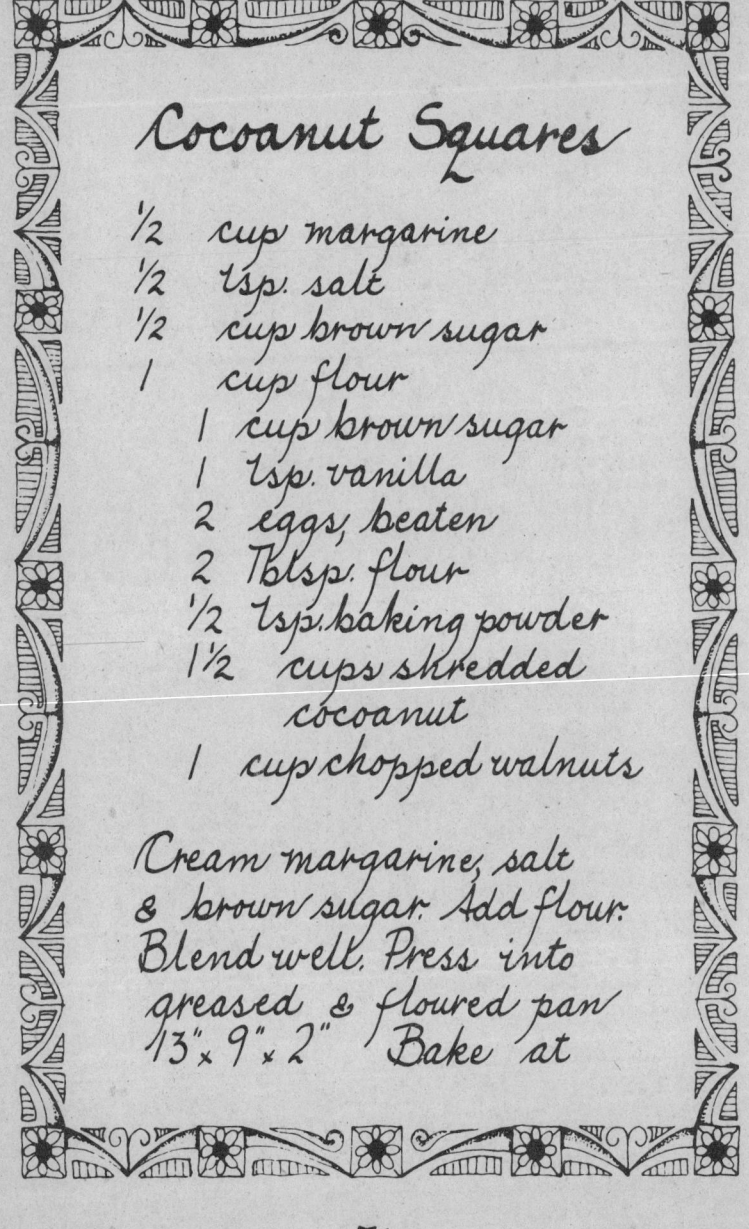

½ cup margarine
½ tsp. salt
½ cup brown sugar
1 cup flour
1 cup brown sugar
1 tsp. vanilla
2 eggs, beaten
2 Tblsp. flour
½ tsp. baking powder
1½ cups shredded cocoanut
1 cup chopped walnuts

Cream margarine, salt & brown sugar. Add flour. Blend well. Press into greased & floured pan 13" x 9" x 2". Bake at

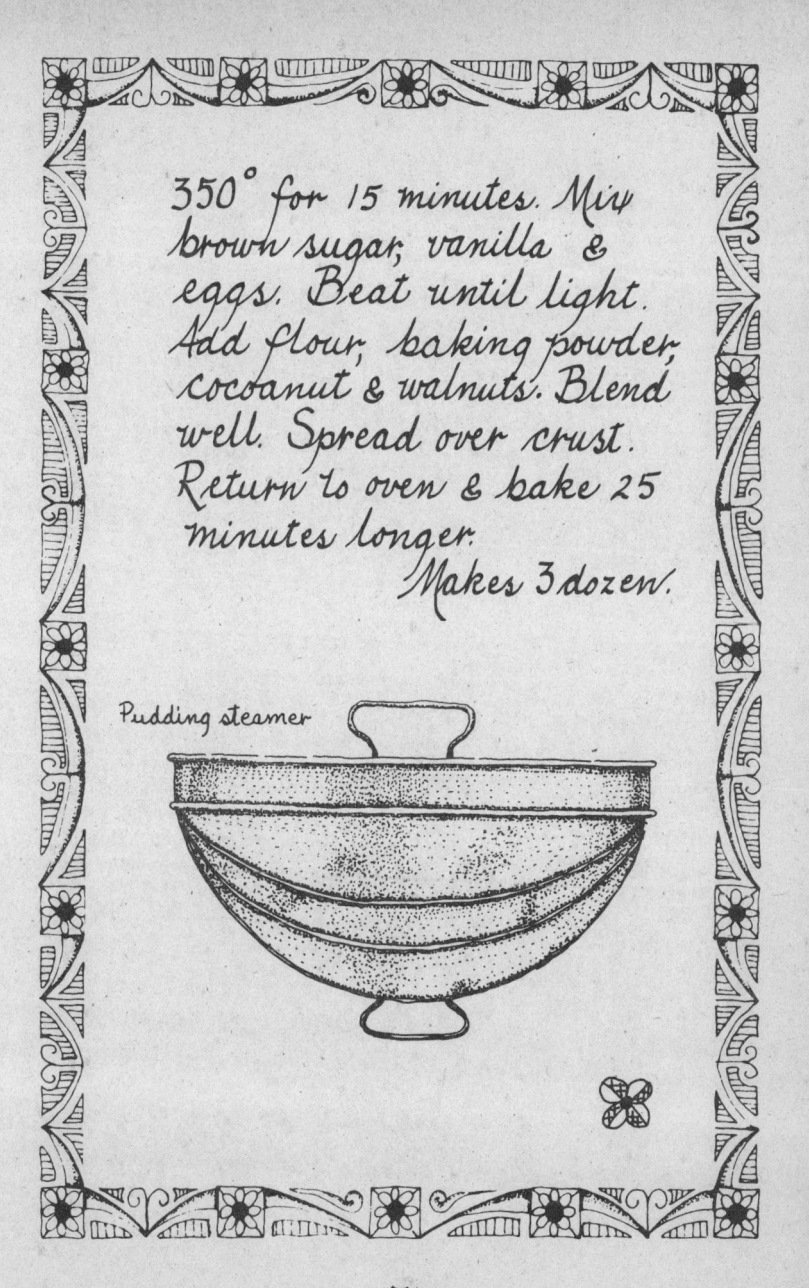

350° for 15 minutes. Mix brown sugar, vanilla & eggs. Beat until light. Add flour, baking powder, cocoanut & walnuts. Blend well. Spread over crust. Return to oven & bake 25 minutes longer.
     Makes 3 dozen.

Pudding steamer

Cranberry Squares

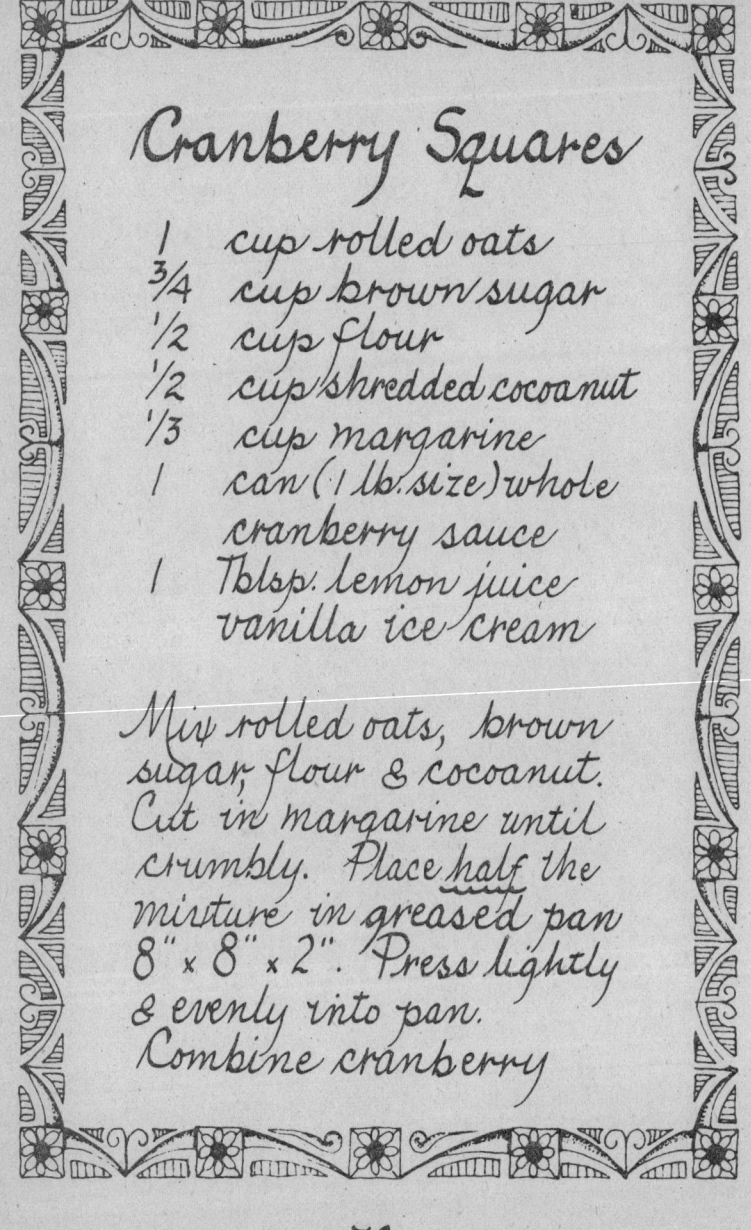

1	cup rolled oats
3/4	cup brown sugar
1/2	cup flour
1/2	cup shredded cocoanut
1/3	cup margarine
1	can (1 lb. size) whole cranberry sauce
1	Tblsp. lemon juice
	vanilla ice cream

Mix rolled oats, brown sugar, flour & cocoanut. Cut in margarine until crumbly. Place half the mixture in greased pan 8" x 8" x 2". Press lightly & evenly into pan. Combine cranberry sauce with lemon juice. Pour on top of mixture in pan. Top with remaining crumb mixture. Press down lightly. Bake at 350° about 40 minutes. Serve with a dollop of ice cream.   Makes 9.

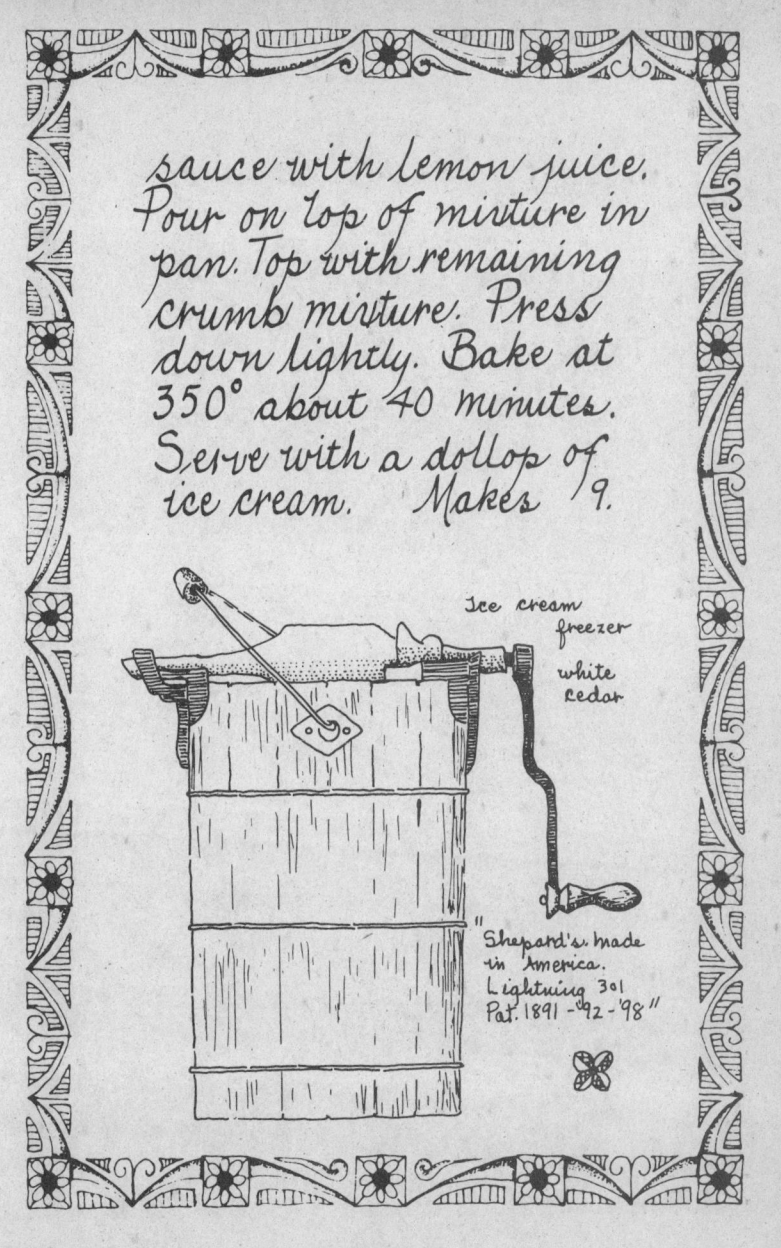

Ice cream freezer
white cedar

"Shepard's made in America. Lightning 301 Pat. 1891-'92-'98"

Creamy Peanut Squares

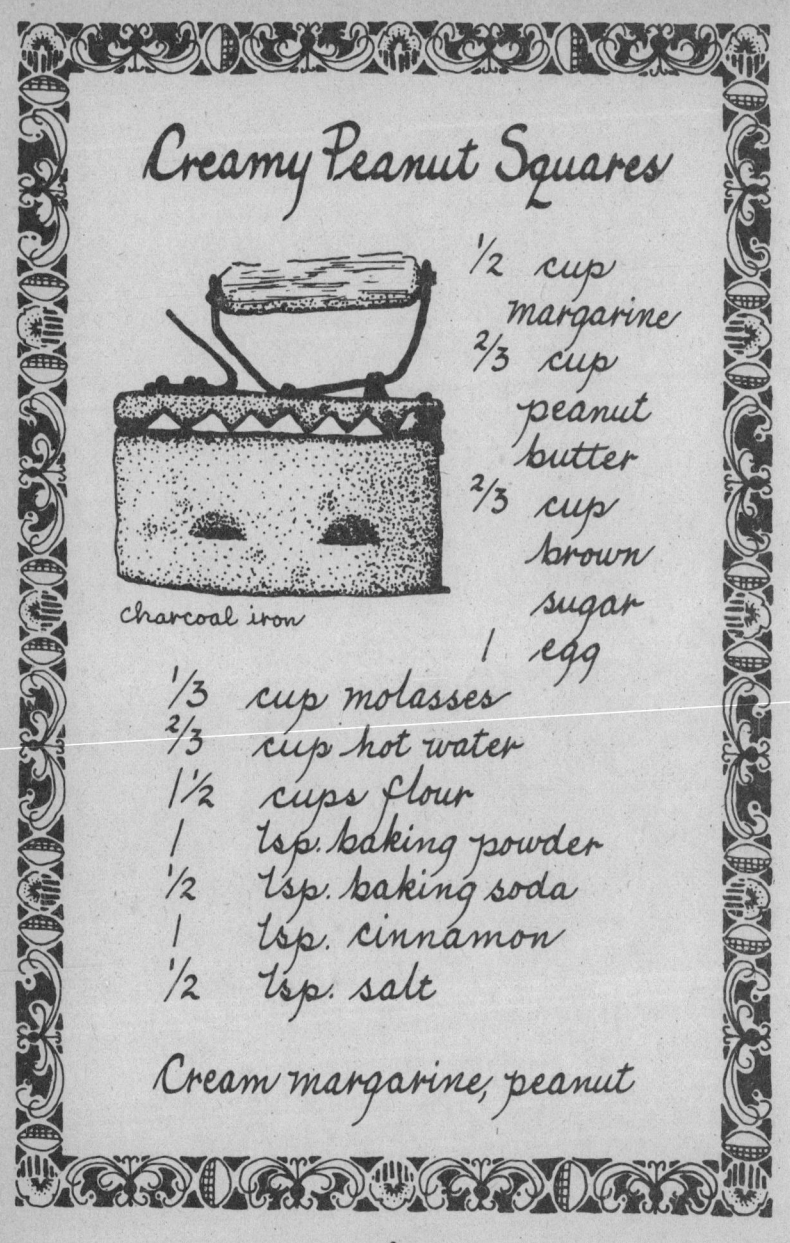

½ cup margarine
⅔ cup peanut butter
⅔ cup brown sugar
1 egg
⅓ cup molasses
⅔ cup hot water
1½ cups flour
1 tsp. baking powder
½ tsp. baking soda
1 tsp. cinnamon
½ tsp. salt

Cream margarine, peanut

charcoal iron

butter & sugar. Add egg & molasses. Blend well. Sift flour, baking powder, soda, cinnamon & salt. Add to first mixture alternately with hot water. Pour into well-greased 13"x 9"x 2" pan. Bake at 350° 25-30 min. Makes 24.

Sad (heavy) iron

wooden handle

top view of cast iron base

metal

Date Squares

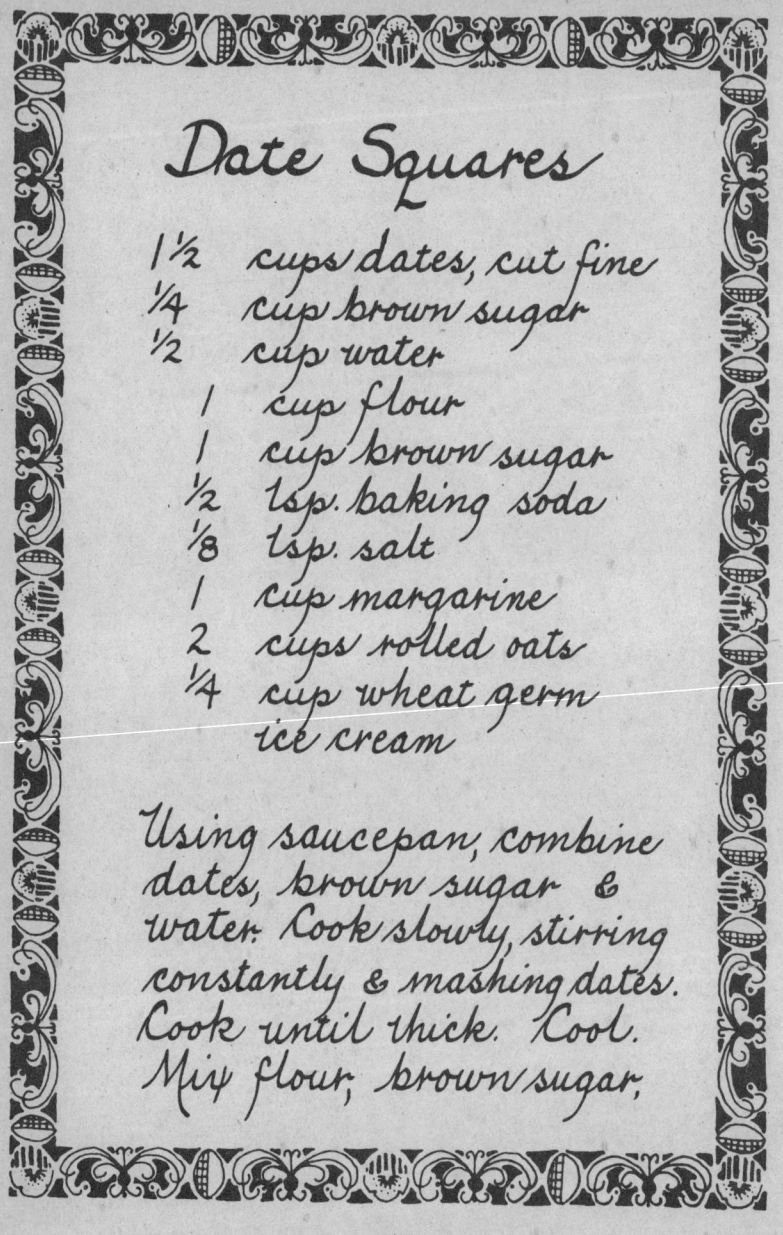

1½   cups dates, cut fine
¼   cup brown sugar
½   cup water
1   cup flour
1   cup brown sugar
½   tsp. baking soda
⅛   tsp. salt
1   cup margarine
2   cups rolled oats
¼   cup wheat germ
    ice cream

Using saucepan, combine dates, brown sugar & water. Cook slowly, stirring constantly & mashing dates. Cook until thick. Cool. Mix flour, brown sugar,

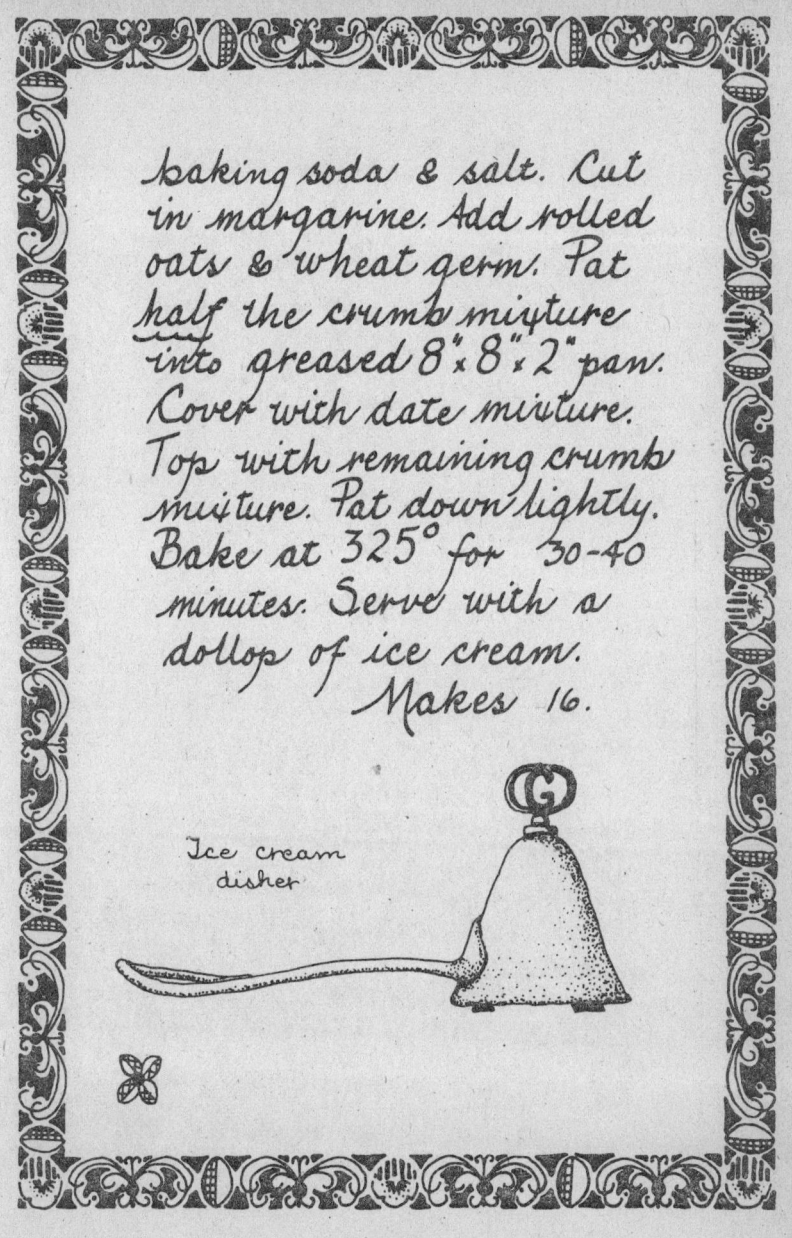

baking soda & salt. Cut in margarine. Add rolled oats & wheat germ. Pat half the crumb mixture into greased 8"x 8"x 2" pan. Cover with date mixture. Top with remaining crumb mixture. Pat down lightly. Bake at 325° for 30-40 minutes. Serve with a dollop of ice cream.
    Makes 16.

Ice cream disher

Filbert Squares

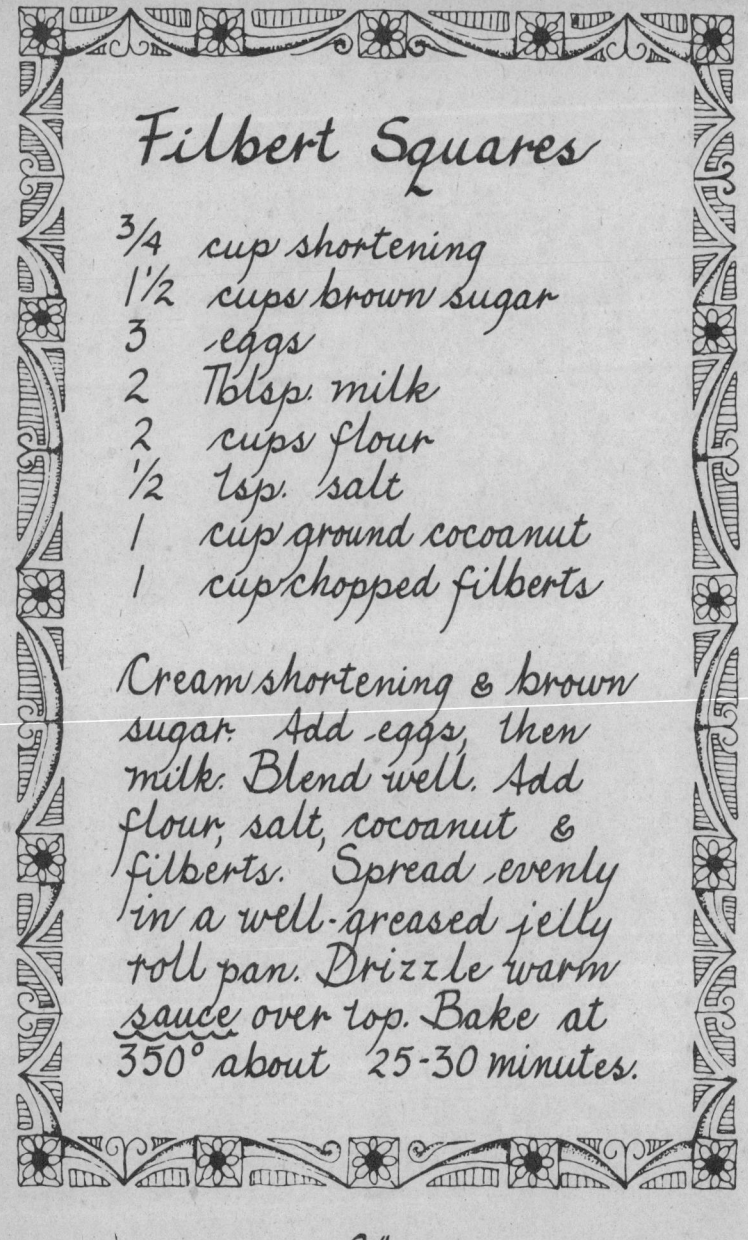

3/4 cup shortening
1½ cups brown sugar
3 eggs
2 Tblsp. milk
2 cups flour
½ tsp. salt
1 cup ground cocoanut
1 cup chopped filberts

Cream shortening & brown sugar. Add eggs, then milk. Blend well. Add flour, salt, cocoanut & filberts. Spread evenly in a well-greased jelly roll pan. Drizzle warm sauce over top. Bake at 350° about 25-30 minutes.

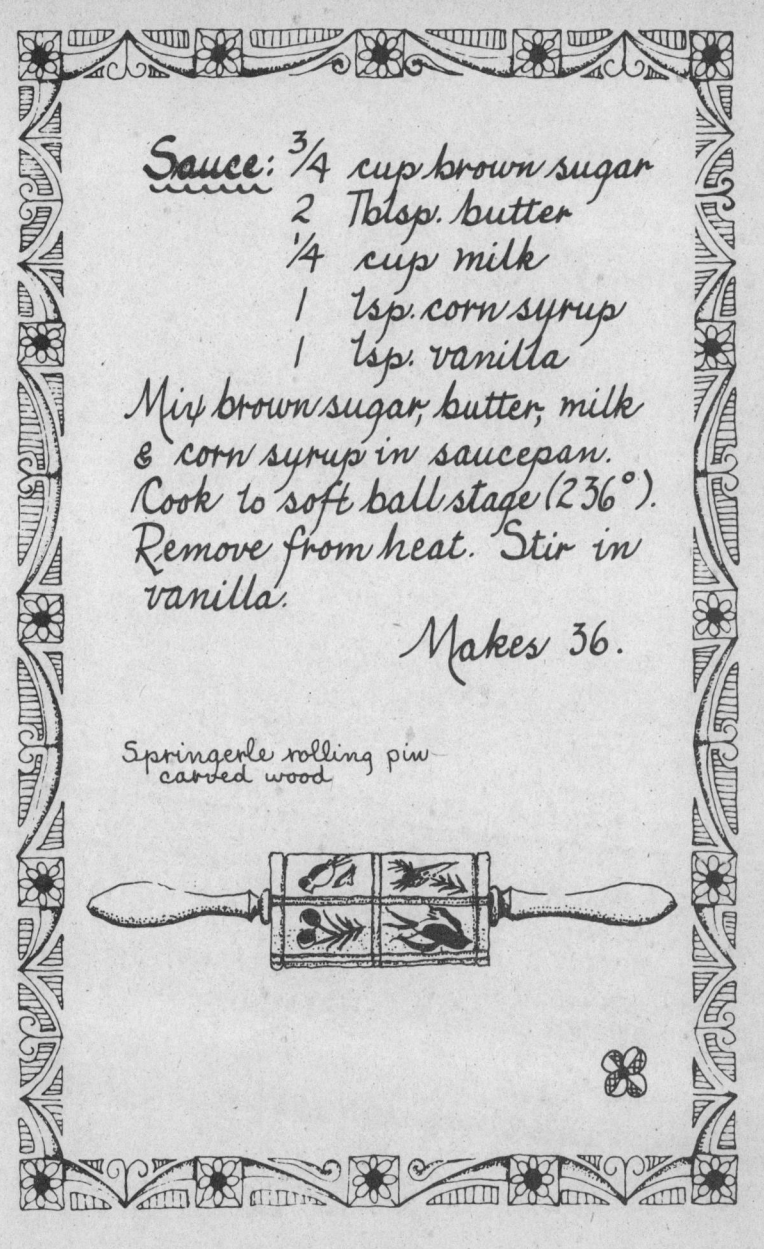

Sauce: 3/4 cup brown sugar
2 Tblsp. butter
1/4 cup milk
1 tsp. corn syrup
1 tsp. vanilla

Mix brown sugar, butter, milk & corn syrup in saucepan. Cook to soft ball stage (236°). Remove from heat. Stir in vanilla.

            Makes 36.

Springerle rolling pin
carved wood

Honey Squares

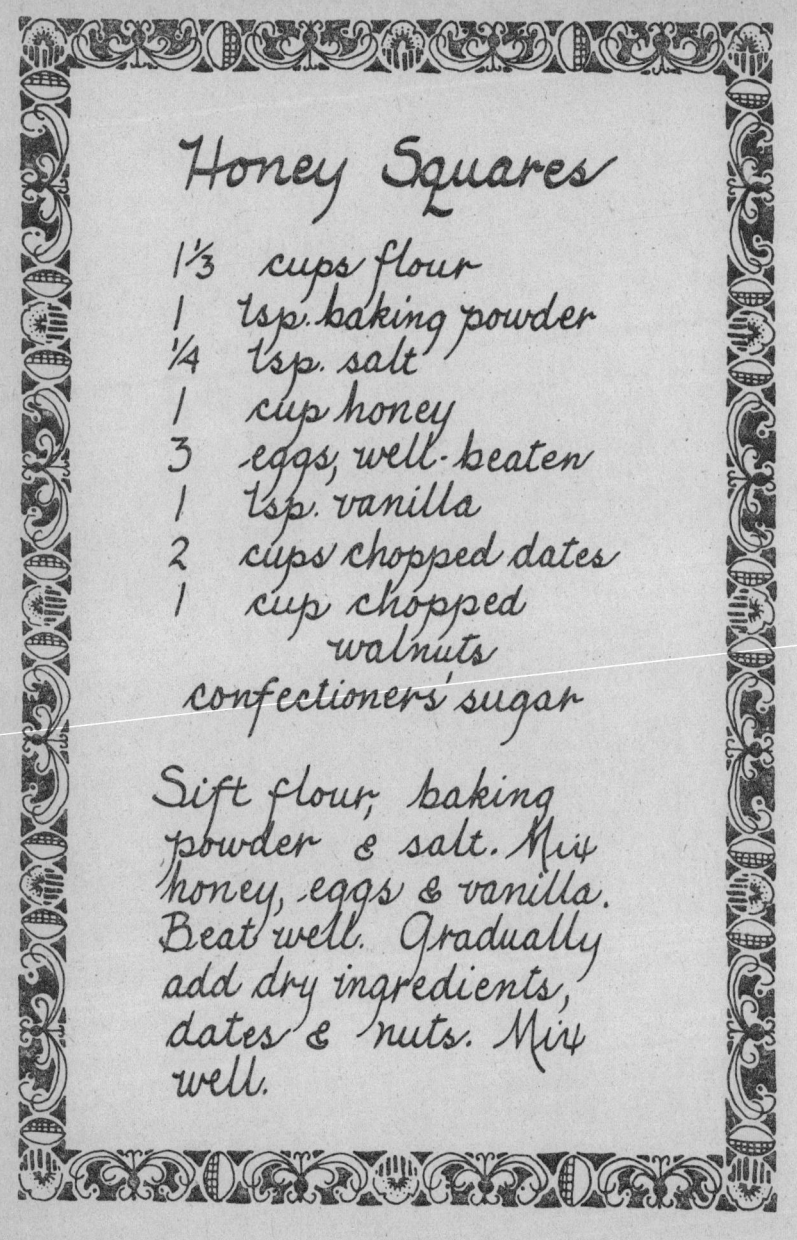

1⅓ cups flour
1 tsp. baking powder
¼ tsp. salt
1 cup honey
3 eggs, well-beaten
1 tsp. vanilla
2 cups chopped dates
1 cup chopped walnuts
confectioners' sugar

Sift flour, baking powder & salt. Mix honey, eggs & vanilla. Beat well. Gradually add dry ingredients, dates & nuts. Mix well.

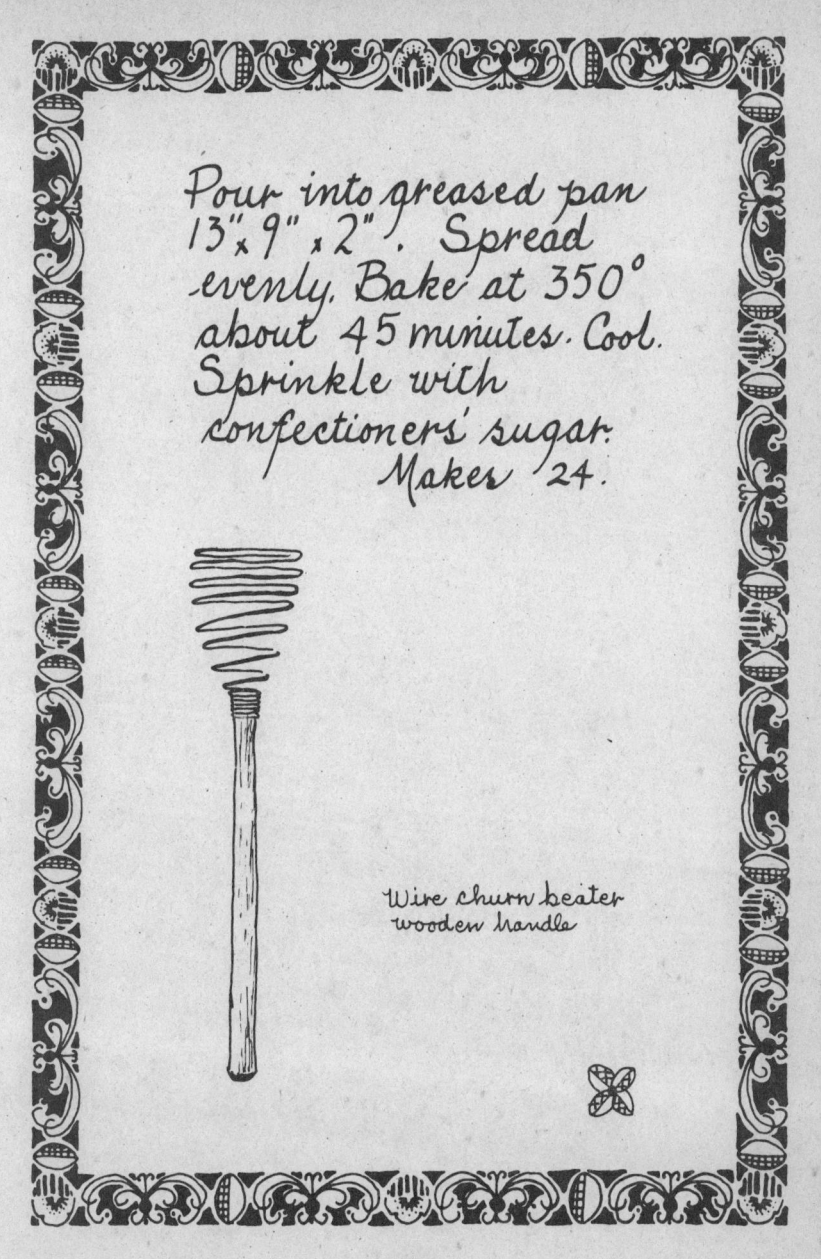

Pour into greased pan
13"x 9" x 2". Spread
evenly. Bake at 350°
about 45 minutes. Cool.
Sprinkle with
confectioners' sugar.
    Makes 24.

Wire churn beater
wooden handle

Honey Almond Squares

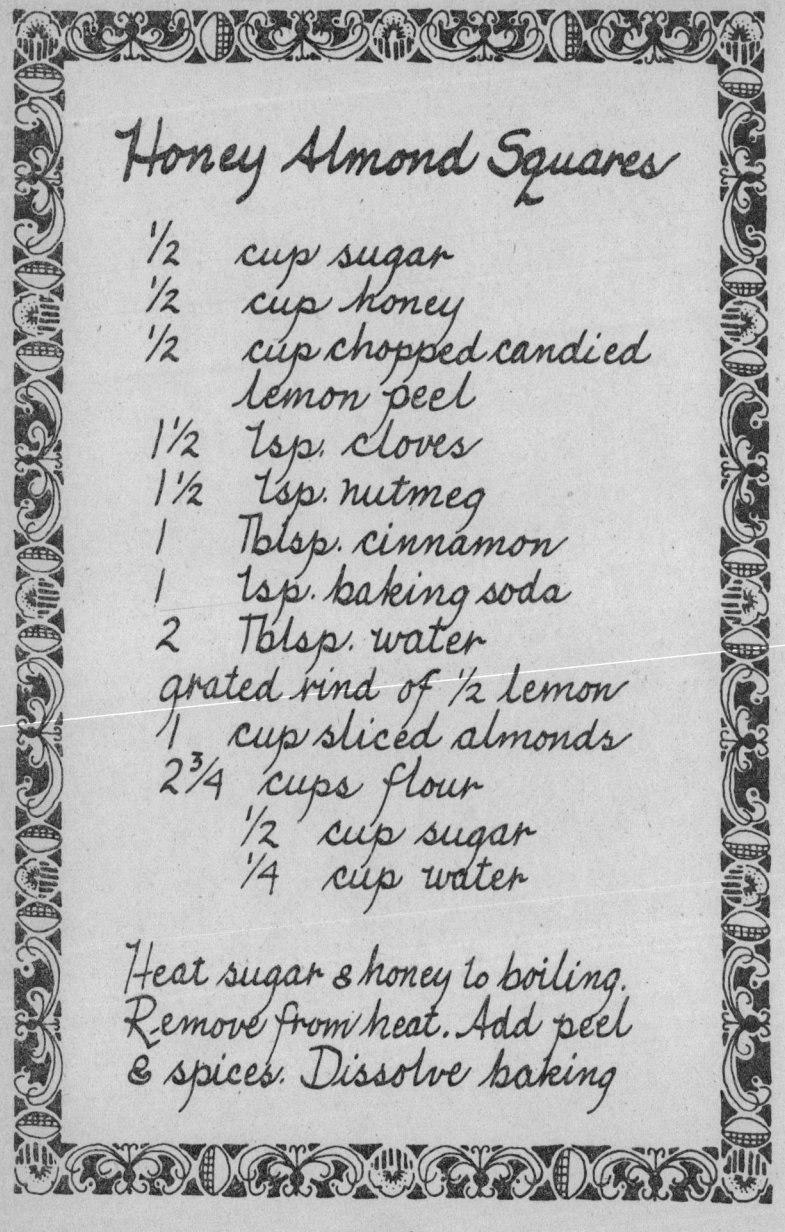

½ cup sugar
½ cup honey
½ cup chopped candied lemon peel
1½ tsp. cloves
1½ tsp. nutmeg
1 Tblsp. cinnamon
1 tsp. baking soda
2 Tblsp. water
grated rind of ½ lemon
1 cup sliced almonds
2¾ cups flour
½ cup sugar
¼ cup water

Heat sugar & honey to boiling. Remove from heat. Add peel & spices. Dissolve baking soda in water. Add to mixture. Add rind, almonds & flour. Mix well. Press into 2 greased pans 9"x 9"x 2". Bake at 350° 25 min. Cool slightly. Pour glaze over top. <u>Glaze</u>: Cook sugar & water until mixture spins a thread (230°-234°). Makes 2 dozen.

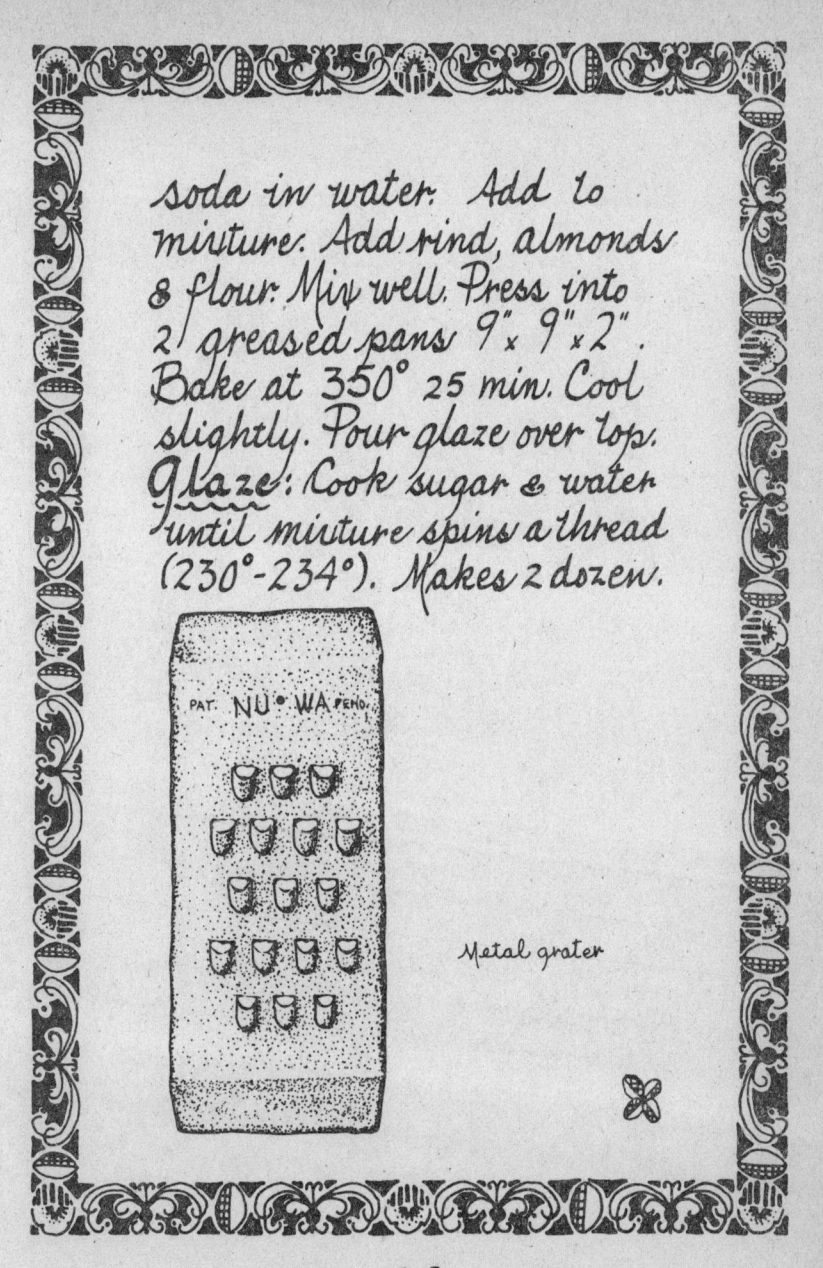

Metal grater

Mincemeat Squares

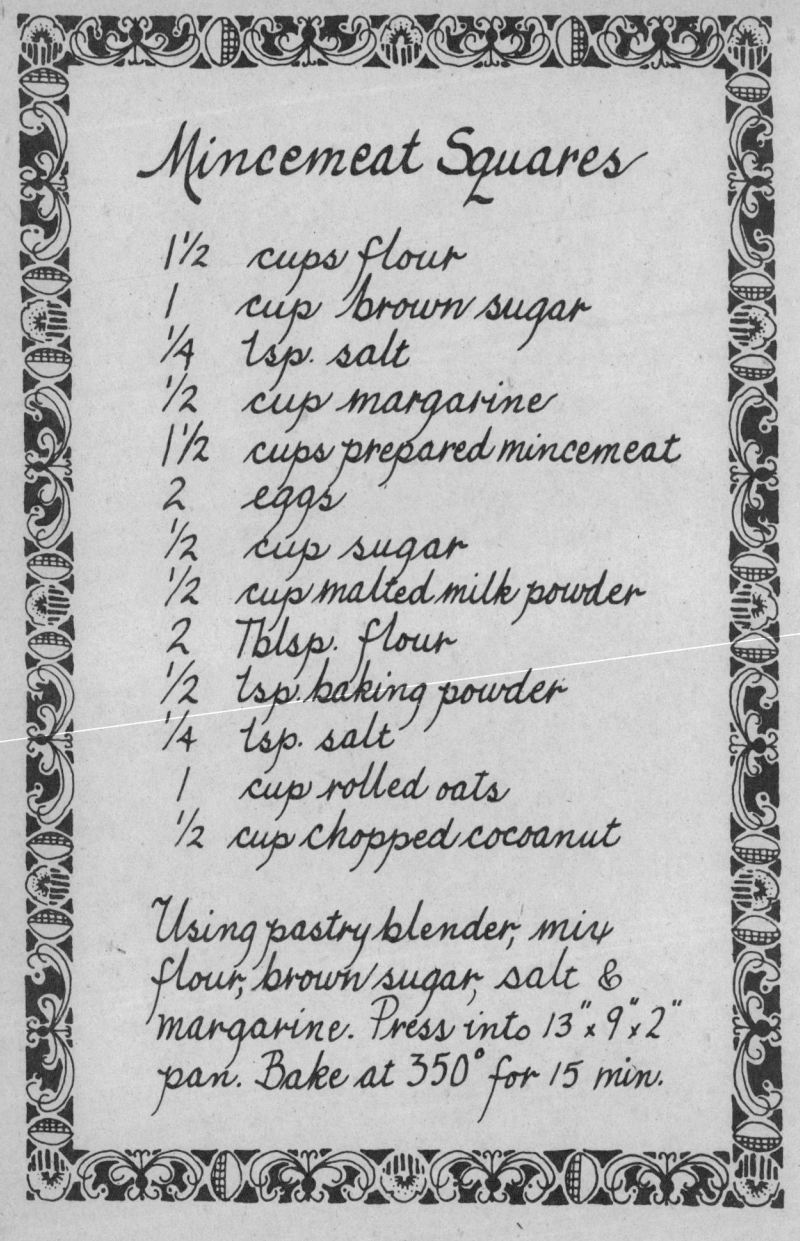

1½ cups flour
1 cup brown sugar
¼ tsp. salt
½ cup margarine
1½ cups prepared mincemeat
2 eggs
½ cup sugar
½ cup malted milk powder
2 Tblsp. flour
½ tsp. baking powder
¼ tsp. salt
1 cup rolled oats
½ cup chopped cocoanut

Using pastry blender, mix flour, brown sugar, salt & margarine. Press into 13" x 9" x 2" pan. Bake at 350° for 15 min.

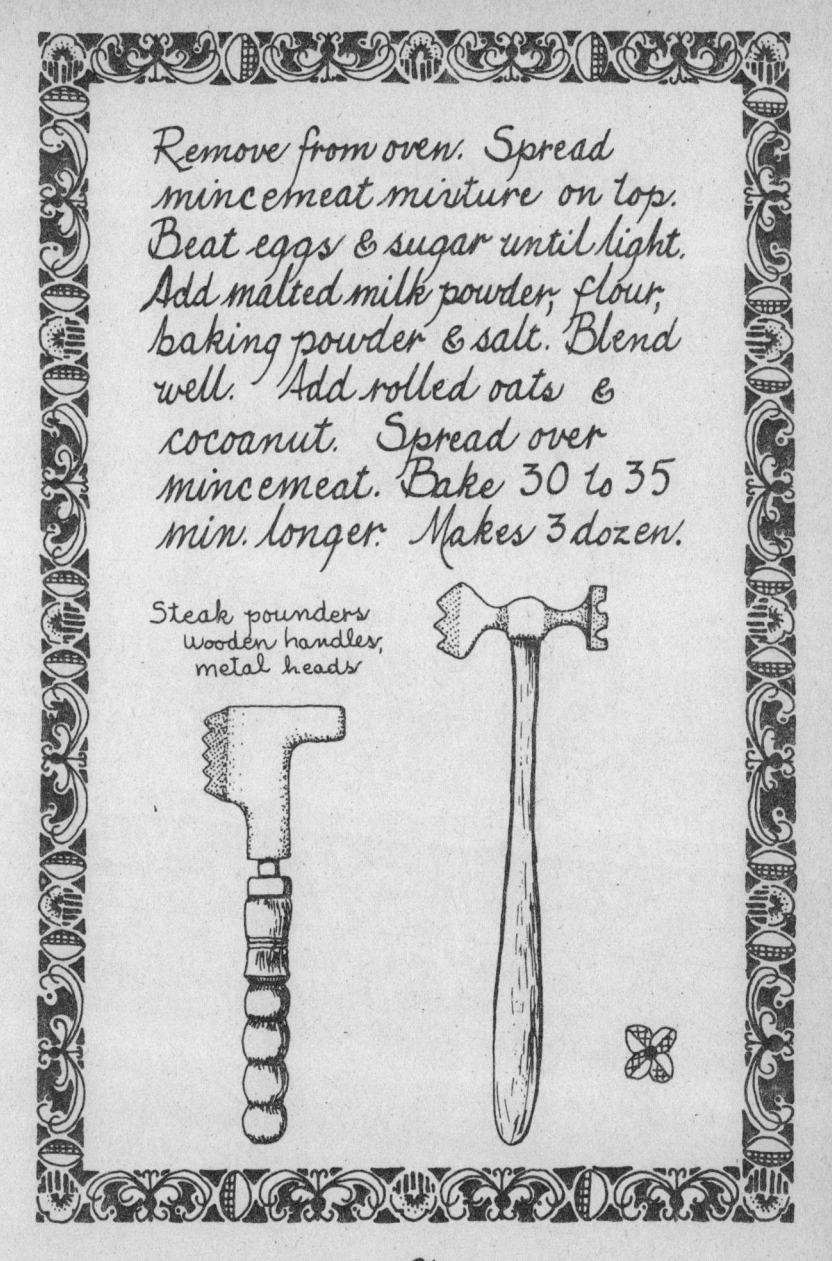

Remove from oven. Spread mincemeat mixture on top. Beat eggs & sugar until light. Add malted milk powder, flour, baking powder & salt. Blend well. Add rolled oats & cocoanut. Spread over mincemeat. Bake 30 to 35 min. longer. Makes 3 dozen.

Steak pounders wooden handles, metal heads

Orange Candy Squares

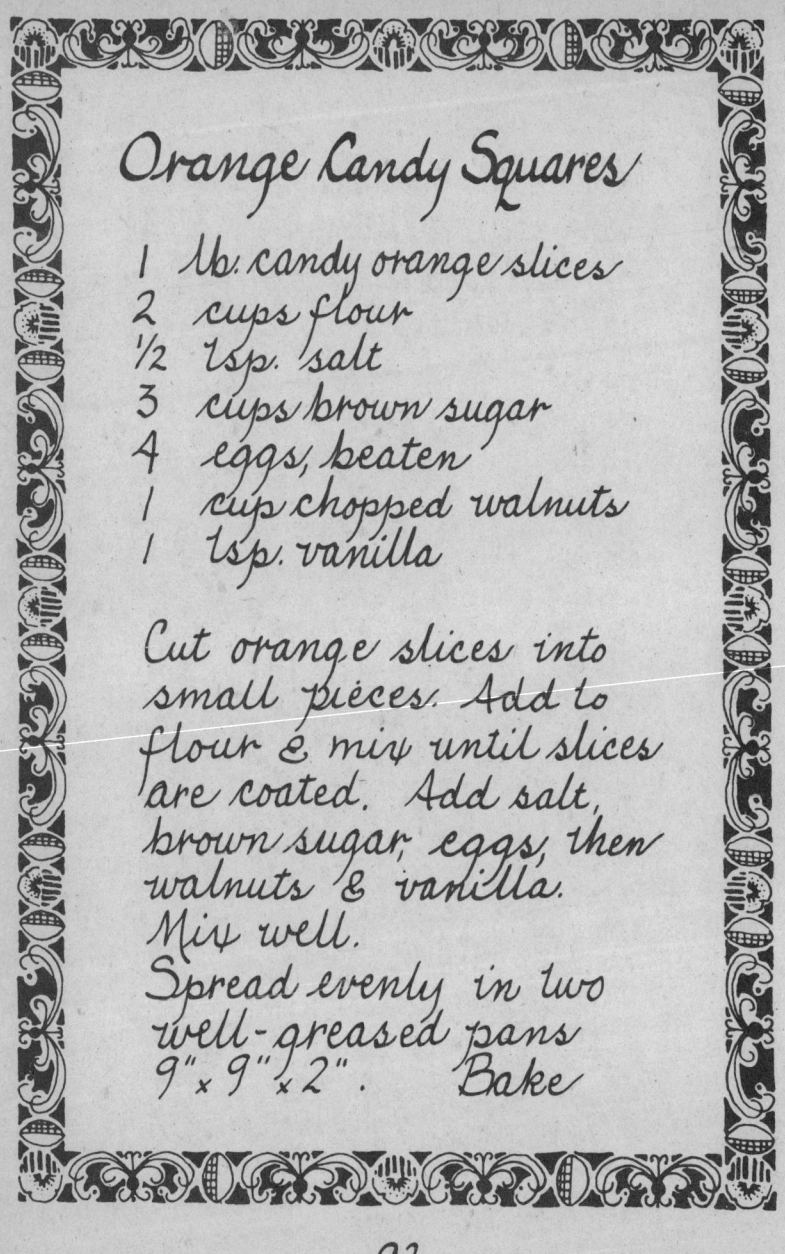

1 lb. candy orange slices
2 cups flour
½ tsp. salt
3 cups brown sugar
4 eggs, beaten
1 cup chopped walnuts
1 tsp. vanilla

Cut orange slices into small pieces. Add to flour & mix until slices are coated. Add salt, brown sugar, eggs, then walnuts & vanilla. Mix well.
Spread evenly in two well-greased pans 9" x 9" x 2". Bake

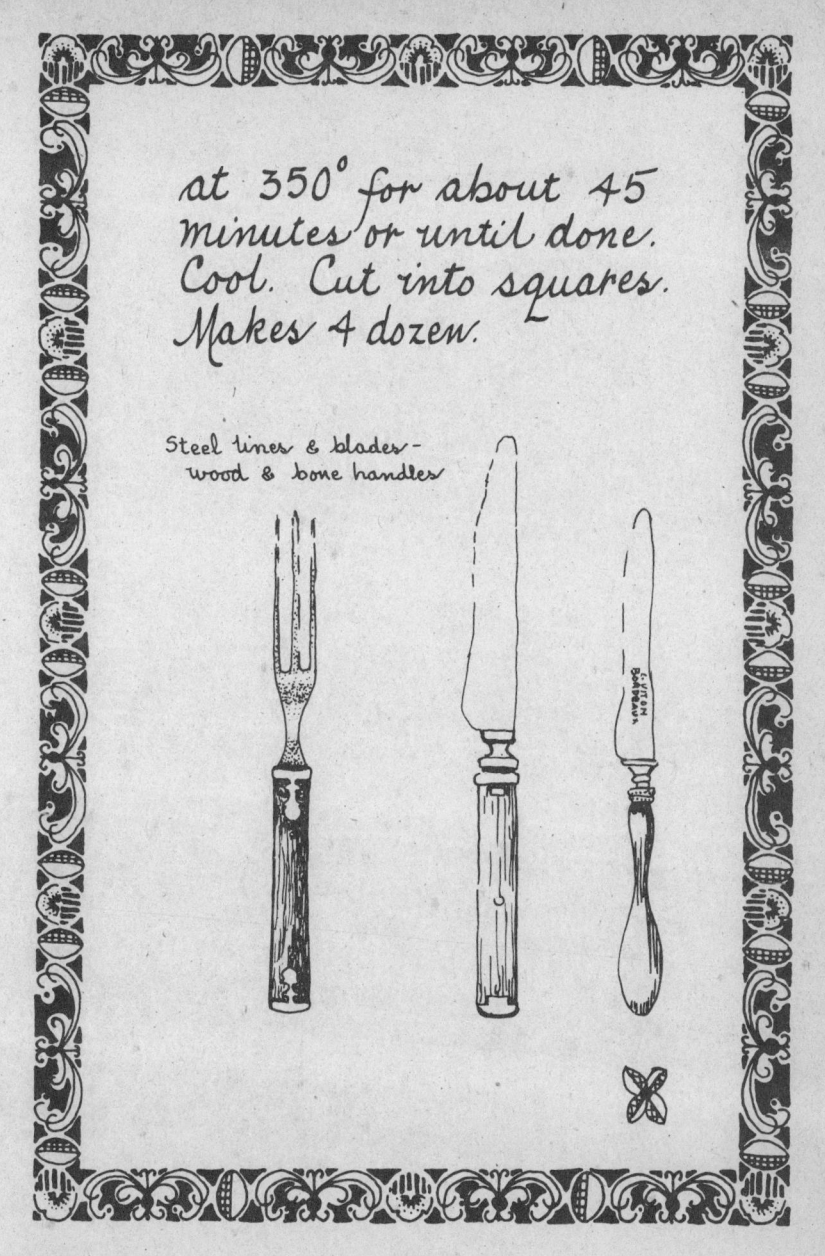

at 350° for about 45 minutes or until done. Cool. Cut into squares. Makes 4 dozen.

Steel tines & blades — wood & bone handles

Pecan Squares

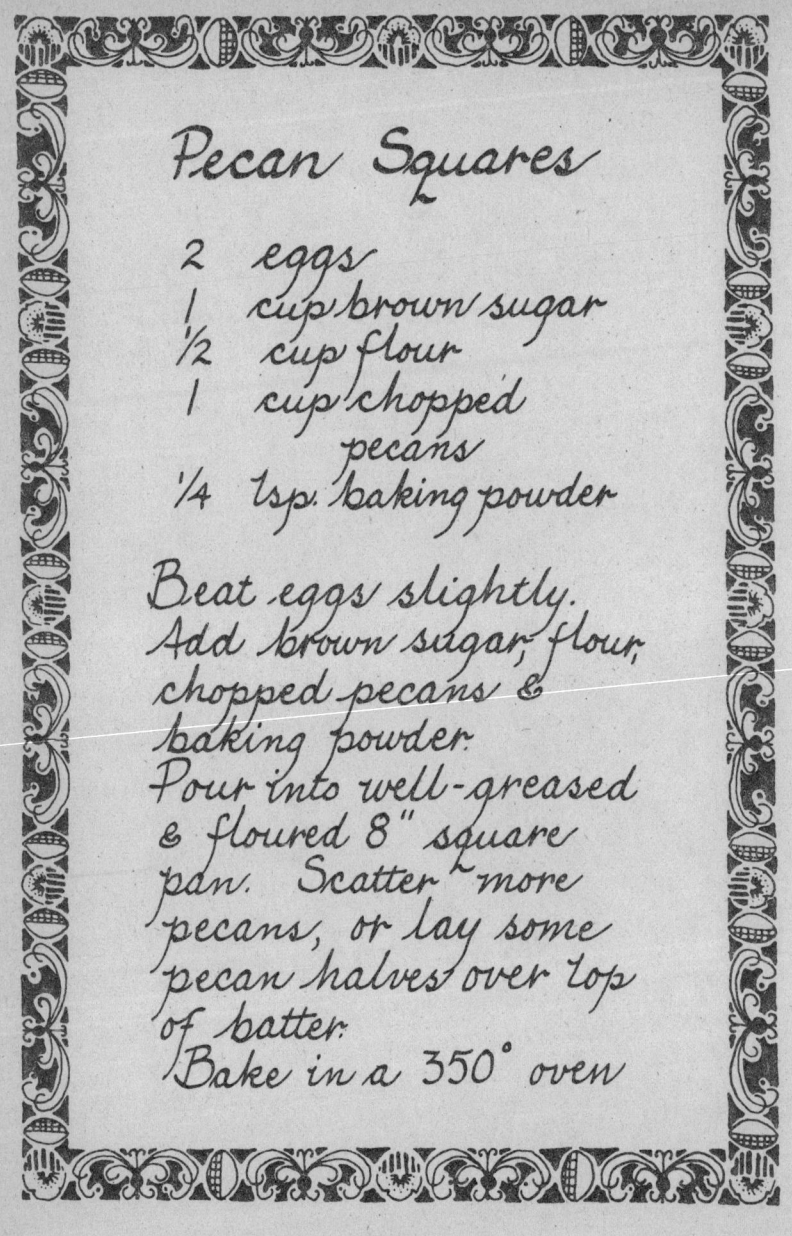

2 eggs
1 cup brown sugar
½ cup flour
1 cup chopped pecans
¼ tsp. baking powder

Beat eggs slightly. Add brown sugar, flour, chopped pecans & baking powder. Pour into well-greased & floured 8" square pan. Scatter more pecans, or lay some pecan halves over top of batter. Bake in a 350° oven

about 15-20 minutes.
  Makes 2 dozen.

Tea caddy. Tin.
   "Ridgways 5 o'clock tea.
   Chief depot: King William St.
   London, Eng. By appointment
   to the late Queen Victoria.
   U.S.A. office: San Francisco & Los Angeles"

Pineapple Squares

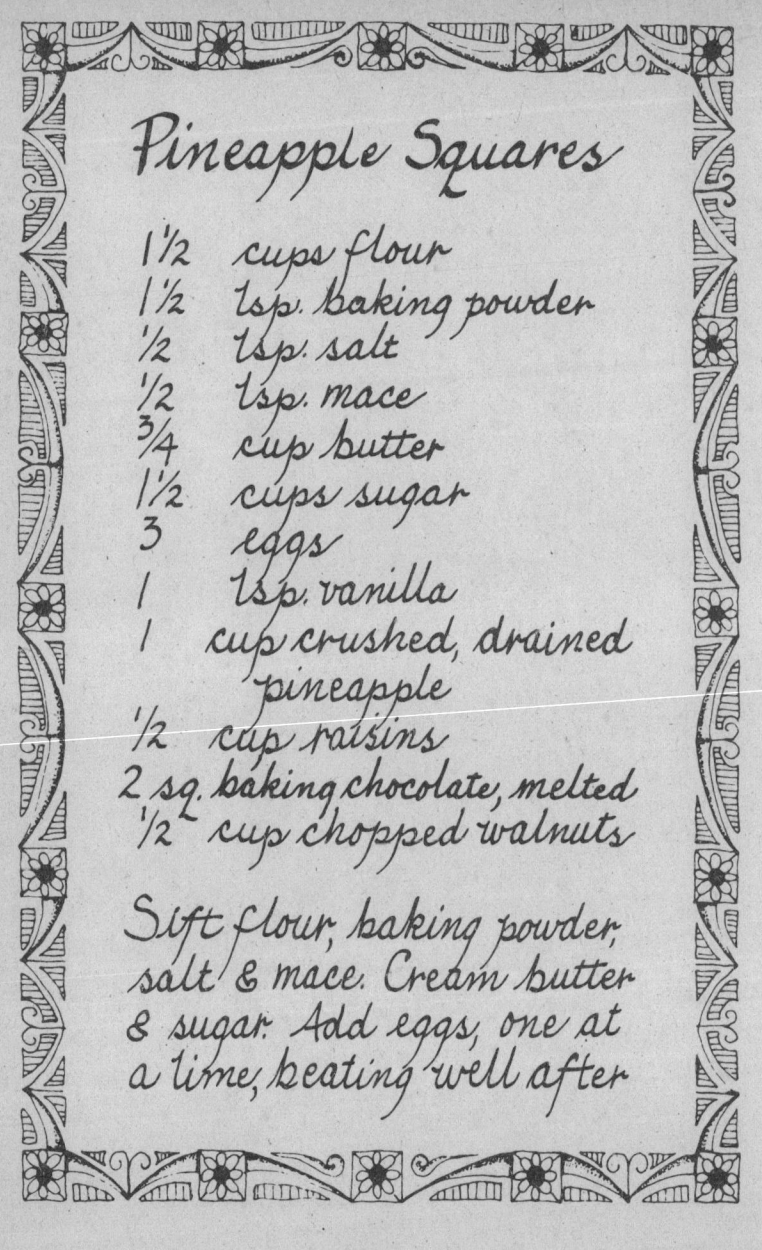

1½ cups flour
1½ tsp. baking powder
½ tsp. salt
½ tsp. mace
¾ cup butter
1½ cups sugar
3 eggs
1 tsp. vanilla
1 cup crushed, drained pineapple
½ cup raisins
2 sq. baking chocolate, melted
½ cup chopped walnuts

Sift flour, baking powder, salt & mace. Cream butter & sugar. Add eggs, one at a time, beating well after each. Add vanilla & dry ingredients. Blend well. Put 1 cup dough in another bowl. Add to it pineapple & raisins. To first bowl, add chocolate & nuts. Spread ½ chocolate dough in greased 13"x 9"x 2" pan. Cover with pineapple dough, then rest of chocolate dough. Bake at 375°, 45-50 min. Makes 28.

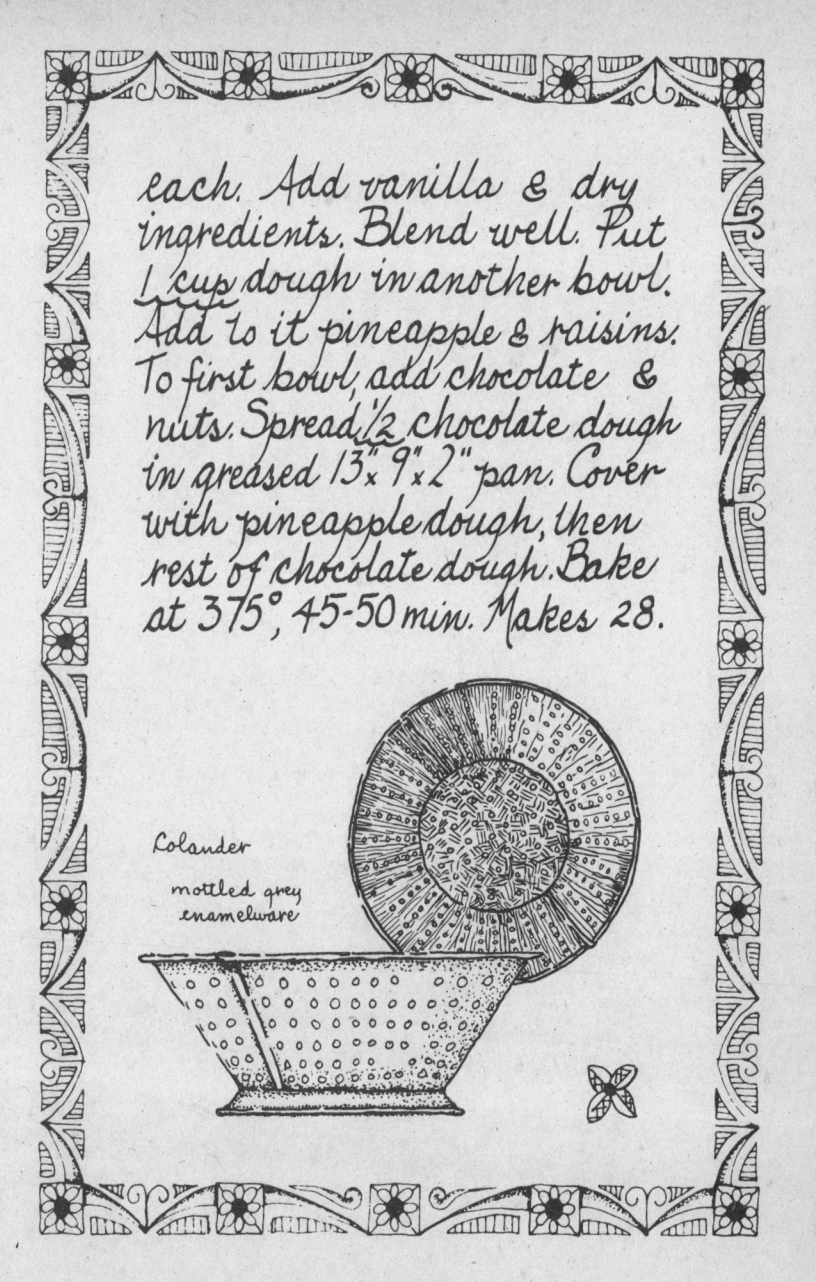

Colander
mottled grey enamelware

Toffee Squares

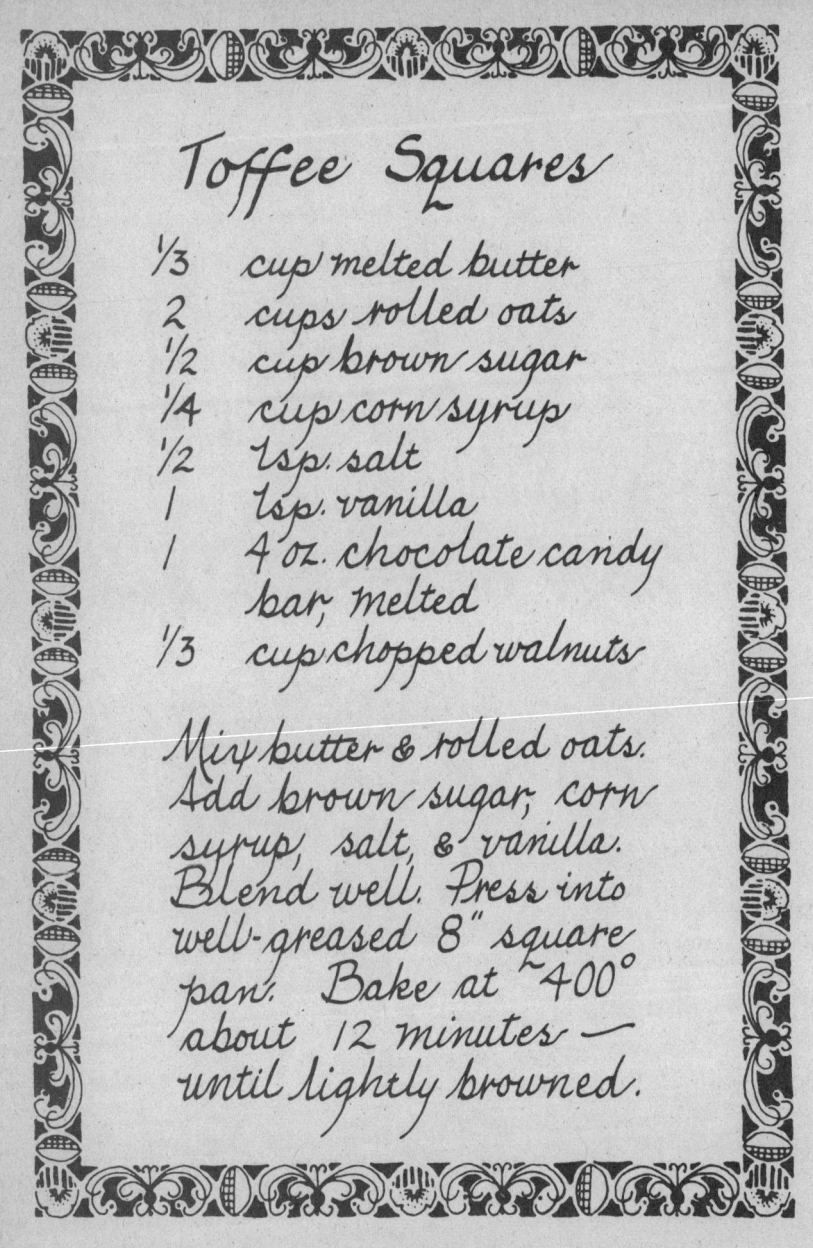

- 1/3 cup melted butter
- 2 cups rolled oats
- 1/2 cup brown sugar
- 1/4 cup corn syrup
- 1/2 tsp. salt
- 1 tsp. vanilla
- 1 4 oz. chocolate candy bar, melted
- 1/3 cup chopped walnuts

Mix butter & rolled oats. Add brown sugar, corn syrup, salt, & vanilla. Blend well. Press into well-greased 8" square pan. Bake at 400° about 12 minutes — until lightly browned.

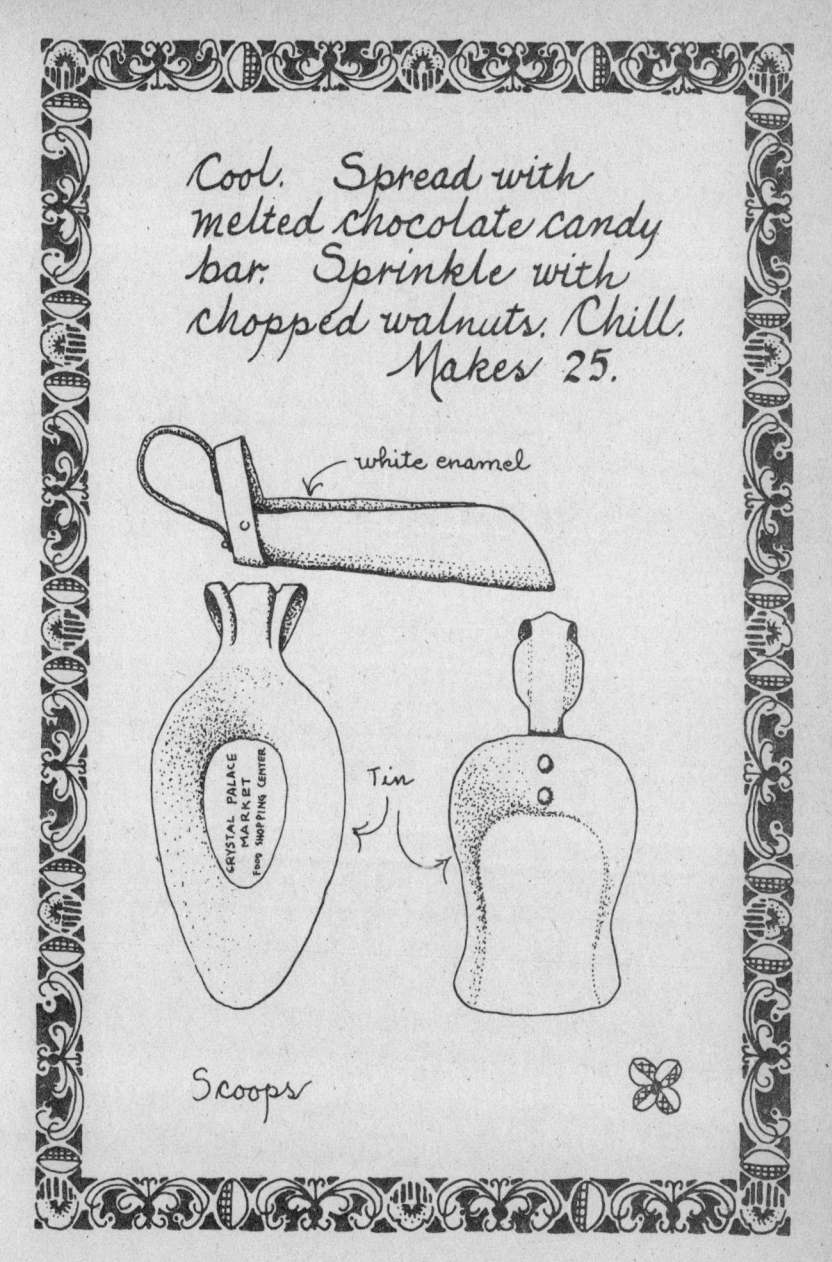

Cool. Spread with melted chocolate candy bar. Sprinkle with chopped walnuts. Chill. Makes 25.

white enamel

Tin

CRYSTAL PALACE MARKET FOOD SHOPPING CENTER

Scoops

Pies

Hints: Pie Crusts

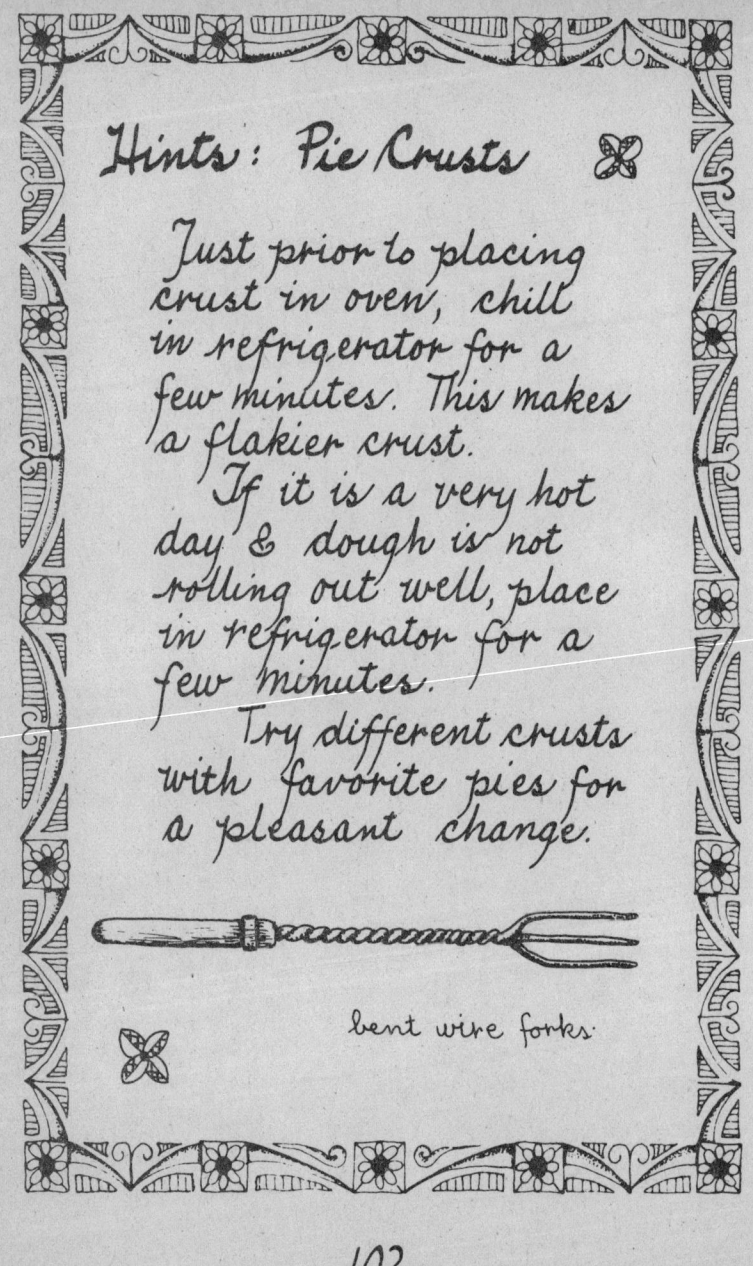

Just prior to placing crust in oven, chill in refrigerator for a few minutes. This makes a flakier crust.

If it is a very hot day & dough is not rolling out well, place in refrigerator for a few minutes.

Try different crusts with favorite pies for a pleasant change.

bent wire forks

To use leftover pie crust:

Roll out into a rectangle. Brush with melted or softened butter. Sprinkle with brown sugar, cinnamon, raisins & nuts. (Or — chopped dates, currants, dried chopped apricots, prunes, pears, etc.) Roll up into a cylinder. Wet edges to seal & press firmly together. Prick with fork. Bake at 400° about 10 min.

To bake crust without filling:

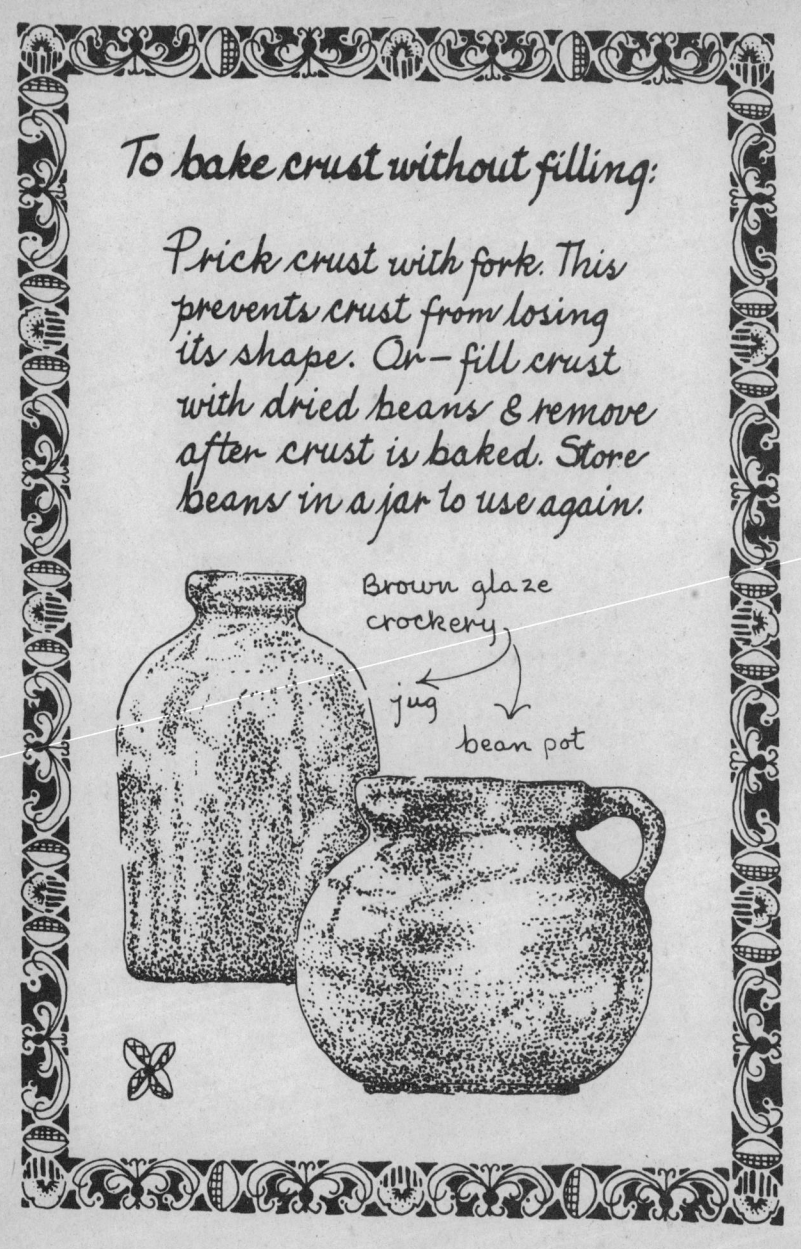

Prick crust with fork. This prevents crust from losing its shape. Or – fill crust with dried beans & remove after crust is baked. Store beans in a jar to use again.

Brown glaze crockery

jug

bean pot

To make lattice strips:

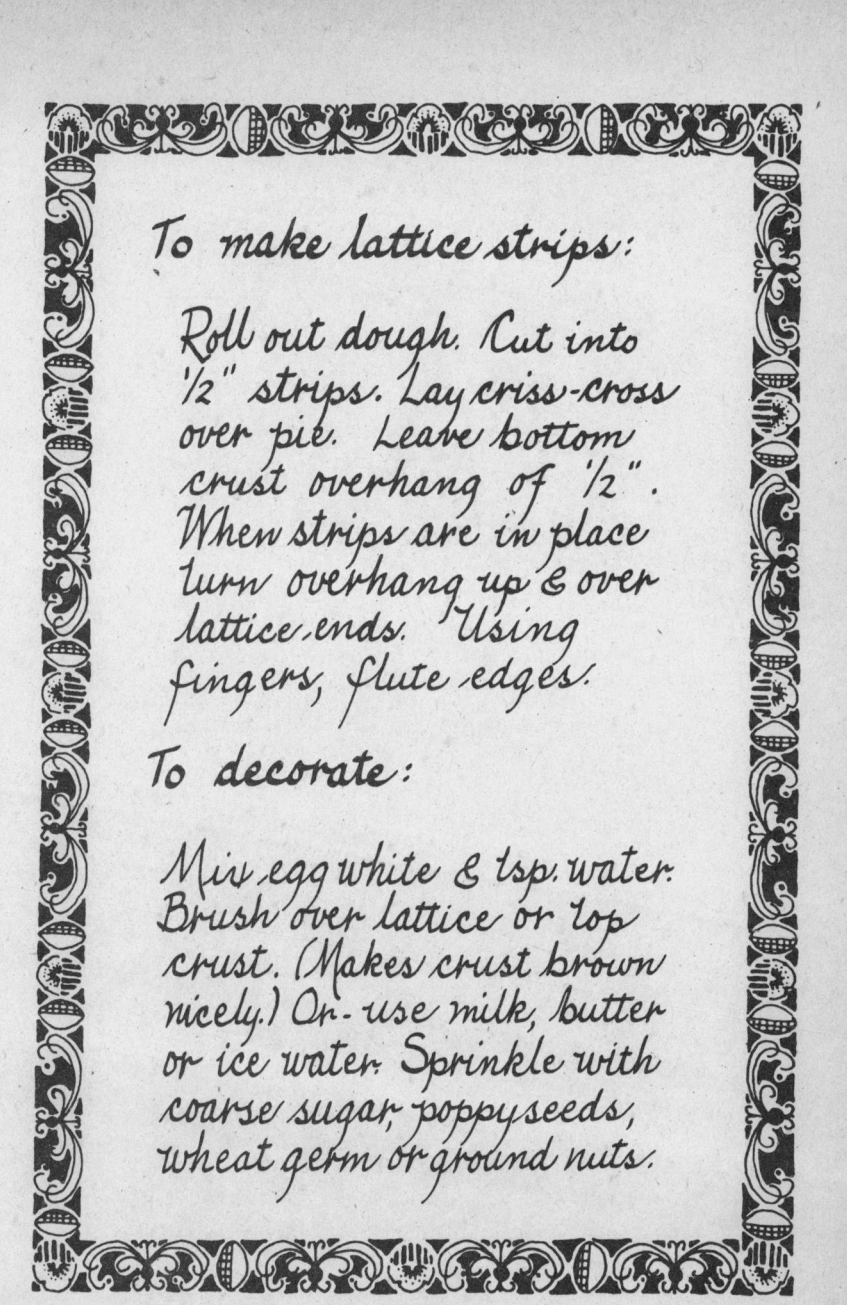

Roll out dough. Cut into ½" strips. Lay criss-cross over pie. Leave bottom crust overhang of ½". When strips are in place turn overhang up & over lattice ends. Using fingers, flute edges.

To decorate:

Mix egg white & tsp. water. Brush over lattice or top crust. (Makes crust brown nicely.) Or - use milk, butter or ice water. Sprinkle with coarse sugar, poppy seeds, wheat germ or ground nuts.

Plain Crust - 1 double or 2 single 8" or 9"

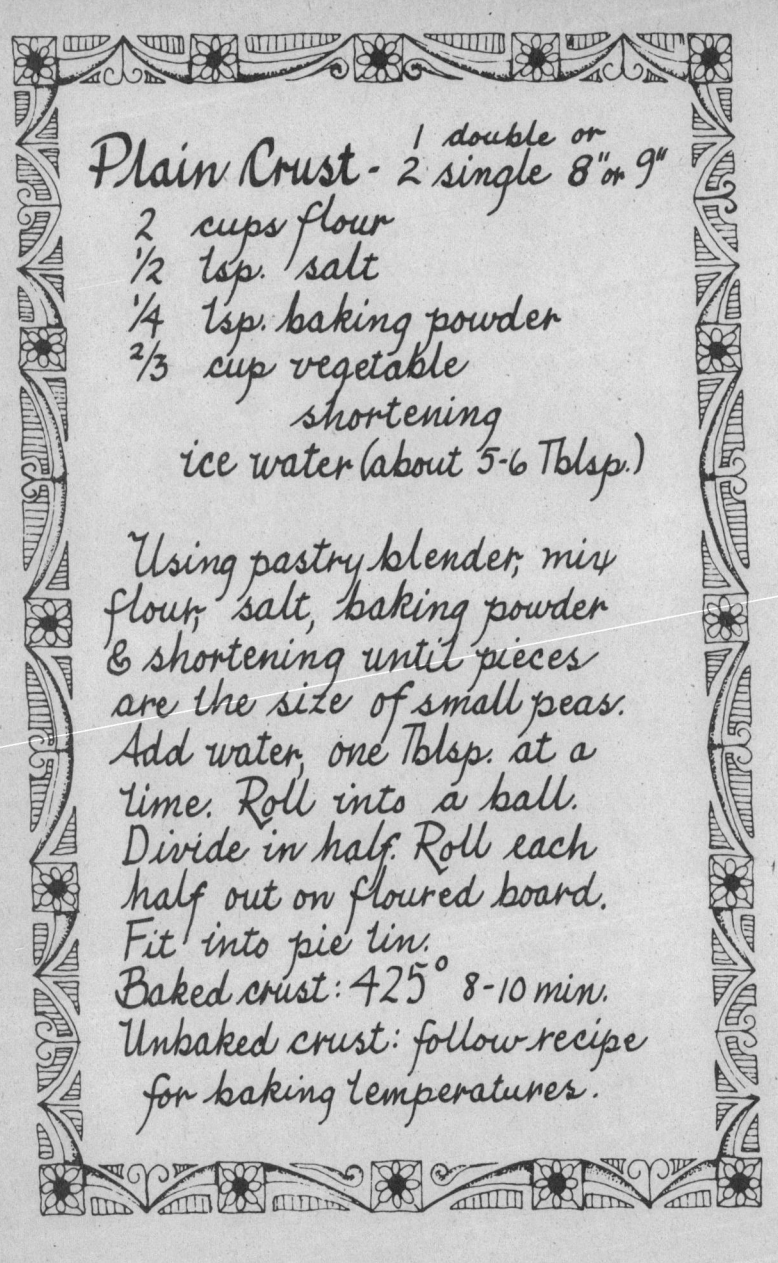

- 2 cups flour
- ½ tsp. salt
- ¼ tsp. baking powder
- ⅔ cup vegetable shortening
- ice water (about 5-6 Tblsp.)

Using pastry blender, mix flour, salt, baking powder & shortening until pieces are the size of small peas. Add water, one Tblsp. at a time. Roll into a ball. Divide in half. Roll each half out on floured board. Fit into pie tin.
Baked crust: 425° 8-10 min.
Unbaked crust: follow recipe for baking temperatures.

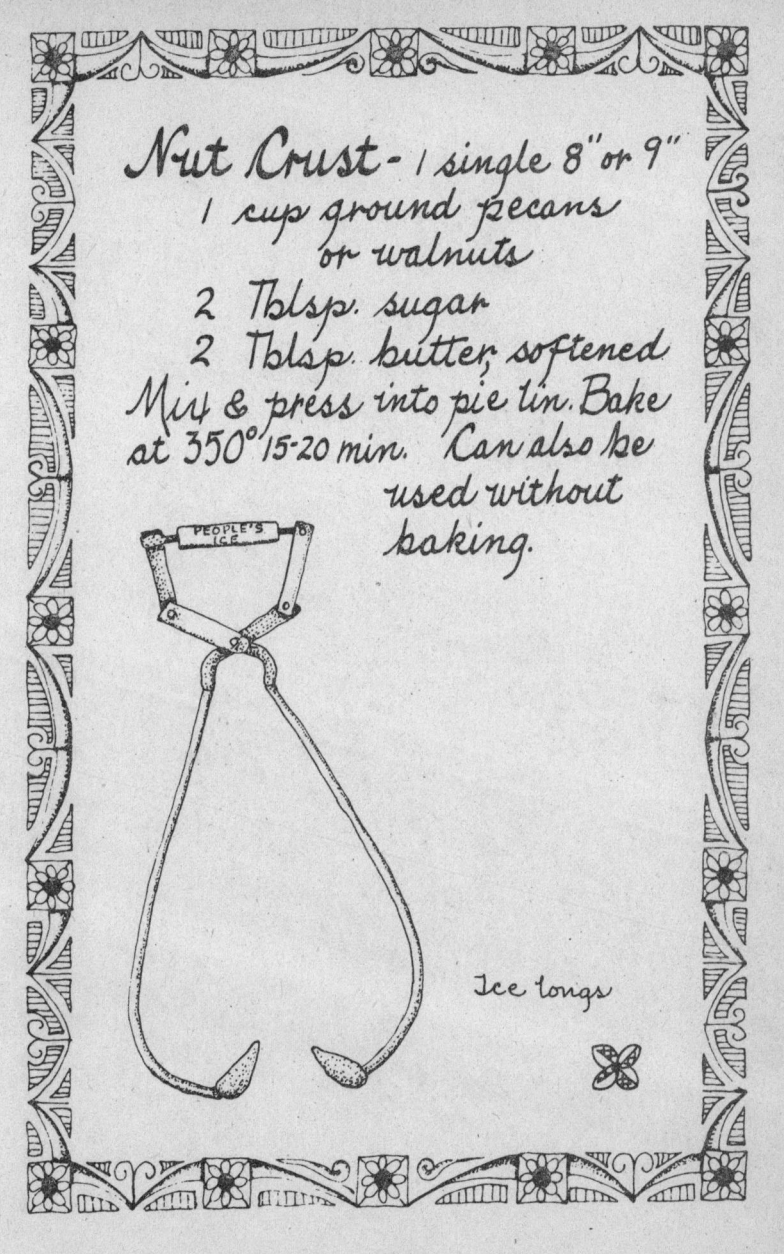

Nut Crust – 1 single 8" or 9"
   1 cup ground pecans
         or walnuts
   2 Tblsp. sugar
   2 Tblsp. butter, softened
Mix & press into pie tin. Bake at 350° 15-20 min. Can also be used without baking.

Ice tongs

Lard Crust - 1 double or 2 single 8" or 9"

- 2½ cups flour
- 1 tsp. salt
- ⅔ cup lard
- ⅓ cup (about) ice water

Using pastry blender, mix flour, salt & lard until the size of small peas. Gradually stir in water. Roll into a ball & divide in 2. Roll out on floured board. Fit into pie tin.
Baked crust: 425° 8-10 min.
Unbaked crust: follow recipe

Easy Crust - 1 single 8" or 9"

- 1 cup flour
- ¼ tsp. salt
- ¾ Tblsp. sugar
- ½ cup butter
- 1 egg

Using pastry blender, mix flour, salt, sugar & butter until the size of small peas. Stir in egg. Pat evenly into pie tin.
Baked crust: 350° 30-35 min.
Unbaked crust: follow recipe

label — A.K. FAIRBANK & CO. PURE REFINED FAMILY LARD CHICAGO

Tin lard cup

Never Fail Crust — 1 double or 2 single 8" or 9"

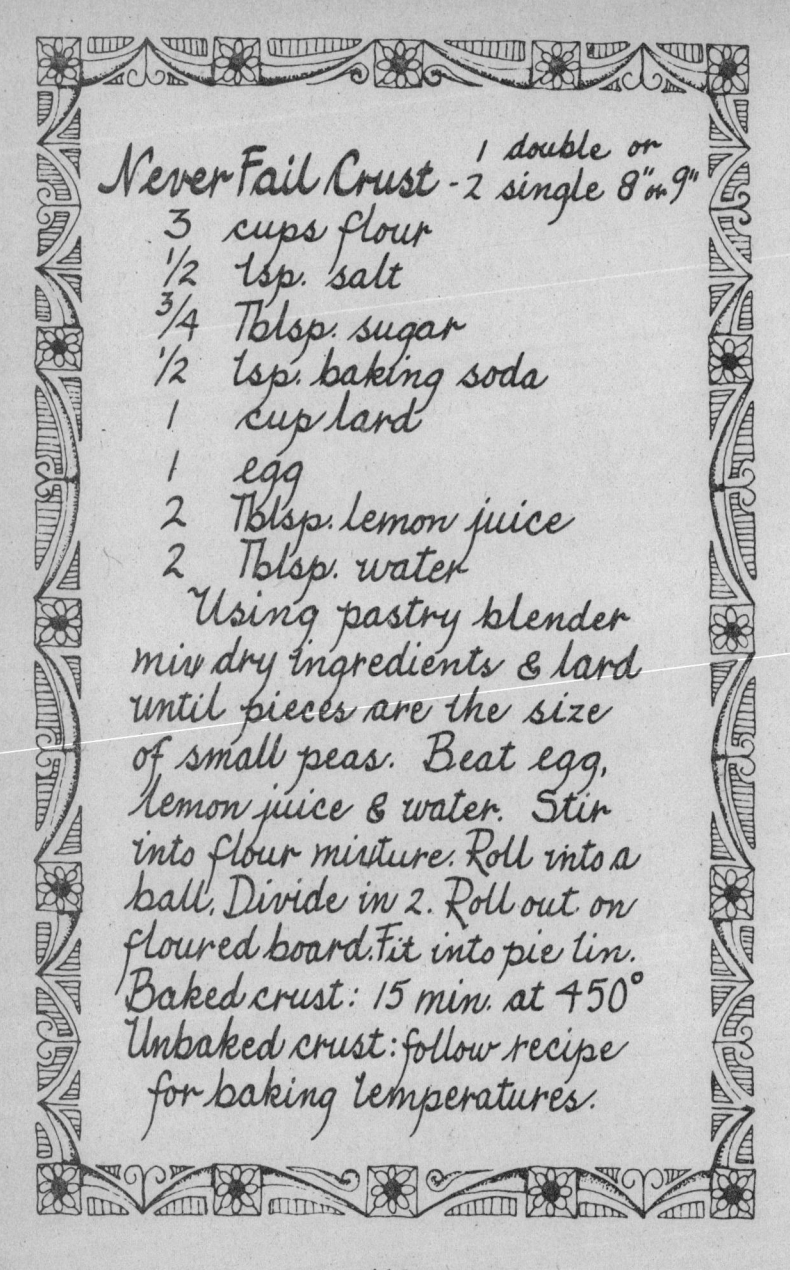

- 3 cups flour
- 1/2 tsp. salt
- 3/4 Tblsp. sugar
- 1/2 tsp. baking soda
- 1 cup lard
- 1 egg
- 2 Tblsp. lemon juice
- 2 Tblsp. water

Using pastry blender mix dry ingredients & lard until pieces are the size of small peas. Beat egg, lemon juice & water. Stir into flour mixture. Roll into a ball. Divide in 2. Roll out on floured board. Fit into pie tin.

Baked crust: 15 min. at 450°
Unbaked crust: follow recipe for baking temperatures.

wood firkin

to store butter, cheese or lard

Almond Cracker Crust

1 single 8" or 9"

- ¼ cup ground almonds
- 16 graham crackers, rolled fine
- ¼ cup butter, melted
- ¼ tsp. almond extract
- 1 Tblsp. cream

Mix all ingredients well. Press into pie tin. Bake 8 min. at 450°

Orange Crust – 1 double or 2 single 8" or 9"

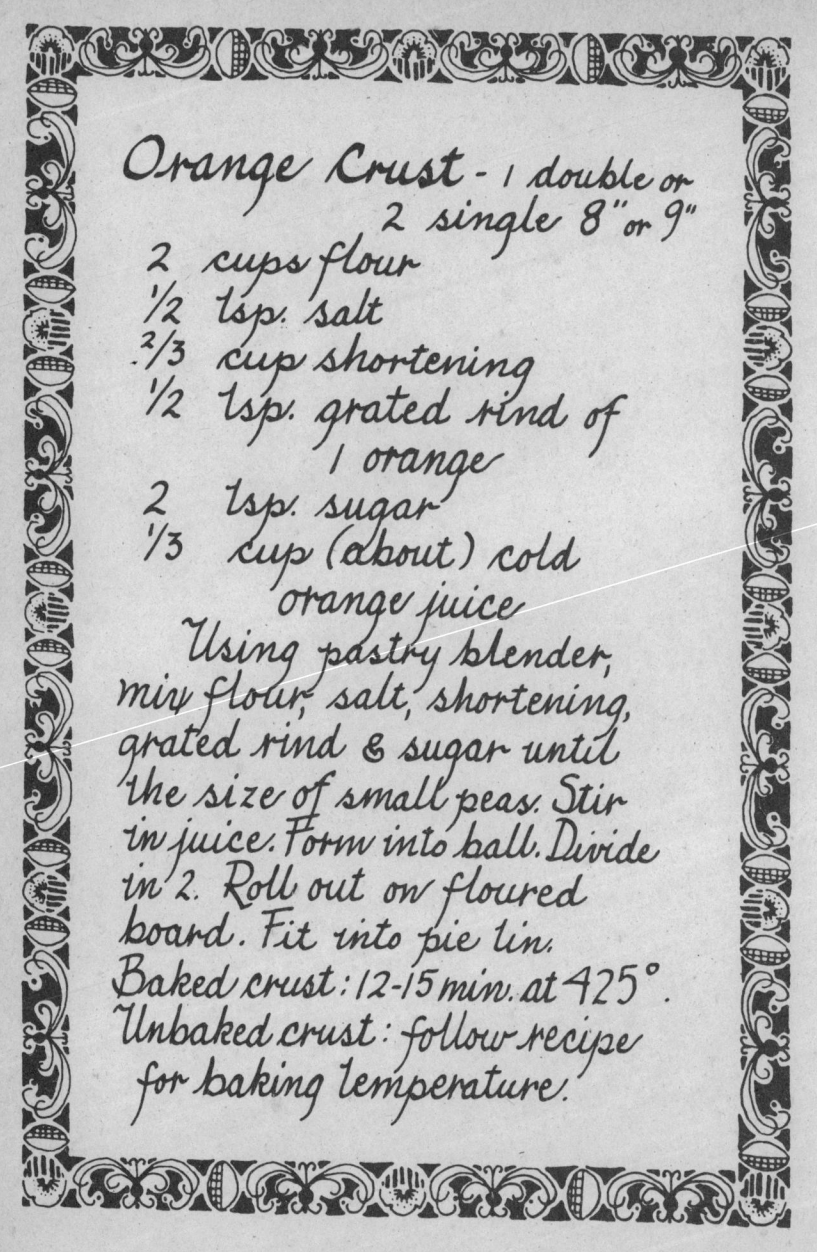

- 2 cups flour
- 1/2 tsp. salt
- 2/3 cup shortening
- 1/2 tsp. grated rind of 1 orange
- 2 tsp. sugar
- 1/3 cup (about) cold orange juice

Using pastry blender, mix flour, salt, shortening, grated rind & sugar until the size of small peas. Stir in juice. Form into ball. Divide in 2. Roll out on floured board. Fit into pie tin. Baked crust: 12-15 min. at 425°. Unbaked crust: follow recipe for baking temperature.

Ice picks

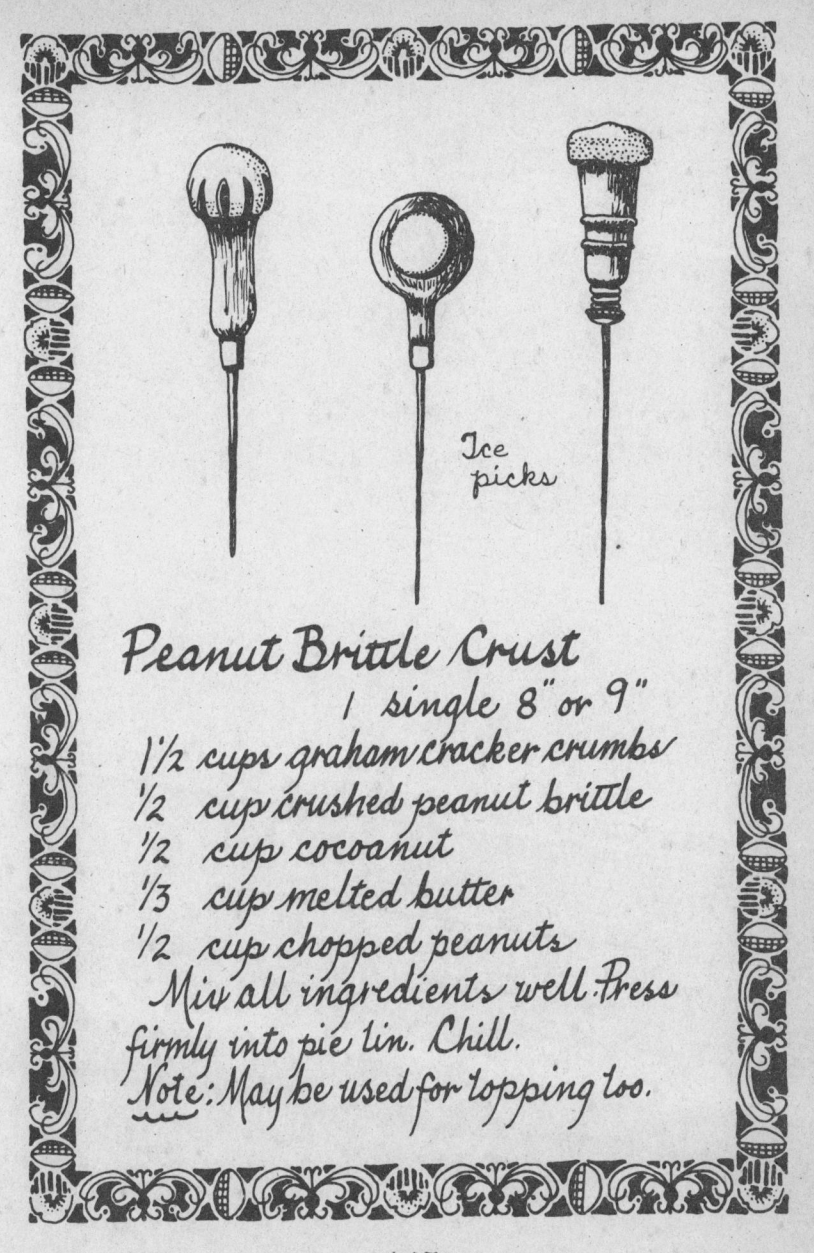

Peanut Brittle Crust
1 single 8" or 9"

1½ cups graham cracker crumbs
½ cup crushed peanut brittle
½ cup cocoanut
⅓ cup melted butter
½ cup chopped peanuts

Mix all ingredients well. Press firmly into pie tin. Chill.
Note: May be used for topping too.

Whole Wheat Crust - 1 double or 2 single 9" or 8"
 2 cups whole wheat pastry flour
 1 tsp. salt
 ½ cup safflower oil
 ¼ cup (about) ice water

Using pastry blender, mix flour, salt & oil. Stir in water. Roll into a ball. Divide in 2. Roll out on floured board. Fit into pie tin.
Baked crust: 8-10 min. at 425°
Unbaked crust: follow recipe

Cocoa Crust - 1 single 9" or 8"
 2 Tblsp. instant cocoa
 3 Tblsp. boiling water
 1¼ cups flour
 ½ tsp. salt
 ½ cup vegetable shortening

Dissolve cocoa in boiling water. Set aside. Using

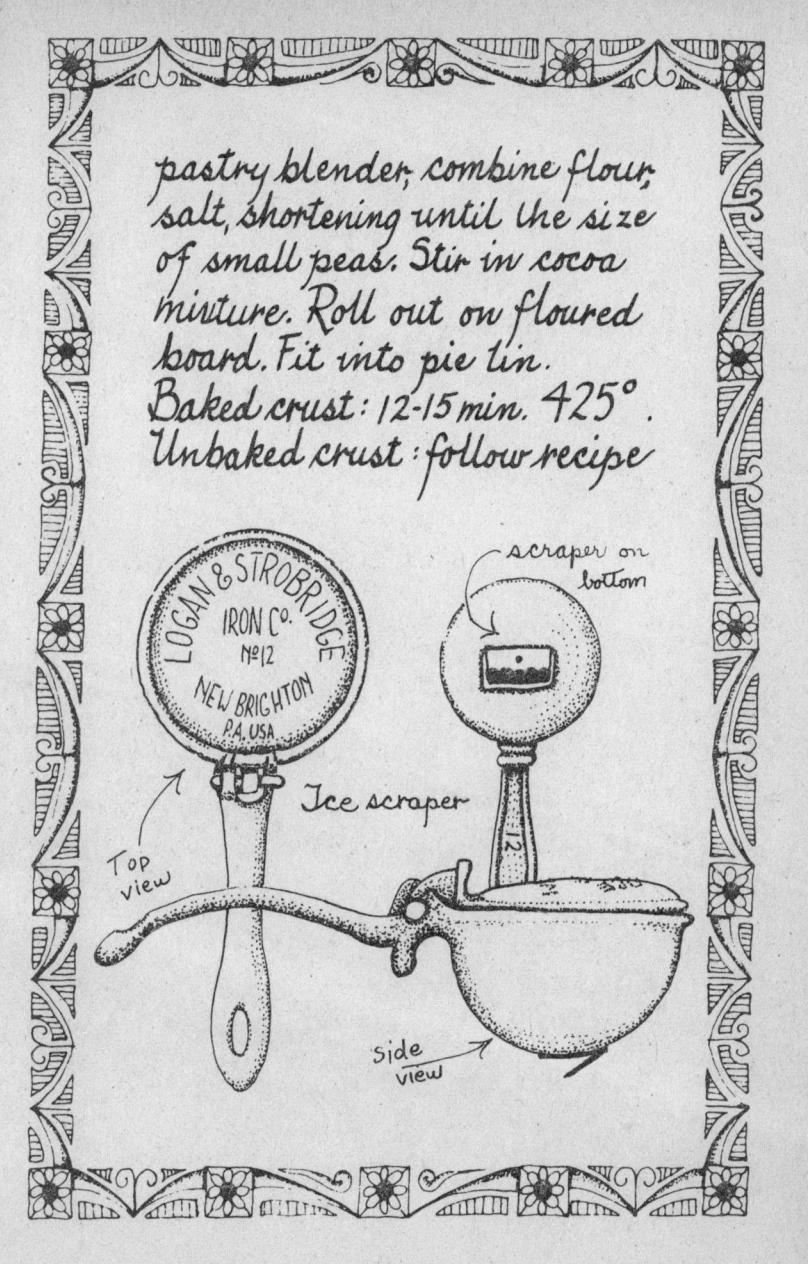

pastry blender, combine flour, salt, shortening until the size of small peas. Stir in cocoa mixture. Roll out on floured board. Fit into pie tin.
Baked crust: 12-15 min. 425°.
Unbaked crust: follow recipe

LOGAN & STROBRIDGE IRON CO. Nº 12 NEW BRIGHTON P.A. USA

Top view

scraper on bottom

Ice scraper

side view

Ice picks

Perfect Meringue

3 egg whites
3 Tblsp. ice water
1 tsp. baking powder
  pinch of salt
6 Tblsp. sugar

Mix egg whites, water, baking powder & salt. Beat until stiff. Gradually add sugar & beat until very stiff. Spread on pie filling, being sure to touch meringue to crust. (Keeps meringue from shrinking.) Bake in a 425° oven (and be sure to watch it constantly) until golden brown. It takes about 5 minutes.

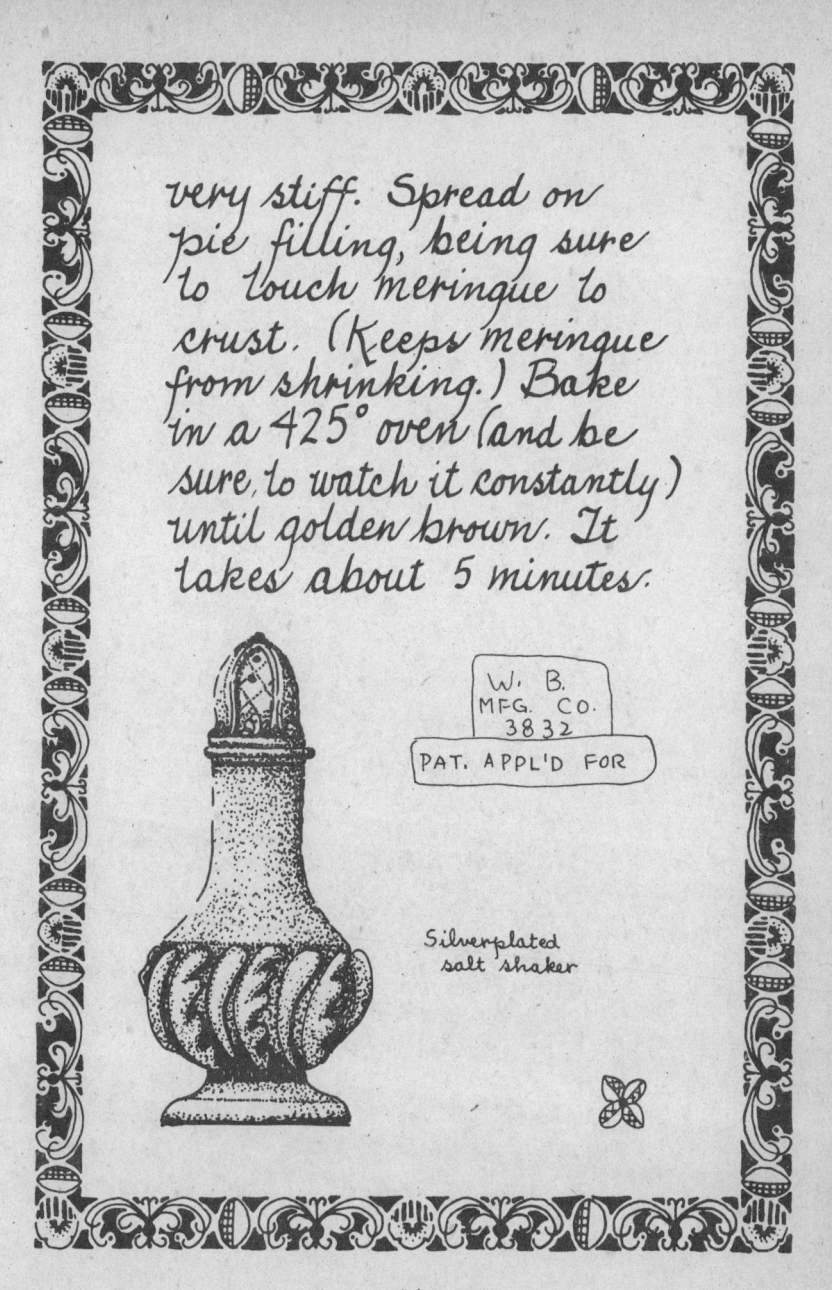

W. B. MFG. CO. 3832
PAT. APPL'D FOR

Silverplated salt shaker

front *back*

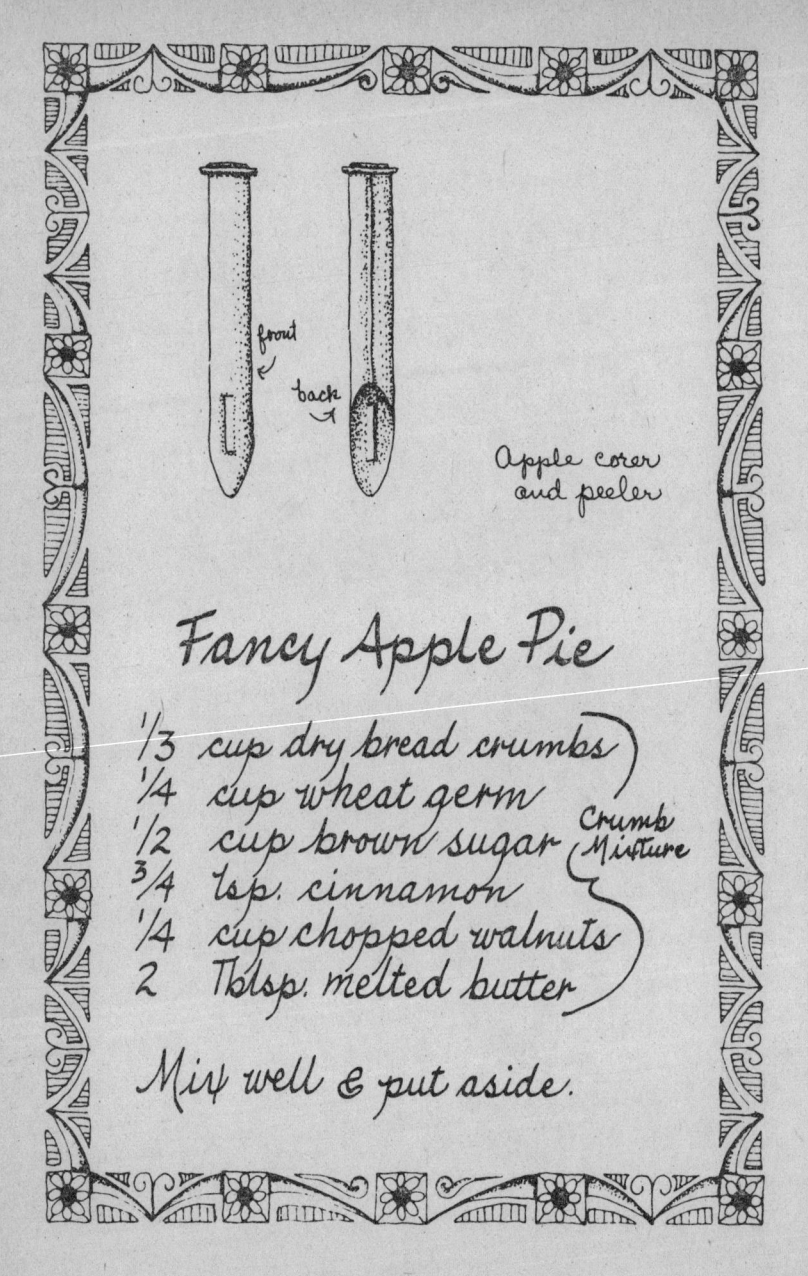

Apple corer and peeler

Fancy Apple Pie

- 1/3 cup dry bread crumbs
- 1/4 cup wheat germ
- 1/2 cup brown sugar
- 3/4 tsp. cinnamon
- 1/4 cup chopped walnuts
- 2 Tblsp. melted butter

} Crumb Mixture

Mix well & put aside.

½ cup brown sugar
2 Tblsp. flour
⅛ tsp. salt   Filling
4 cups sliced tart apples
1 unbaked pie crust 9"
(Try Lard Crust p. 108)

Mix brown sugar, flour, salt & apples. Put into unbaked pie crust. Cover with aluminum foil. Be sure to turn foil under edge of pie tin to seal. Bake in a 450° oven about 10 min., then 350° for 30 min. more. Remove from oven & remove foil. Spread with crumb mixture. Bake 10 min. — until brown.

Dried Apple Pie

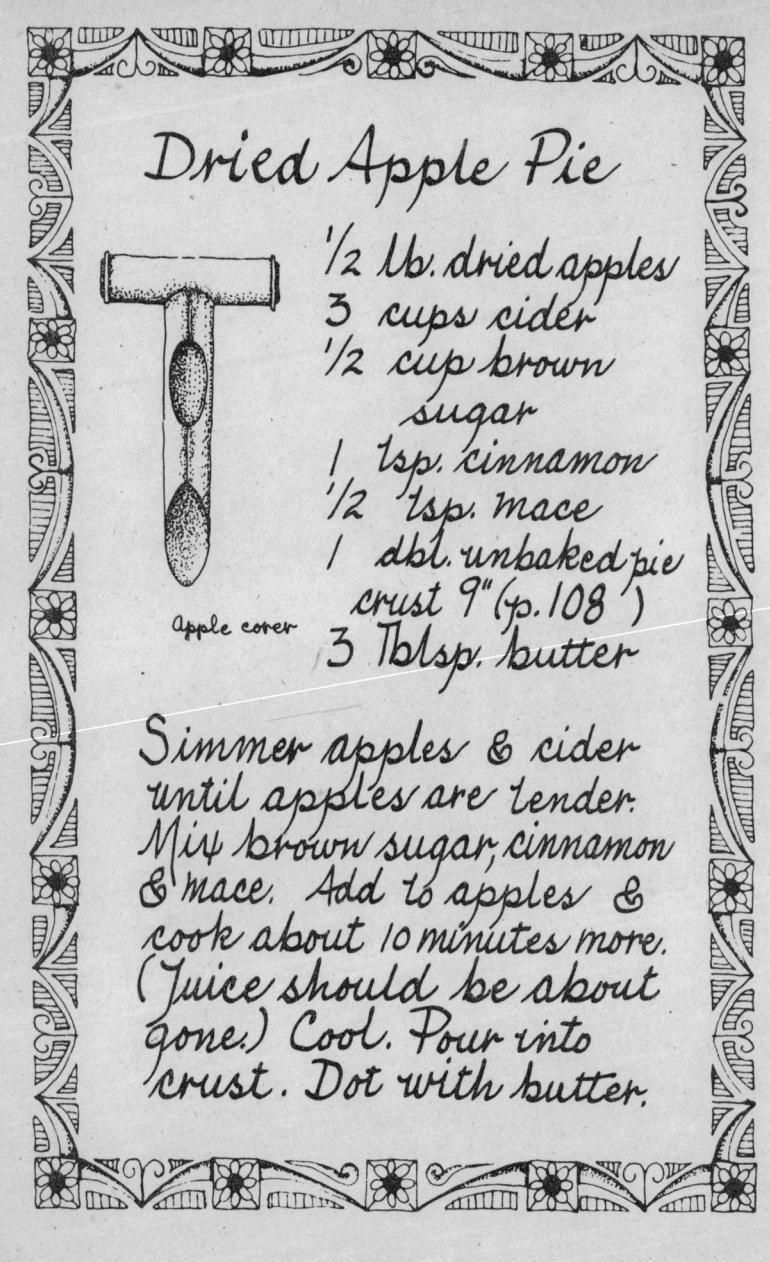

½ lb. dried apples
3 cups cider
½ cup brown sugar
1 tsp. cinnamon
½ tsp. mace
1 dbl. unbaked pie crust 9" (p. 108)
3 Tblsp. butter

apple corer

Simmer apples & cider until apples are tender. Mix brown sugar, cinnamon & mace. Add to apples & cook about 10 minutes more. (Juice should be about gone.) Cool. Pour into crust. Dot with butter.

Cover with top crust or lattice strips. Bake in a 425° oven for 30 to 40 minutes — until crust is light brown.

Blue & white enameled cooking pot

Apple Butter Pie

½ cup brown sugar
3 egg yolks
½ cup apple butter
½ cup milk
1 cup cider
½ tsp. salt
1½ tsp. cinnamon
½ tsp. nutmeg
⅛ tsp. cloves
1 Tblsp. gelatine
½ cup cold water
3 egg whites
2 Tblsp. sugar
1 baked pie crust 9"
   (Try Never Fail p. 110)
sweetened whipped cream

Cook brown sugar, yolks,

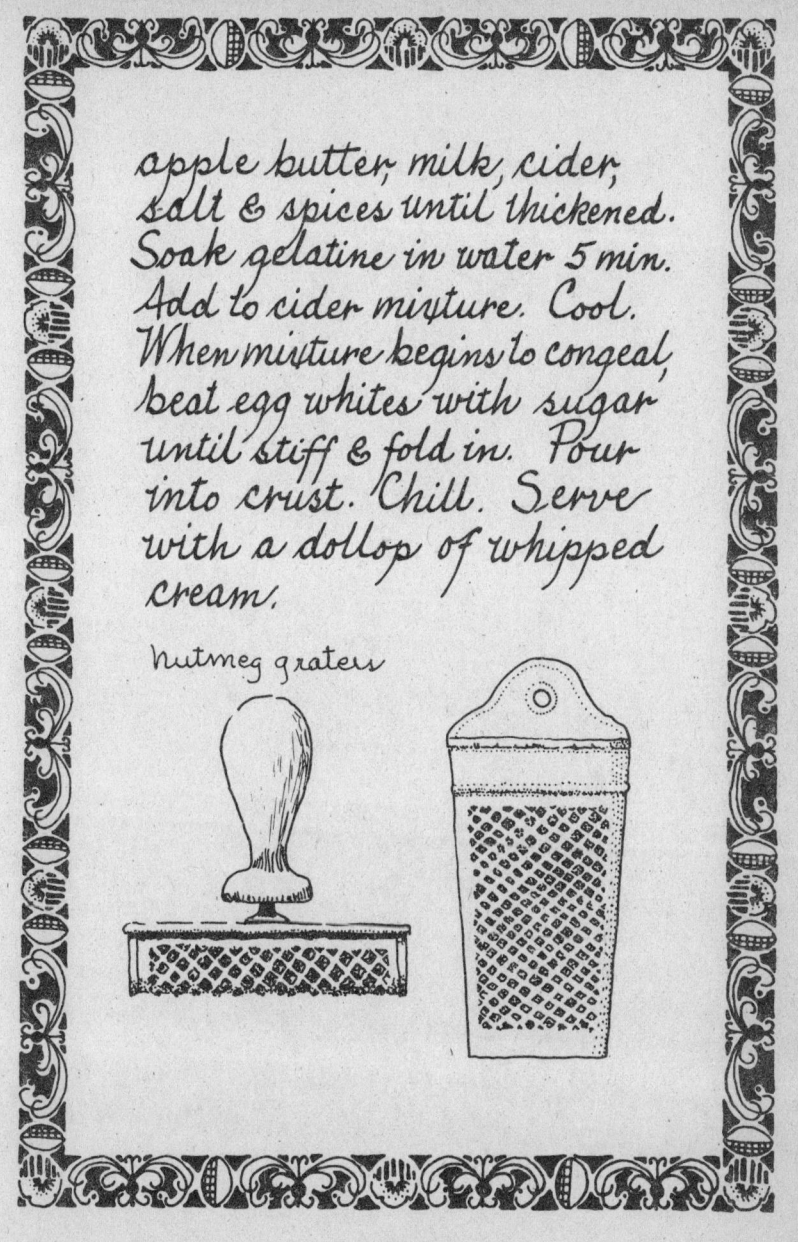

apple butter, milk, cider, salt & spices until thickened. Soak gelatine in water 5 min. Add to cider mixture. Cool. When mixture begins to congeal, beat egg whites with sugar until stiff & fold in. Pour into crust. Chill. Serve with a dollop of whipped cream.

nutmeg graters

Pear Anise Pie

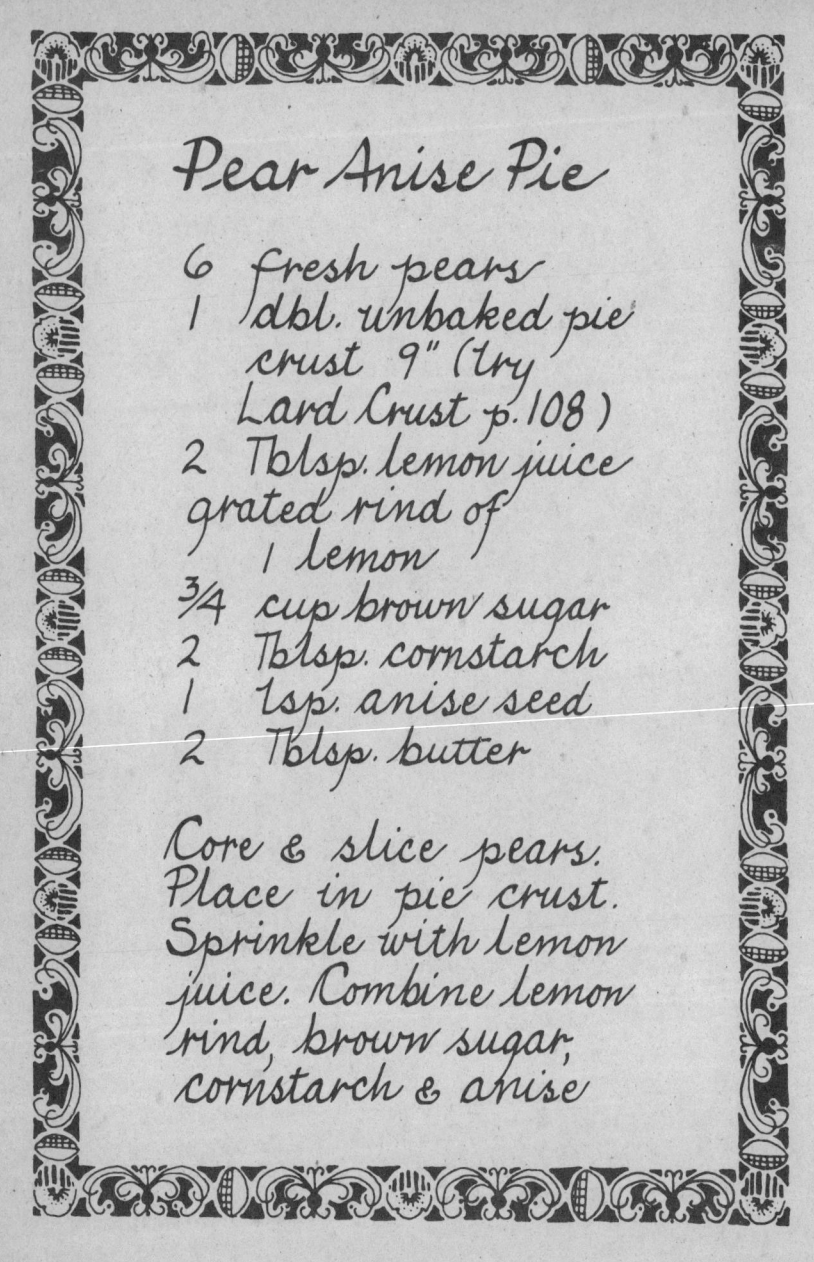

6 fresh pears
1 dbl. unbaked pie crust 9" (try Lard Crust p. 108)
2 Tblsp. lemon juice
grated rind of 1 lemon
3/4 cup brown sugar
2 Tblsp. cornstarch
1 tsp. anise seed
2 Tblsp. butter

Core & slice pears. Place in pie crust. Sprinkle with lemon juice. Combine lemon rind, brown sugar, cornstarch & anise seed. Pour evenly over pears. Dot with butter. Cover with top crust. Prick crust with fork. Bake at 425° about 35-45 minutes.

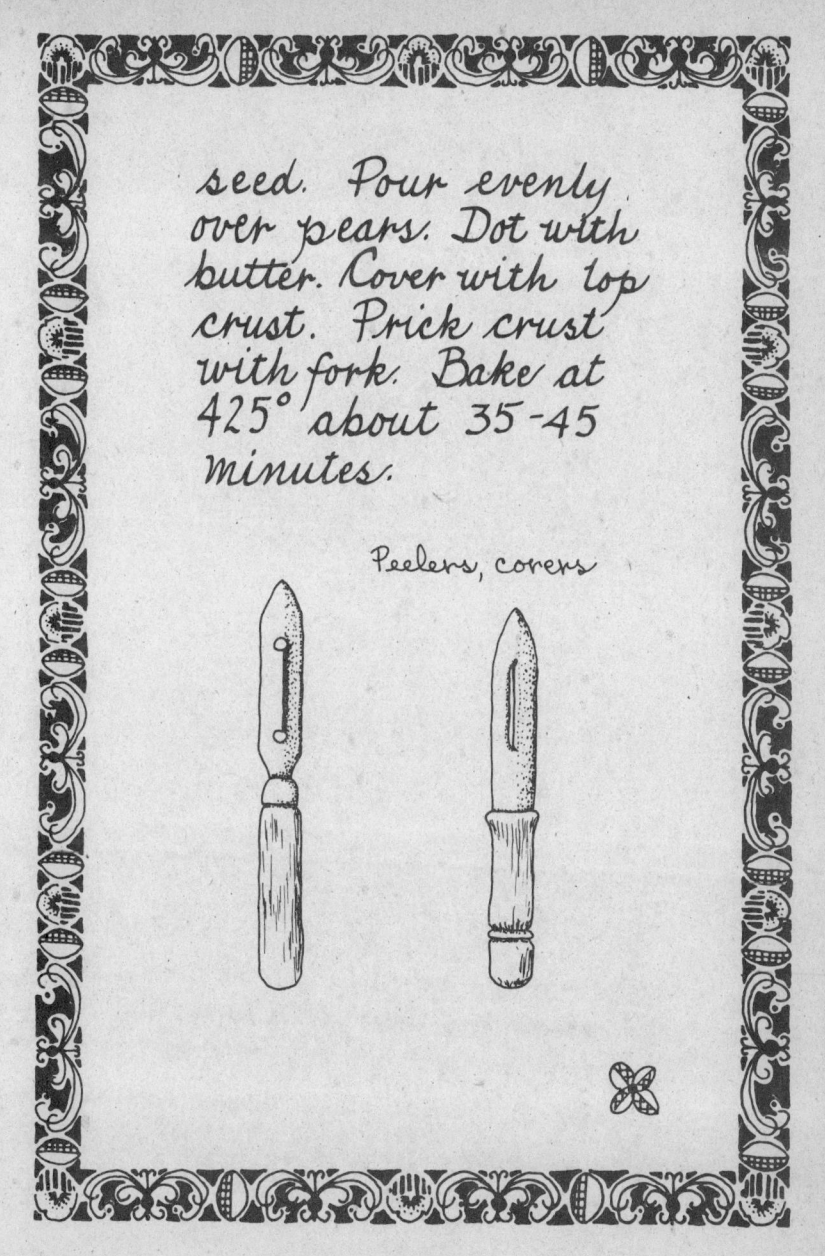

Peelers, corers

Banana Cream Pie

- 2/3 cup sugar
- 1/2 cup flour
- 1/8 tsp. salt
- 1 cup milk
- 1 cup evaporated milk
- 2 eggs, beaten
- 1 tsp. vanilla
- 1/2 tsp. almond extract
- 2 bananas, mashed
- 2 bananas, sliced
- 1 baked pie crust 9"

(Try Almond Cracker p. 111)

Mix sugar, flour & salt. Scald the 2 milks together. Gradually add milk to flour mixture. Cook, stirring constantly, about 5 min.

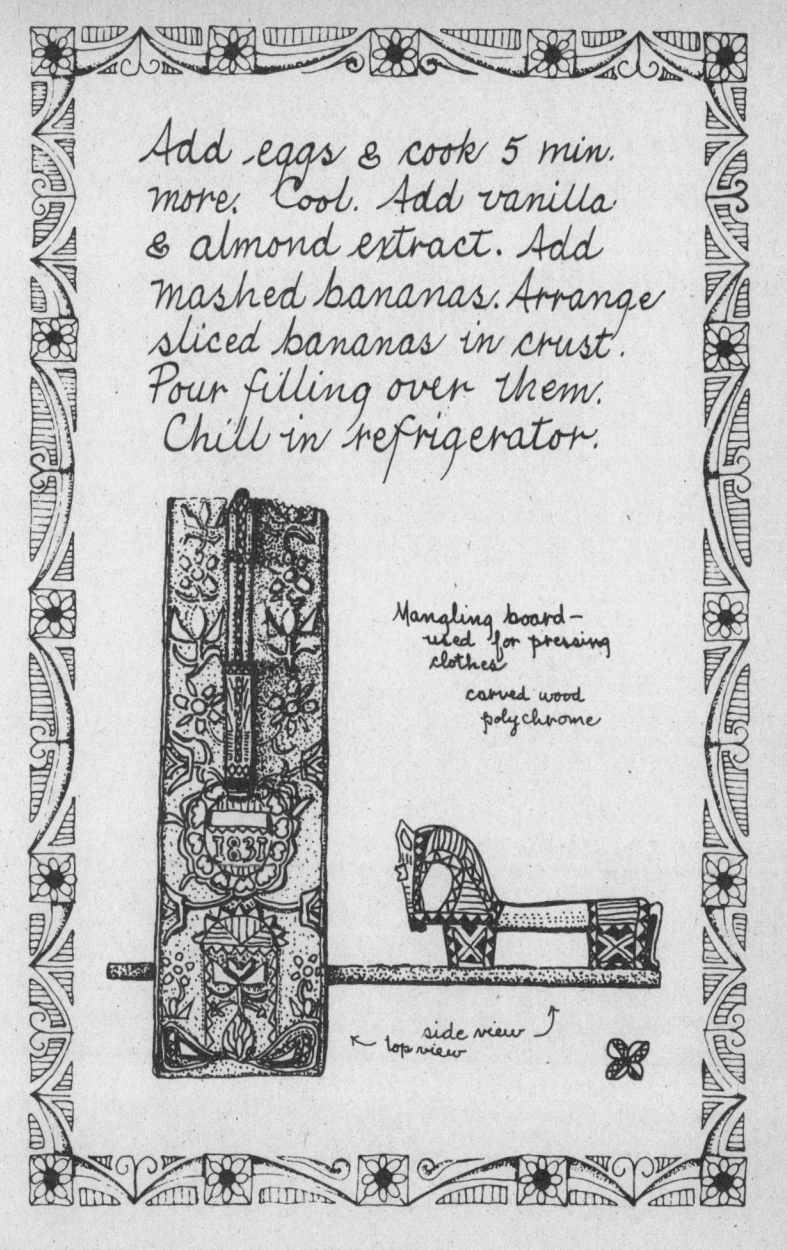

Add eggs & cook 5 min. more. Cool. Add vanilla & almond extract. Add mashed bananas. Arrange sliced bananas in crust. Pour filling over them. Chill in refrigerator.

Mangling board – used for pressing clothes
carved wood polychrome

← top view   side view →

Banana Marshmallow Pie

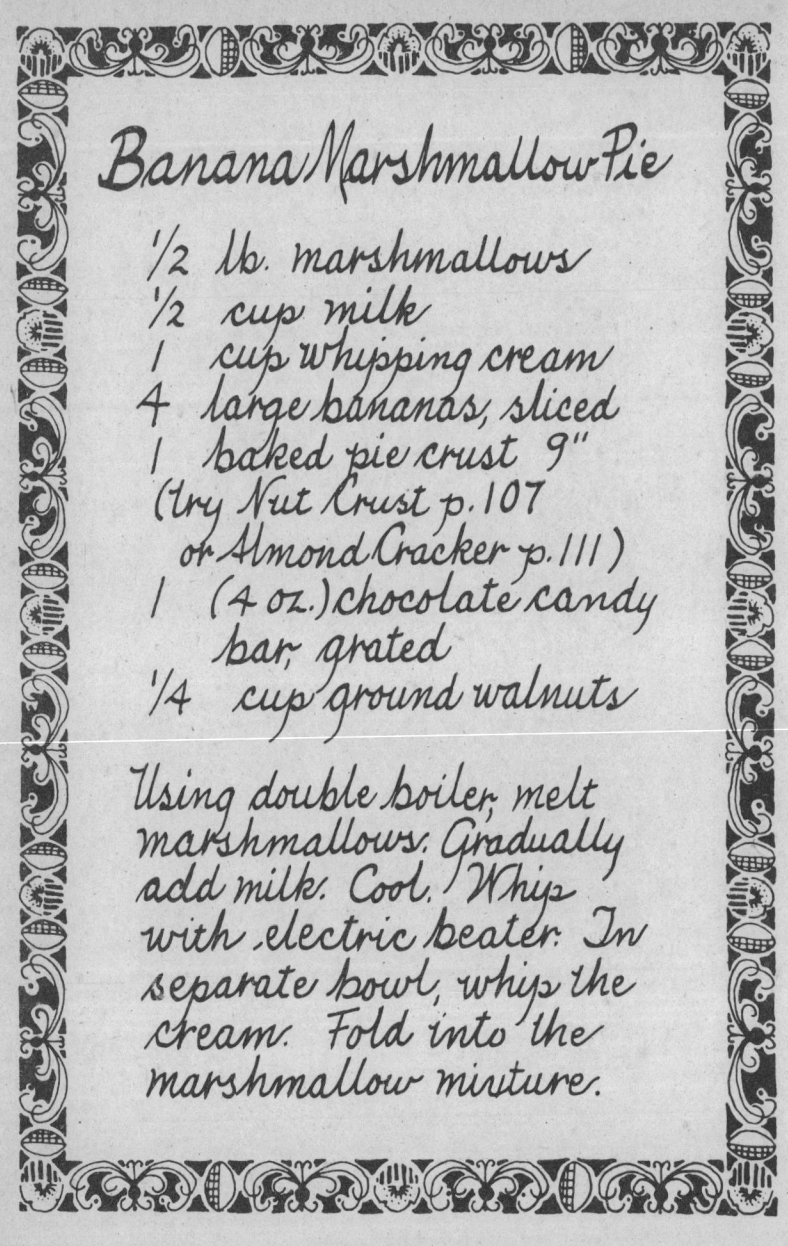

½ lb. marshmallows
½ cup milk
1 cup whipping cream
4 large bananas, sliced
1 baked pie crust 9"
(try Nut Crust p. 107
   or Almond Cracker p. 111)
1 (4 oz.) chocolate candy
   bar, grated
¼ cup ground walnuts

Using double boiler, melt marshmallows. Gradually add milk. Cool. Whip with electric beater. In separate bowl, whip the cream. Fold into the marshmallow mixture.

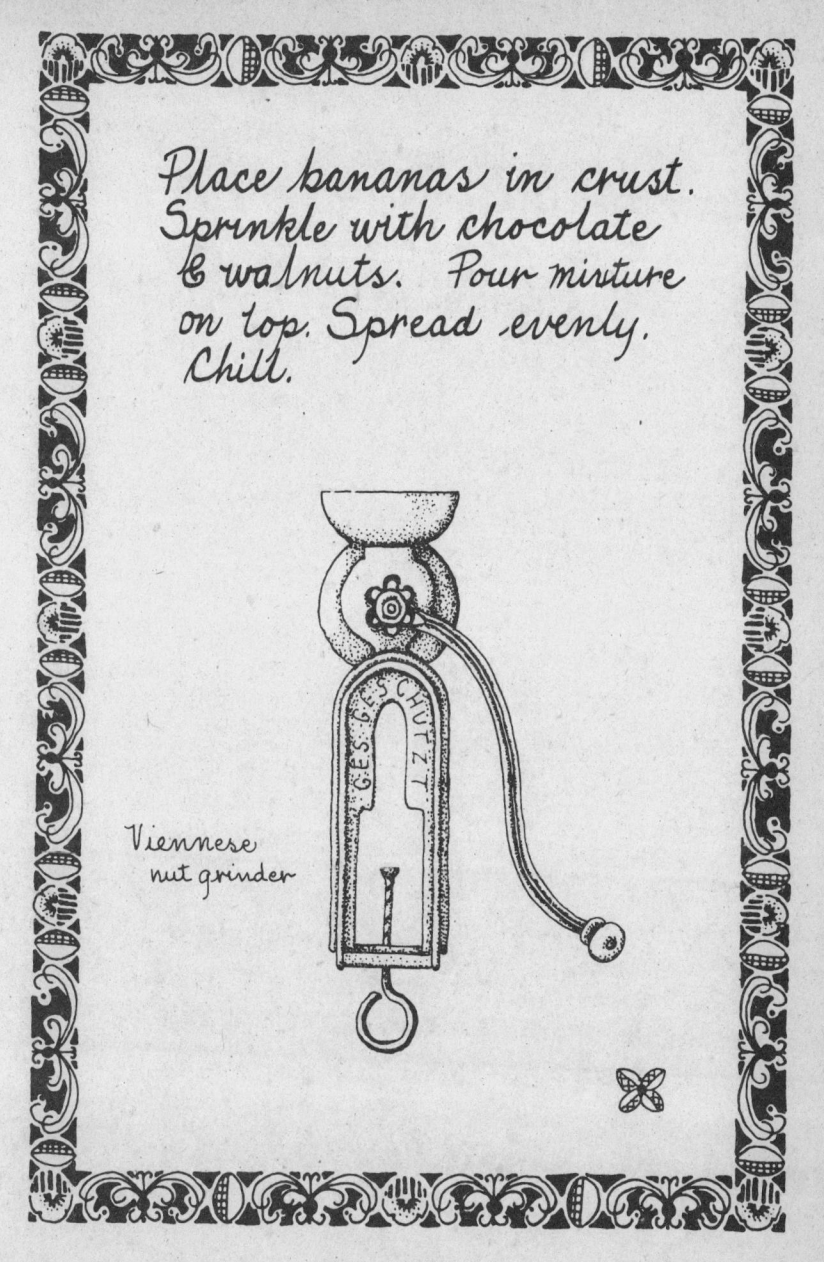

Place bananas in crust. Sprinkle with chocolate & walnuts. Pour mixture on top. Spread evenly. Chill.

Viennese nut grinder

Dried Apricot Pie

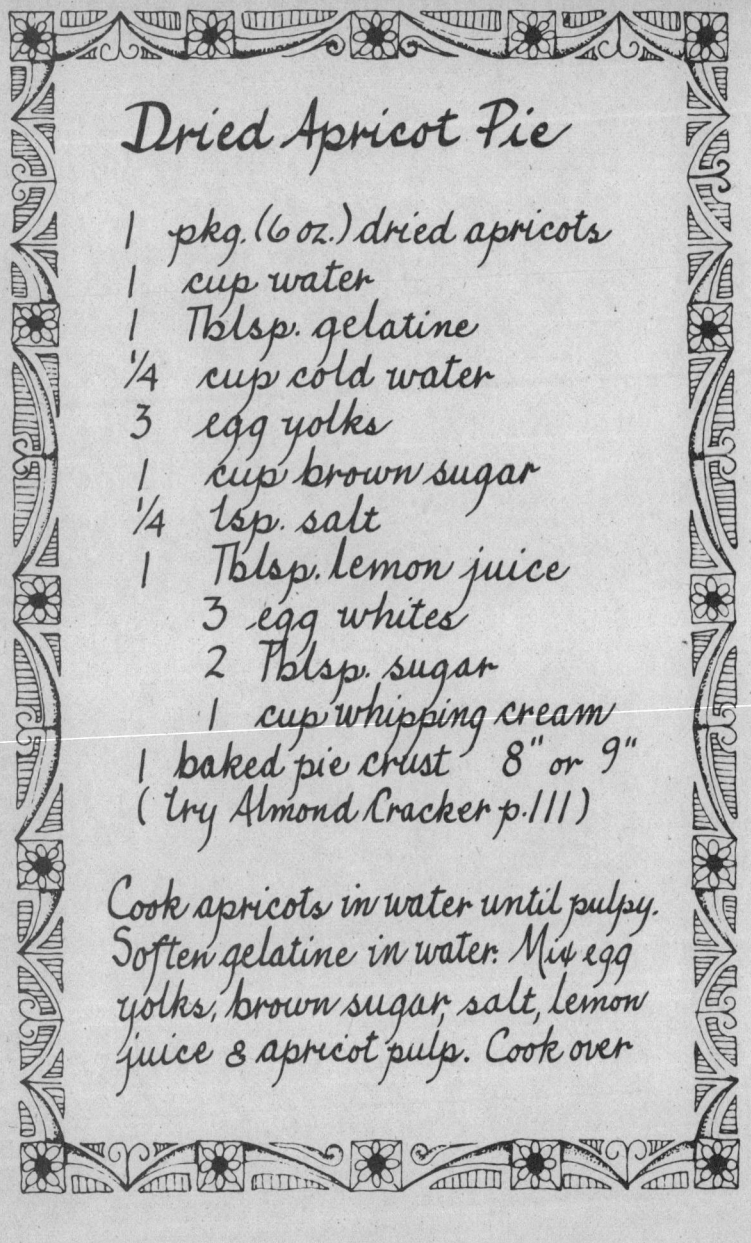

1 pkg. (6 oz.) dried apricots
1 cup water
1 Tblsp. gelatine
1/4 cup cold water
3 egg yolks
1 cup brown sugar
1/4 tsp. salt
1 Tblsp. lemon juice
3 egg whites
2 Tblsp. sugar
1 cup whipping cream
1 baked pie crust 8" or 9"
(try Almond Cracker p. 111)

Cook apricots in water until pulpy. Soften gelatine in water. Mix egg yolks, brown sugar, salt, lemon juice & apricot pulp. Cook over low heat. Stir constantly until thick. Add gelatine. Chill until firm. Beat egg whites & sugar until stiff. Whip cream; put ½ aside. Fold egg whites into ½ the cream, then into filling mixture. Pour into crust. Top with remaining ½ of the cream.

Cast iron porcelain lined preserving kettle

Clark & Co. Patent

Fresh Peach or Apricot Pie

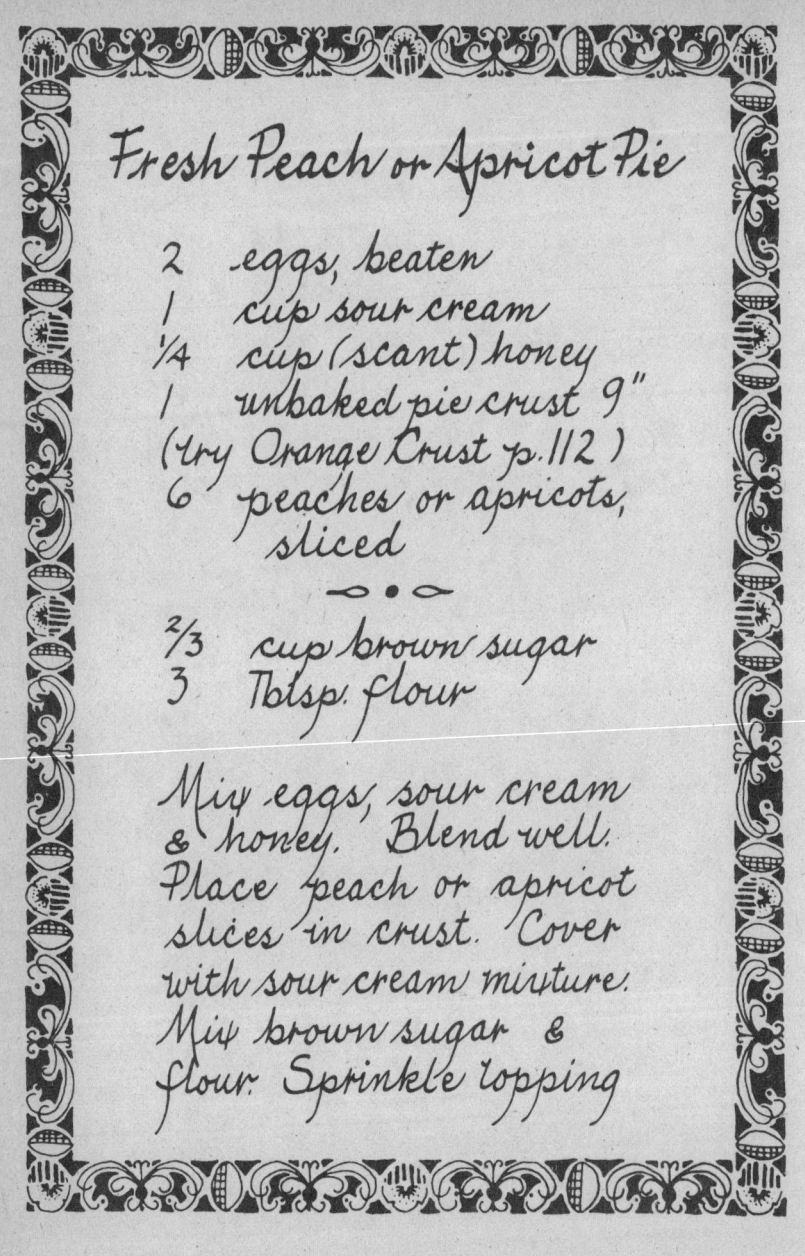

2 eggs, beaten
1 cup sour cream
¼ cup (scant) honey
1 unbaked pie crust 9"
(try Orange Crust p. 112)
6 peaches or apricots, sliced

— • —

⅔ cup brown sugar
3 Tblsp. flour

Mix eggs, sour cream & honey. Blend well. Place peach or apricot slices in crust. Cover with sour cream mixture. Mix brown sugar & flour. Sprinkle topping

over sour cream mixture.
Bake at 425° for 10 min.,
then 300° about 30 min.
more.

Embroidered linen
doily – ordered from
Corticelli Home Needlework
Magazine 1890.

Blueberry Peach Pie

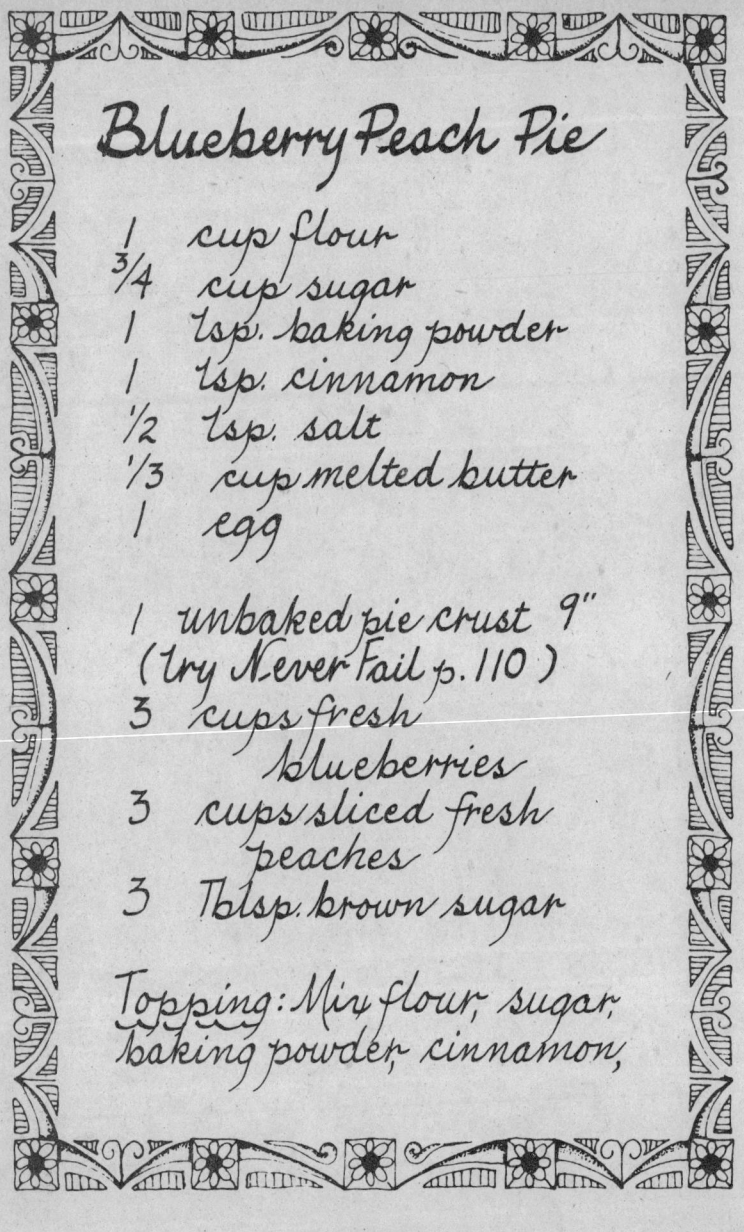

1 cup flour
3/4 cup sugar
1 tsp. baking powder
1 tsp. cinnamon
1/2 tsp. salt
1/3 cup melted butter
1 egg

1 unbaked pie crust 9"
(Try Never Fail p. 110)
3 cups fresh blueberries
3 cups sliced fresh peaches
3 Tblsp. brown sugar

Topping: Mix flour, sugar, baking powder, cinnamon,

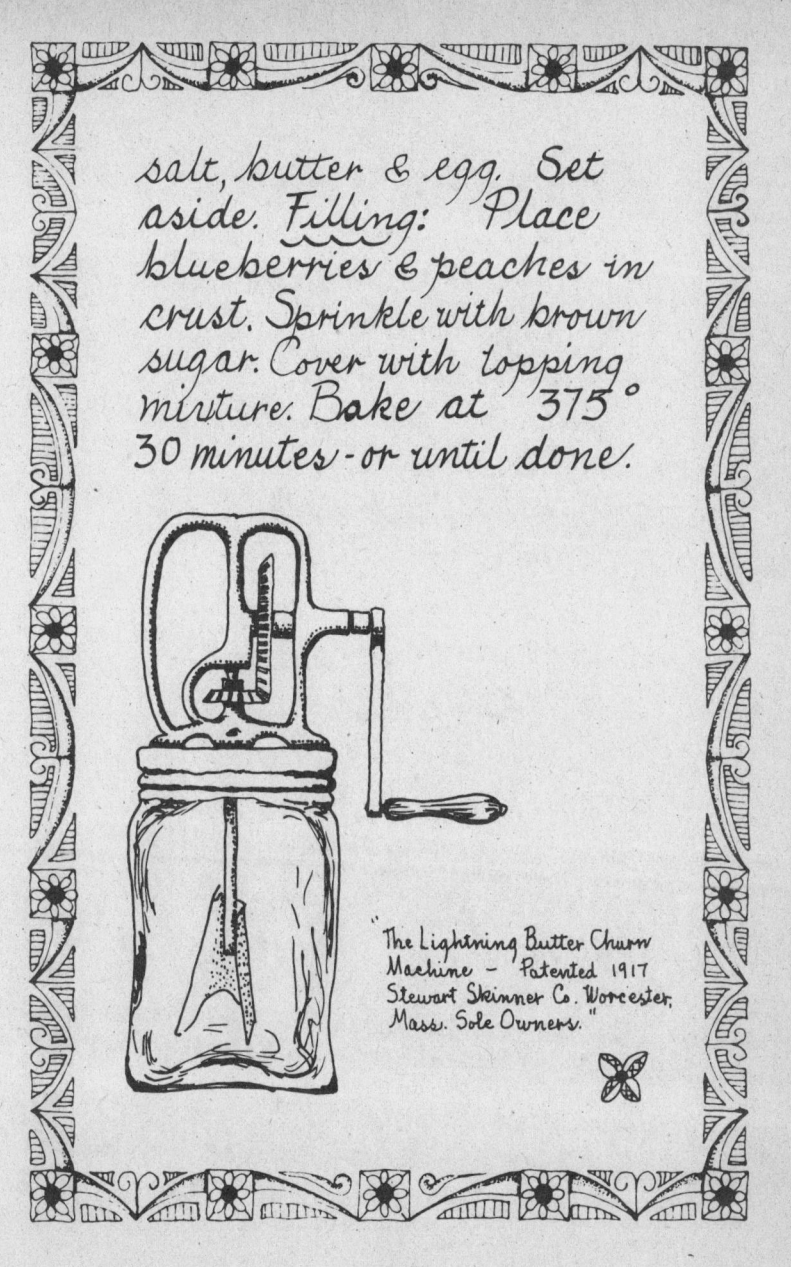

salt, butter & egg. Set aside. Filling: Place blueberries & peaches in crust. Sprinkle with brown sugar. Cover with topping mixture. Bake at 375° 30 minutes - or until done.

"The Lightning Butter Churn Machine - Patented 1917 Stewart Skinner Co. Worcester, Mass. Sole Owners."

Blueberry Pie

4 cups blueberries
1/4 cup flour
1 1/2 cups sugar
1 tsp. cinnamon
1/2 tsp. nutmeg
1 double unbaked pie crust 9" (try Never Fail p. 110)
1 Tblsp. lemon juice
2 Tblsp. butter

Mix blueberries with flour, sugar, cinnamon & nutmeg. Pour into bottom crust. Sprinkle with lemon juice. Dot with butter. Cover with top crust or lattice

strips. Bake at 450°
for 10 minutes, then
350° about 40 minutes
more.

Tart pan
folded tin strips
riveted
wire handles

Fresh Berry Pie

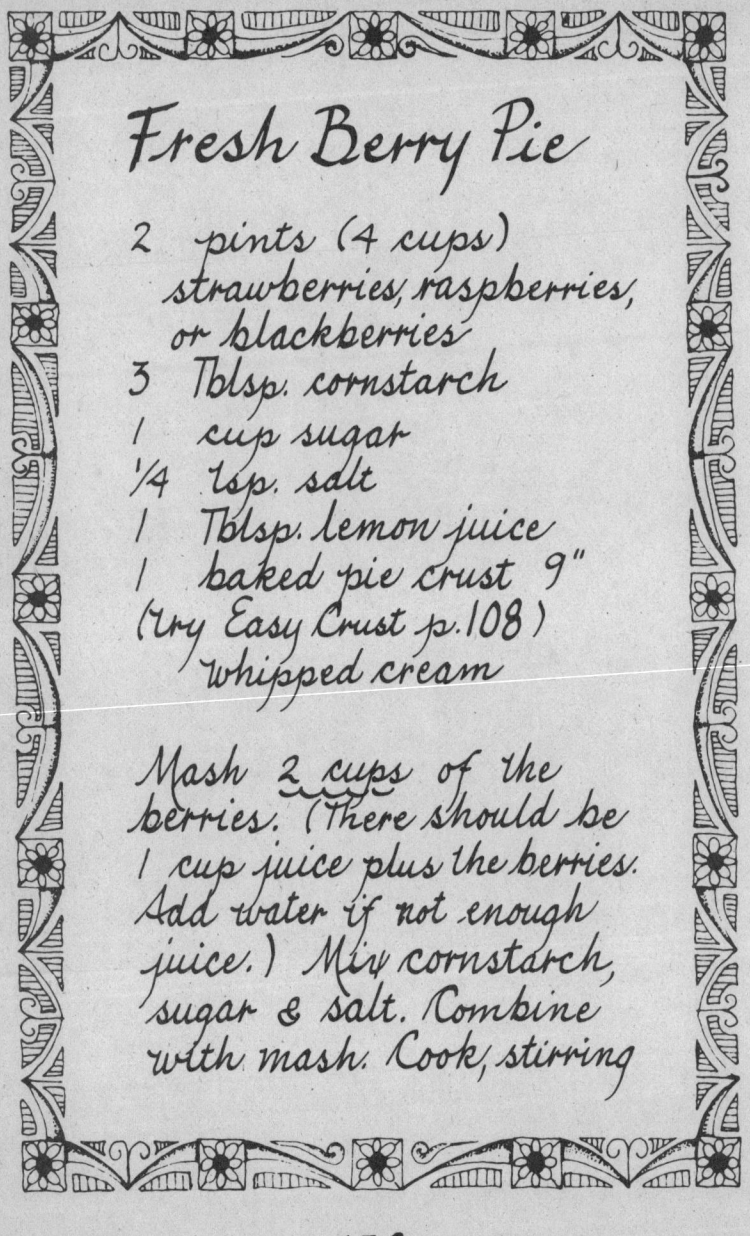

2 pints (4 cups) strawberries, raspberries, or blackberries
3 Tblsp. cornstarch
1 cup sugar
1/4 tsp. salt
1 Tblsp. lemon juice
1 baked pie crust 9"
(try Easy Crust p. 108)
  whipped cream

Mash 2 cups of the berries. (There should be 1 cup juice plus the berries. Add water if not enough juice.) Mix cornstarch, sugar & salt. Combine with mash. Cook, stirring constantly, until thick & clear. Add lemon juice. Cool. Fill crust with the 2 cups whole berries. Pour cooked mixture on top. Chill. Serve with whipped cream.

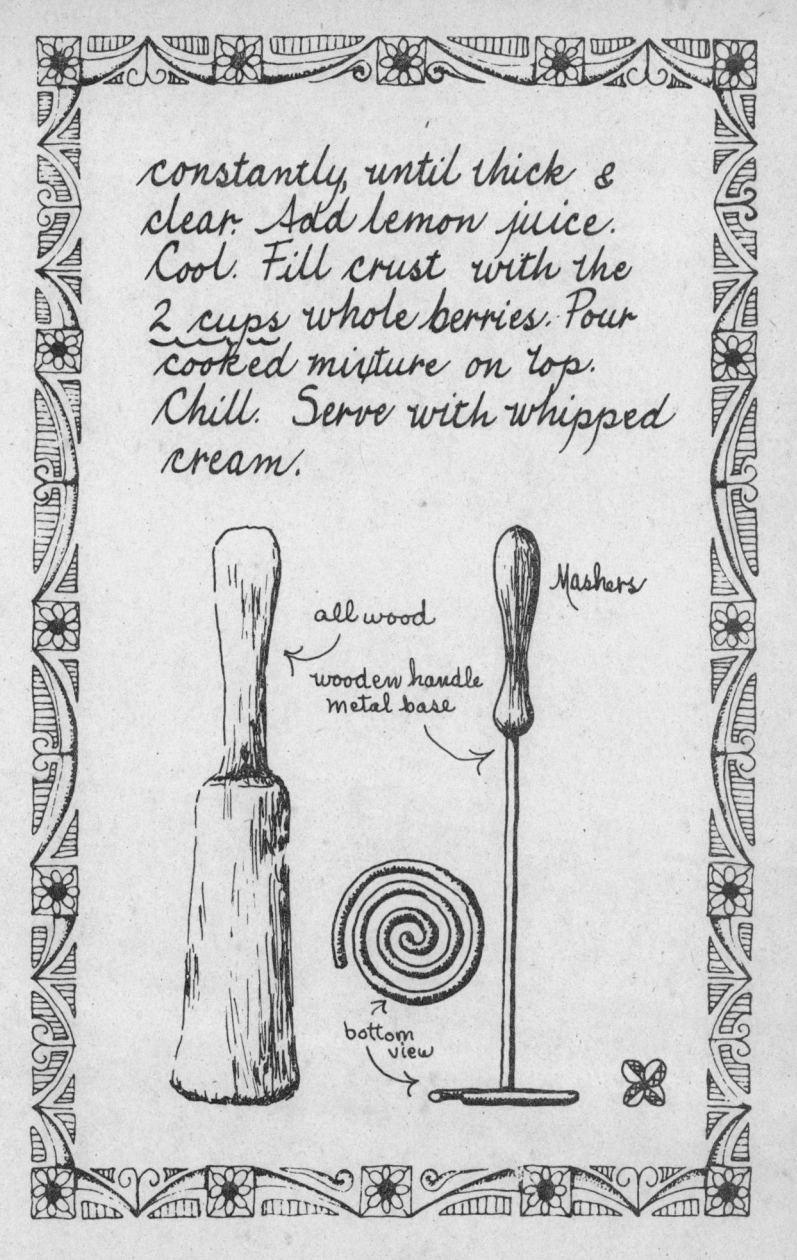

Mashers

all wood

wooden handle metal base

bottom view

Mixed Fruit Pie

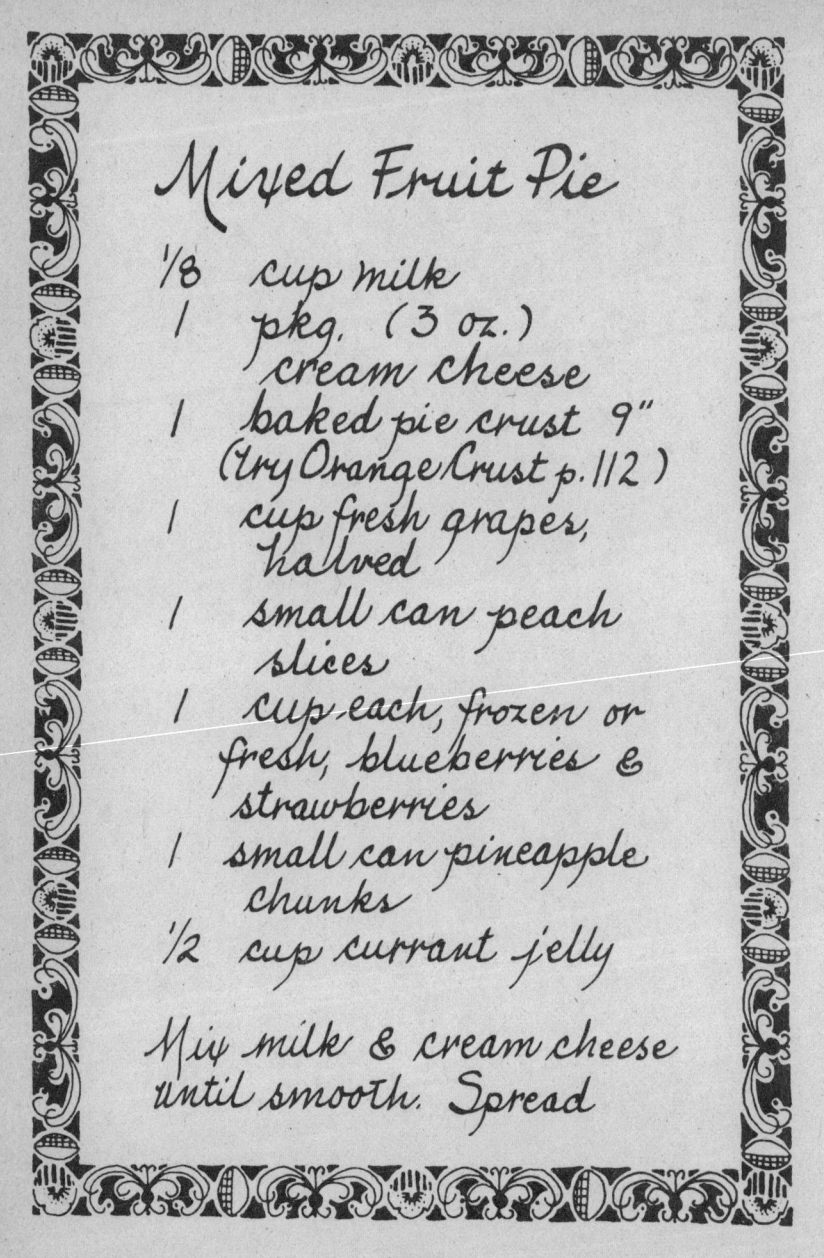

1/8 cup milk
1 pkg. (3 oz.) cream cheese
1 baked pie crust 9" (try Orange Crust p. 112)
1 cup fresh grapes, halved
1 small can peach slices
1 cup each, frozen or fresh, blueberries & strawberries
1 small can pineapple chunks
1/2 cup currant jelly

Mix milk & cream cheese until smooth. Spread

evenly on bottom crust.
Drain fruits & arrange
in circles - grapes along
edge of crust, then peaches,
blueberries, strawberries
& pineapple. Melt jelly slowly
over low heat. Cool
slightly. Pour
over fruit.
Chill.

Wire fruit jar
holder for
canning

Cherry Pie

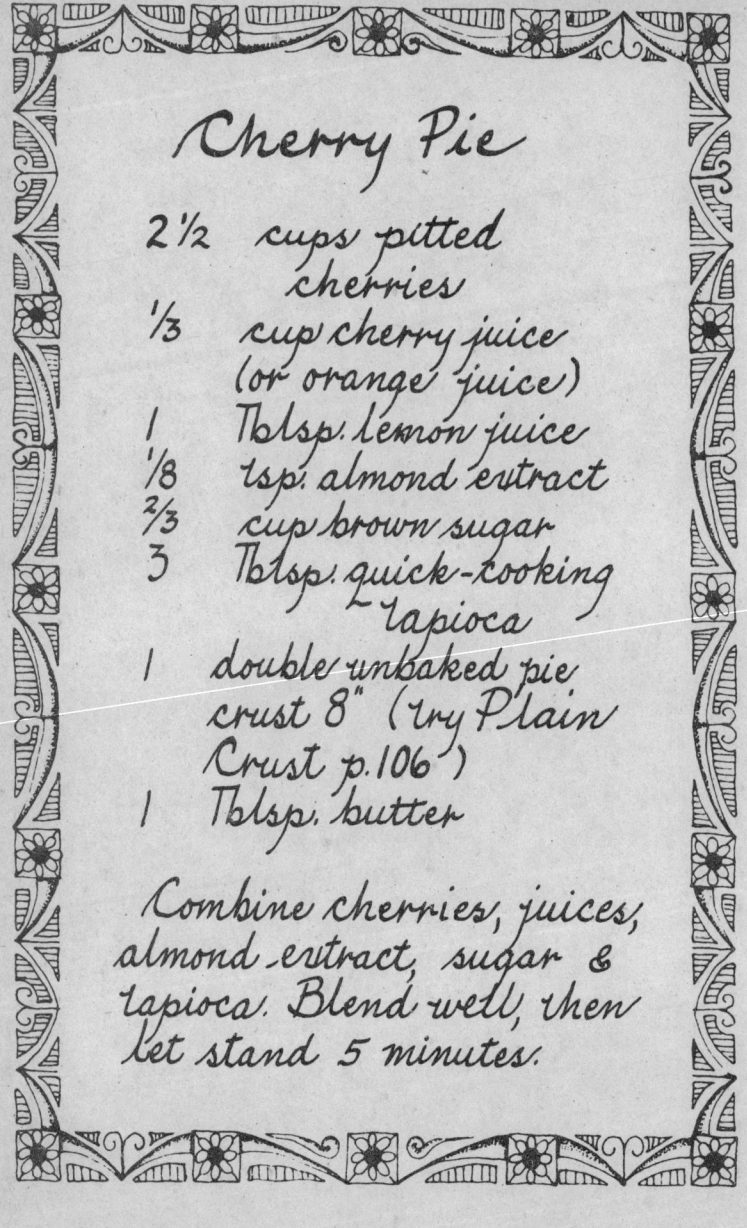

2½ cups pitted cherries
⅓ cup cherry juice (or orange juice)
1 Tblsp. lemon juice
⅛ tsp. almond extract
⅔ cup brown sugar
3 Tblsp. quick-cooking tapioca
1 double unbaked pie crust 8" (try Plain Crust p. 106)
1 Tblsp. butter

Combine cherries, juices, almond extract, sugar & tapioca. Blend well, then let stand 5 minutes.

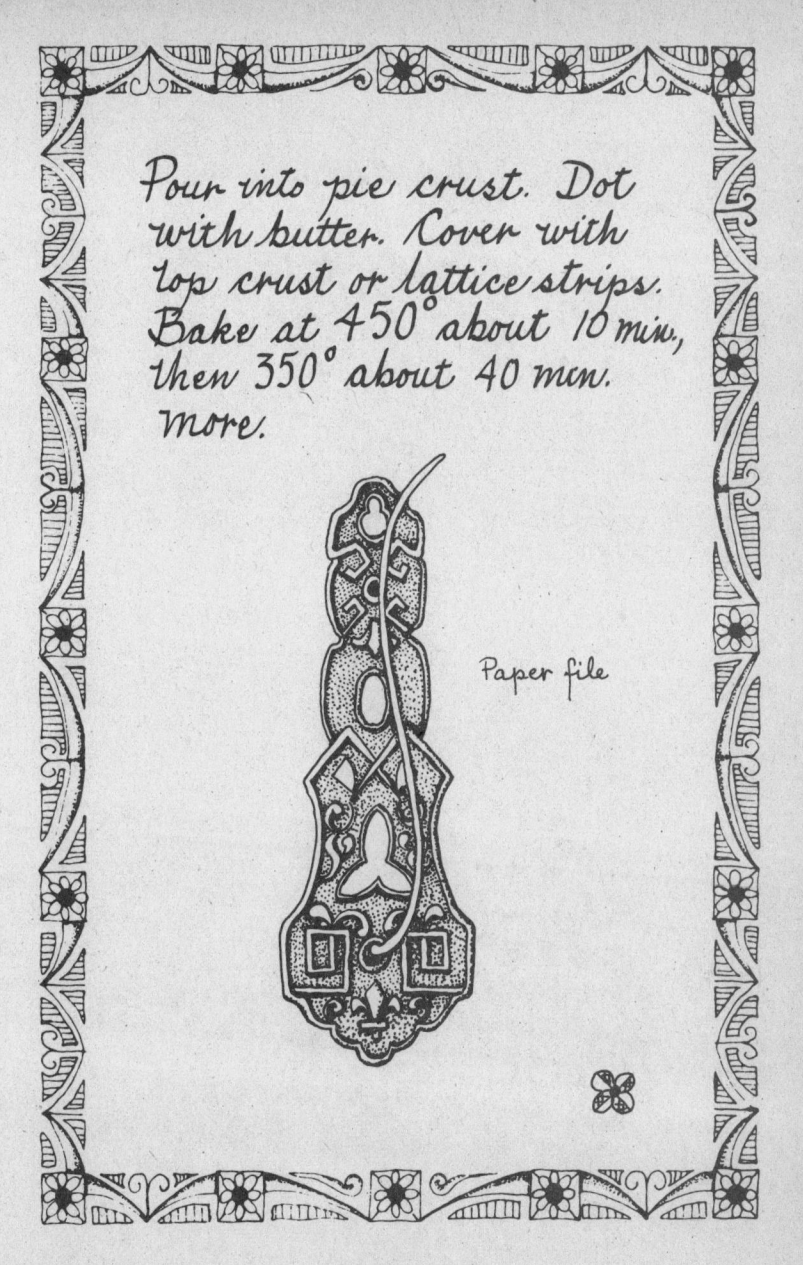

Pour into pie crust. Dot with butter. Cover with top crust or lattice strips. Bake at 450° about 10 min., then 350° about 40 min. more.

Paper file

Concord Grape Pie

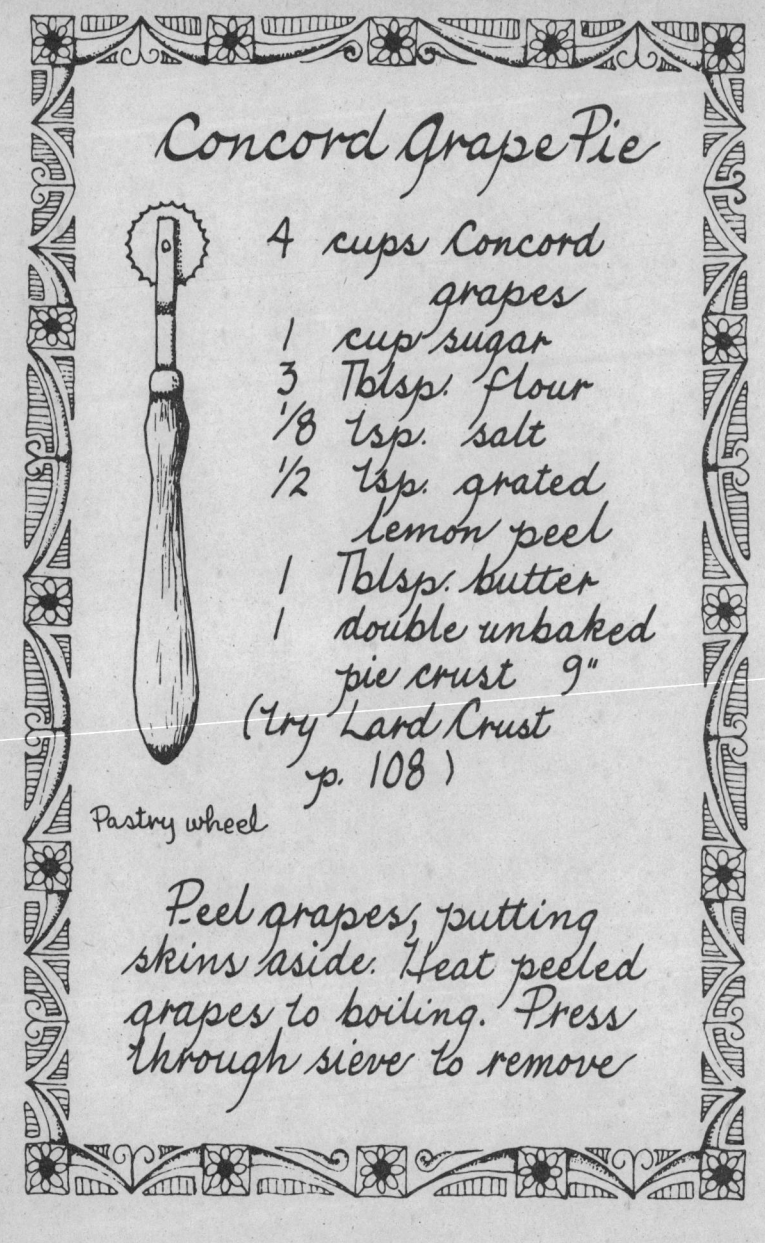

4 cups Concord grapes
1 cup sugar
3 Tblsp. flour
1/8 tsp. salt
1/2 tsp. grated lemon peel
1 Tblsp. butter
1 double unbaked pie crust 9"
(Try Lard Crust p. 108)

Pastry wheel

Peel grapes, putting skins aside. Heat peeled grapes to boiling. Press through sieve to remove seeds. Chop skins in wooden bowl. Mix sugar, flour, salt, lemon peel. Add grape pulp & skins. Pour into crust. Dot with butter. Cover with top crust or lattice strips. Bake at 400°, 25-30 min.

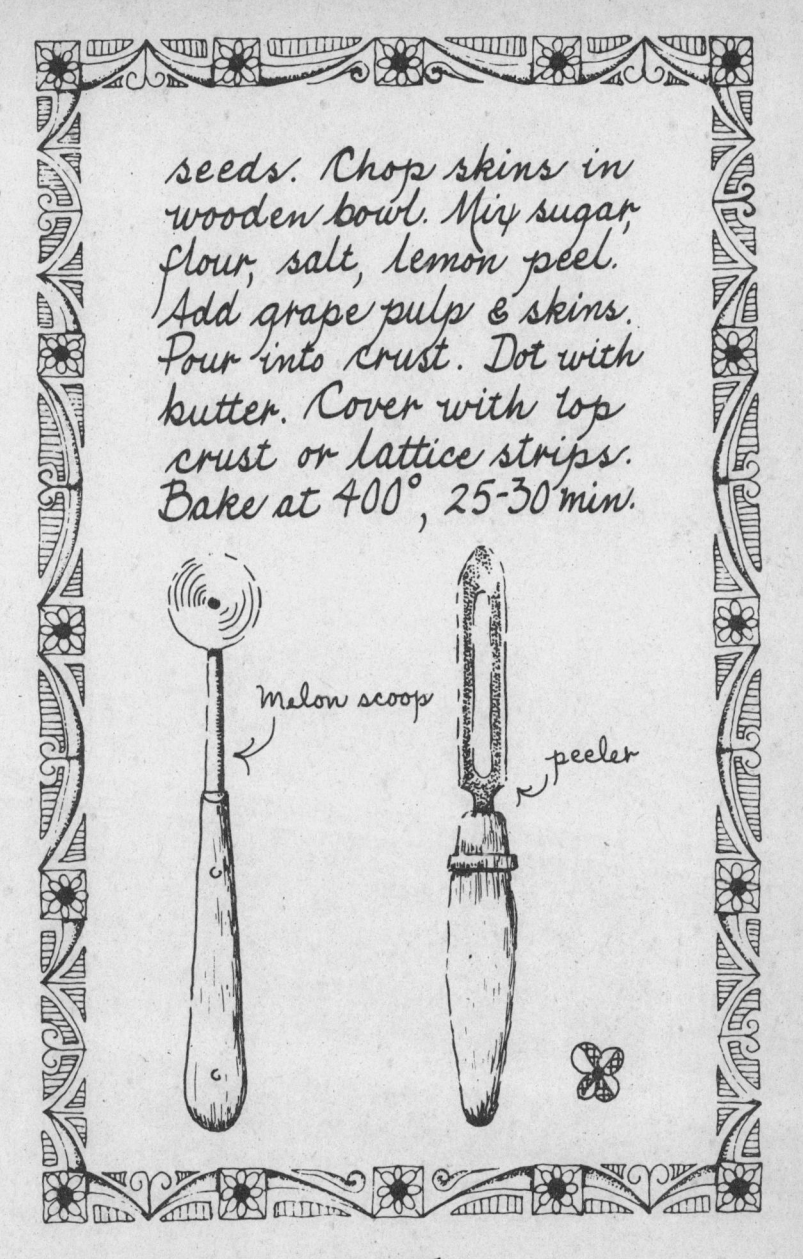

melon scoop

peeler

Cranberry Pie

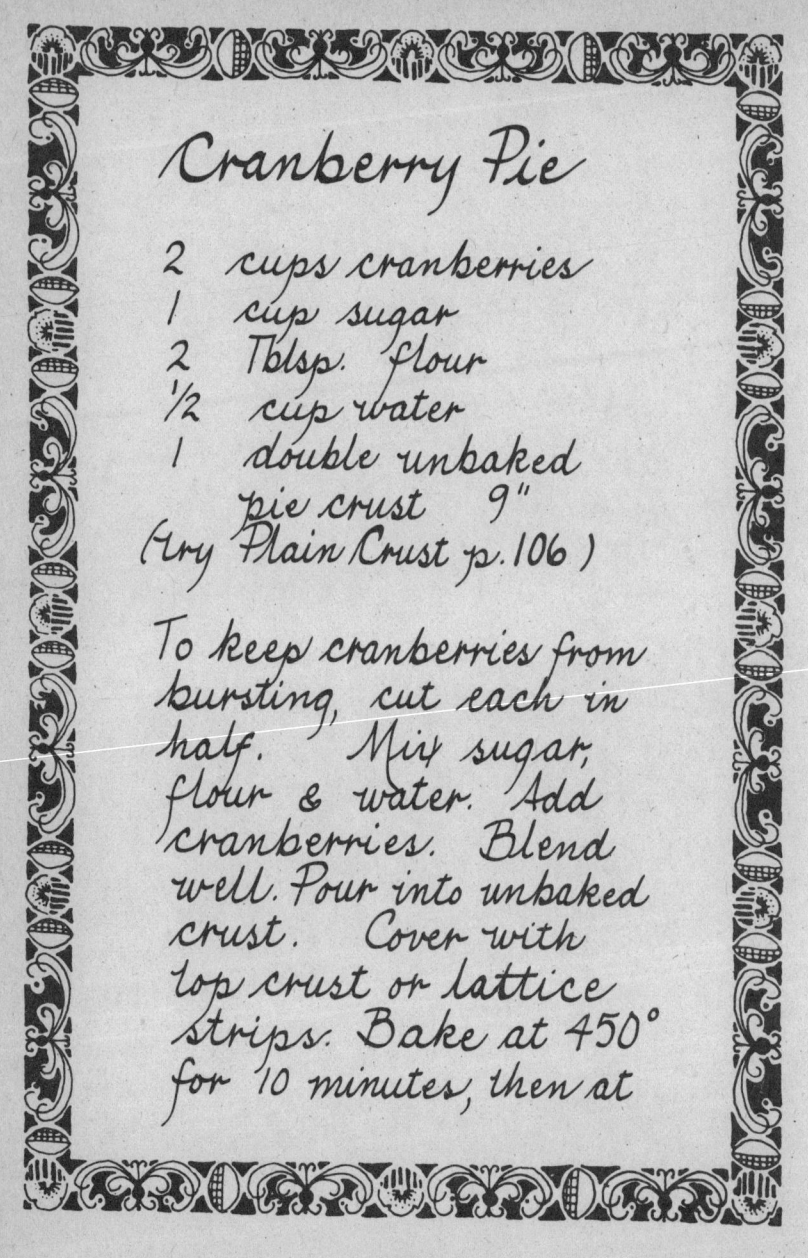

2 cups cranberries
1 cup sugar
2 Tblsp. flour
½ cup water
1 double unbaked pie crust 9"
(try Plain Crust p. 106)

To keep cranberries from bursting, cut each in half. Mix sugar, flour & water. Add cranberries. Blend well. Pour into unbaked crust. Cover with top crust or lattice strips. Bake at 450° for 10 minutes, then at

350° about 30 minutes more, or until done.

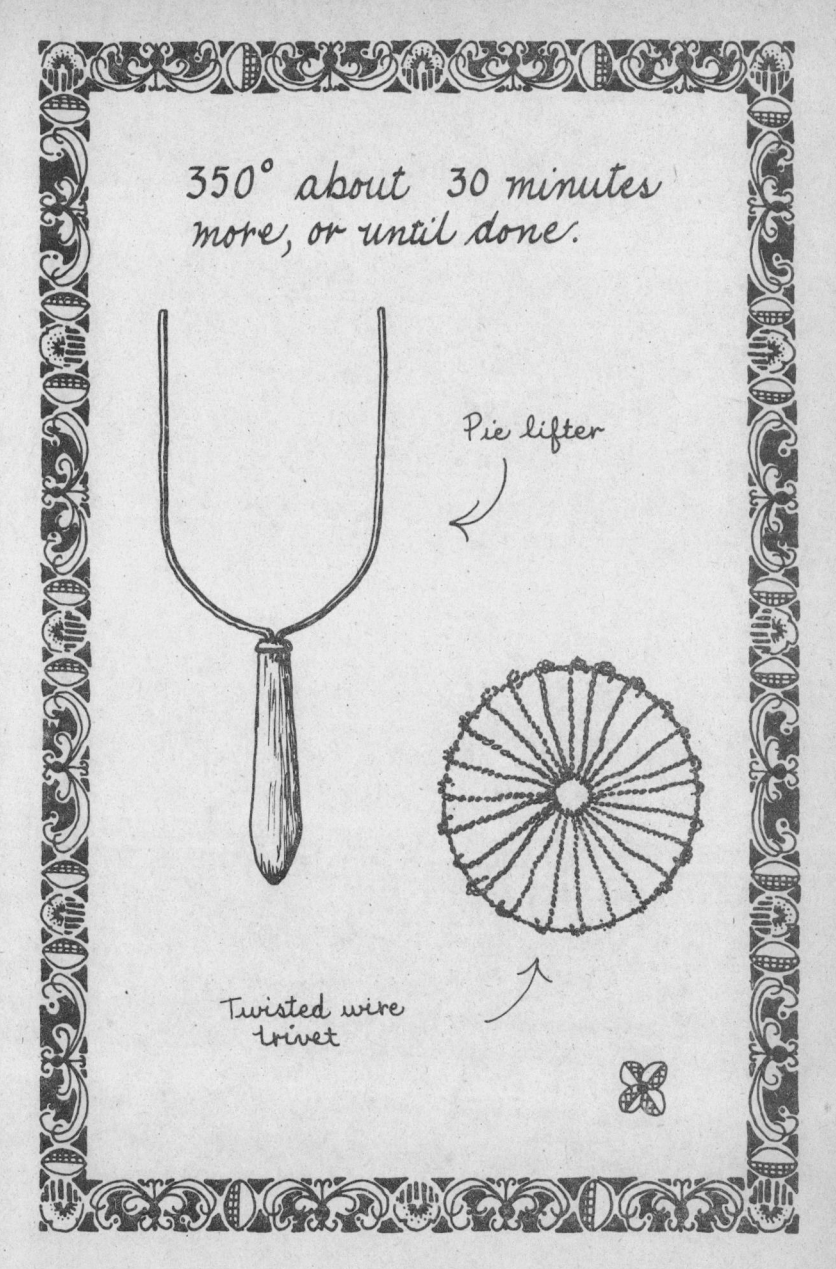

Pie lifter

Twisted wire trivet

Prune Pie

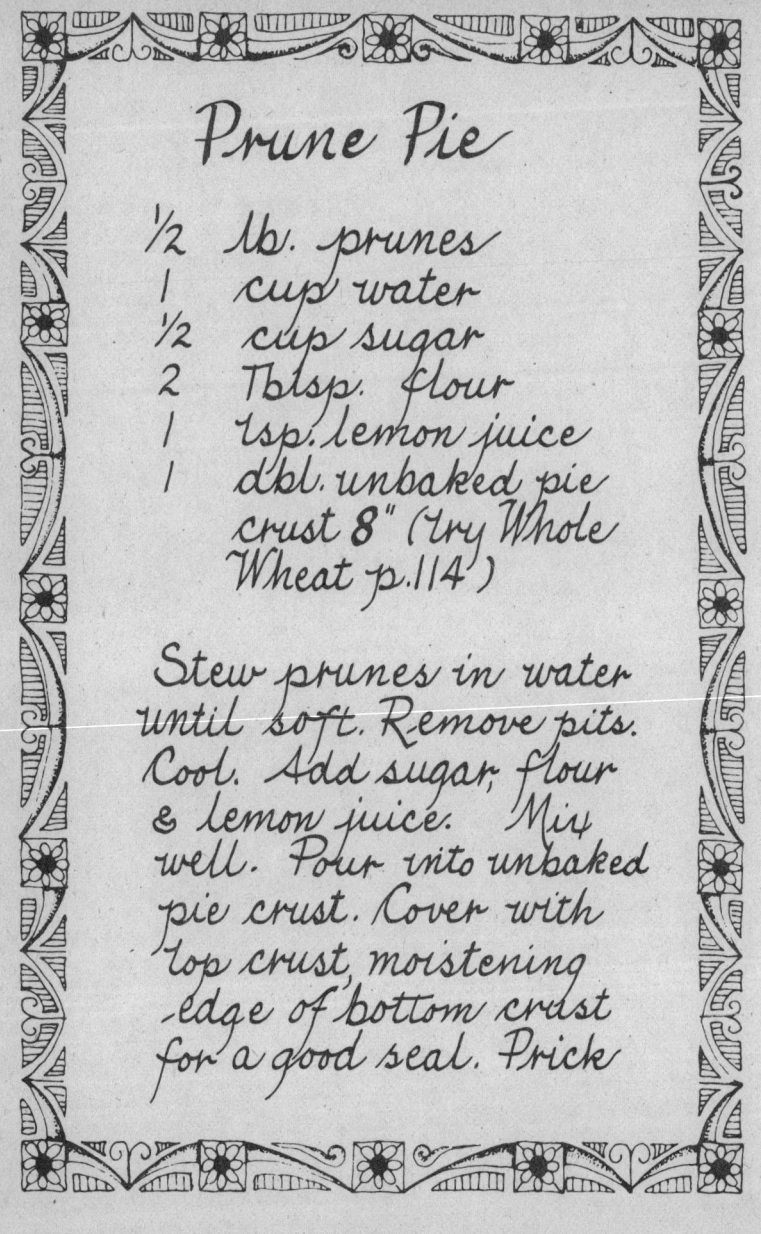

½   lb. prunes
1   cup water
½   cup sugar
2   Tbsp. flour
1   tsp. lemon juice
1   dbl. unbaked pie crust 8" (Try Whole Wheat p.114)

Stew prunes in water until soft. Remove pits. Cool. Add sugar, flour & lemon juice. Mix well. Pour into unbaked pie crust. Cover with top crust, moistening edge of bottom crust for a good seal. Prick top crust. Bake at 425° for 10 minutes, then 350° for about 20-30 minutes more.

Cast iron stove kettle

Ripe Currant Pie

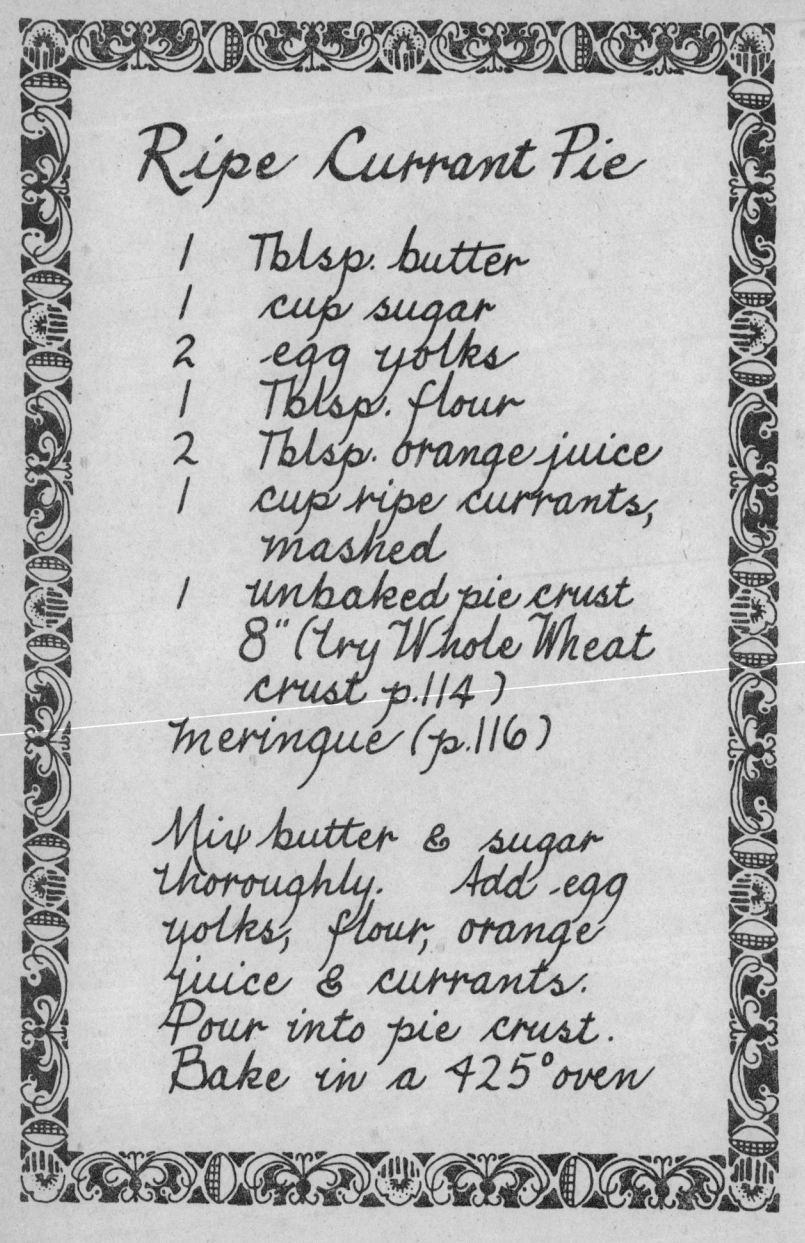

1 Tblsp. butter
1 cup sugar
2 egg yolks
1 Tblsp. flour
2 Tblsp. orange juice
1 cup ripe currants, mashed
1 unbaked pie crust 8" (try Whole Wheat crust p.114)
Meringue (p.116)

Mix butter & sugar thoroughly. Add egg yolks, flour, orange juice & currants. Pour into pie crust. Bake in a 425° oven

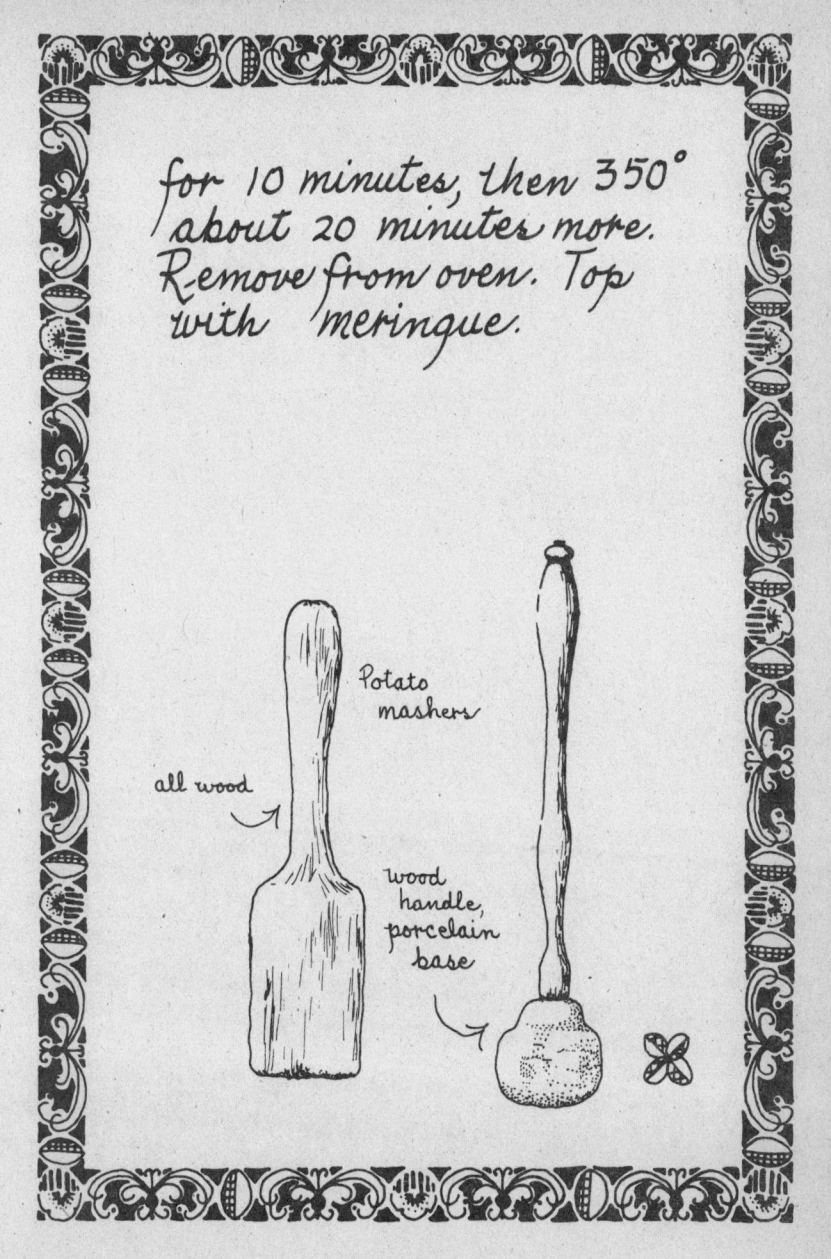

for 10 minutes, then 350°
about 20 minutes more.
Remove from oven. Top
with meringue.

Potato mashers

all wood

wood handle, porcelain base

Raisin Pie

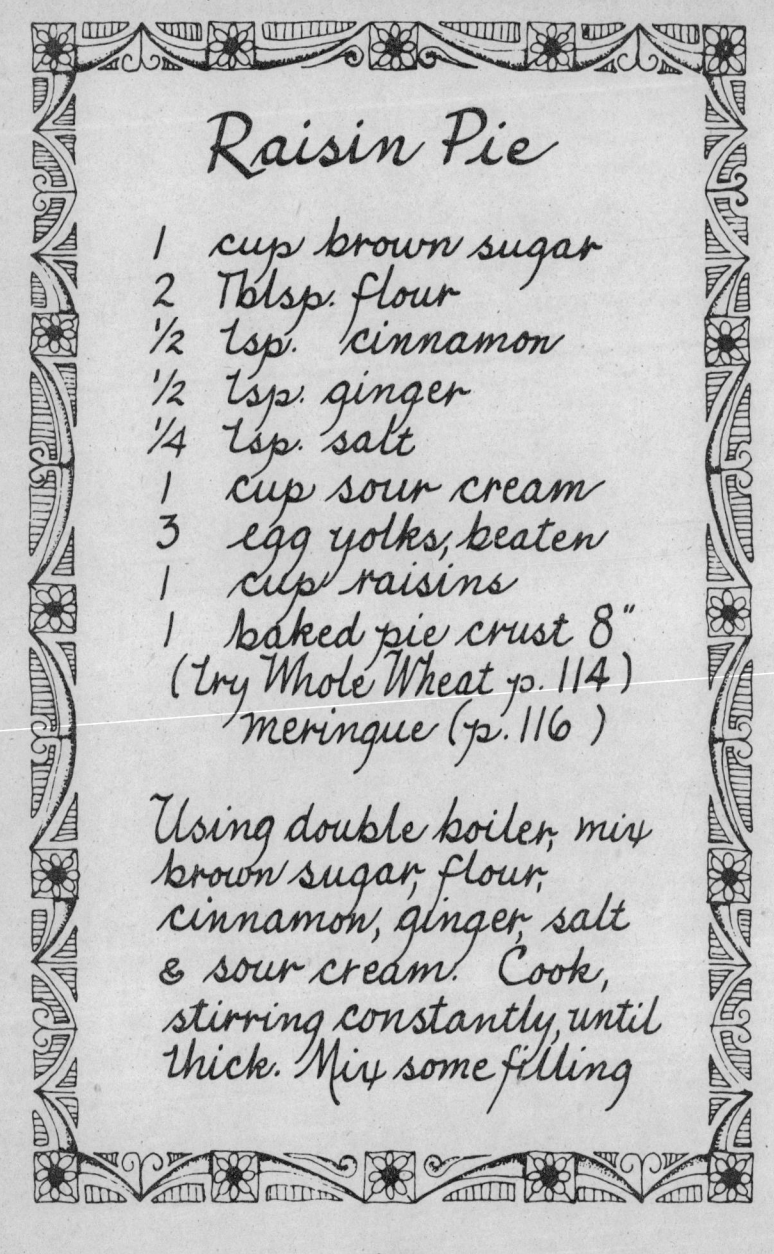

1 cup brown sugar
2 Tblsp. flour
½ tsp. cinnamon
½ tsp. ginger
¼ tsp. salt
1 cup sour cream
3 egg yolks, beaten
1 cup raisins
1 baked pie crust 8"
(try Whole Wheat p. 114)
    meringue (p. 116)

Using double boiler, mix brown sugar, flour, cinnamon, ginger, salt & sour cream. Cook, stirring constantly, until thick. Mix some filling with egg yolks, then more until yolks can be added to filling smoothly. Cook 5 min. more. Add raisins. Cool. Pour into baked crust. Top with meringue.

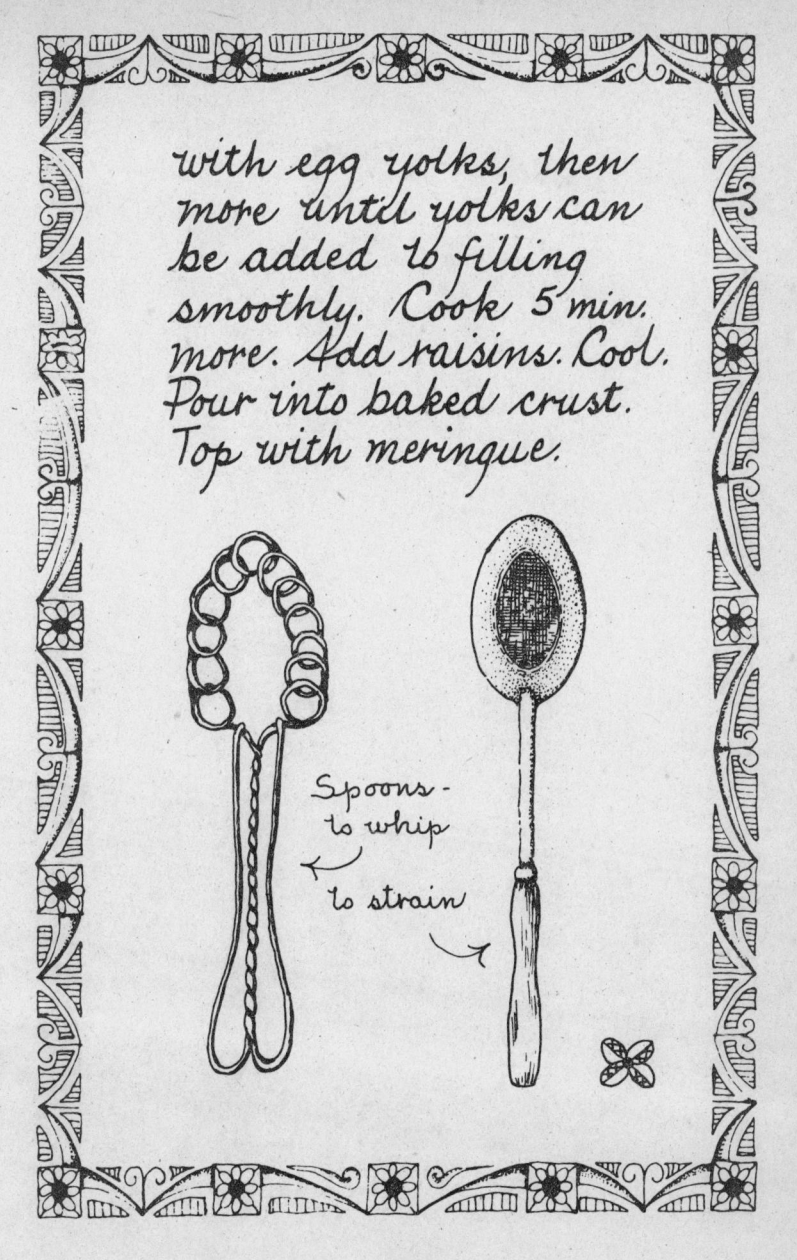

Spoons —
to whip
to strain

Rhubarb Custard Pie

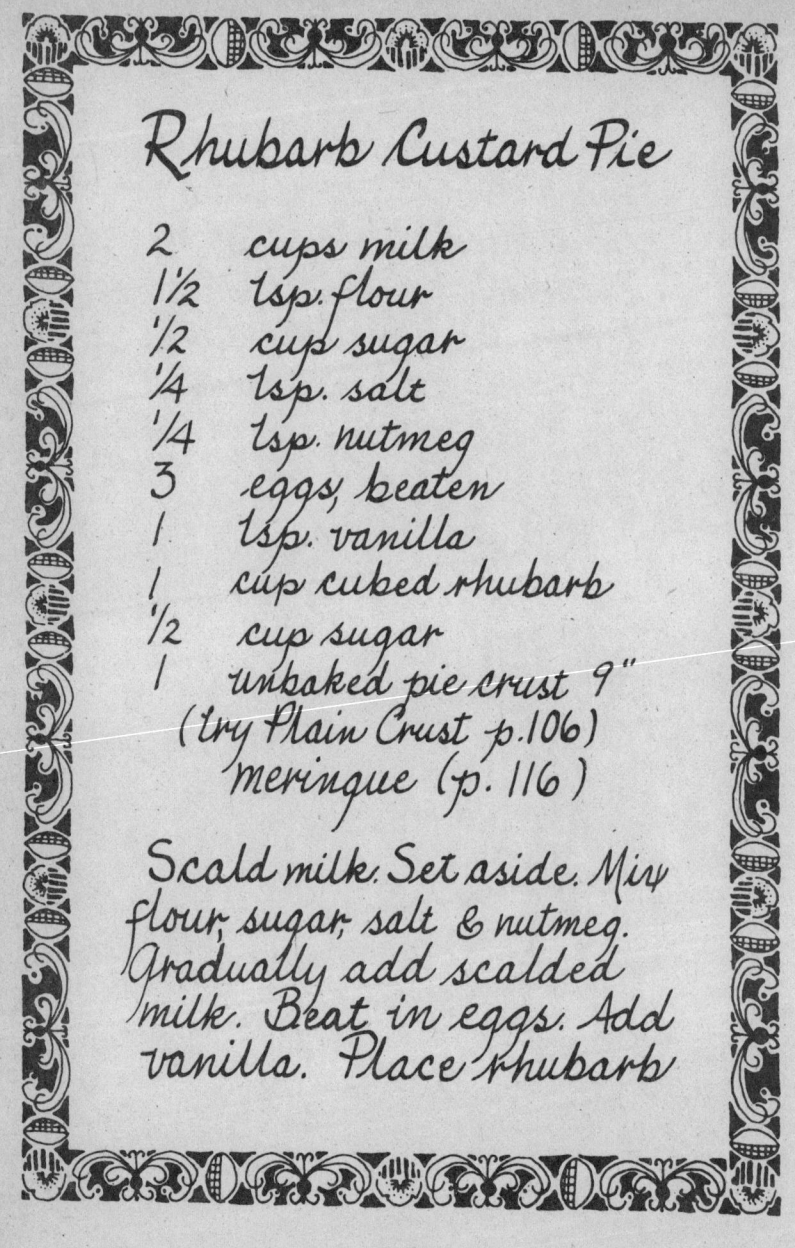

2 cups milk
1½ tsp. flour
½ cup sugar
¼ tsp. salt
¼ tsp. nutmeg
3 eggs, beaten
1 tsp. vanilla
1 cup cubed rhubarb
½ cup sugar
1 unbaked pie crust 9"
 (try Plain Crust p.106)
 meringue (p. 116)

Scald milk. Set aside. Mix flour, sugar, salt & nutmeg. Gradually add scalded milk. Beat in eggs. Add vanilla. Place rhubarb in bottom crust. Sprinkle with sugar. Pour custard mixture on top. Bake at 350° about 45 min., or until knife inserted in center comes out clean. Top with meringue.

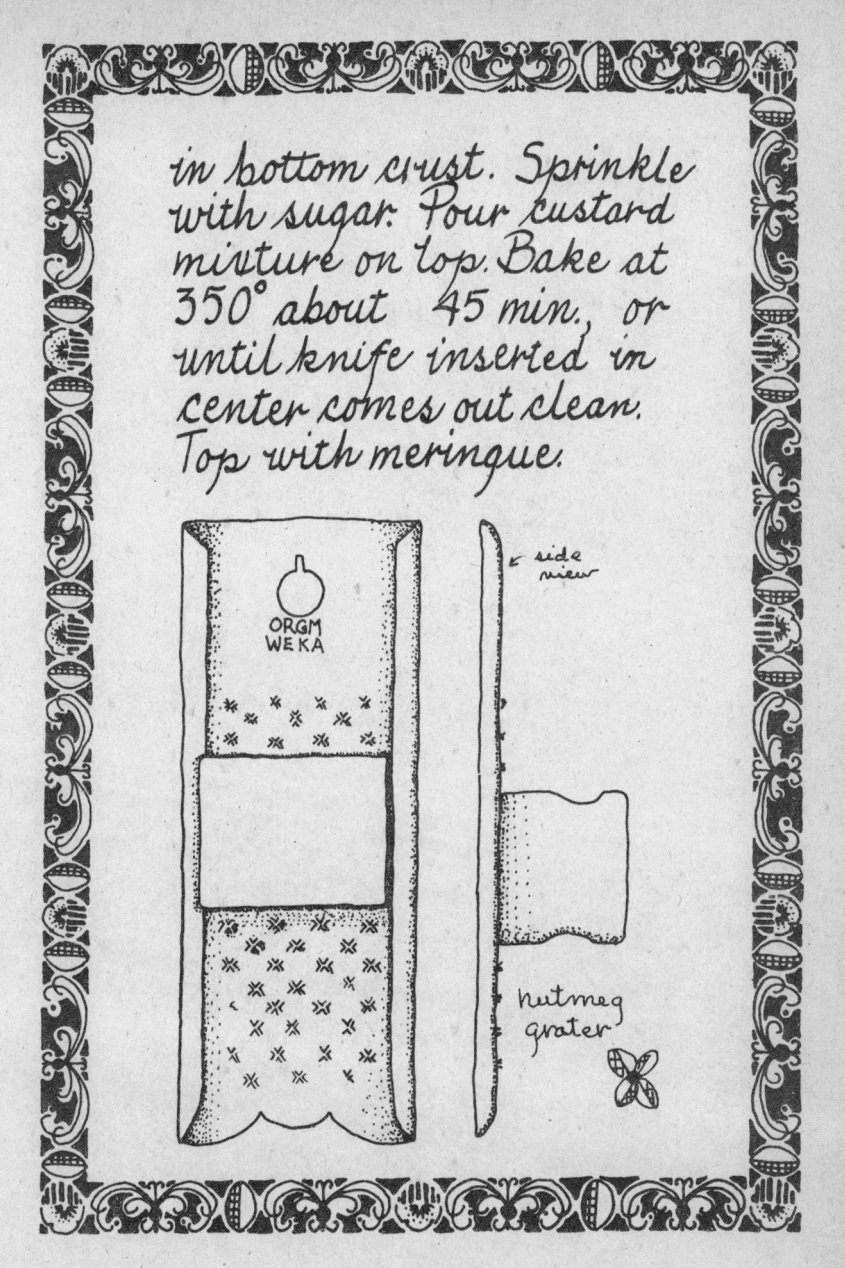

nutmeg grater
← side view
ORGM WEKA

Rich Lemon Pie

½ cup lemon juice
6 tsp. grated lemon rind (or grated rind from 2 lemons)
2 cups sugar
1 cup butter
4 eggs
1 baked pie crust 8" or 9" (try Easy Crust p. 108)
sweetened whipped cream

Using a double boiler, combine lemon juice, lemon rind, sugar & butter. Heat until butter is melted. Beat eggs & add to mixture, stirring constantly, until it becomes thick (about 15 minutes). Cool. Pour into baked pie crust. Serve with a dollop of whipped cream.

Lemon squeezer
Cast iron handle
aluminum cup

← top view

side view →

Fresh Lime Pie

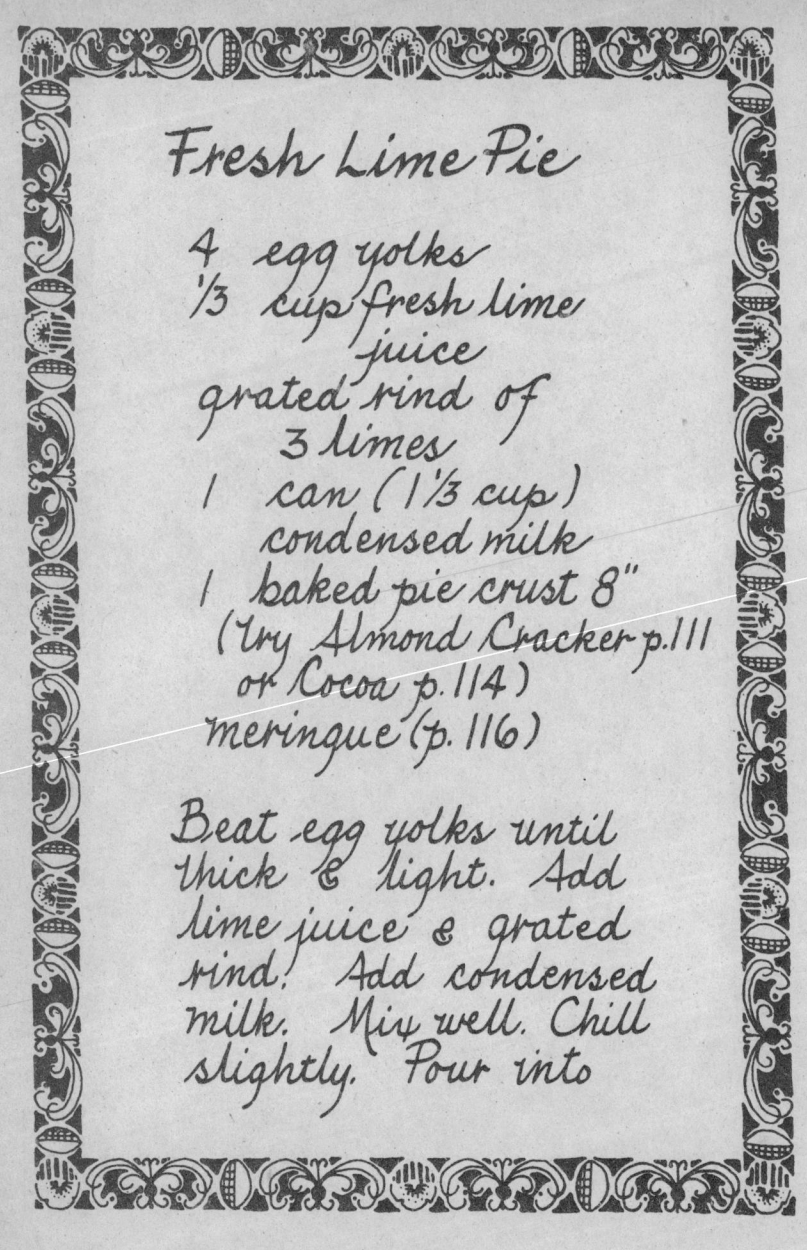

4 egg yolks
1/3 cup fresh lime
    juice
grated rind of
    3 limes
1 can (1 1/3 cup)
    condensed milk
1 baked pie crust 8"
   (try Almond Cracker p.111
    or Cocoa p.114)
meringue (p.116)

Beat egg yolks until thick & light. Add lime juice & grated rind. Add condensed milk. Mix well. Chill slightly. Pour into pie crust. Cover with meringue & bake until lightly browned. Store in refrigerator.

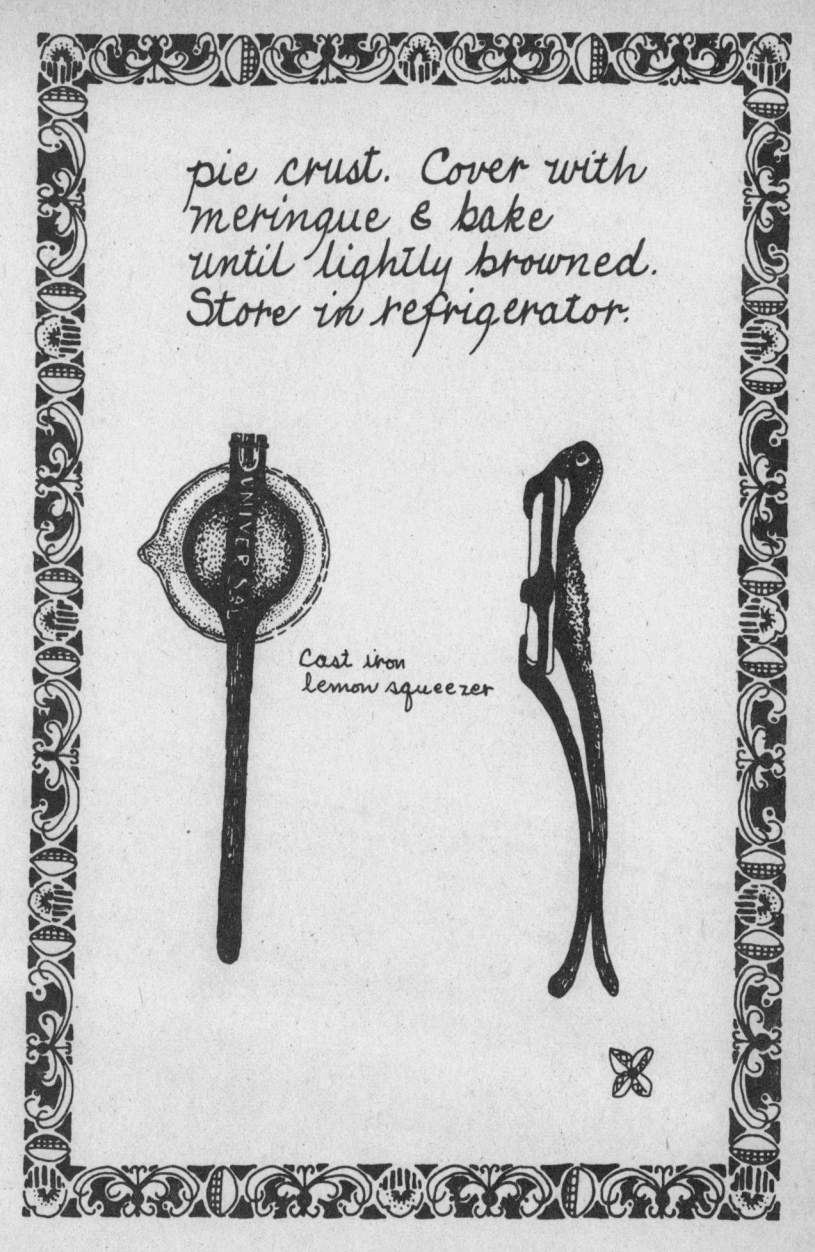

Cast iron lemon squeezer

Pineapple Pie

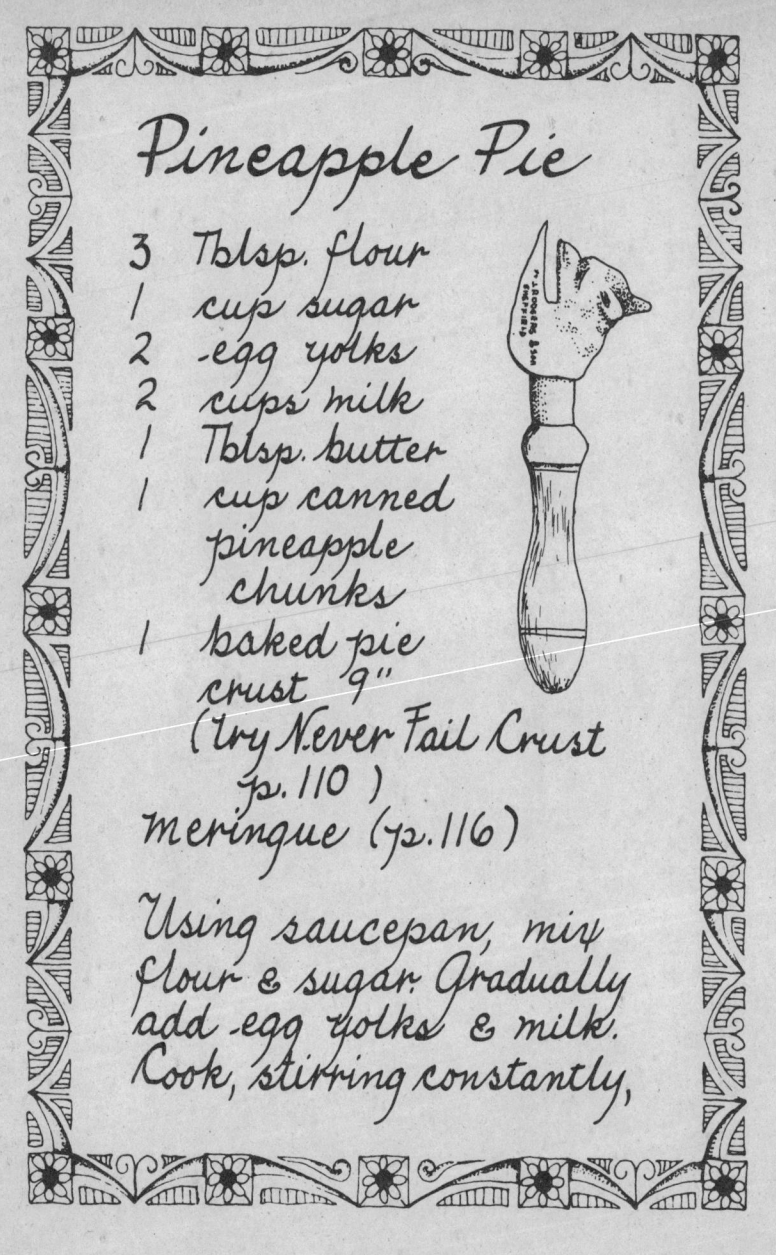

3 Tblsp. flour
1 cup sugar
2 egg yolks
2 cups milk
1 Tblsp. butter
1 cup canned pineapple chunks
1 baked pie crust 9" (try Never Fail Crust p. 110)
Meringue (p. 116)

Using saucepan, mix flour & sugar. Gradually add egg yolks & milk. Cook, stirring constantly, until thick (about 20 minutes). Add butter & drained pineapple chunks. Pour into pie crust. Cover with meringue.

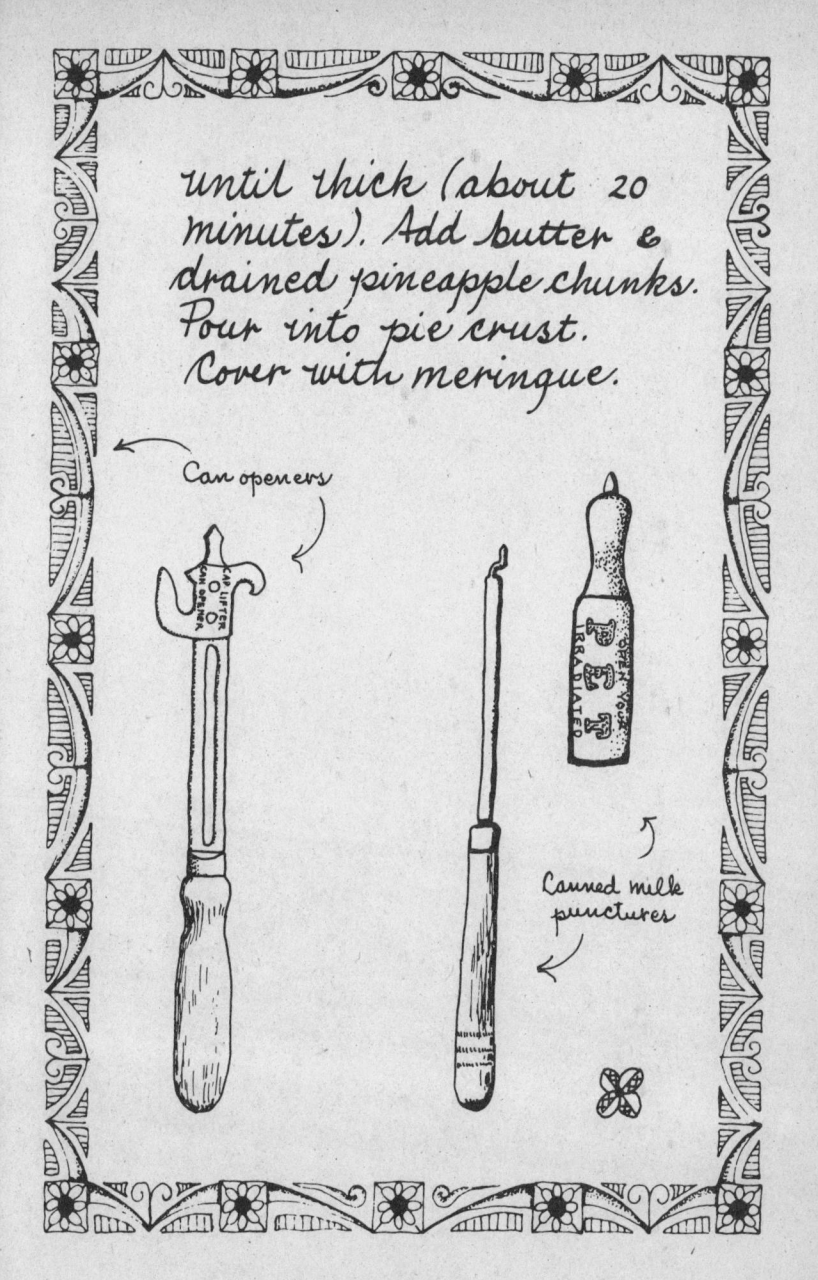

← Can openers

↑ Canned milk punctures ←

Baked Alaska Pie

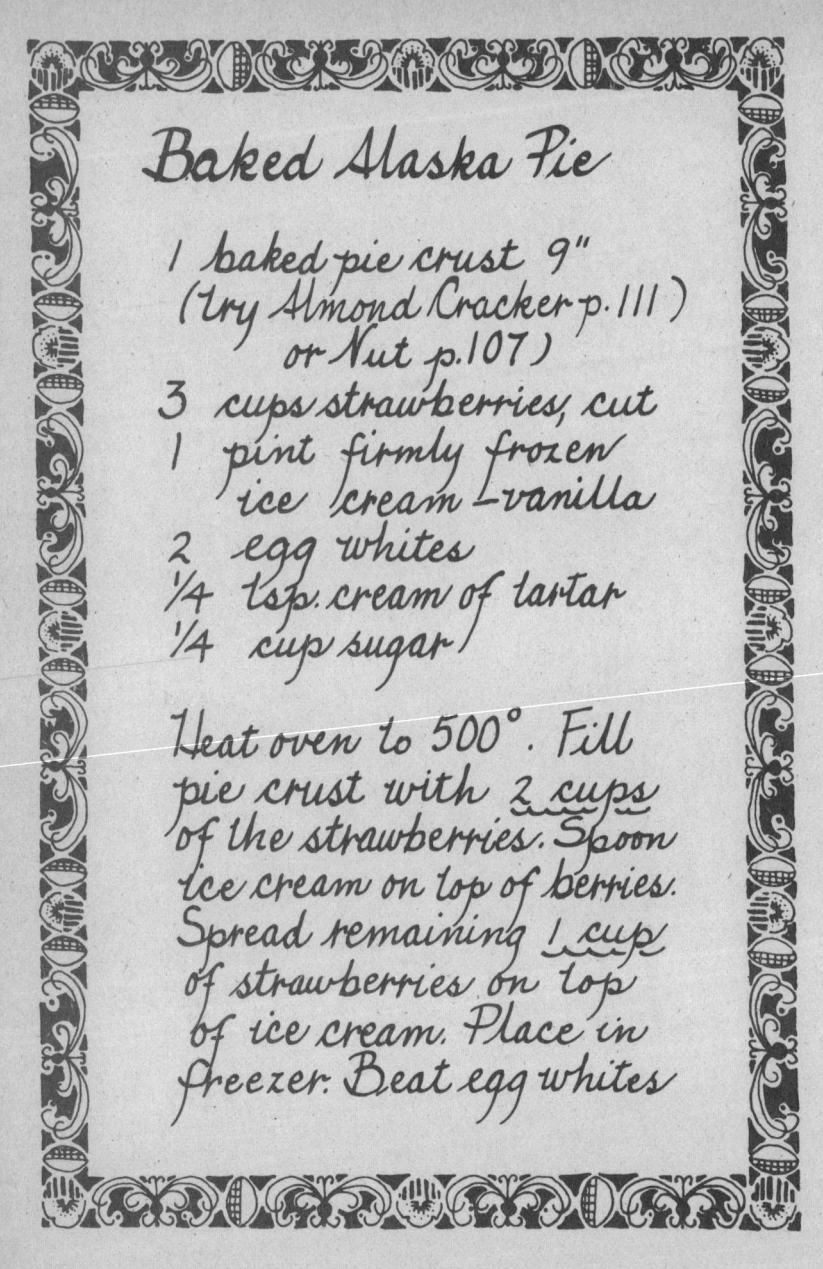

1 baked pie crust 9"
(Try Almond Cracker p.111)
or Nut p.107)
3 cups strawberries, cut
1 pint firmly frozen
 ice cream — vanilla
2 egg whites
¼ tsp. cream of tartar
¼ cup sugar

Heat oven to 500°. Fill pie crust with 2 cups of the strawberries. Spoon ice cream on top of berries. Spread remaining 1 cup of strawberries on top of ice cream. Place in freezer. Beat egg whites

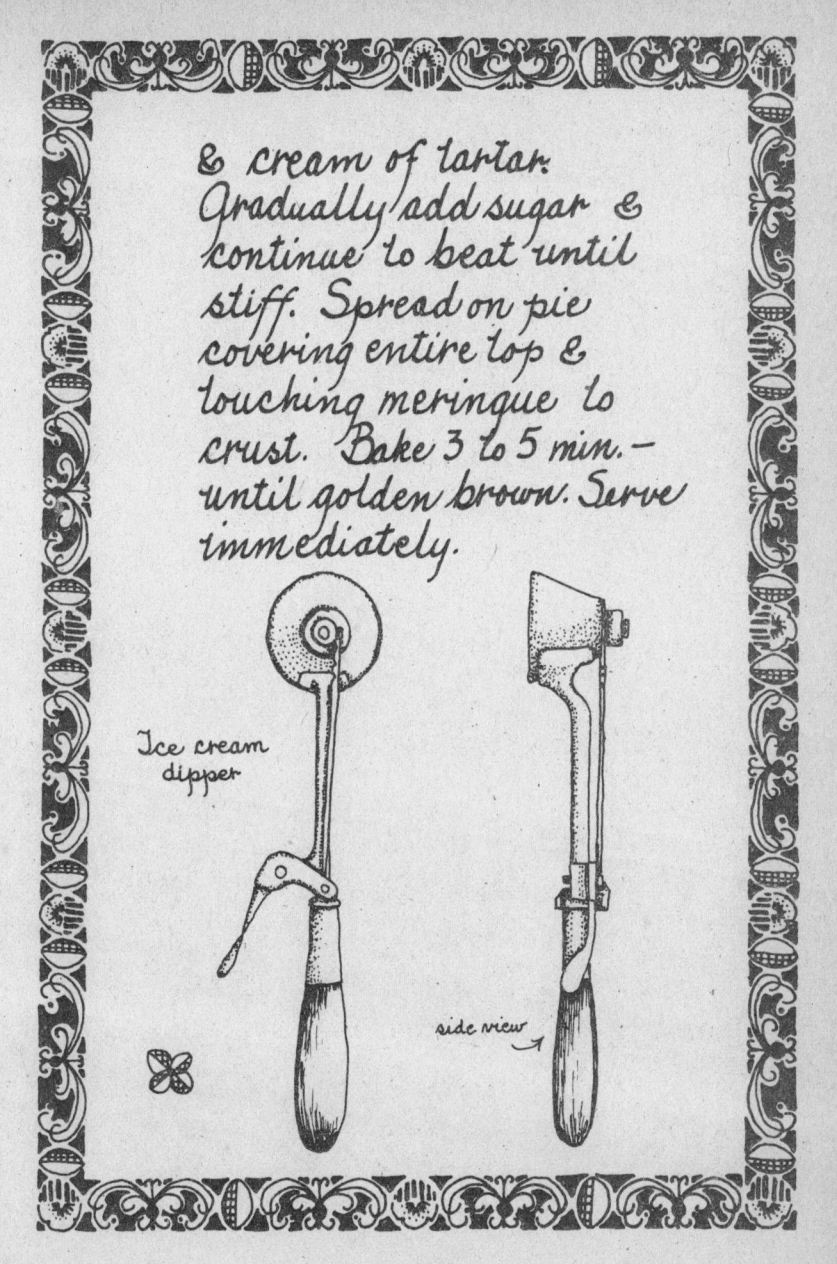

& cream of tartar. Gradually add sugar & continue to beat until stiff. Spread on pie covering entire top & touching meringue to crust. Bake 3 to 5 min. — until golden brown. Serve immediately.

Ice cream dipper

side view

Date Nut Pie

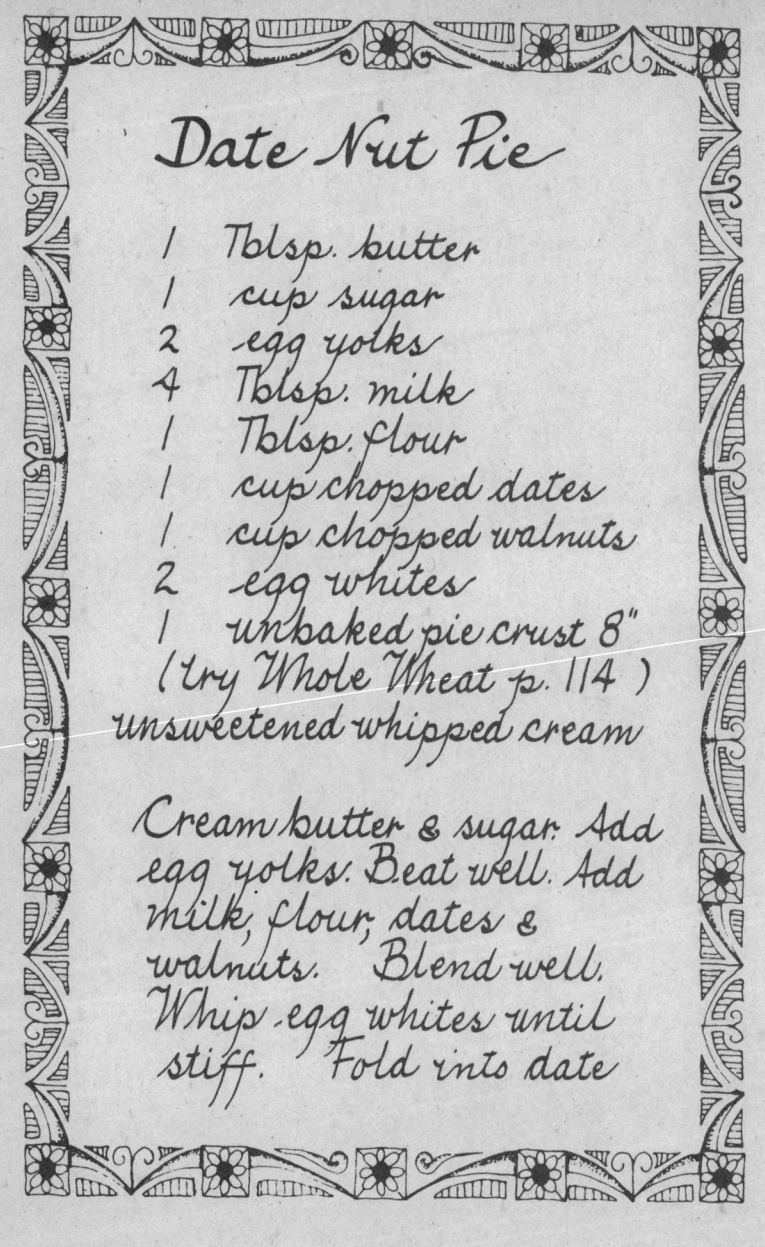

1 Tblsp. butter
1 cup sugar
2 egg yolks
4 Tblsp. milk
1 Tblsp. flour
1 cup chopped dates
1 cup chopped walnuts
2 egg whites
1 unbaked pie crust 8"
(try Whole Wheat p. 114)
unsweetened whipped cream

Cream butter & sugar. Add egg yolks. Beat well. Add milk, flour, dates & walnuts. Blend well. Whip egg whites until stiff. Fold into date mixture. Pour into pie crust. Bake at 300° about 45 minutes. Cool. Serve with a dollop of whipped cream.

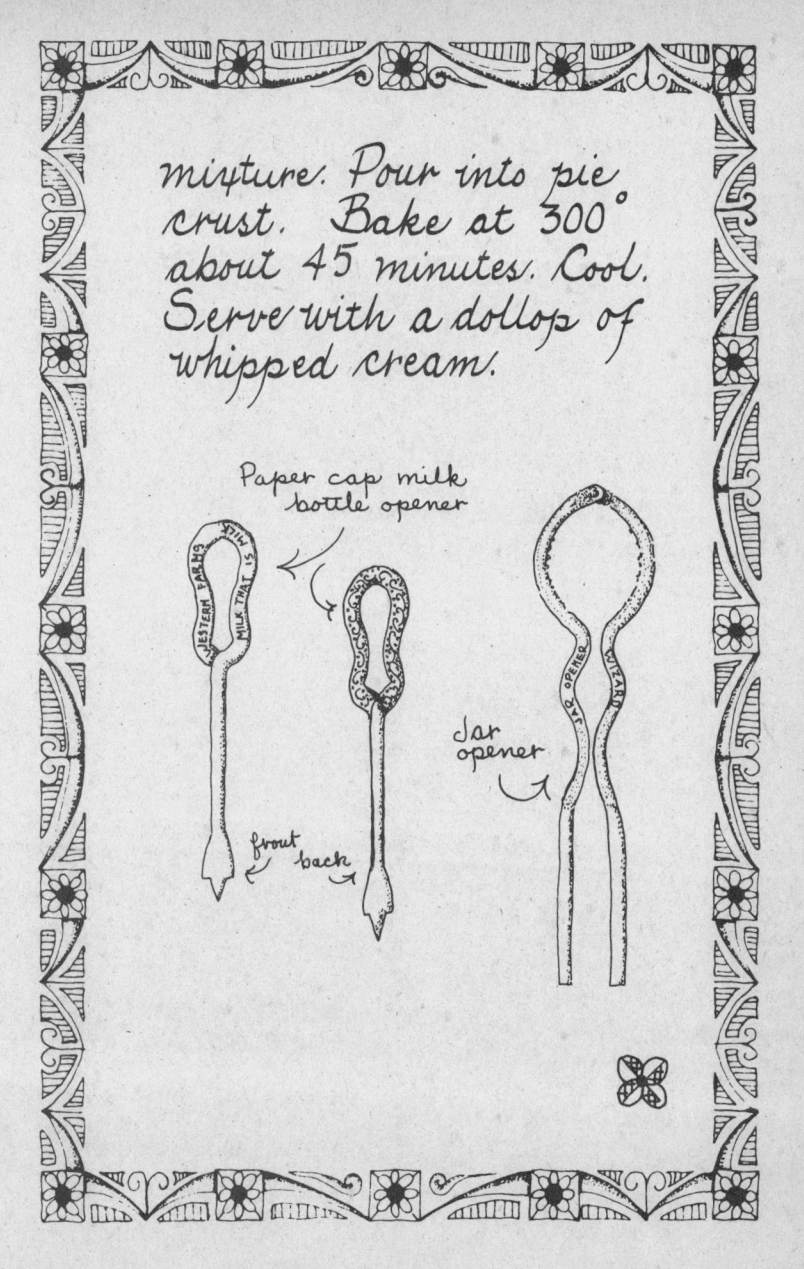

Paper cap milk bottle opener

front   back

Jar opener

Pumpkin Pecan Pie

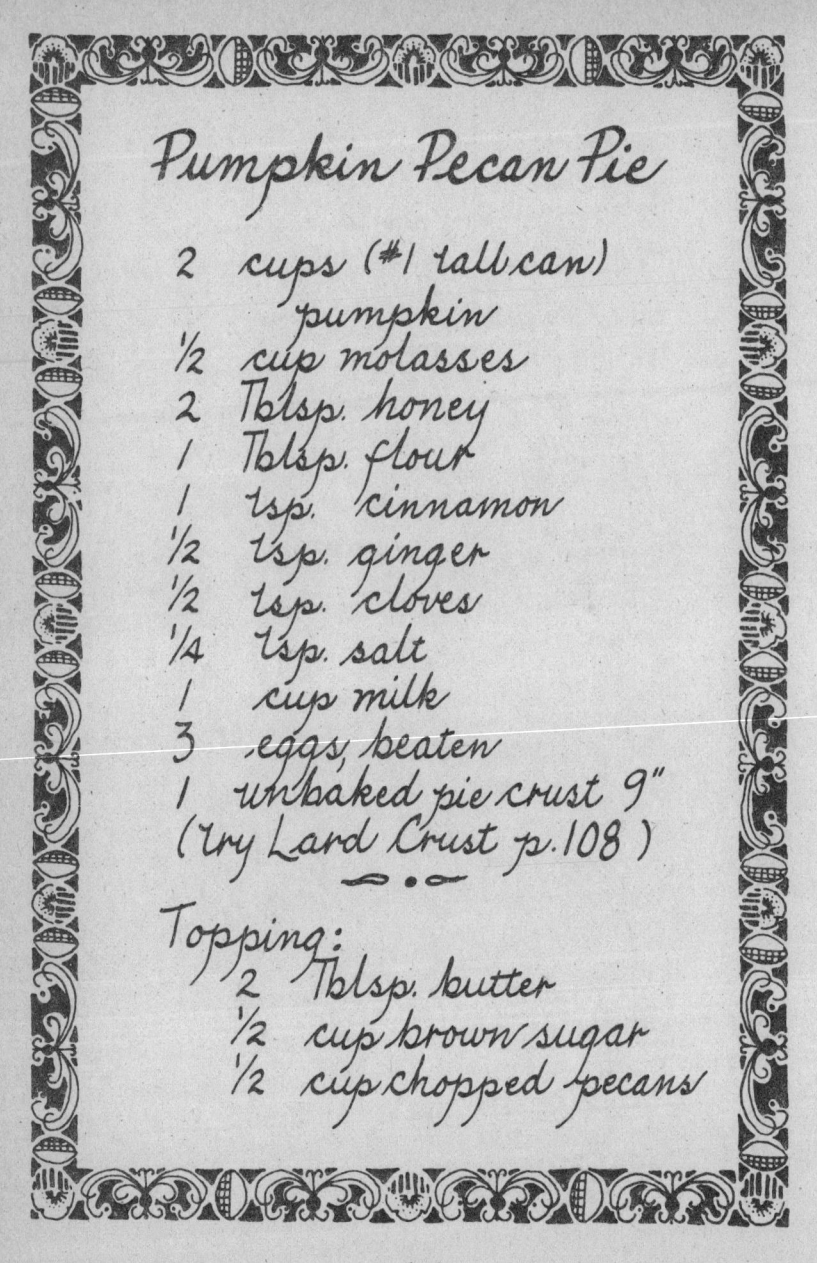

2 cups (#1 tall can) pumpkin
½ cup molasses
2 Tblsp. honey
1 Tblsp. flour
1 tsp. cinnamon
½ tsp. ginger
½ tsp. cloves
¼ tsp. salt
1 cup milk
3 eggs, beaten
1 unbaked pie crust 9"
(Try Lard Crust p. 108)

Topping:
2 Tblsp. butter
½ cup brown sugar
½ cup chopped pecans

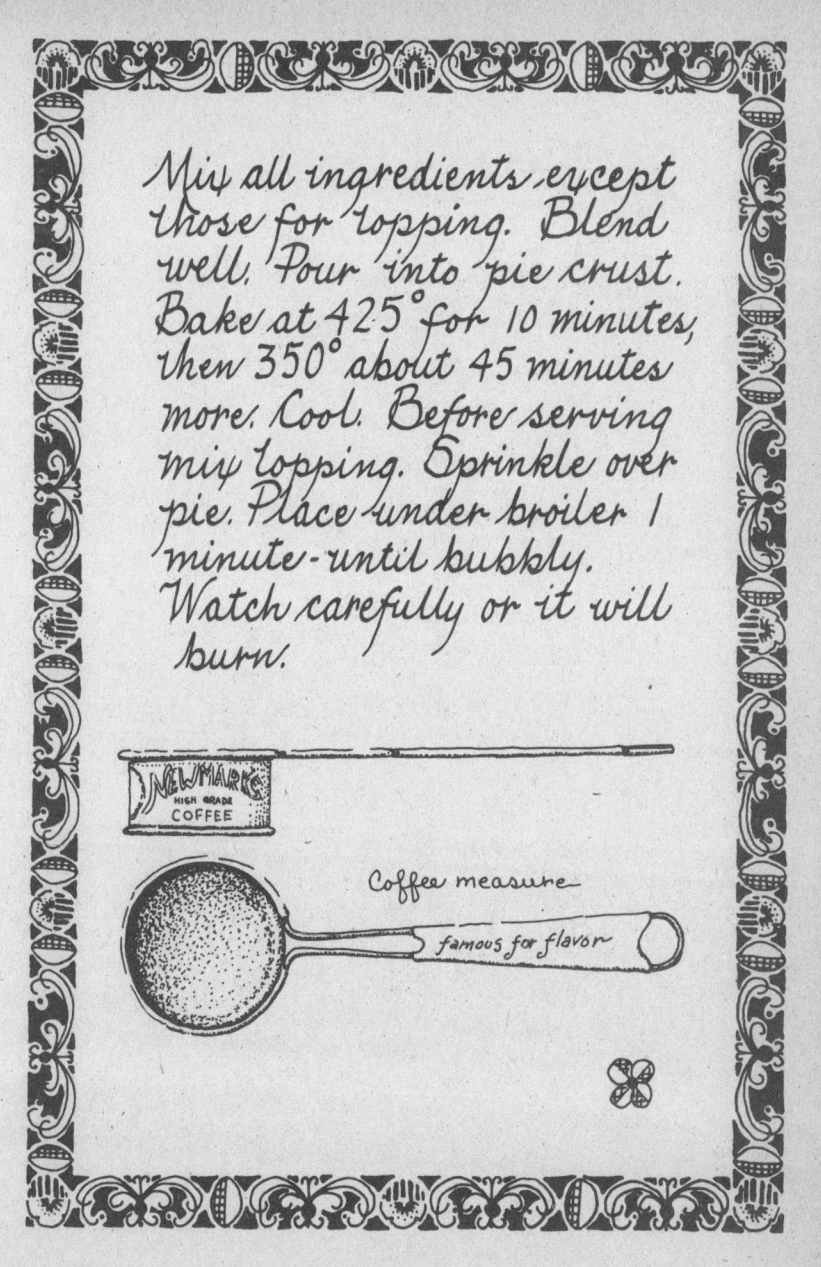

Mix all ingredients except those for topping. Blend well. Pour into pie crust. Bake at 425° for 10 minutes, then 350° about 45 minutes more. Cool. Before serving mix topping. Sprinkle over pie. Place under broiler 1 minute - until bubbly. Watch carefully or it will burn.

Coffee measure — famous for flavor

Peanut Pie

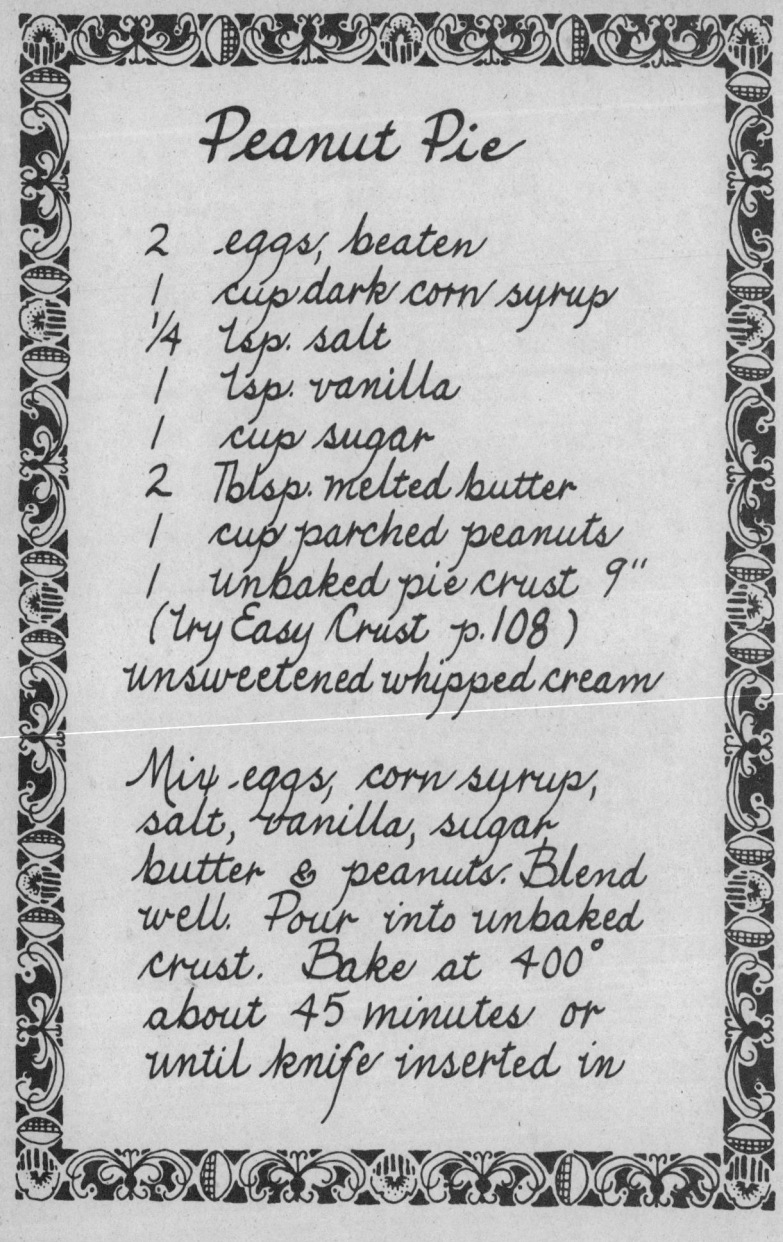

2 eggs, beaten
1 cup dark corn syrup
1/4 tsp. salt
1 tsp. vanilla
1 cup sugar
2 Tbsp. melted butter
1 cup parched peanuts
1 unbaked pie crust 9"
(Try Easy Crust p. 108)
unsweetened whipped cream

Mix eggs, corn syrup, salt, vanilla, sugar, butter & peanuts. Blend well. Pour into unbaked crust. Bake at 400° about 45 minutes or until knife inserted in center of pie comes out clean. Cool. Serve with a dollop of whipped cream.

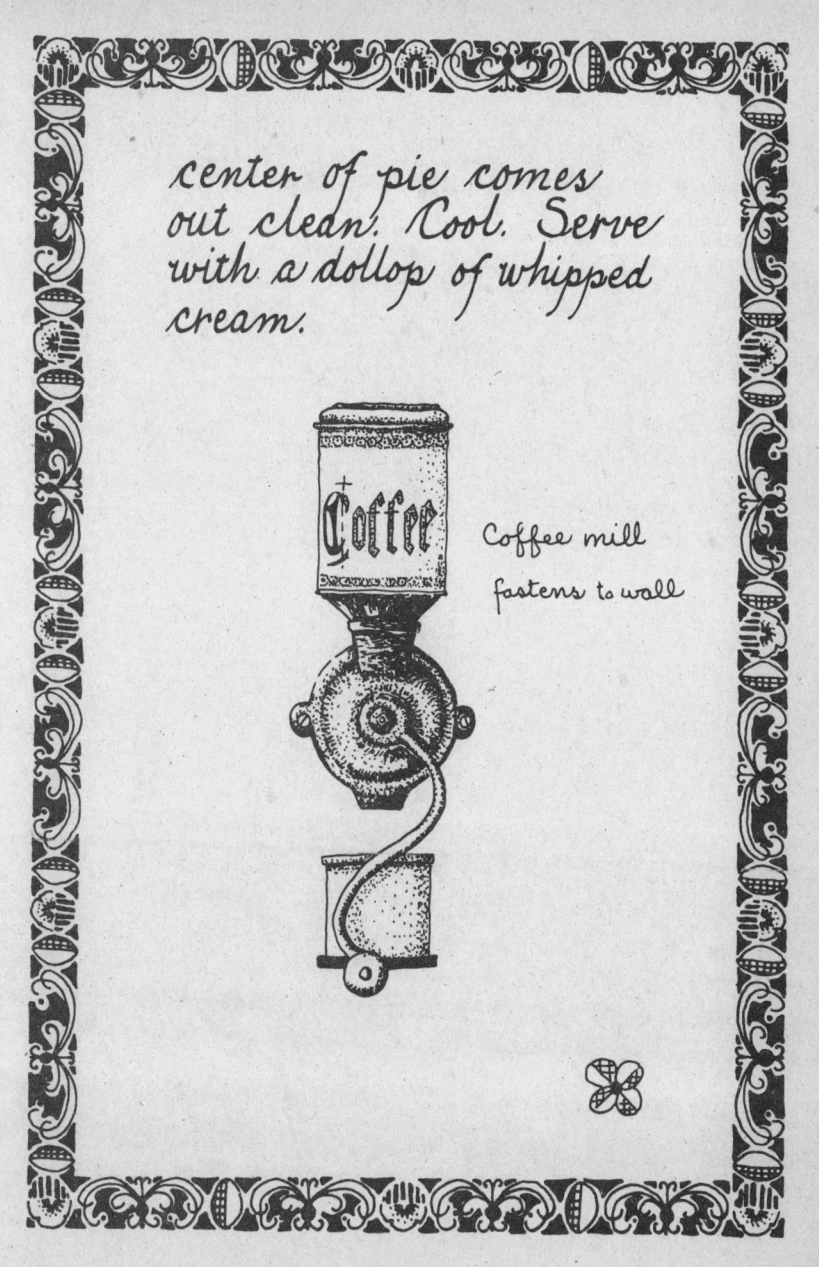

Coffee mill fastens to wall

Peanut Butter Pie

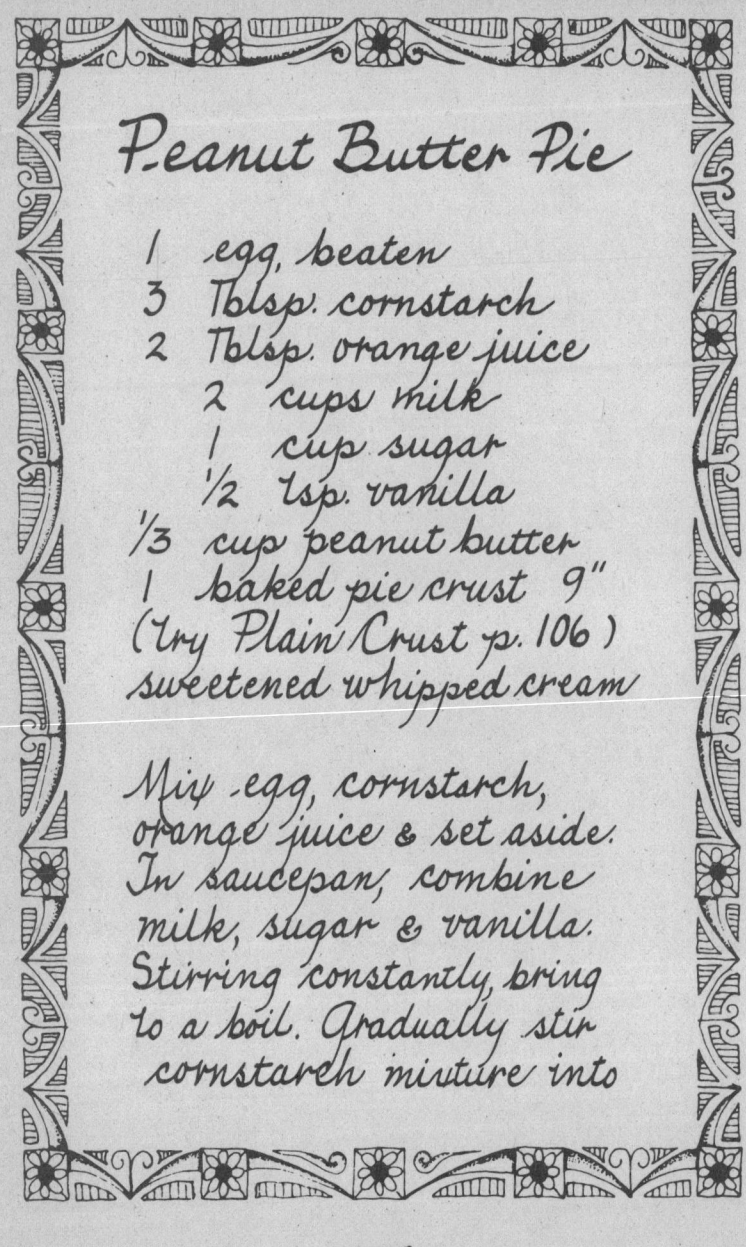

1 egg, beaten
3 Tblsp. cornstarch
2 Tblsp. orange juice
2 cups milk
1 cup sugar
½ tsp. vanilla
⅓ cup peanut butter
1 baked pie crust 9"
(Try Plain Crust p. 106)
sweetened whipped cream

Mix egg, cornstarch, orange juice & set aside. In saucepan, combine milk, sugar & vanilla. Stirring constantly, bring to a boil. Gradually stir cornstarch mixture into milk mixture. Cook until thick. Remove from heat. Add peanut butter. Pour into crust. Chill. Top with whipped cream.

galvanized iron milk can with chain

Peanut Brittle Pie

1 Tblsp. gelatine
1/4 cup cold water
1 pkg. butterscotch pudding mix
2 cups milk
2 eggs, separated
2 Tblsp. butter
2 Tblsp. sugar
1 cup whipping cream
3/4 cup crushed peanut brittle
1 baked pie crust 9"
(Try Peanut Brittle p. 113)

Soften gelatine in water. Combine pudding mix & milk. Cook to directions on package. Beat egg yolks. Gradually add to pudding & cook 2 minutes, stirring constantly. Blend in gelatine. Remove from heat. Add butter. Cool. Beat egg whites until soft peaks form. Gradually add sugar & beat until stiff. Whip the cream; put aside ½ & fold egg whites into other ½, then fold in peanut brittle & pudding mixture. Pour into crust. Spread the cream put aside on top. Chill.

Not-So-Sweet Pecan Pie

3 egg yolks
1½ cups sugar
1½ tsp. cinnamon
¾ tsp. cloves
1 cup pecan halves
½ cup raisins
1½ Tblsp. melted butter
3 egg whites, stiffly beaten
1½ Tblsp. vinegar
1 unbaked pie crust 8"
  (try Lard Crust p. 108)
unsweetened whipped cream

Beat egg yolks until thick. Mix sugar & spices. Add to yolks & beat well. Add pecan halves, raisins & butter. Fold beaten egg whites into pecan mixture. Add vinegar. Pour into crust. Bake at 400° for 10 min., then 350° for 25-30 min. more. Serve with dollop of whipped cream.

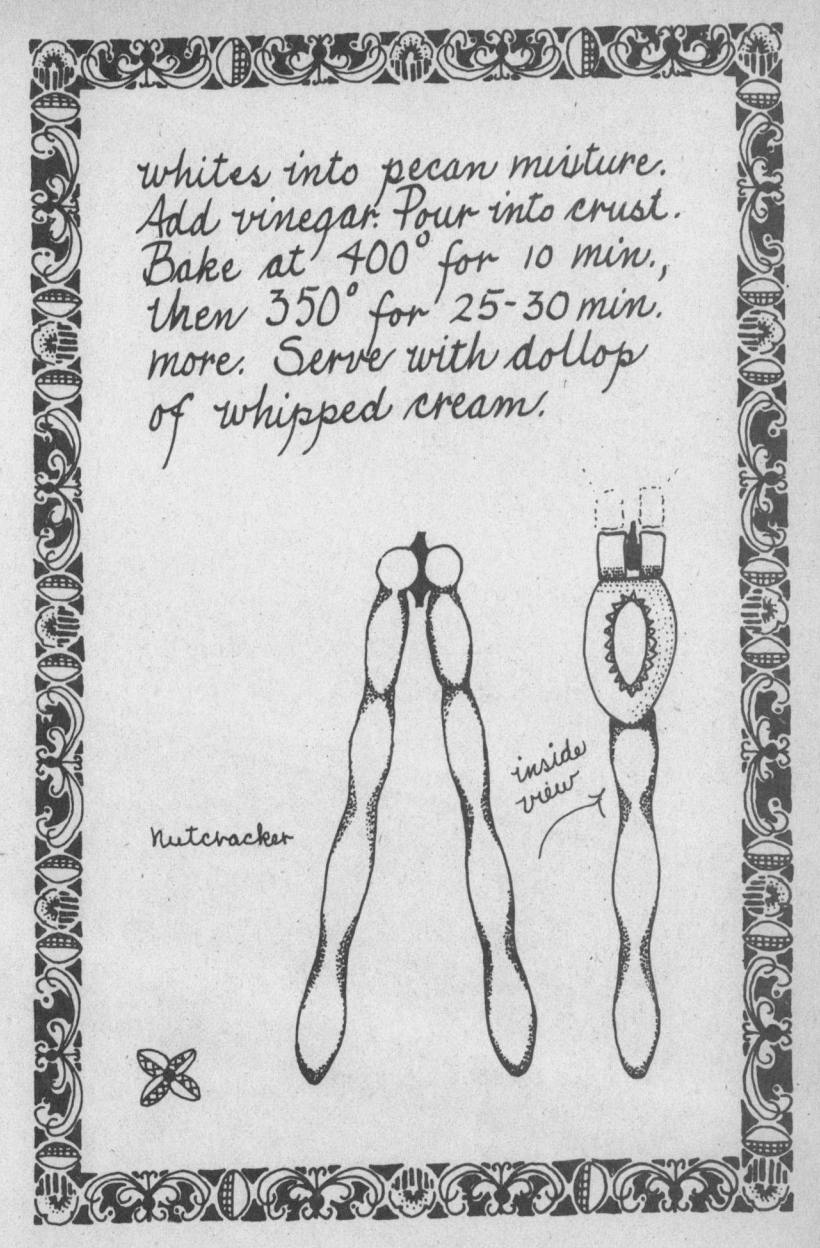

Nutcracker

inside view

Walnut Pie

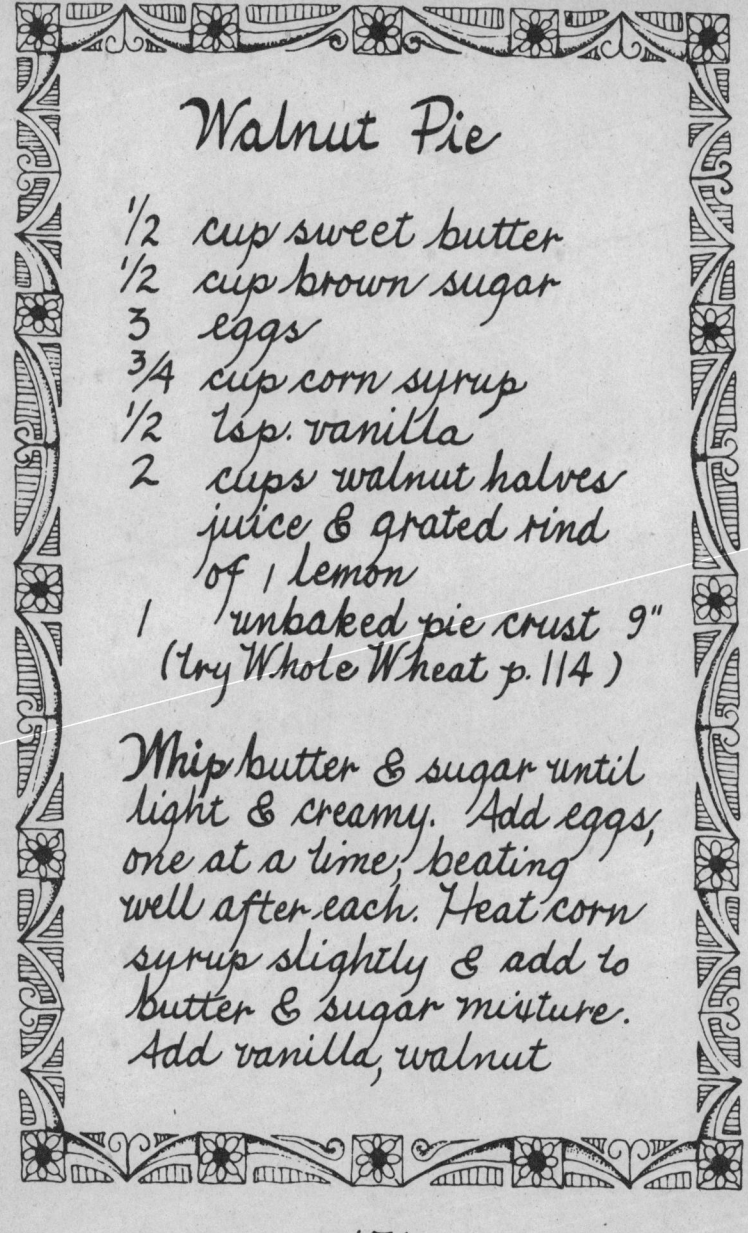

½ cup sweet butter
½ cup brown sugar
3 eggs
¾ cup corn syrup
½ tsp. vanilla
2 cups walnut halves
juice & grated rind of 1 lemon
1 unbaked pie crust 9"
(try Whole Wheat p. 114)

Whip butter & sugar until light & creamy. Add eggs, one at a time, beating well after each. Heat corn syrup slightly & add to butter & sugar mixture. Add vanilla, walnut halves, lemon juice & rind. Pour into unbaked pie crust. Bake in a 375° oven about 45 min. or until firm. Serve warm.

grater

Buttermilk Pie

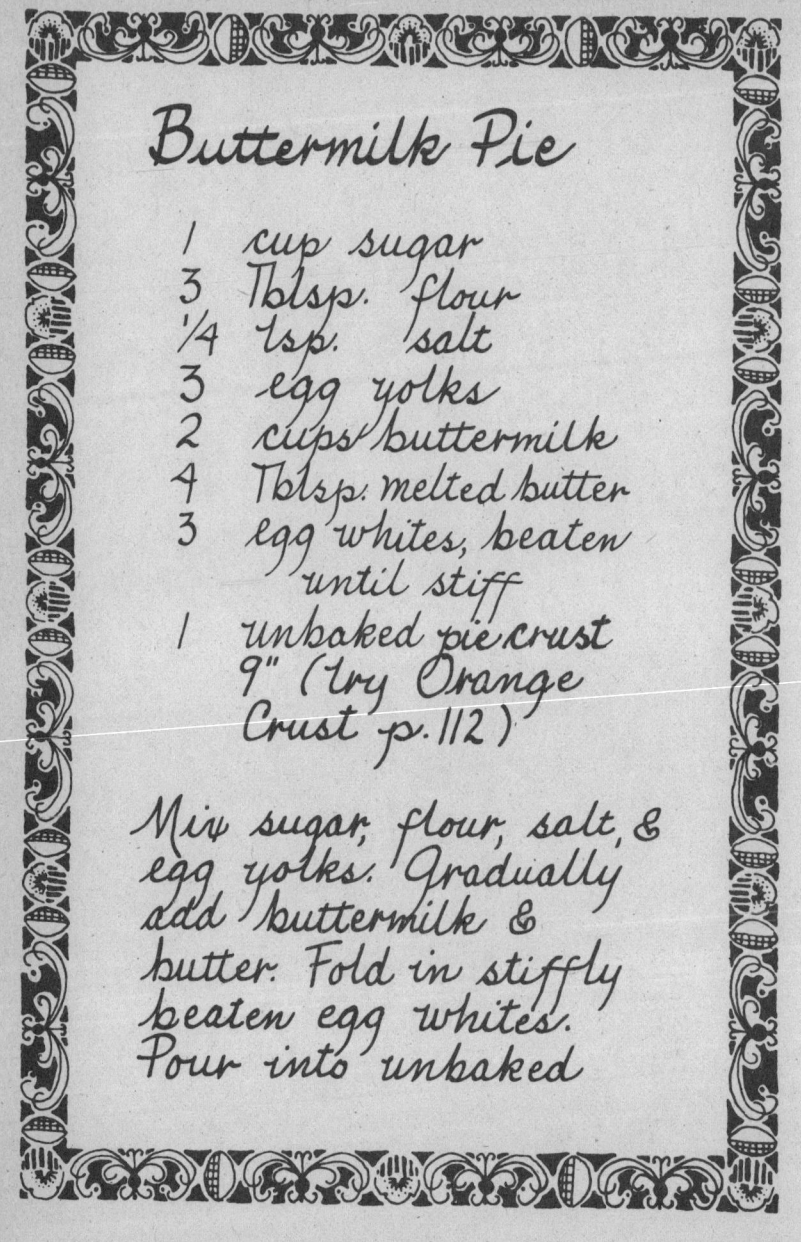

1 cup sugar
3 Tblsp. flour
¼ tsp. salt
3 egg yolks
2 cups buttermilk
4 Tblsp. melted butter
3 egg whites, beaten until stiff
1 unbaked pie crust 9" (try Orange Crust p. 112)

Mix sugar, flour, salt, & egg yolks. Gradually add buttermilk & butter. Fold in stiffly beaten egg whites. Pour into unbaked crust. Bake at 450° for 5 minutes, then 350° for about 40 minutes more.

Canning jar   Milk bottle

Cocoanut Cream Pie

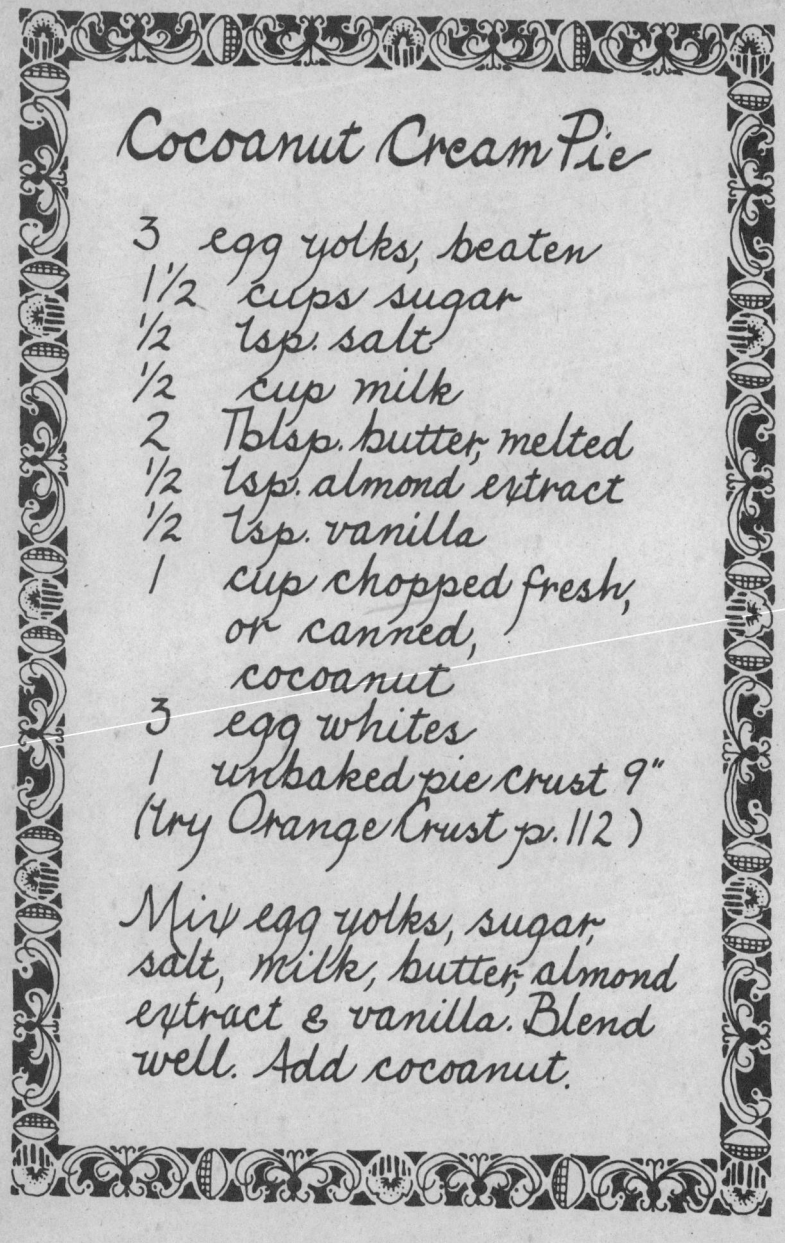

3 egg yolks, beaten
1½ cups sugar
½ tsp. salt
½ cup milk
2 Tblsp. butter, melted
½ tsp. almond extract
½ tsp. vanilla
1 cup chopped fresh, or canned, cocoanut
3 egg whites
1 unbaked pie crust 9"
(Try Orange Crust p. 112)

Mix egg yolks, sugar, salt, milk, butter, almond extract & vanilla. Blend well. Add cocoanut.

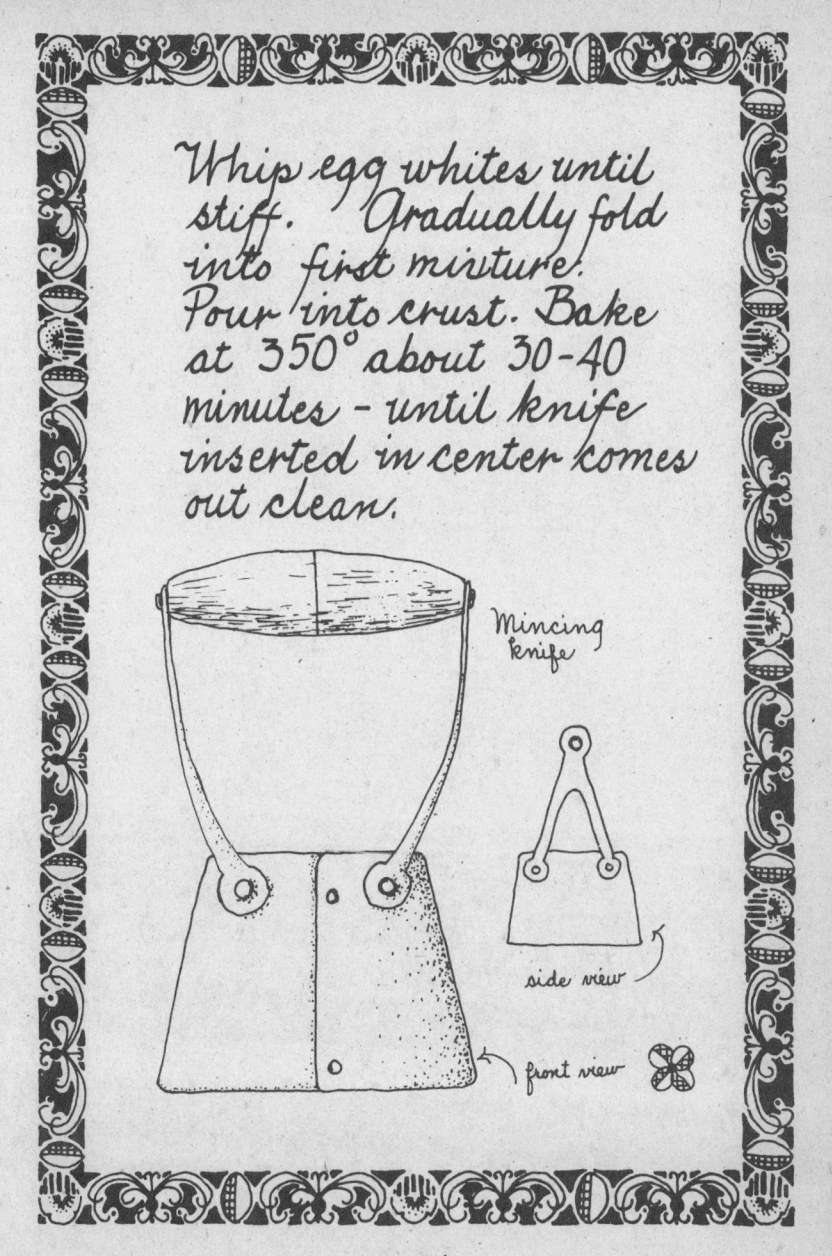

Whip egg whites until stiff. Gradually fold into first mixture. Pour into crust. Bake at 350° about 30-40 minutes – until knife inserted in center comes out clean.

Mincing knife

side view

front view

Cheese Pie

1 large pkg. (8 oz.) cream cheese
1 pint cottage cheese
½ cup sugar
2 Tblsp. flour
2 eggs, beaten
1 tsp. vanilla
1 unbaked pie crust 9" (Try Almond Cracker Crust p. 111)
½ pint sour cream, sweetened

Soften cream cheese. Put cottage cheese through a sieve, then mix with cream cheese. Add sugar, flour & beaten eggs.

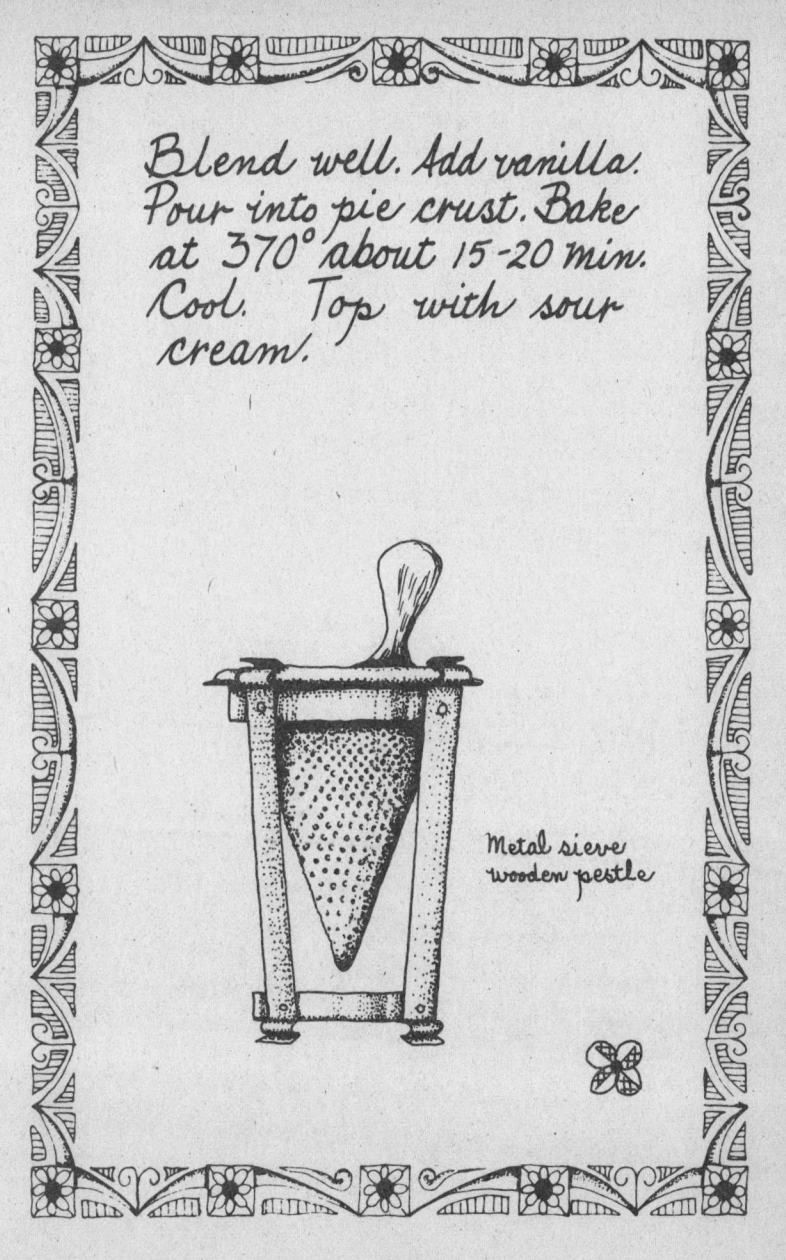

Blend well. Add vanilla. Pour into pie crust. Bake at 370° about 15-20 min. Cool. Top with sour cream.

Metal sieve wooden pestle

Chess Pie

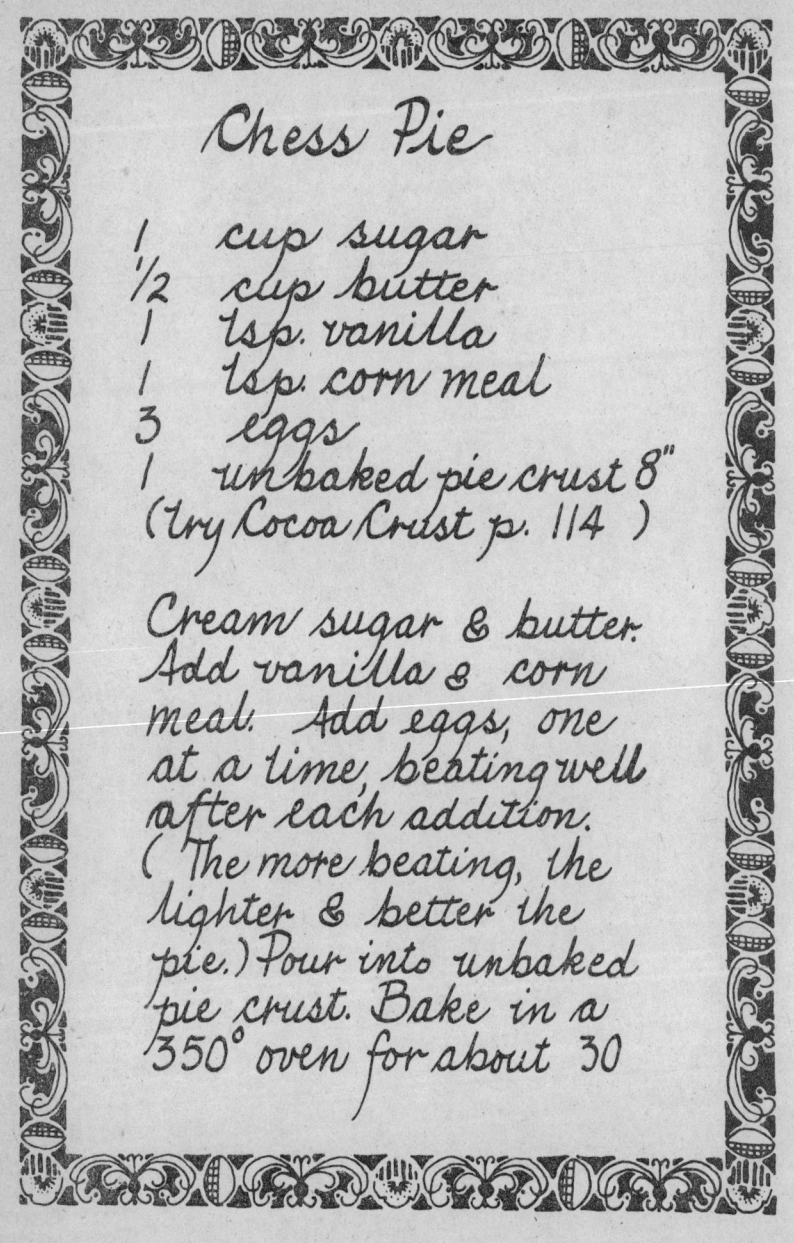

1 cup sugar
1/2 cup butter
1 tsp. vanilla
1 tsp. corn meal
3 eggs
1 unbaked pie crust 8"
(Try Cocoa Crust p. 114)

Cream sugar & butter. Add vanilla & corn meal. Add eggs, one at a time, beating well after each addition. (The more beating, the lighter & better the pie.) Pour into unbaked pie crust. Bake in a 350° oven for about 30 minutes — or until knife inserted in center comes out clean.

"Mixes {shortening with flour / butter with sugar
Removes eggs, veg., from HOT WATER.
Crushes berries, etc. Mashes & whips potatoes. Separates whites of eggs from yolks. Pat. Pend. Made in USA."

Frozen Chocolate Pie

16 marshmallows
1 chocolate almond candy bar (4½ oz.)
½ cup evaporated milk, undiluted
1 cup whipping cream
1 baked pie crust 8" or 9" (Try Almond Cracker p. 111 or Nut Crust p. 107)

Melt marshmallows in double boiler. Add chocolate bar & evaporated milk. Stir until chocolate is melted. Cool. In separate bowl, whip cream until stiff, but not butter. Fold in marshmallow &

chocolate mixture. Pour into pie crust. Freeze until ready to use.

TEPCO USA CHINA

1882
GREENWOOD CHINA
TRENTON, N.J.
1878
REG. U.S. PAT. OFF.

K.T. & K.
S — V
CHINA.
26 8 3

white ironstone china

Chocolate Mint Pie

1 pkg. (6 oz.) semi-sweet chocolate bits
3 Tblsp. milk
2 Tblsp. sugar
4 egg yolks
1 tsp. vanilla
¼ tsp. mint extract
4 egg whites
1 baked pie crust 8"
(try Easy Crust p. 108)
sweetened whipped cream

Melt chocolate over hot water. Gradually add milk & sugar. Add egg yolks, one at a time, beating well after each. Add vanilla & mint.

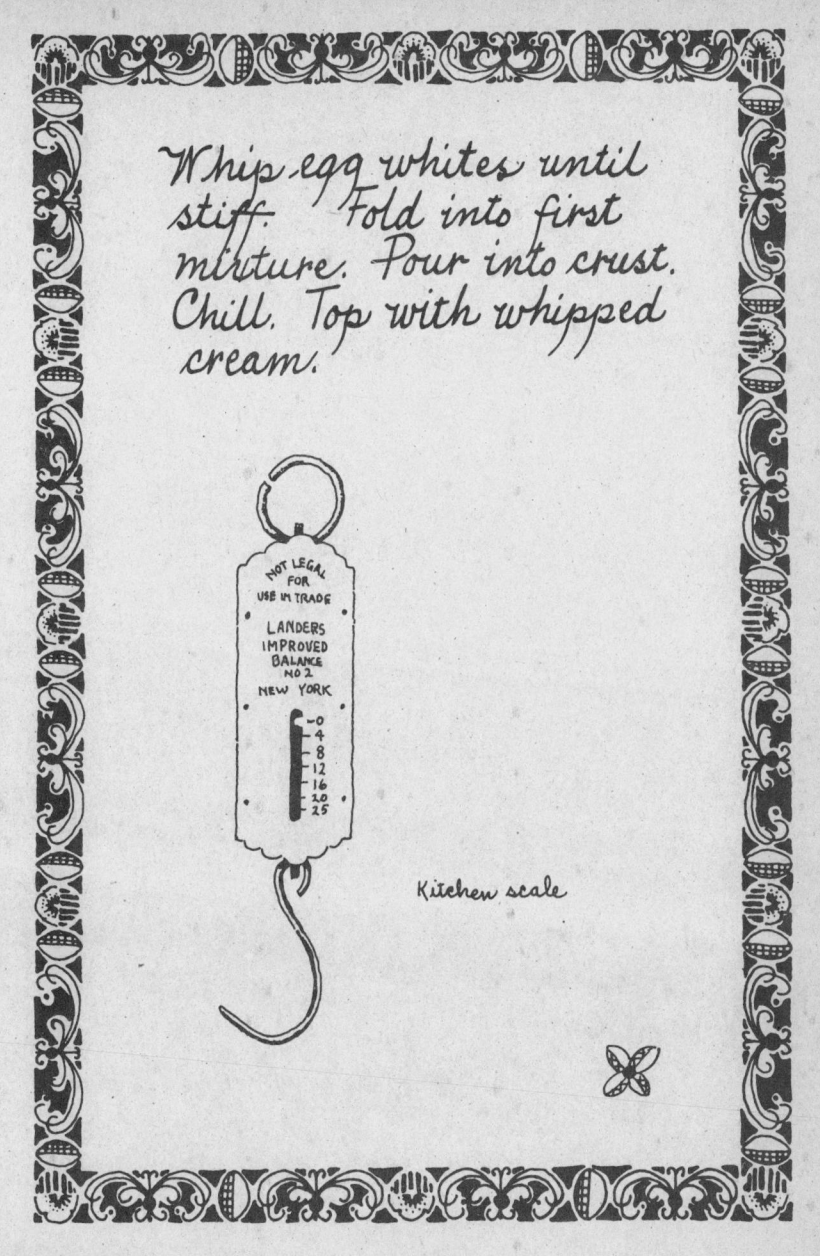

Whip egg whites until stiff. Fold into first mixture. Pour into crust. Chill. Top with whipped cream.

Kitchen scale

Molasses Pie

2 cups molasses
3 eggs, beaten
1 Tblsp. butter, melted
½ tsp. lemon juice
1 unbaked pie crust 9" (try Whole Wheat p. 114)

∽ ◦ ∽

1 cup flour
½ cup sugar
2 Tblsp. butter

Ice chisel

Mix molasses, eggs, butter & lemon juice. Blend well. Pour into crust. Mix flour, sugar

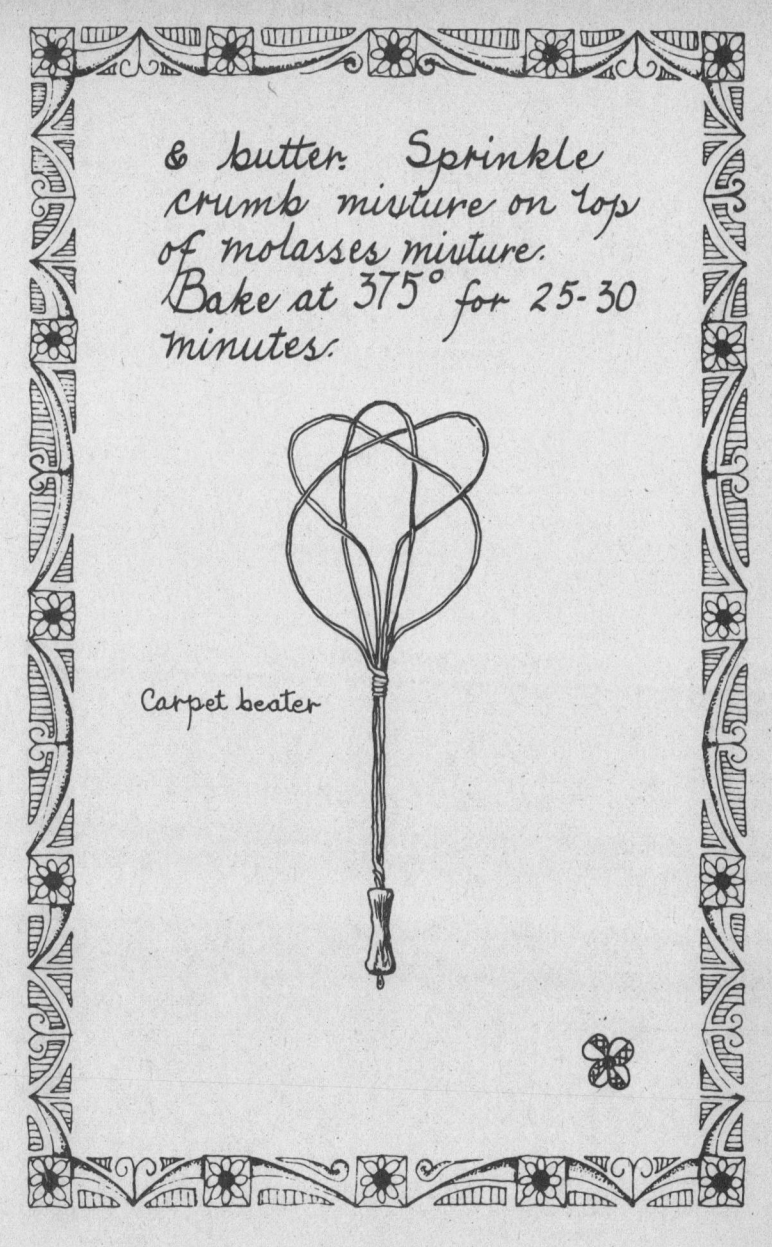

& butter. Sprinkle crumb mixture on top of molasses mixture. Bake at 375° for 25-30 minutes.

Carpet beater

Shoofly Pie

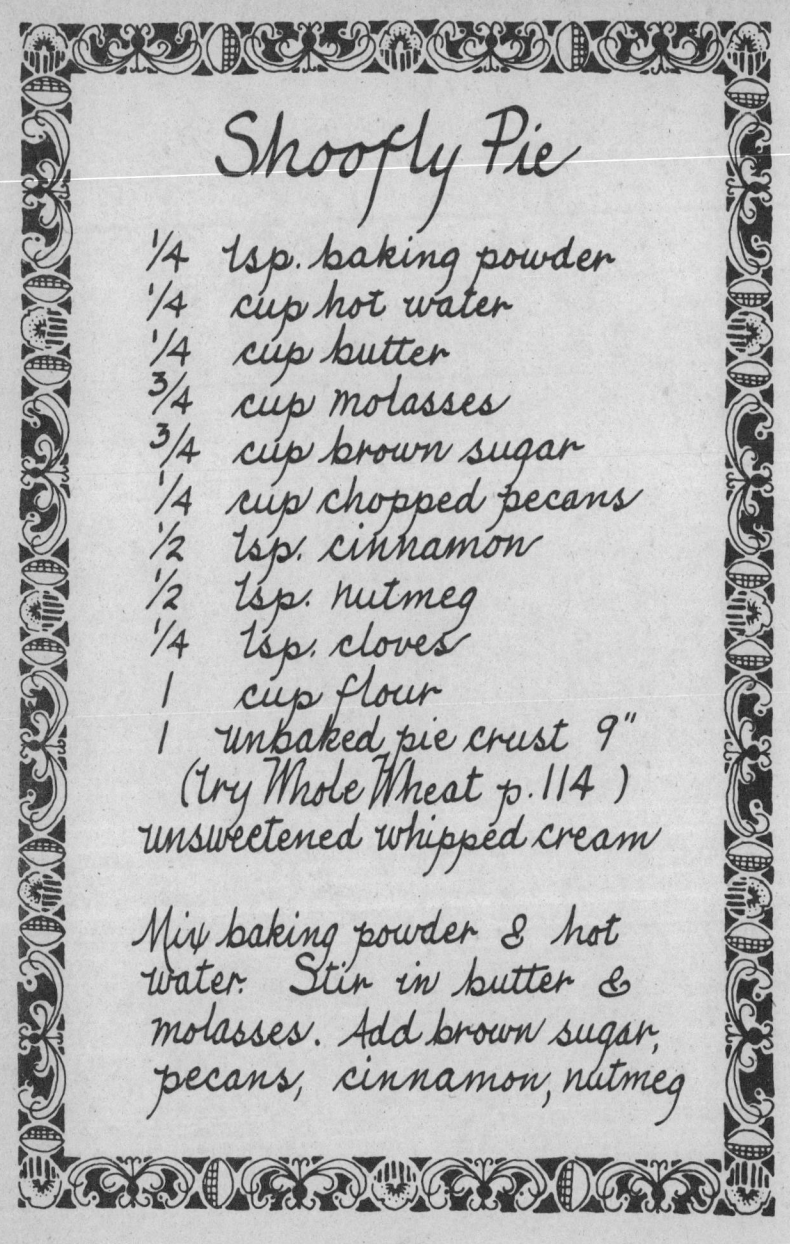

1/4 tsp. baking powder
1/4 cup hot water
1/4 cup butter
3/4 cup molasses
3/4 cup brown sugar
1/4 cup chopped pecans
1/2 tsp. cinnamon
1/2 tsp. nutmeg
1/4 tsp. cloves
1 cup flour
1 unbaked pie crust 9"
(try Whole Wheat p. 114)
unsweetened whipped cream

Mix baking powder & hot water. Stir in butter & molasses. Add brown sugar, pecans, cinnamon, nutmeg

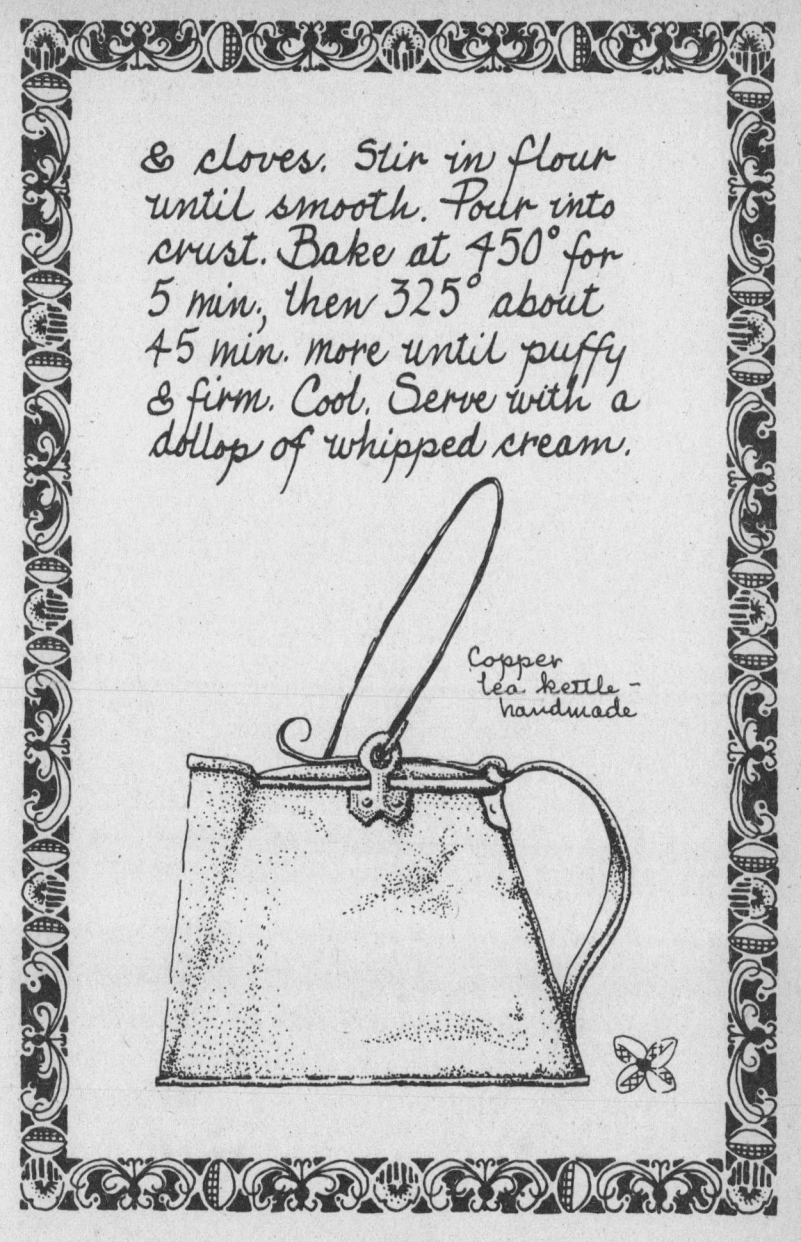

& cloves. Stir in flour until smooth. Pour into crust. Bake at 450° for 5 min., then 325° about 45 min. more until puffy & firm. Cool. Serve with a dollop of whipped cream.

Copper tea kettle - handmade

Sweet Potato Pie

- 1/4 cup butter
- 1/2 cup brown sugar
- 1 1/2 cups cooked, mashed sweet potatoes
- 3 eggs, beaten
- 1/3 cup corn syrup
- 1/3 cup milk
- 1/2 tsp. salt
- 1/2 tsp. cinnamon
- 1/2 tsp. nutmeg
- 1 tsp. vanilla
- 1 unbaked pie crust 9"

(Try Whole Wheat Crust p. 114)

Cream butter, brown sugar & sweet potatoes. Add eggs. Mix well. Add corn syrup, milk, salt, cinnamon, nutmeg & vanilla. Pour into unbaked crust. Bake at 425° for 10 min., then 325° for 35-45 min. or until knife inserted in middle of pie comes out clean.

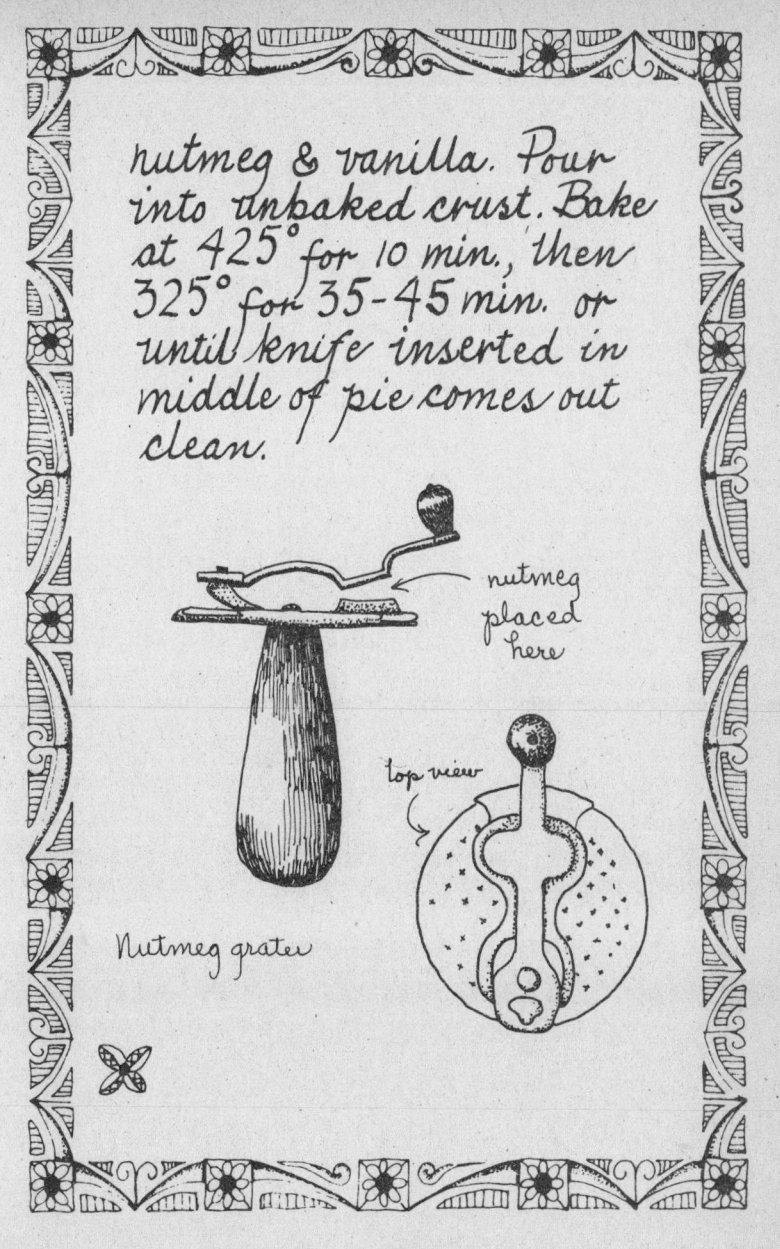

nutmeg placed here

Nutmeg grater

top view

Yeast Breads

Hints: Yeast Breads

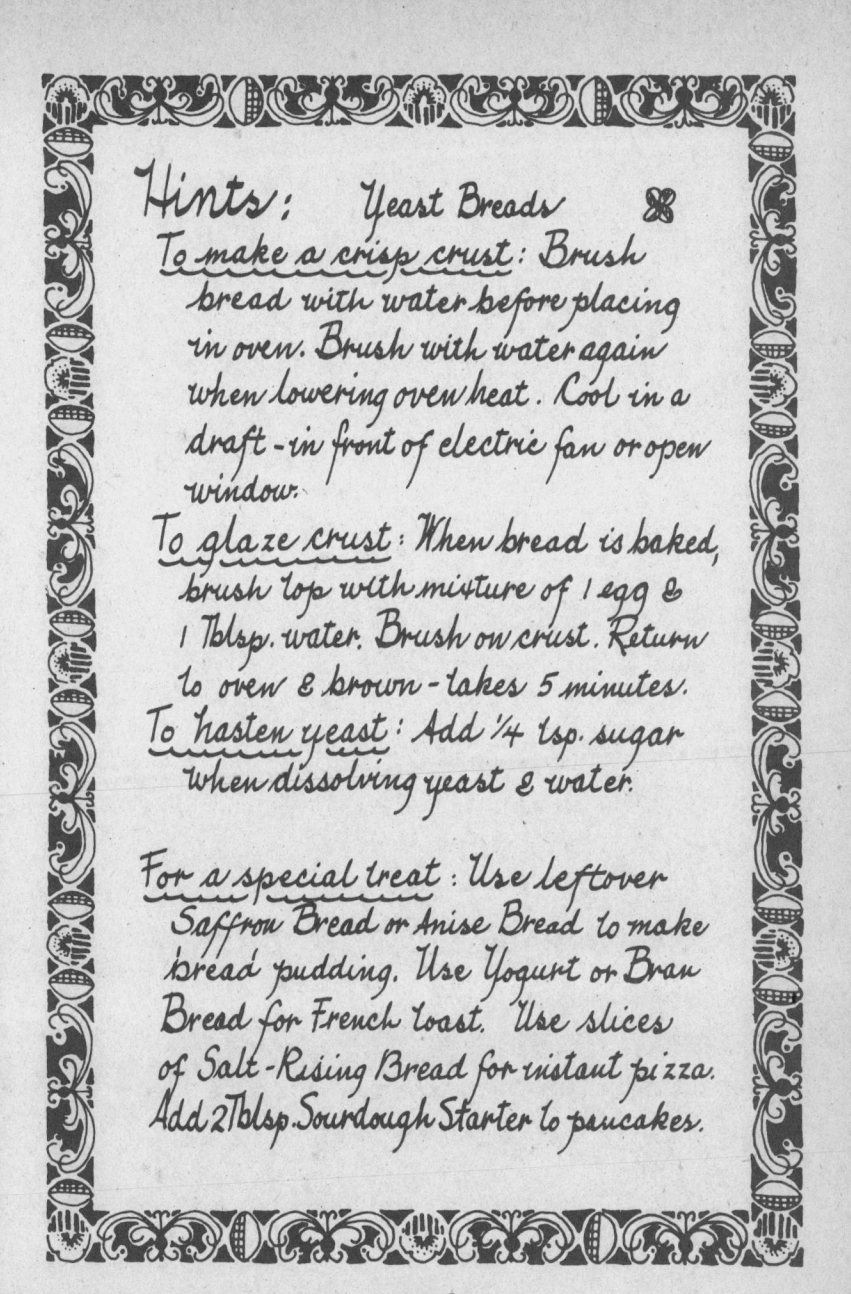

<u>To make a crisp crust</u>: Brush bread with water before placing in oven. Brush with water again when lowering oven heat. Cool in a draft - in front of electric fan or open window.

<u>To glaze crust</u>: When bread is baked, brush top with mixture of 1 egg & 1 Tblsp. water. Brush on crust. Return to oven & brown - takes 5 minutes.

<u>To hasten yeast</u>: Add ¼ tsp. sugar when dissolving yeast & water.

<u>For a special treat</u>: Use leftover Saffron Bread or Anise Bread to make bread pudding. Use Yogurt or Bran Bread for French toast. Use slices of Salt-Rising Bread for instant pizza. Add 2 Tblsp. Sourdough Starter to pancakes.

Anise Bread
1 large loaf

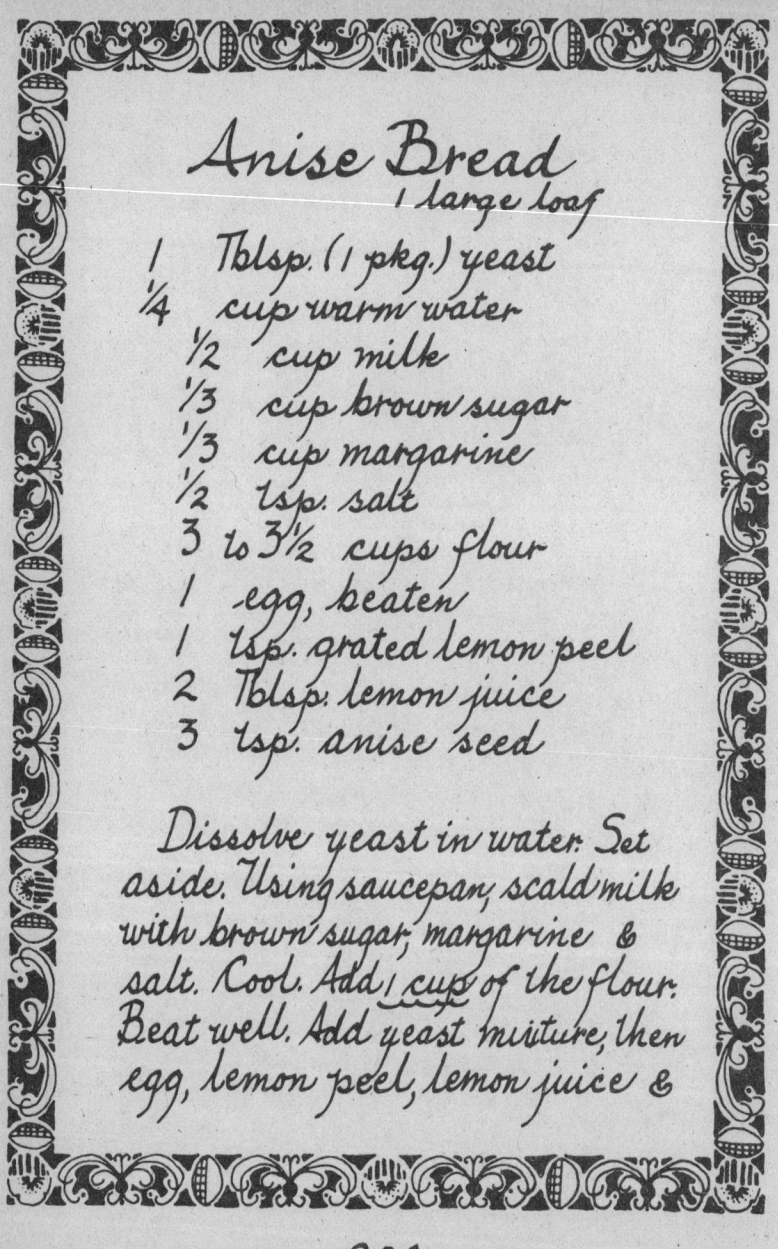

- 1 Tblsp. (1 pkg.) yeast
- 1/4 cup warm water
- 1/2 cup milk
- 1/3 cup brown sugar
- 1/3 cup margarine
- 1/2 tsp. salt
- 3 to 3 1/2 cups flour
- 1 egg, beaten
- 1 tsp. grated lemon peel
- 2 Tblsp. lemon juice
- 3 tsp. anise seed

Dissolve yeast in water. Set aside. Using saucepan, scald milk with brown sugar, margarine & salt. Cool. Add 1 cup of the flour. Beat well. Add yeast mixture, then egg, lemon peel, lemon juice &

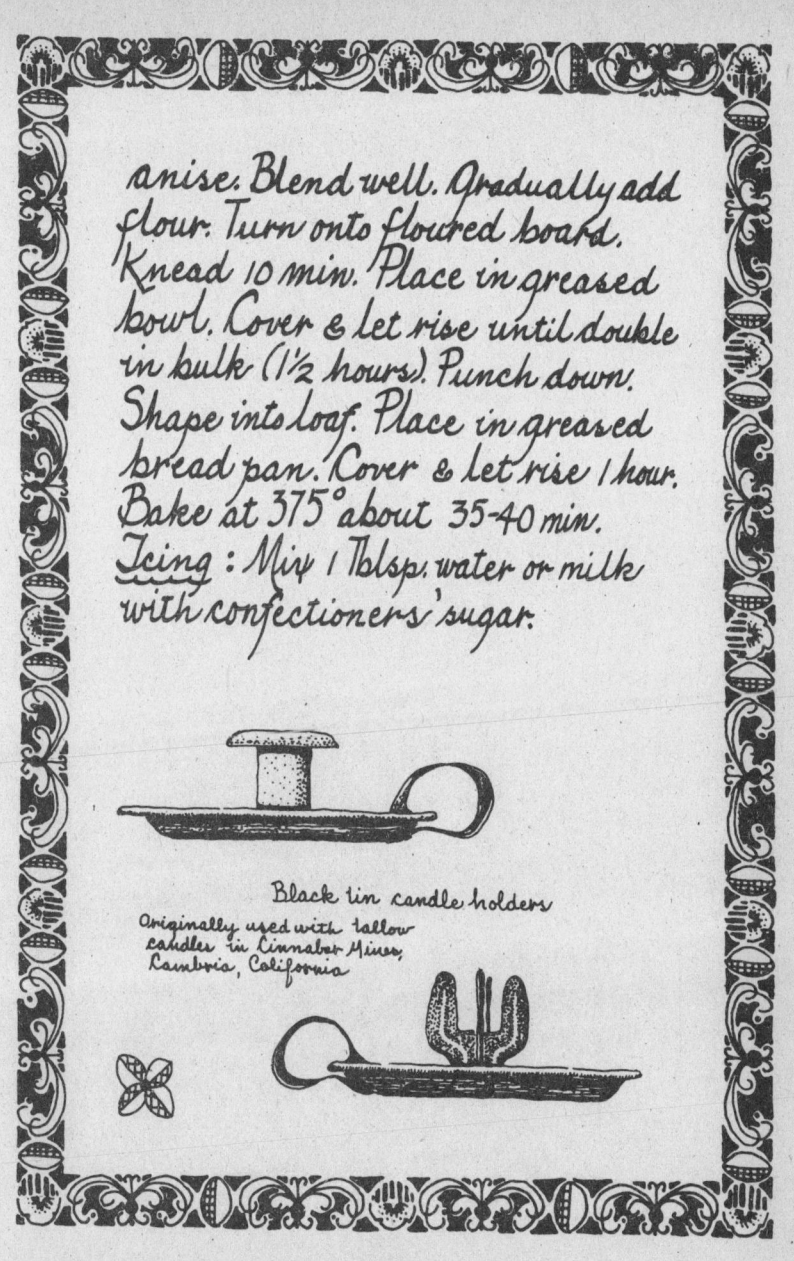

anise. Blend well. Gradually add flour. Turn onto floured board. Knead 10 min. Place in greased bowl. Cover & let rise until double in bulk (1½ hours). Punch down. Shape into loaf. Place in greased bread pan. Cover & let rise 1 hour. Bake at 375° about 35-40 min.
<u>Icing</u>: Mix 1 Tblsp. water or milk with confectioners' sugar.

Black tin candle holders
Originally used with tallow candles in Cinnabar Mines, Cambria, California

Bran Bread
2 loaves

2 Tblsp. (2 pkgs.) yeast
1 cup warm water
  1 cup boiling water
  1 cup margarine
  1/3 cup honey
  1/3 cup molasses
  1 cup shredded bran
    (all-bran cereal)
1½ tsp. salt
2 eggs, well-beaten
2 cups whole wheat flour
4 cups (about) white flour

Dissolve yeast in warm water. Set aside. Pour boiling water over margarine. Stir in honey, molasses, bran & salt. Cool. Add eggs & yeast mixture. Add whole wheat

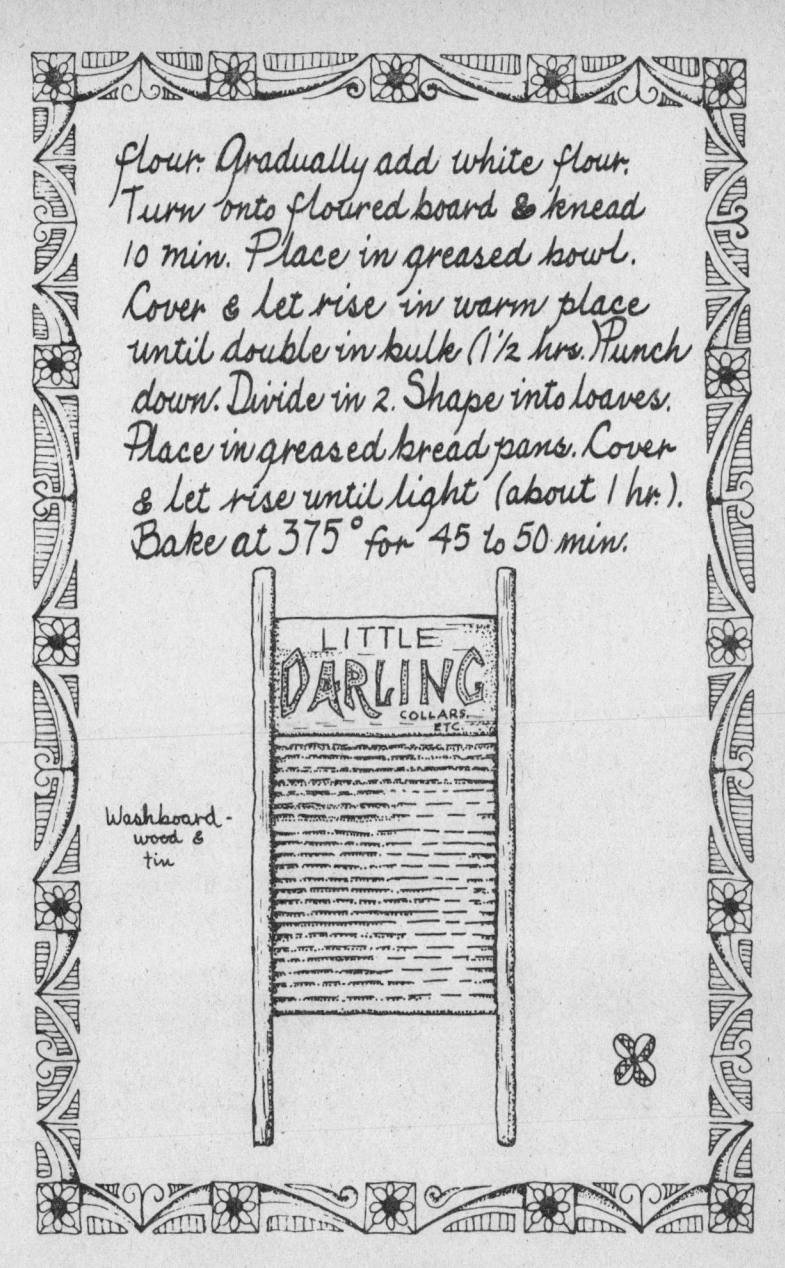

flour. Gradually add white flour.
Turn onto floured board & knead
10 min. Place in greased bowl.
Cover & let rise in warm place
until double in bulk (1½ hrs.) Punch
down. Divide in 2. Shape into loaves.
Place in greased bread pans. Cover
& let rise until light (about 1 hr.).
Bake at 375° for 45 to 50 min.

Washboard - wood & tin

Coarse Rye Bread
4 small loaves

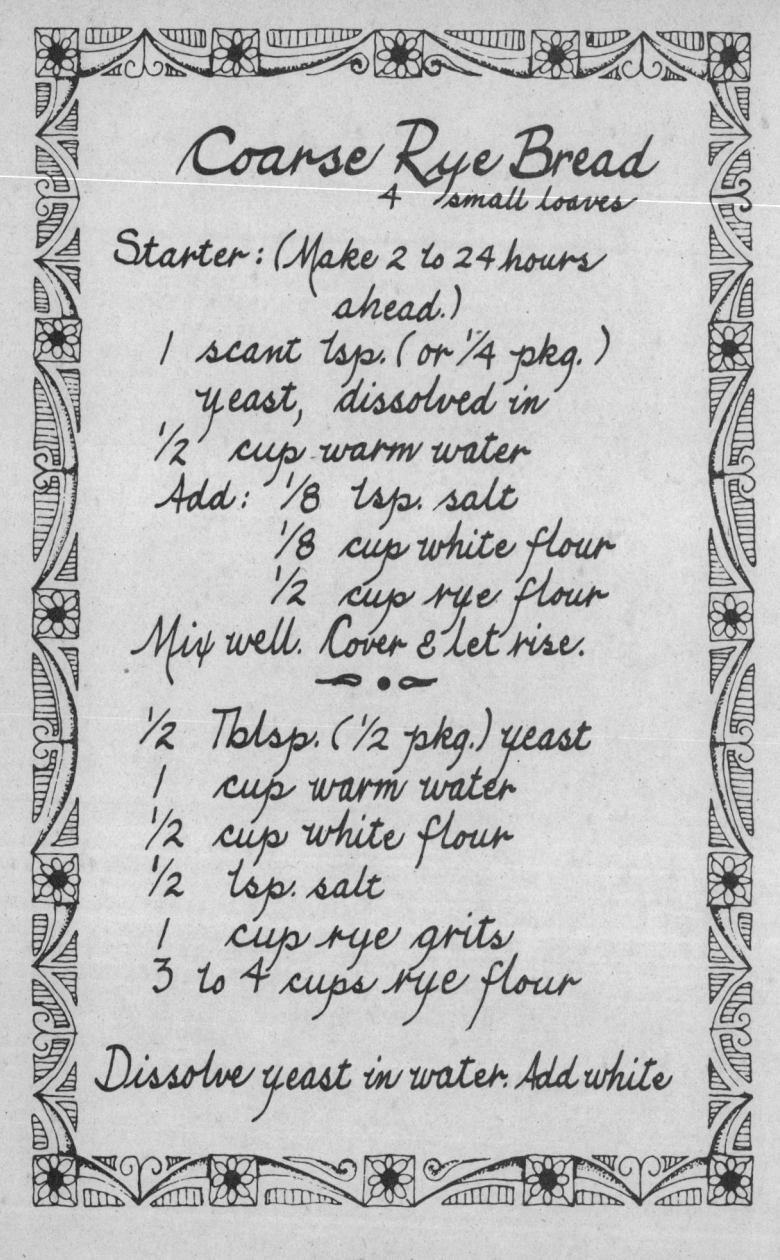

Starter: (Make 2 to 24 hours ahead.)
1 scant tsp. (or ¼ pkg.) yeast, dissolved in
½ cup warm water
Add: ⅛ tsp. salt
⅛ cup white flour
½ cup rye flour
Mix well. Cover & let rise.

—•—

½ Tblsp. (½ pkg.) yeast
1 cup warm water
½ cup white flour
½ tsp. salt
1 cup rye grits
3 to 4 cups rye flour

Dissolve yeast in water. Add white

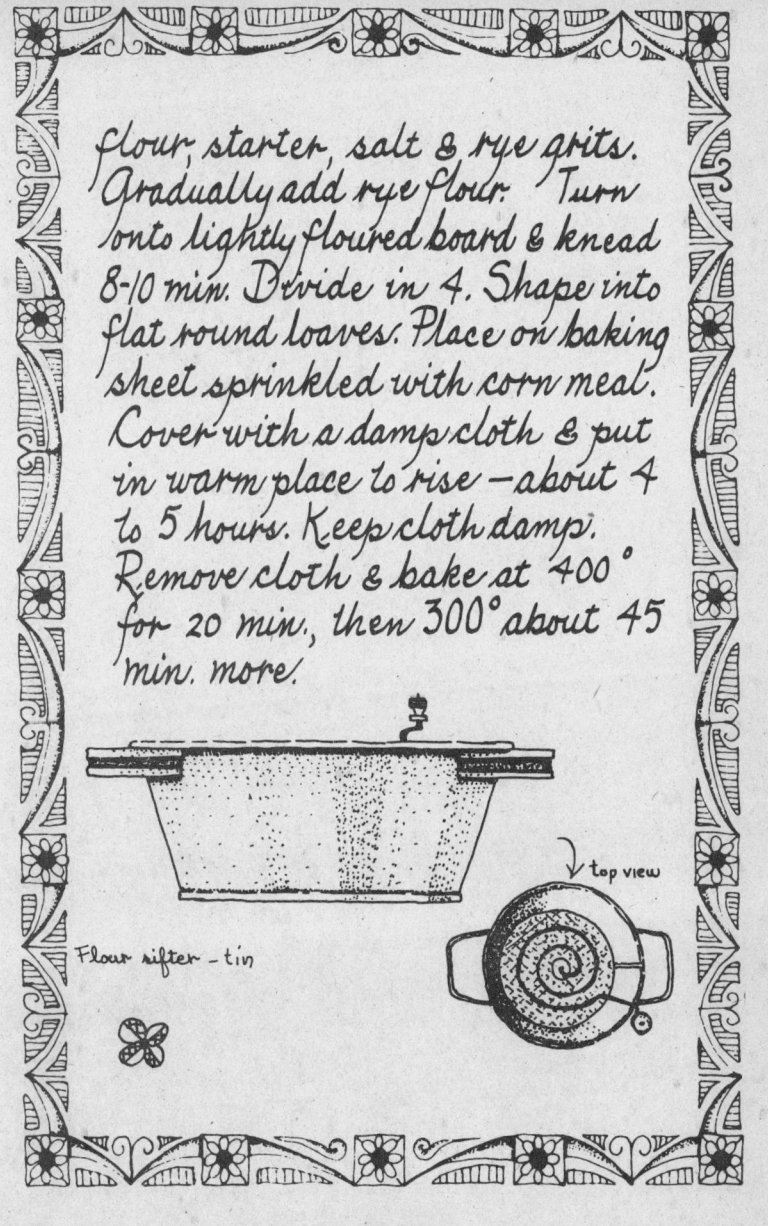

flour, starter, salt & rye grits. Gradually add rye flour. Turn onto lightly floured board & knead 8-10 min. Divide in 4. Shape into flat round loaves. Place on baking sheet sprinkled with corn meal. Cover with a damp cloth & put in warm place to rise — about 4 to 5 hours. Keep cloth damp. Remove cloth & bake at 400° for 20 min., then 300° about 45 min. more.

Flour sifter — tin

top view

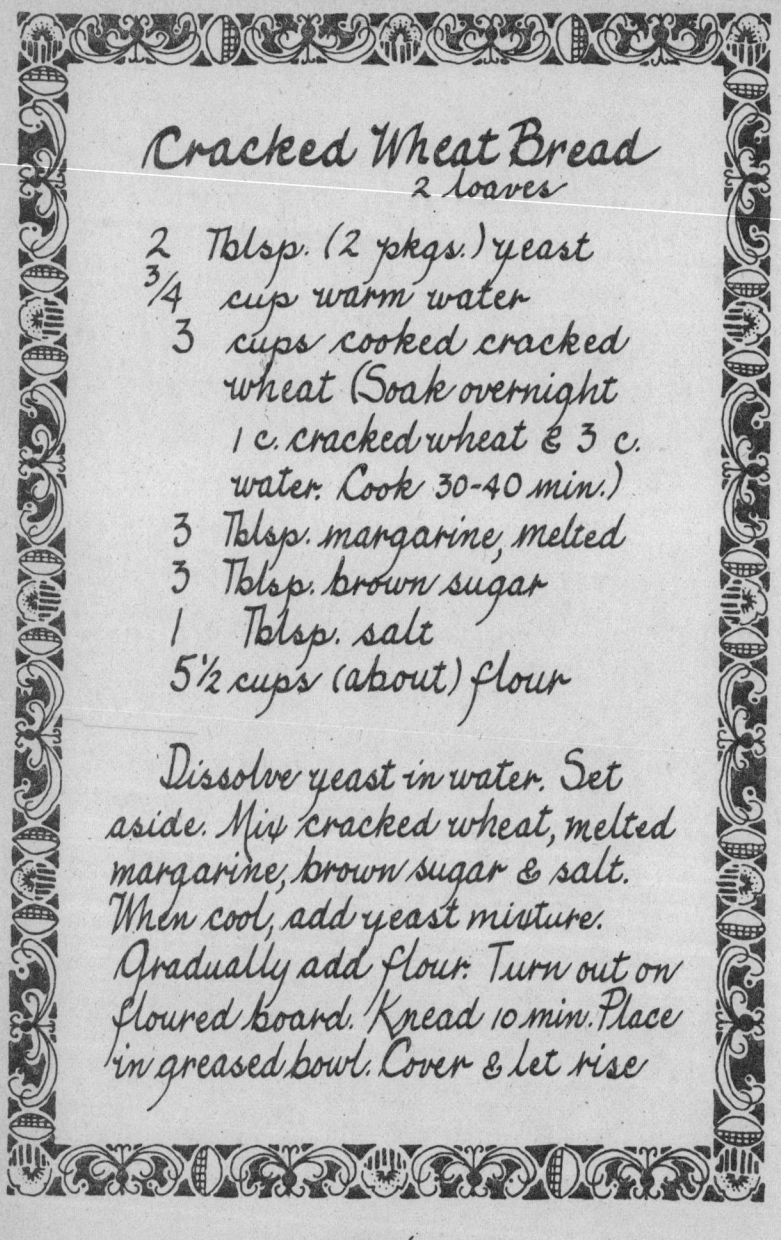

Cracked Wheat Bread
2 loaves

- 2 Tblsp. (2 pkgs.) yeast
- 3/4 cup warm water
- 3 cups cooked cracked wheat (Soak overnight 1 c. cracked wheat & 3 c. water. Cook 30-40 min.)
- 3 Tblsp. margarine, melted
- 3 Tblsp. brown sugar
- 1 Tblsp. salt
- 5½ cups (about) flour

Dissolve yeast in water. Set aside. Mix cracked wheat, melted margarine, brown sugar & salt. When cool, add yeast mixture. Gradually add flour. Turn out on floured board. Knead 10 min. Place in greased bowl. Cover & let rise in a warm place until double in bulk (about 1½ hrs.). Punch down. Divide in 2. Shape into loaves. Place in greased bread pans. Cover & let rise until light (about 1 hr.). Bake at 400° for about 1 hr.

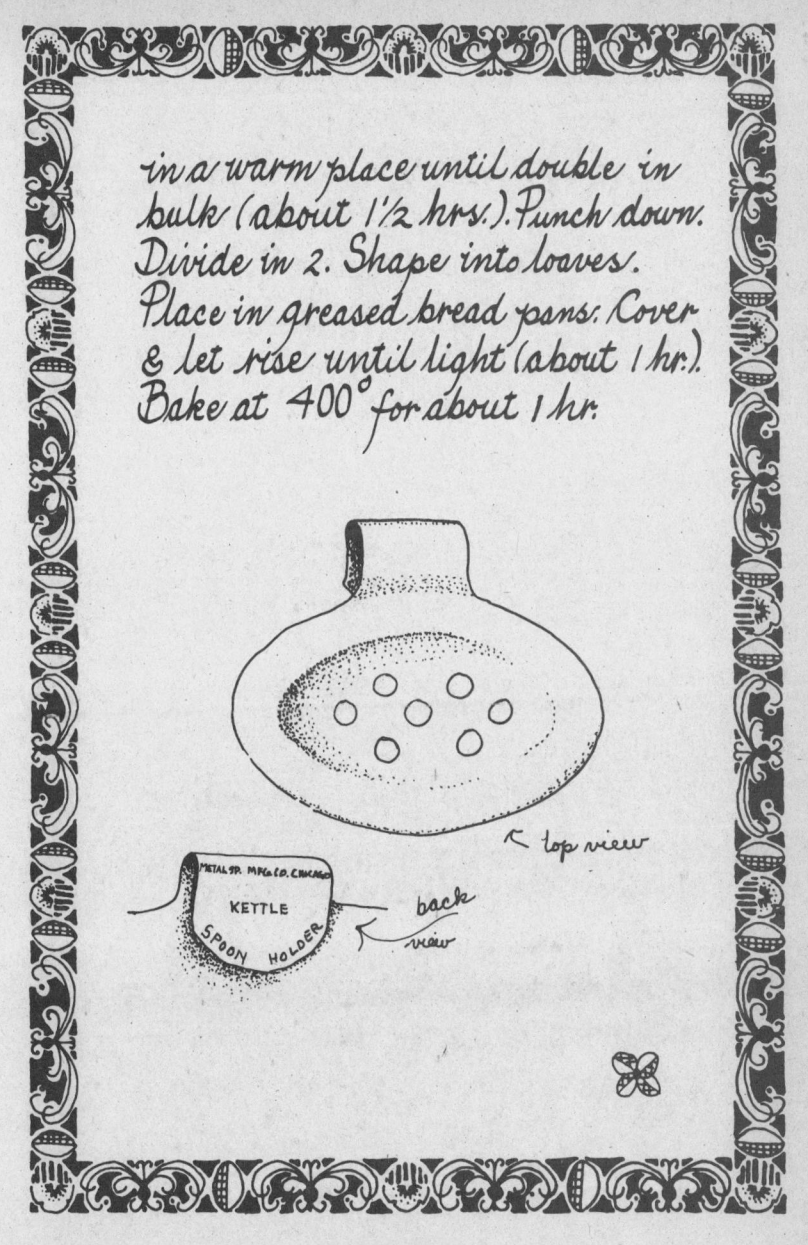

← top view

METAL SP. MFG CO. CHICAGO
KETTLE
SPOON HOLDER
← back view

Easy White Bread
2 loaves

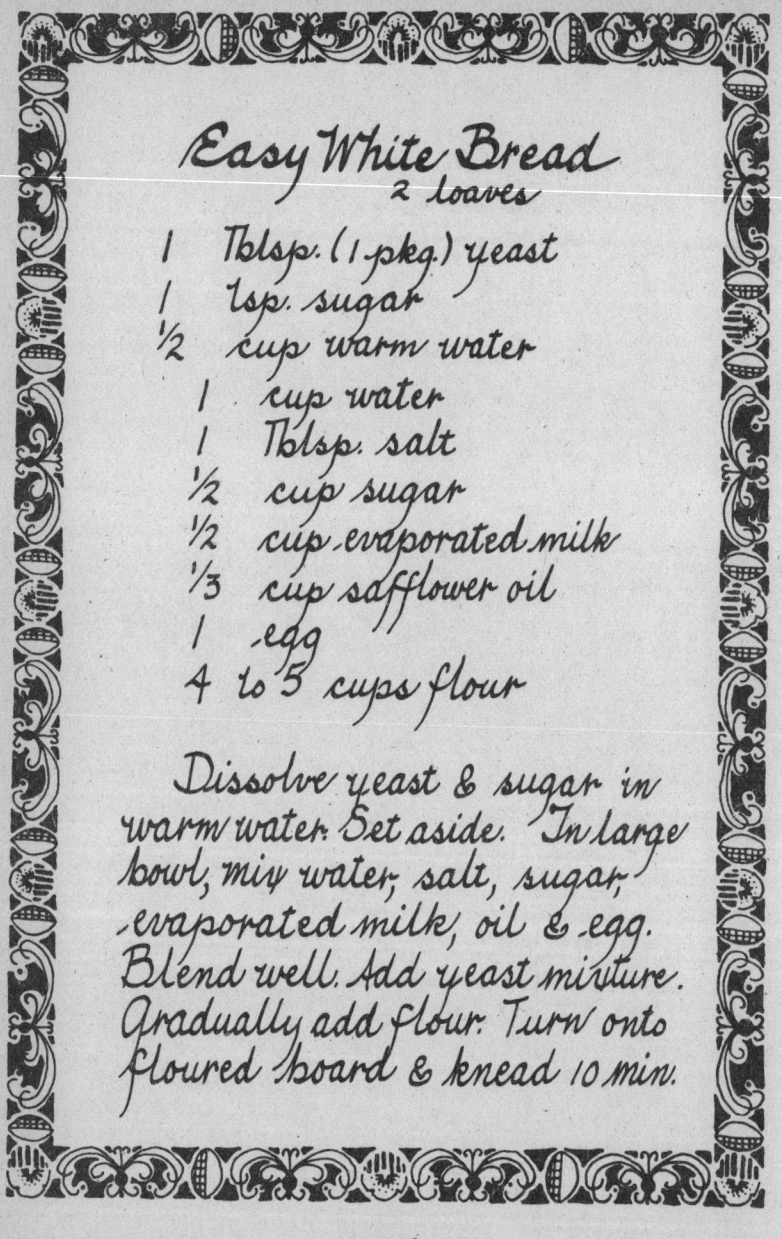

- 1 Tblsp. (1 pkg.) yeast
- 1 tsp. sugar
- ½ cup warm water
- 1 cup water
- 1 Tblsp. salt
- ½ cup sugar
- ½ cup evaporated milk
- ⅓ cup safflower oil
- 1 egg
- 4 to 5 cups flour

Dissolve yeast & sugar in warm water. Set aside. In large bowl, mix water, salt, sugar, evaporated milk, oil & egg. Blend well. Add yeast mixture. Gradually add flour. Turn onto floured board & knead 10 min.

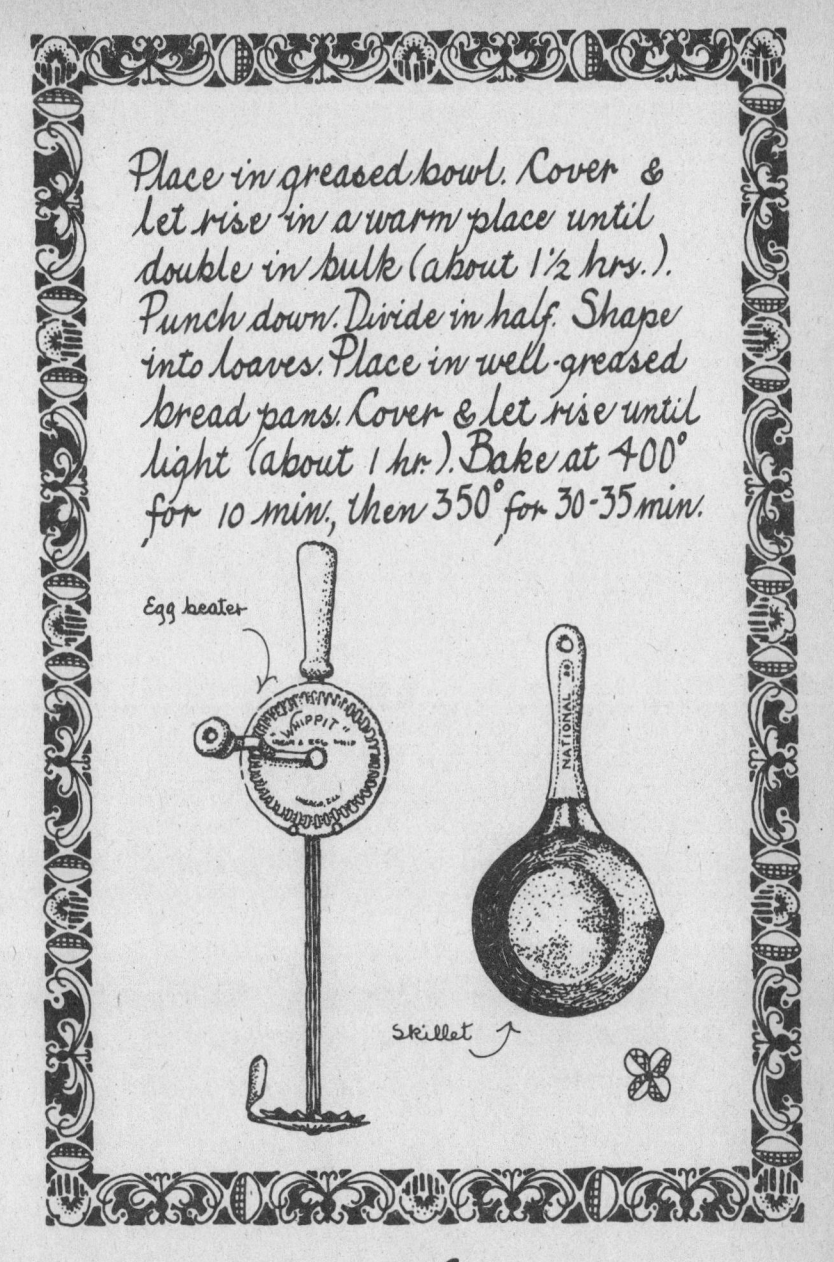

Place in greased bowl. Cover & let rise in a warm place until double in bulk (about 1½ hrs.). Punch down. Divide in half. Shape into loaves. Place in well-greased bread pans. Cover & let rise until light (about 1 hr.). Bake at 400° for 10 min, then 350° for 30-35 min.

Egg beater

Skillet

French Bread
2 loaves

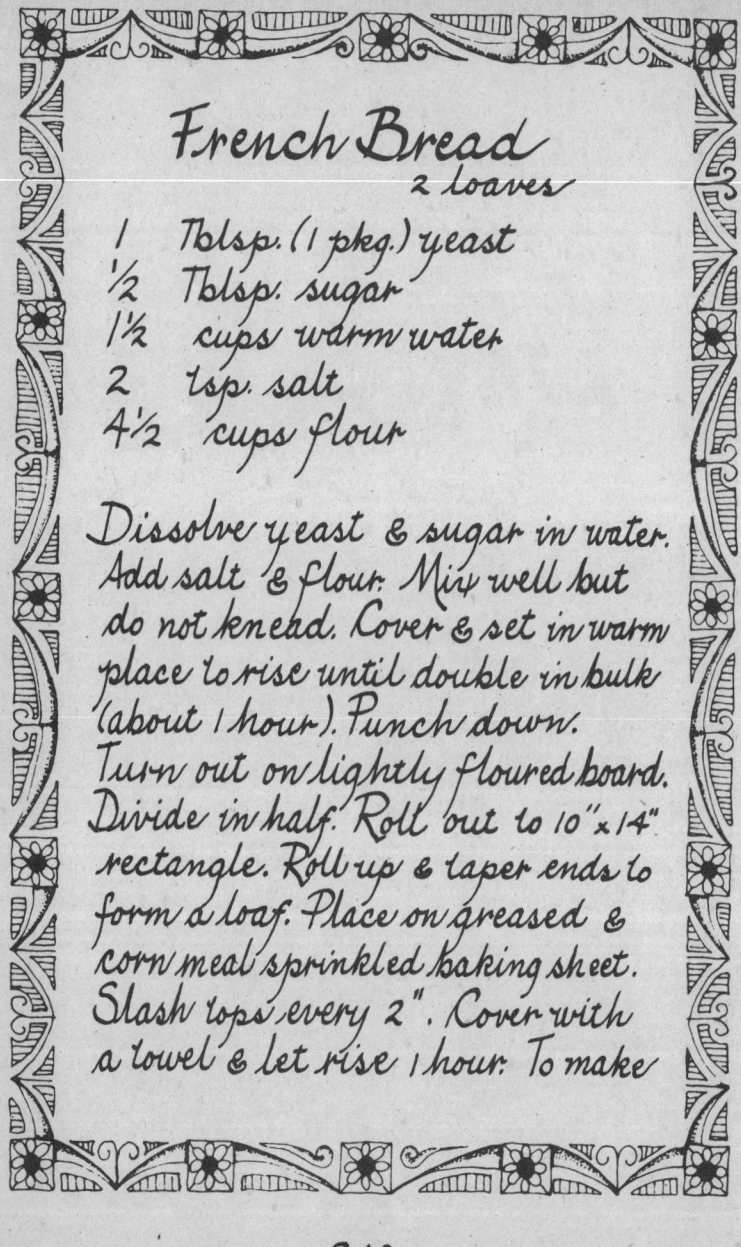

1 Tblsp. (1 pkg.) yeast
½ Tblsp. sugar
1½ cups warm water
2 tsp. salt
4½ cups flour

Dissolve yeast & sugar in water. Add salt & flour. Mix well but do not knead. Cover & set in warm place to rise until double in bulk (about 1 hour). Punch down. Turn out on lightly floured board. Divide in half. Roll out to 10"x14" rectangle. Roll up & taper ends to form a loaf. Place on greased & corn meal sprinkled baking sheet. Slash tops every 2". Cover with a towel & let rise 1 hour. To make loaves crusty, brush lightly with water just before placing in oven. Bake at 400° 10 min., then brush with water again. Lower heat to 350° & bake 40 min. more. Cool loaves quickly in draft or in front of an electric fan to insure a crisp crust.

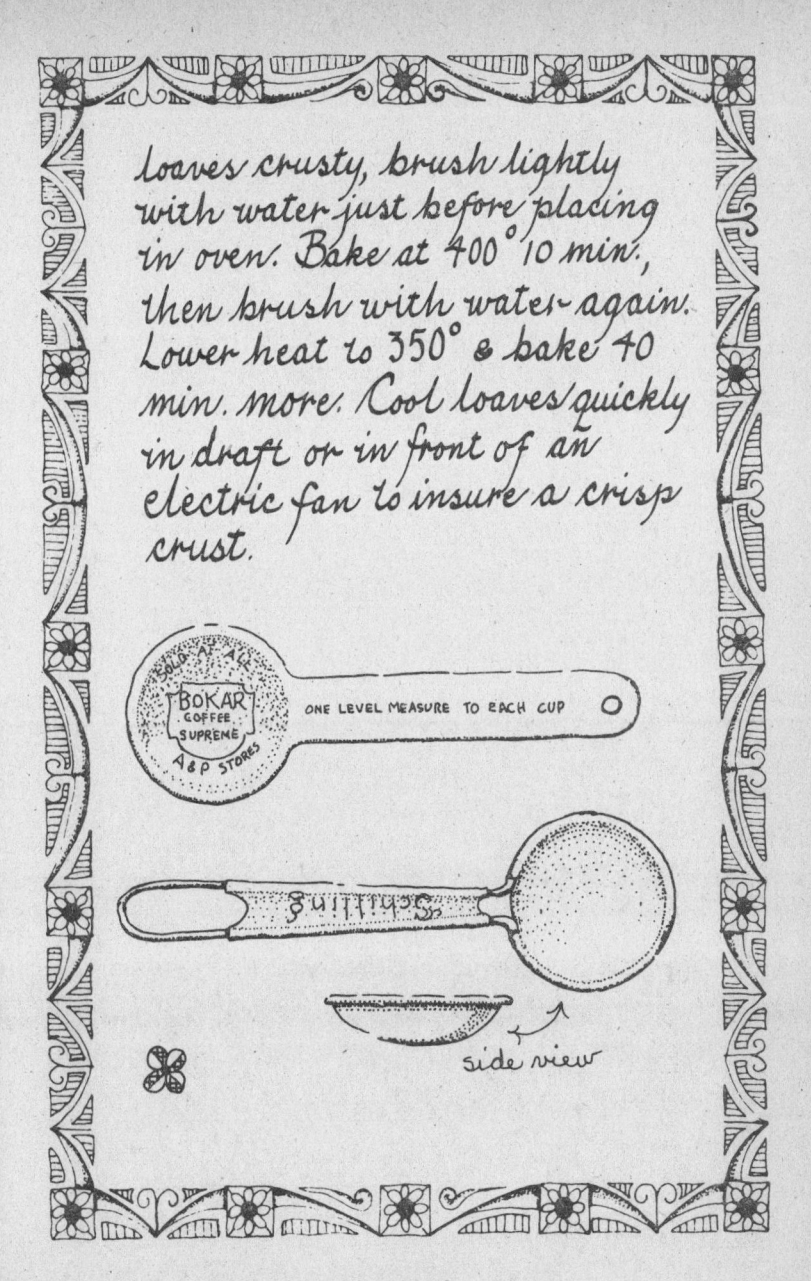

ONE LEVEL MEASURE TO EACH CUP

side view

Gluten Bread
2 loaves

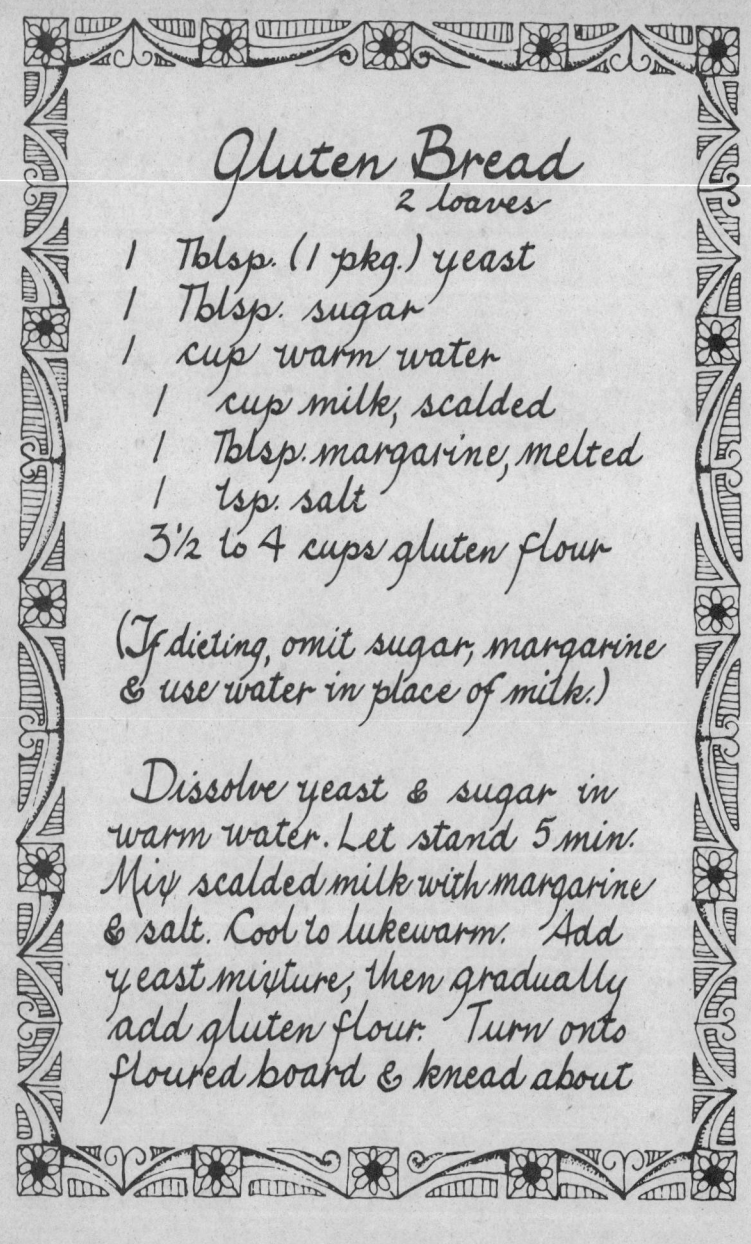

1 Tblsp. (1 pkg.) yeast
1 Tblsp. sugar
1 cup warm water
1 cup milk, scalded
1 Tblsp. margarine, melted
1 tsp. salt
3½ to 4 cups gluten flour

(If dieting, omit sugar, margarine & use water in place of milk.)

Dissolve yeast & sugar in warm water. Let stand 5 min. Mix scalded milk with margarine & salt. Cool to lukewarm. Add yeast mixture, then gradually add gluten flour. Turn onto floured board & knead about

10 min. Place in a greased bowl. Cover & let rise in a warm place until double in bulk (about 1½ hrs.). Punch down. Divide in half. Shape into loaves. Place in greased bread pans. Cover & let rise in warm place until light (about 1 hr.). Bake at 400° about 1 hr.

Spatulas

Nat's Bread
2 loaves

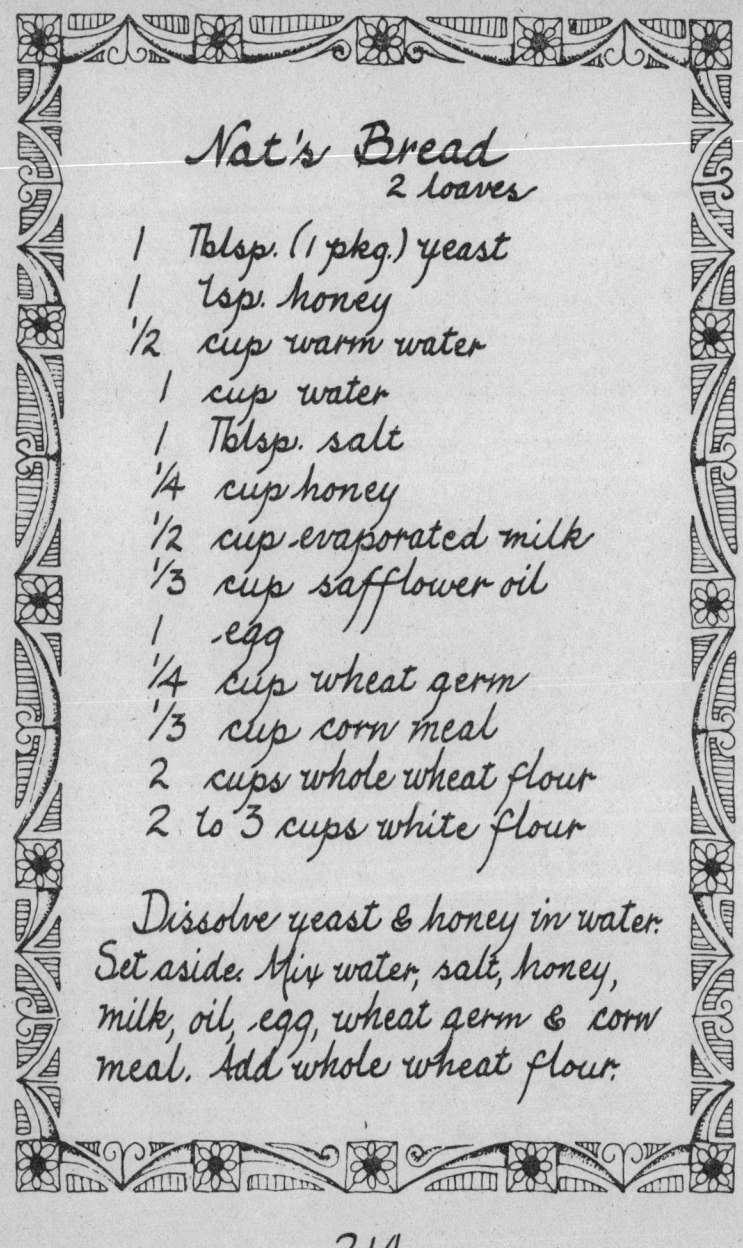

- 1 Tblsp. (1 pkg.) yeast
- 1 Tsp. honey
- 1/2 cup warm water
- 1 cup water
- 1 Tblsp. salt
- 1/4 cup honey
- 1/2 cup evaporated milk
- 1/3 cup safflower oil
- 1 egg
- 1/4 cup wheat germ
- 1/3 cup corn meal
- 2 cups whole wheat flour
- 2 to 3 cups white flour

Dissolve yeast & honey in water. Set aside. Mix water, salt, honey, milk, oil, egg, wheat germ & corn meal. Add whole wheat flour.

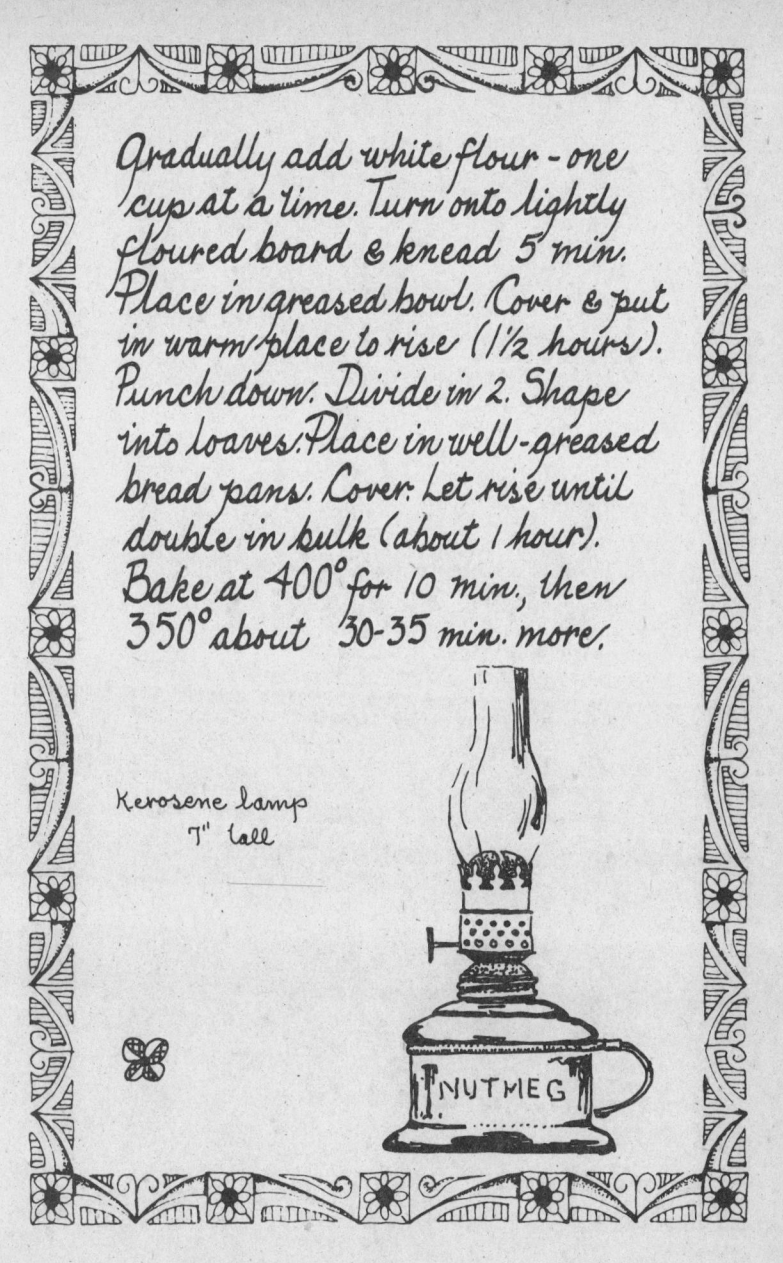

Gradually add white flour – one cup at a time. Turn onto lightly floured board & knead 5 min. Place in greased bowl. Cover & put in warm place to rise (1½ hours). Punch down. Divide in 2. Shape into loaves. Place in well-greased bread pans. Cover. Let rise until double in bulk (about 1 hour). Bake at 400° for 10 min., then 350° about 30-35 min. more.

Kerosene lamp
7" tall

Oatmeal Bread
2 loaves

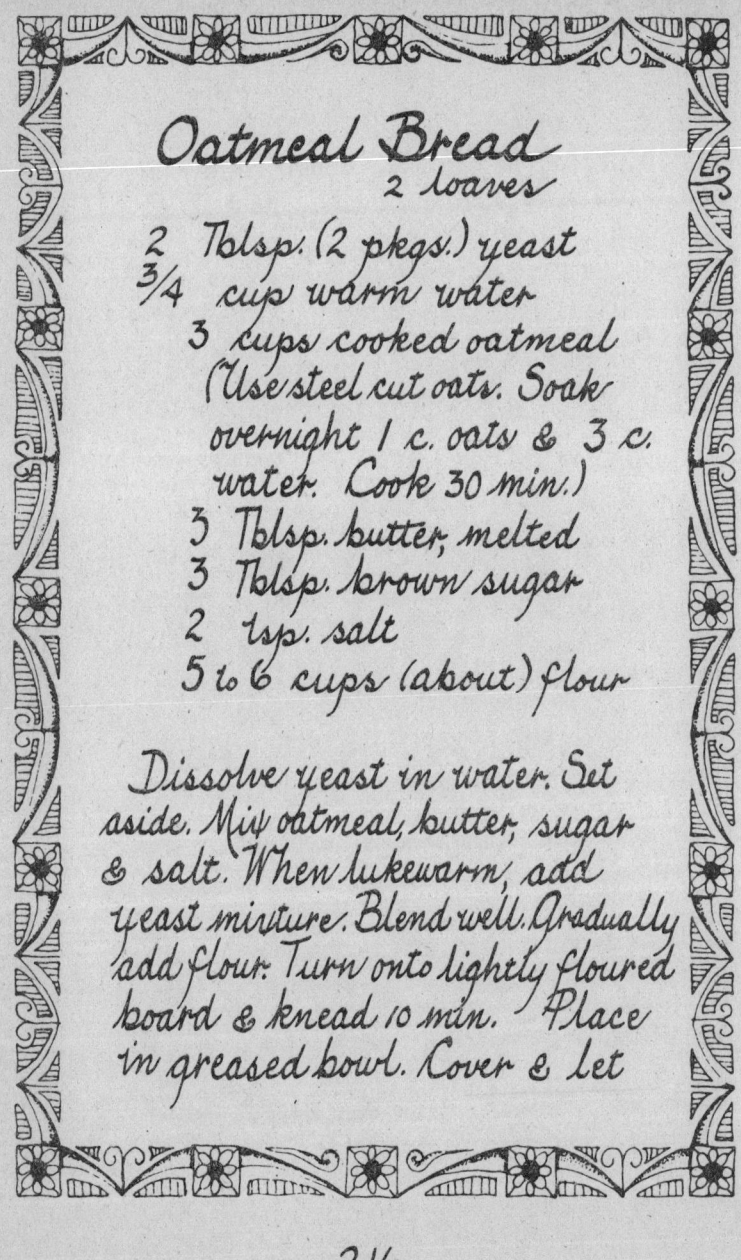

2 Tblsp. (2 pkgs.) yeast
¾ cup warm water
3 cups cooked oatmeal
(Use steel cut oats. Soak overnight 1 c. oats & 3 c. water. Cook 30 min.)
3 Tblsp. butter, melted
3 Tblsp. brown sugar
2 tsp. salt
5 to 6 cups (about) flour

Dissolve yeast in water. Set aside. Mix oatmeal, butter, sugar & salt. When lukewarm, add yeast mixture. Blend well. Gradually add flour. Turn onto lightly floured board & knead 10 min. Place in greased bowl. Cover & let rise in warm place until double in bulk (about 1½ hrs.). Punch down. Divide in 2. Shape into loaves & place in well-greased bread pans. Cover & let rise (about 1 hr.). Bake at 400° about 1 hr.

Mixing bowls – yellow crockery

Polish Easter Bread
1 large loaf

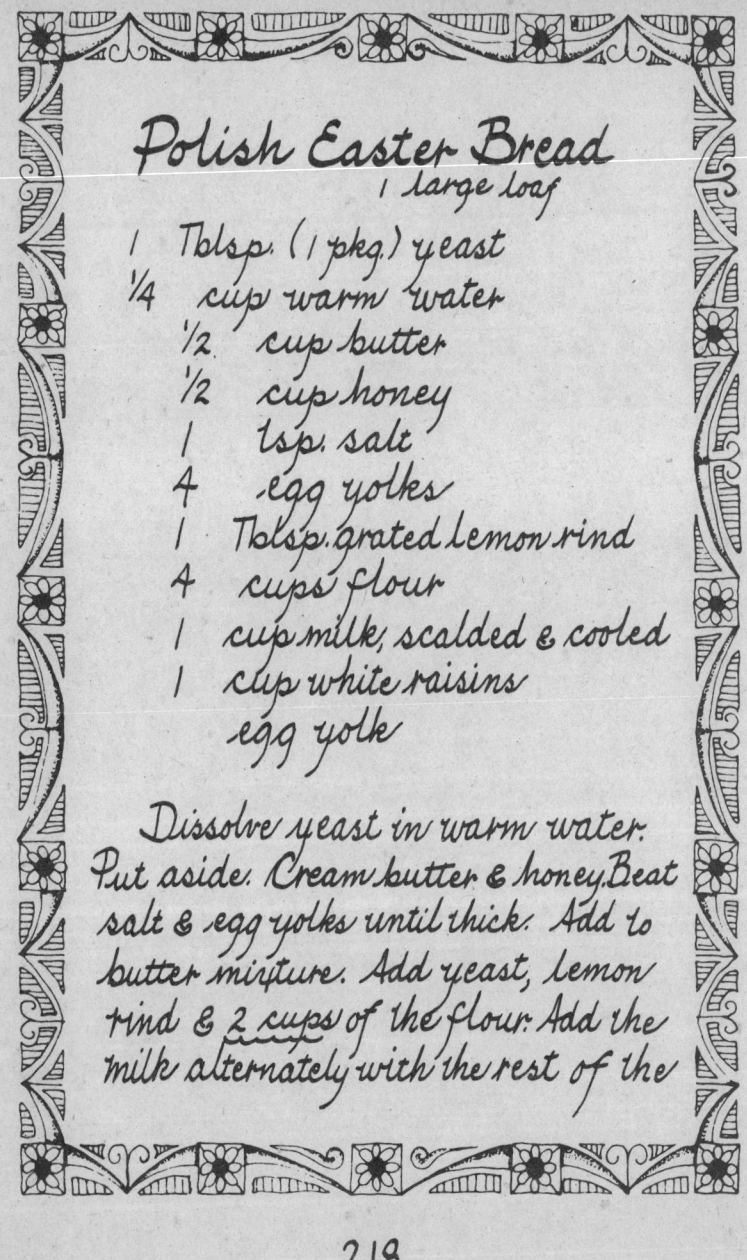

- 1 Tblsp. (1 pkg.) yeast
- 1/4 cup warm water
- 1/2 cup butter
- 1/2 cup honey
- 1 tsp. salt
- 4 egg yolks
- 1 Tblsp. grated lemon rind
- 4 cups flour
- 1 cup milk, scalded & cooled
- 1 cup white raisins
- egg yolk

Dissolve yeast in warm water. Put aside. Cream butter & honey. Beat salt & egg yolks until thick. Add to butter mixture. Add yeast, lemon rind & 2 cups of the flour. Add the milk alternately with the rest of the flour. Add raisins. Turn onto a lightly floured board & knead 5 min. Place in greased bowl. Cover & let rise in a warm place until double in bulk (about 1½ hrs.). Punch down in bowl & let rise again 1 hr. Punch down. Form into long roll & place in a well-greased 10" fluted tube pan - traditional. (Or use ovenproof bowl or large bread pan.) Brush top with egg yolk. Bake at 350° for about 30 minutes.

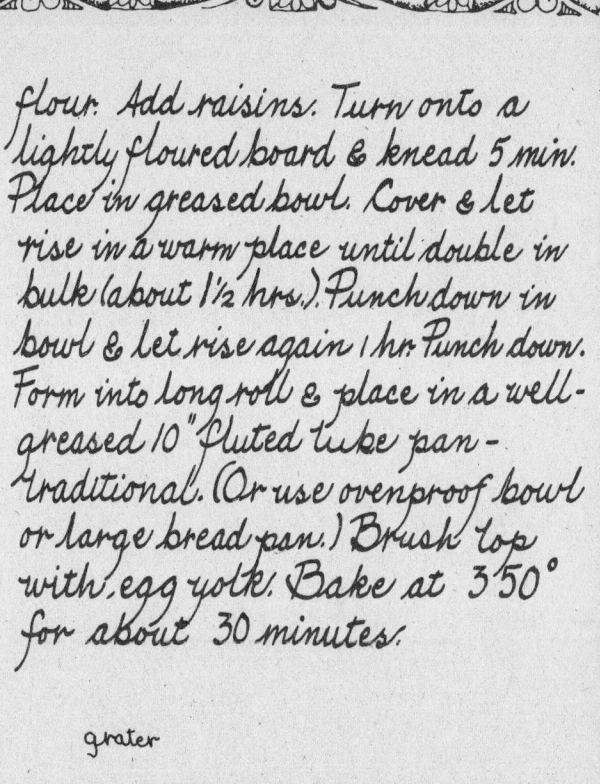

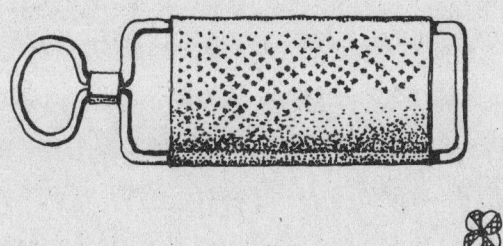

grater

Potato Bread
2 loaves

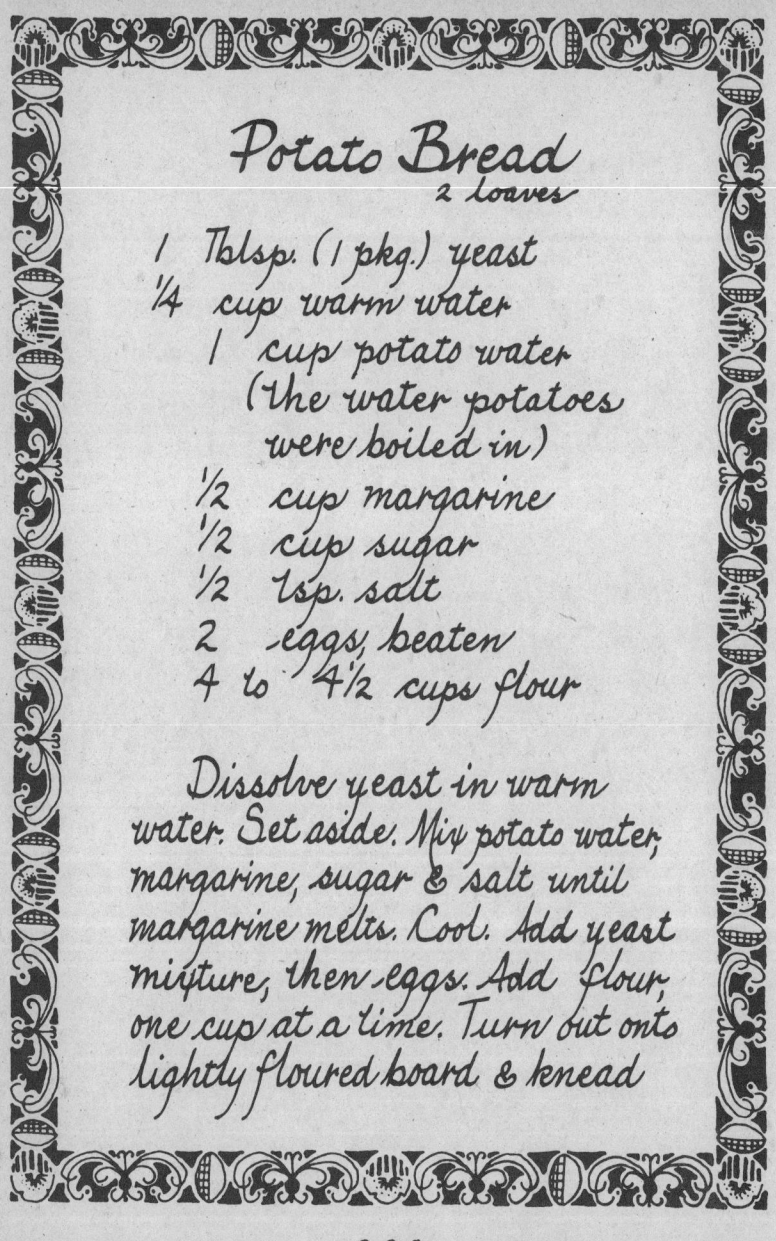

- 1 Tblsp. (1 pkg.) yeast
- 1/4 cup warm water
- 1 cup potato water (the water potatoes were boiled in)
- 1/2 cup margarine
- 1/2 cup sugar
- 1/2 tsp. salt
- 2 eggs, beaten
- 4 to 4 1/2 cups flour

Dissolve yeast in warm water. Set aside. Mix potato water, margarine, sugar & salt until margarine melts. Cool. Add yeast mixture, then eggs. Add flour, one cup at a time. Turn out onto lightly floured board & knead about 10 min. Place in greased & covered bowl in a warm place to rise until double in bulk (about 1½ hours). Punch down. Divide in half. Shape into loaves. Place in well-greased bread pans. Let rise until light (about 1 hour). Bake at 375° about 40 to 50 min.

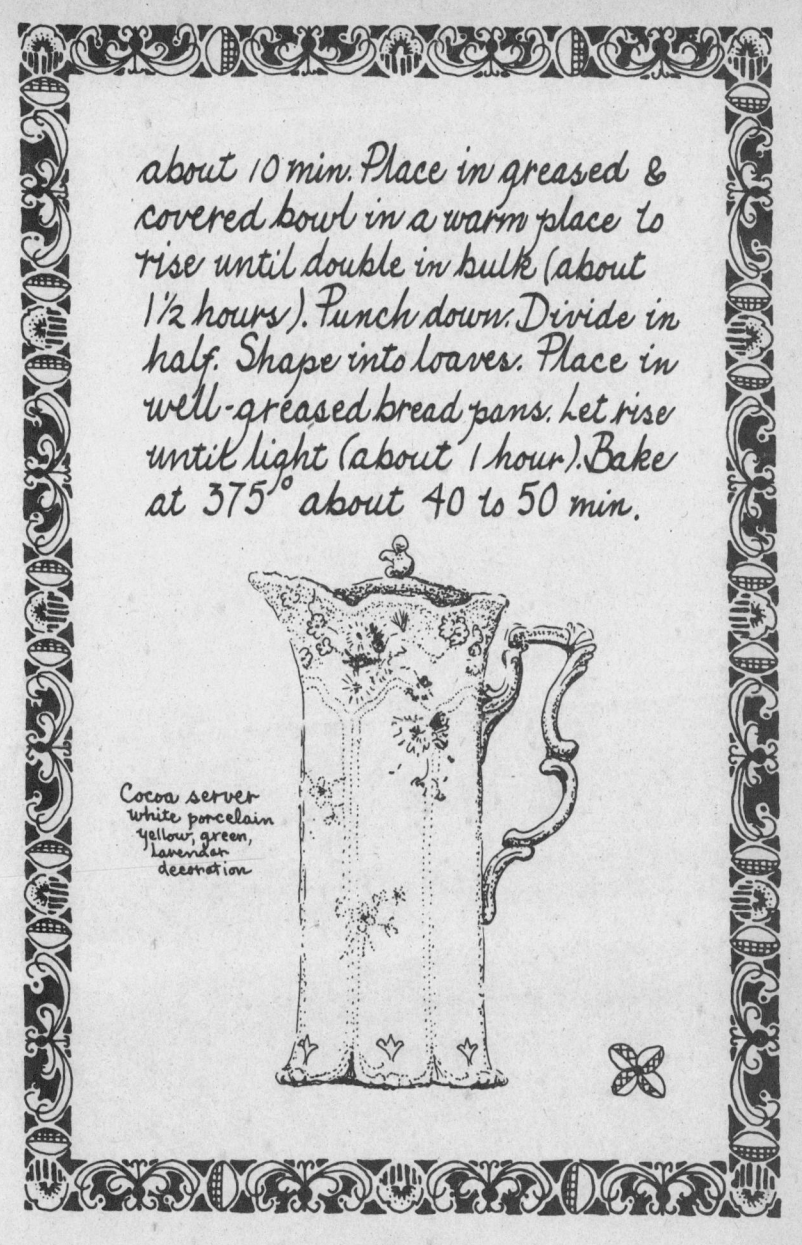

Cocoa server
white porcelain
yellow, green,
Lavendar
decoration

Saffron Bread
2 braided loaves

2 Tblsp. (2 pkgs.) yeast
1 Tblsp. sugar
½ cup warm water
1¼ cup milk, scalded
½ cup butter
⅓ cup sugar
½ tsp. salt
½ tsp. powdered saffron
1 egg
½ cup raisins
4½ to 5 cups flour
egg yolk

Dissolve yeast & sugar in warm water. Put aside. Mix scalded milk & butter. When butter melts, add sugar, salt & saffron. Cool. Add egg, yeast mixture & raisins.

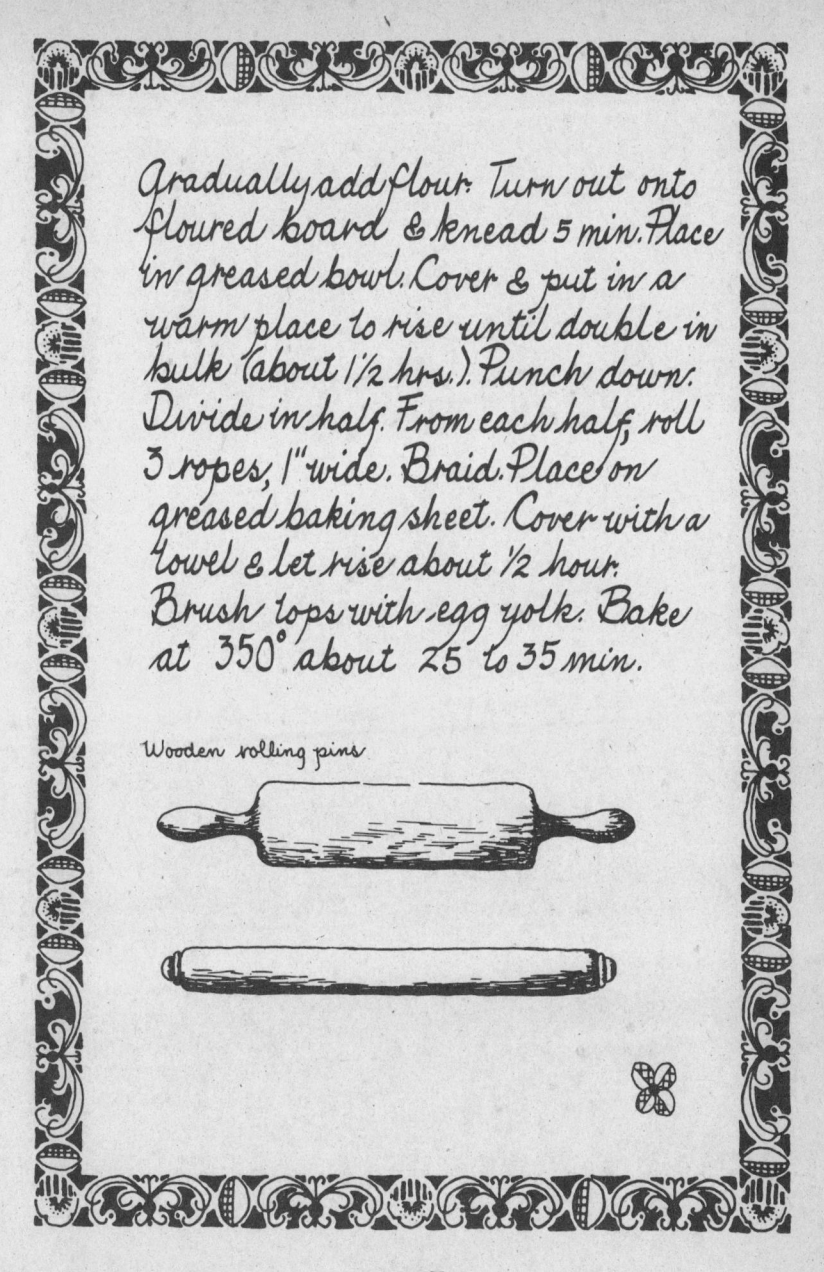

Gradually add flour. Turn out onto floured board & knead 5 min. Place in greased bowl. Cover & put in a warm place to rise until double in bulk (about 1½ hrs.). Punch down. Divide in half. From each half, roll 3 ropes, 1" wide. Braid. Place on greased baking sheet. Cover with a towel & let rise about ½ hour. Brush tops with egg yolk. Bake at 350° about 25 to 35 min.

Wooden rolling pins

Salt-Rising Bread
2 loaves

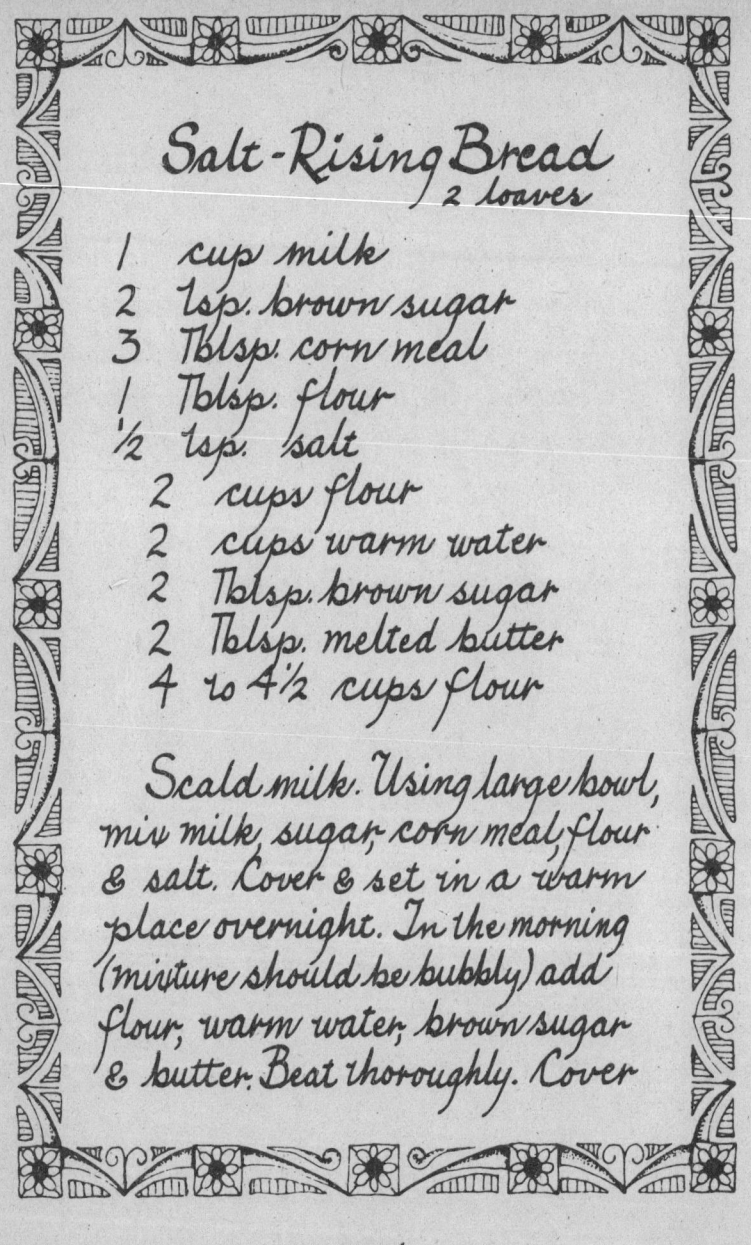

- 1 cup milk
- 2 tsp. brown sugar
- 3 Tblsp. corn meal
- 1 Tblsp. flour
- ½ tsp. salt
- 2 cups flour
- 2 cups warm water
- 2 Tblsp. brown sugar
- 2 Tblsp. melted butter
- 4 to 4½ cups flour

Scald milk. Using large bowl, mix milk, sugar, corn meal, flour & salt. Cover & set in a warm place overnight. In the morning (mixture should be bubbly) add flour, warm water, brown sugar & butter. Beat thoroughly. Cover

& let rise until bubbly (from 1½ to 2½ hours). Add the remaining 4 to 4½ cups of flour. Turn onto floured board & knead 10 min. Shape into loaves. Place in greased bread pans. Cover & let rise until light (about 1½ hours). Bake at 425° for 15 min., then 375° for about 35-40 min. more.

Blue & white enamelware coffee pot

Sourdough Starter

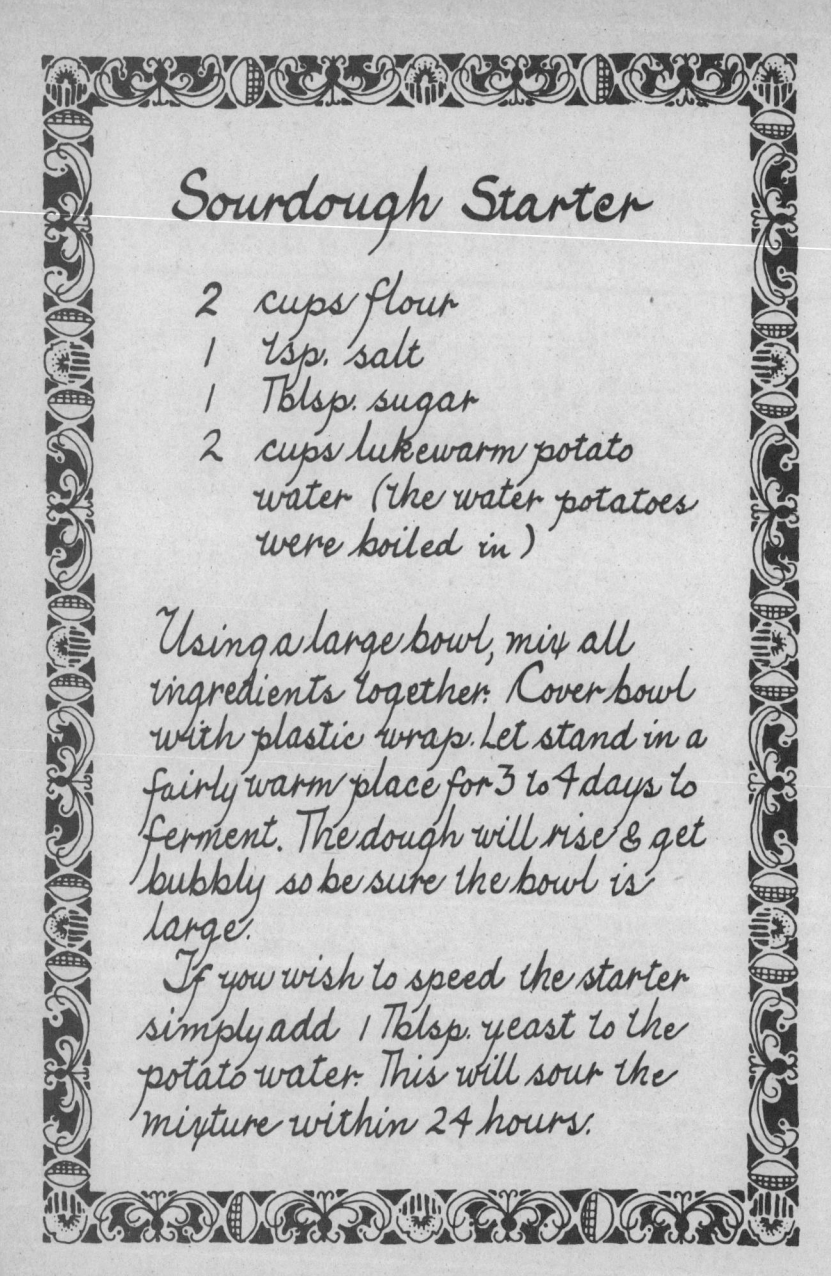

2 cups flour
1 tsp. salt
1 Tblsp. sugar
2 cups lukewarm potato water (the water potatoes were boiled in)

Using a large bowl, mix all ingredients together. Cover bowl with plastic wrap. Let stand in a fairly warm place for 3 to 4 days to ferment. The dough will rise & get bubbly so be sure the bowl is large.

If you wish to speed the starter simply add 1 Tblsp. yeast to the potato water. This will sour the mixture within 24 hours.

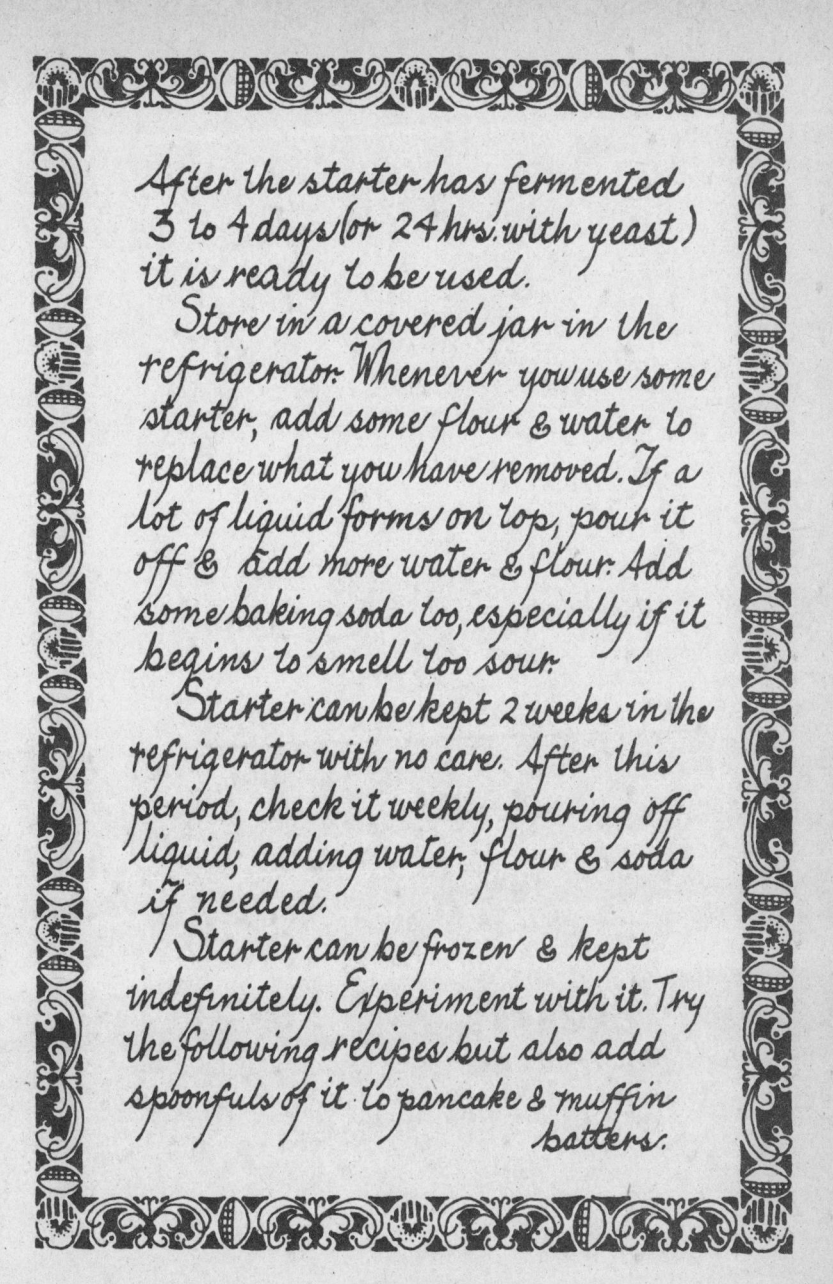

After the starter has fermented 3 to 4 days (or 24 hrs. with yeast) it is ready to be used.

Store in a covered jar in the refrigerator. Whenever you use some starter, add some flour & water to replace what you have removed. If a lot of liquid forms on top, pour it off & add more water & flour. Add some baking soda too, especially if it begins to smell too sour.

Starter can be kept 2 weeks in the refrigerator with no care. After this period, check it weekly, pouring off liquid, adding water, flour & soda if needed.

Starter can be frozen & kept indefinitely. Experiment with it. Try the following recipes but also add spoonfuls of it to pancake & muffin batters.

Sourdough Bread
2 loaves

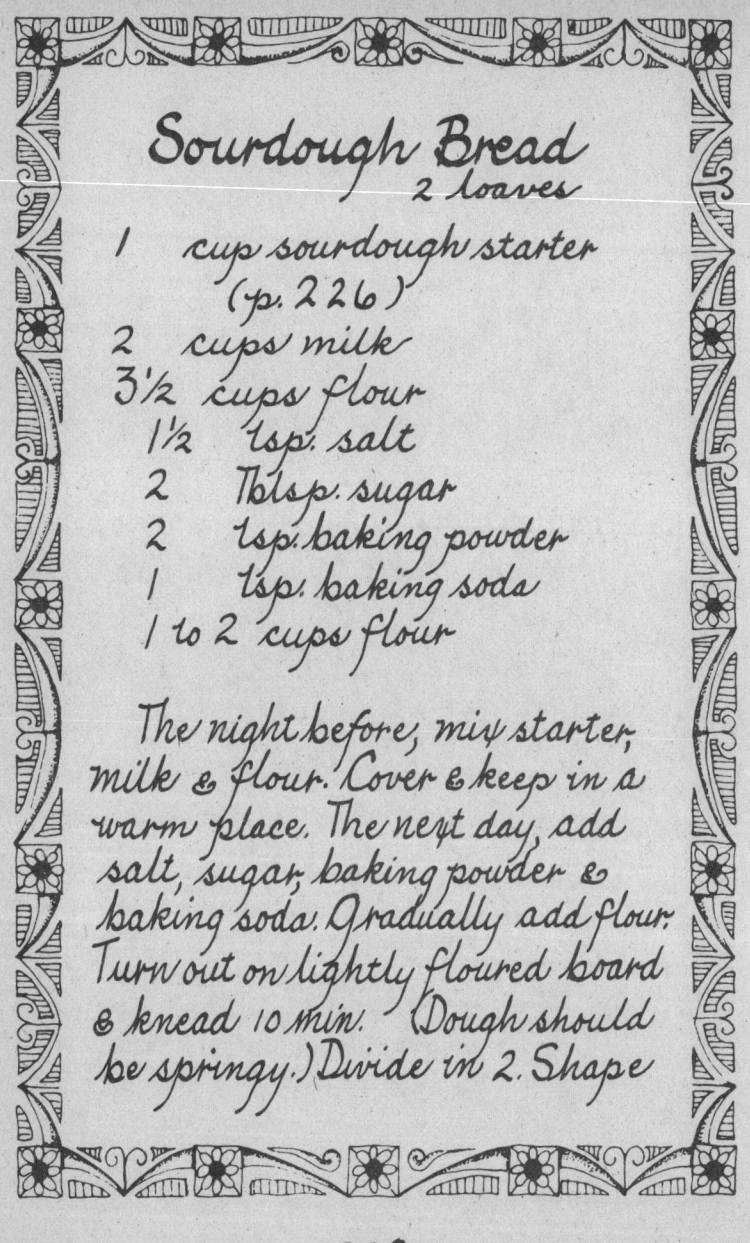

1 cup sourdough starter (p. 226)
2 cups milk
3½ cups flour
1½ tsp. salt
2 Tblsp. sugar
2 tsp. baking powder
1 tsp. baking soda
1 to 2 cups flour

The night before, mix starter, milk & flour. Cover & keep in a warm place. The next day, add salt, sugar, baking powder & baking soda. Gradually add flour. Turn out on lightly floured board & knead 10 min. (Dough should be springy.) Divide in 2. Shape into loaves & place in well-greased bread pans. Let rise until double in bulk (about 2 hours). Bake at 400° for 10 min., then 375° about 30 min. more.

1881
ROGERS
QUADRUPLE
NEW YORK
5902

Child's cup
silver on pewter

Sourdough French Bread
2 loaves

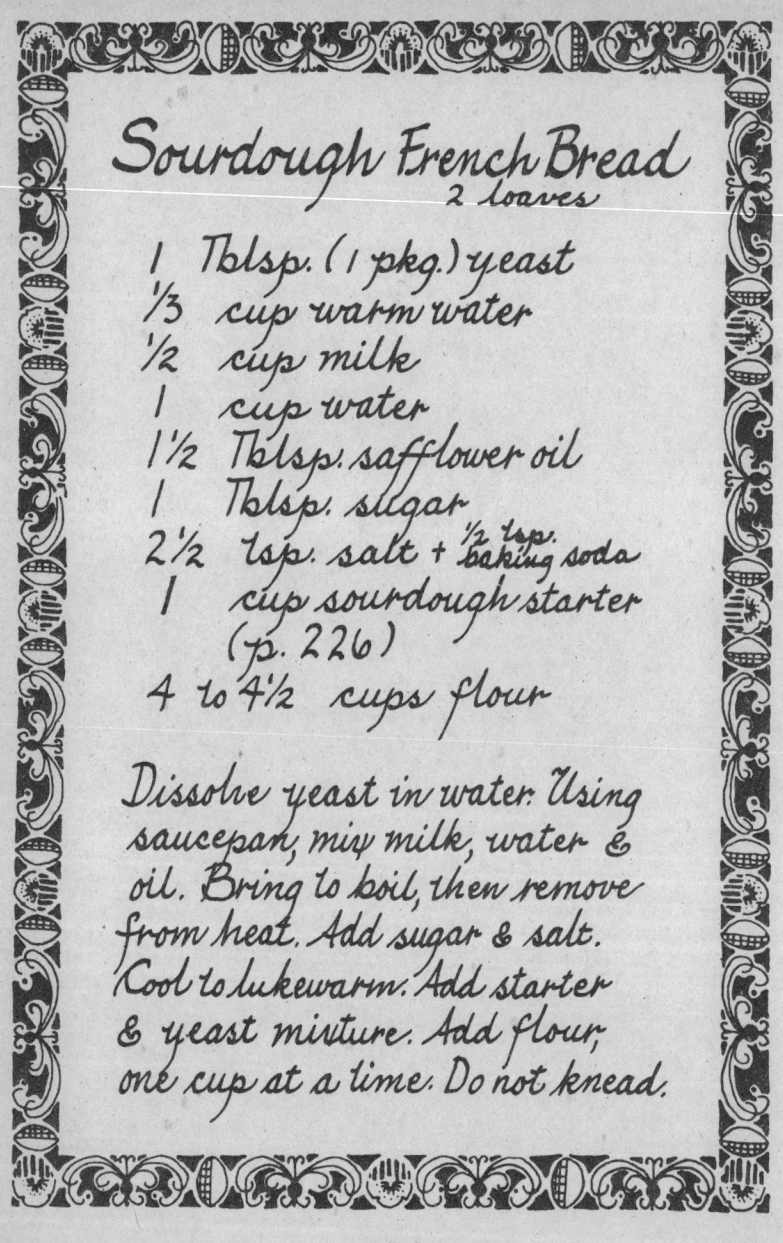

- 1 Tblsp. (1 pkg.) yeast
- 1/3 cup warm water
- 1/2 cup milk
- 1 cup water
- 1 1/2 Tblsp. safflower oil
- 1 Tblsp. sugar
- 2 1/2 tsp. salt + 1/2 tsp. baking soda
- 1 cup sourdough starter (p. 226)
- 4 to 4 1/2 cups flour

Dissolve yeast in water. Using saucepan, mix milk, water & oil. Bring to boil, then remove from heat. Add sugar & salt. Cool to lukewarm. Add starter & yeast mixture. Add flour, one cup at a time. Do not knead.

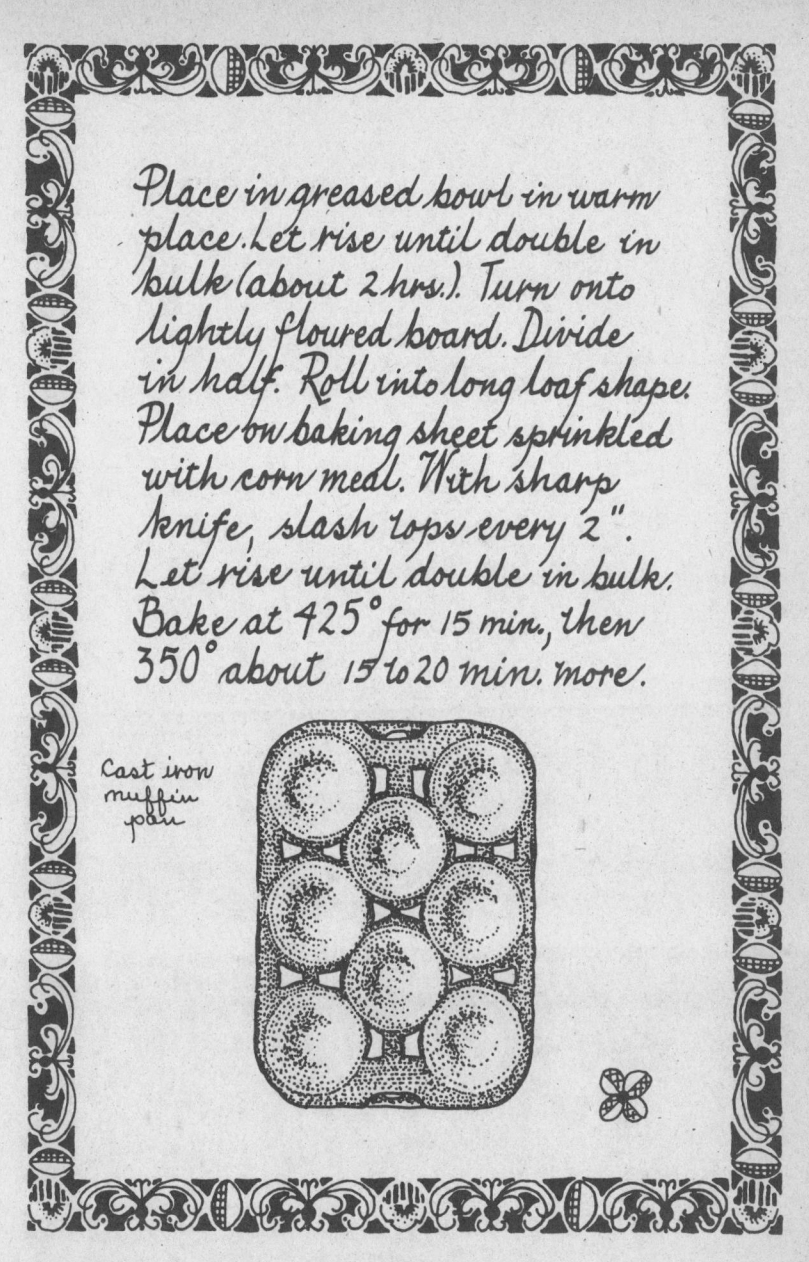

Place in greased bowl in warm place. Let rise until double in bulk (about 2 hrs.). Turn onto lightly floured board. Divide in half. Roll into long loaf shape. Place on baking sheet sprinkled with corn meal. With sharp knife, slash tops every 2". Let rise until double in bulk. Bake at 425° for 15 min., then 350° about 15 to 20 min. more.

Cast iron muffin pan

Sourdough Herb Bread
2 loaves

- 1 cup sourdough starter (p. 226)
- 2 cups milk
- 3 cups whole wheat flour
- 1 tsp. salt
- 1/4 cup brown sugar
- 2 tsp. baking powder
- 1 tsp. baking soda
- 1/2 tsp. ground ginger
- 1/2 tsp. basil
- 1/4 tsp. leaf sage, rubbed
- 1 1/2 to 2 cups whole wheat flour

The night before, using a large bowl, mix starter, milk & whole wheat flour. Cover & put in a warm place.

The next day, add salt, sugar,

baking powder & soda, ginger, basil & sage. Gradually add flour. Turn onto floured board & knead (10 min.) until dough is springy. Divide in 2. Shape into loaves & place in well-greased bread pans. Cover & let rise until double in bulk (about 2 hrs.). Bake at 400° 10 min., 375° 30 min.

Flour sifter

Sourdough Pumpernickel Bread
2 loaves

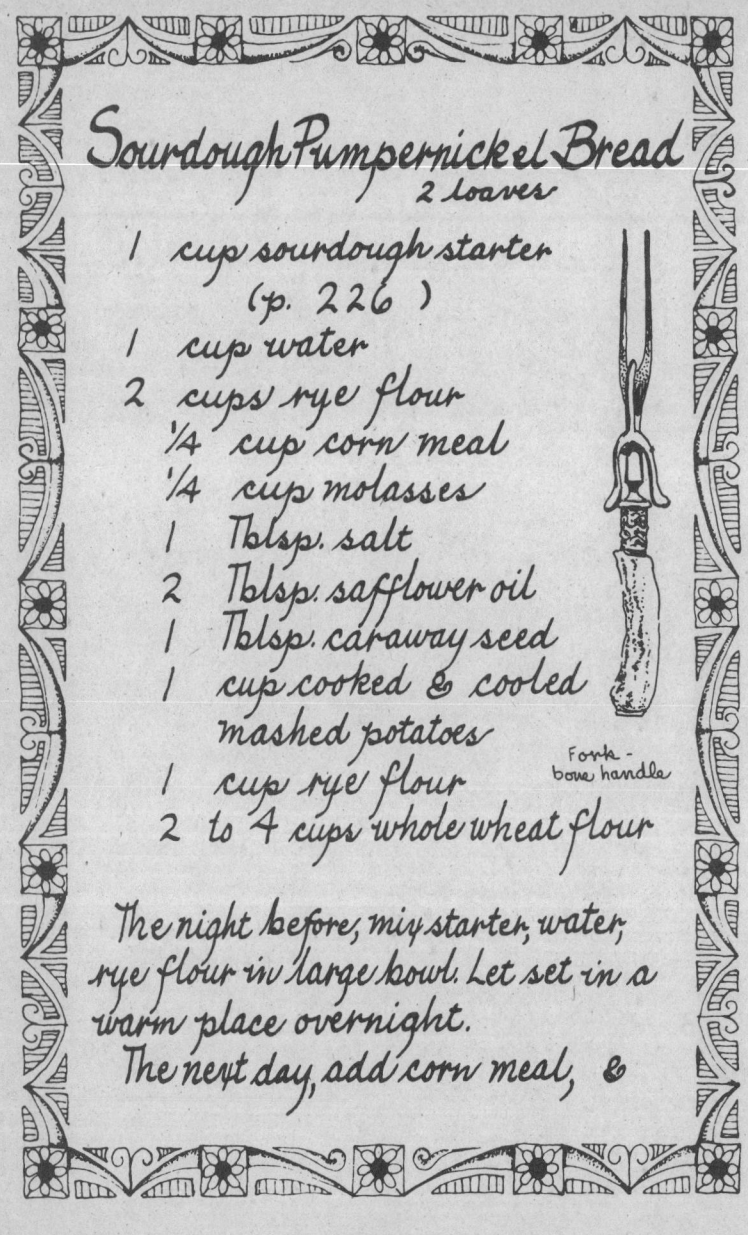

1 cup sourdough starter (p. 226)
1 cup water
2 cups rye flour
¼ cup corn meal
¼ cup molasses
1 Tblsp. salt
2 Tblsp. safflower oil
1 Tblsp. caraway seed
1 cup cooked & cooled mashed potatoes
1 cup rye flour
2 to 4 cups whole wheat flour

Fork - bone handle

The night before, mix starter, water, rye flour in large bowl. Let set in a warm place overnight.

The next day, add corn meal, &

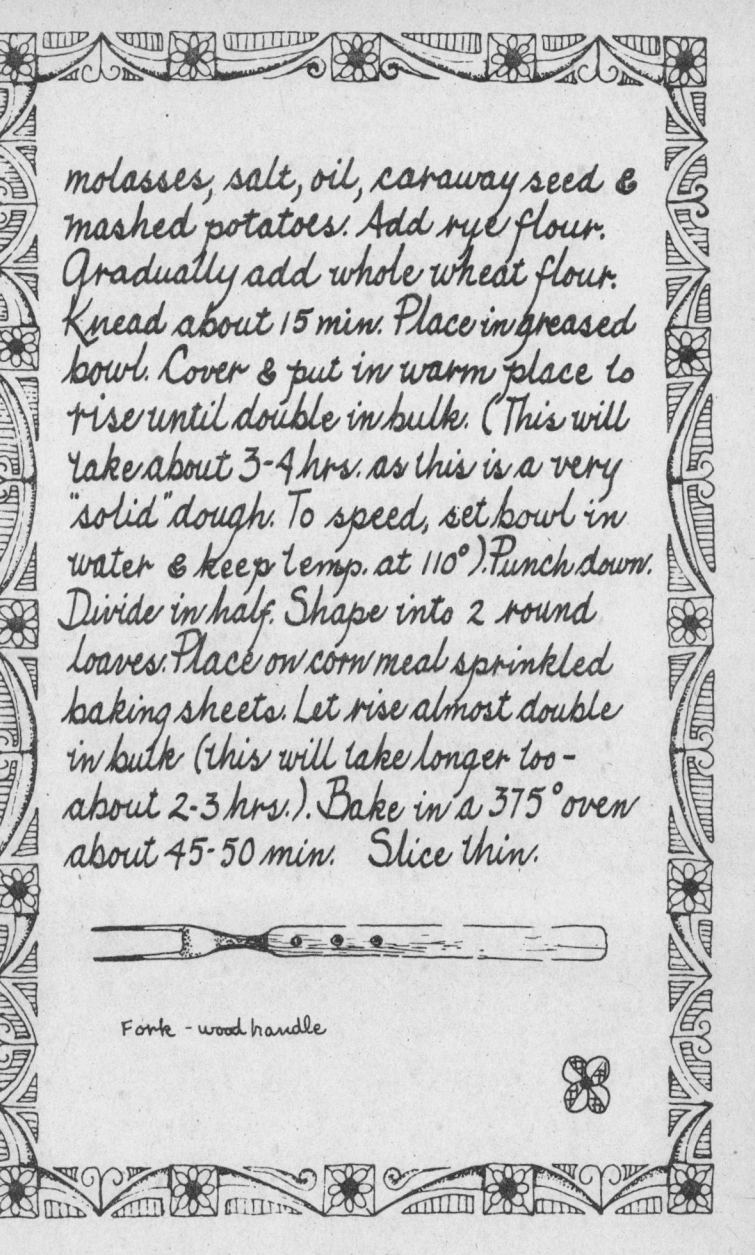

molasses, salt, oil, caraway seed &
mashed potatoes. Add rye flour.
Gradually add whole wheat flour.
Knead about 15 min. Place in greased
bowl. Cover & put in warm place to
rise until double in bulk. (This will
take about 3-4 hrs. as this is a very
"solid" dough. To speed, set bowl in
water & keep temp. at 110°). Punch down.
Divide in half. Shape into 2 round
loaves. Place on corn meal sprinkled
baking sheets. Let rise almost double
in bulk (this will take longer too -
about 2-3 hrs.). Bake in a 375° oven
about 45-50 min.   Slice thin.

Fork - wood handle

Sour Rye Bread
2 loaves

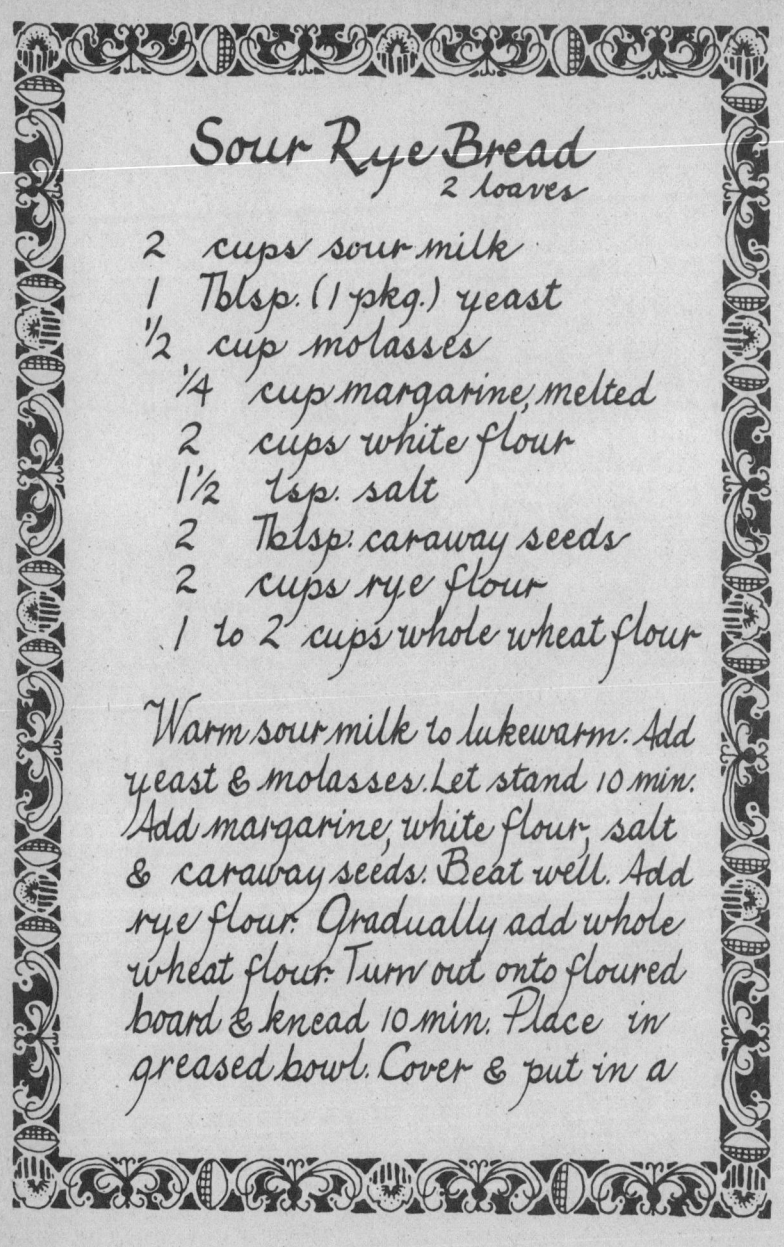

- 2 cups sour milk
- 1 Tblsp. (1 pkg.) yeast
- ½ cup molasses
- ¼ cup margarine, melted
- 2 cups white flour
- 1½ tsp. salt
- 2 Tblsp. caraway seeds
- 2 cups rye flour
- 1 to 2 cups whole wheat flour

Warm sour milk to lukewarm. Add yeast & molasses. Let stand 10 min. Add margarine, white flour, salt & caraway seeds. Beat well. Add rye flour. Gradually add whole wheat flour. Turn out onto floured board & knead 10 min. Place in greased bowl. Cover & put in a warm place to rise until double in bulk (about 2½ hrs.). Punch down. Divide in half. Shape into loaves & place in greased bread pans. (Or - roll dough out into two 10" x 14" rectangles. Roll up into long loaves. Place on well-greased baking sheet sprinkled with corn meal. Slash tops with knife every 2".) Bake at 350° for about 50-60 min.

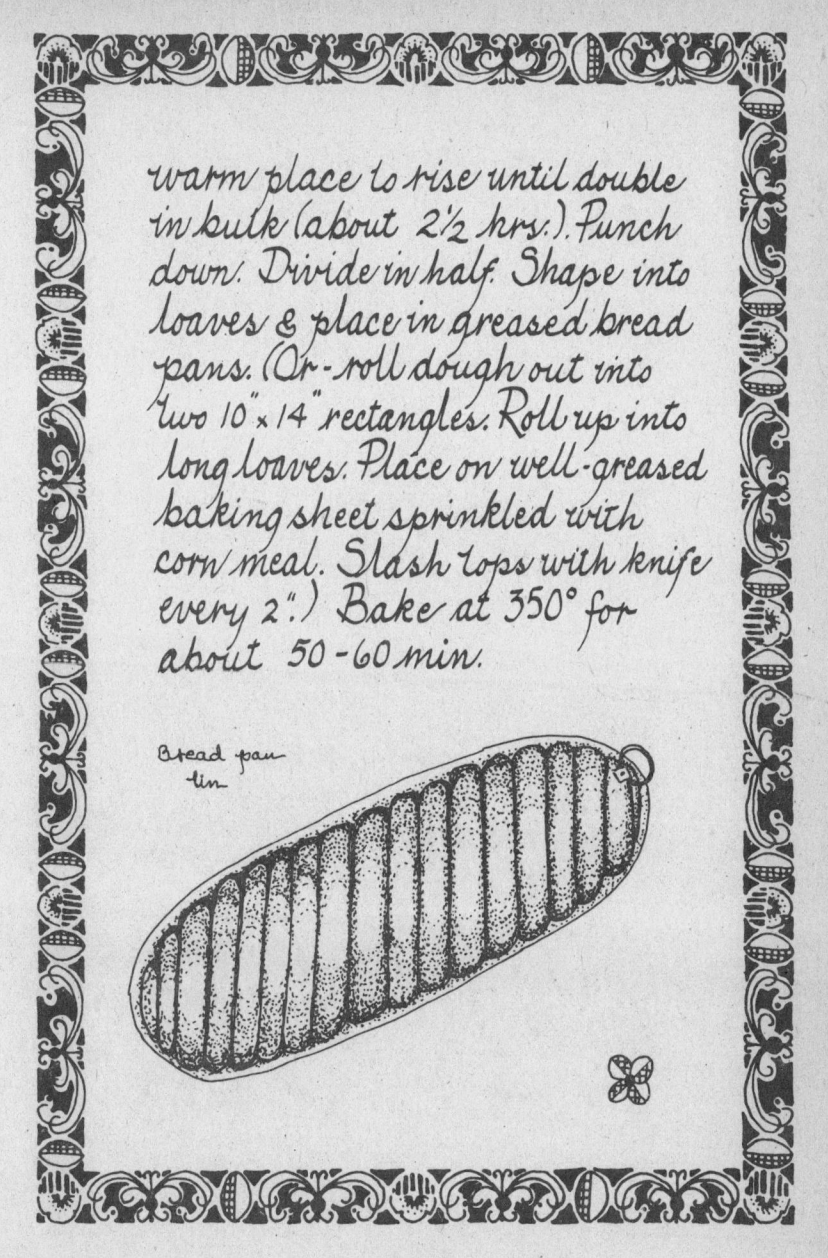

Bread pan tin

Squash Bread
2 loaves

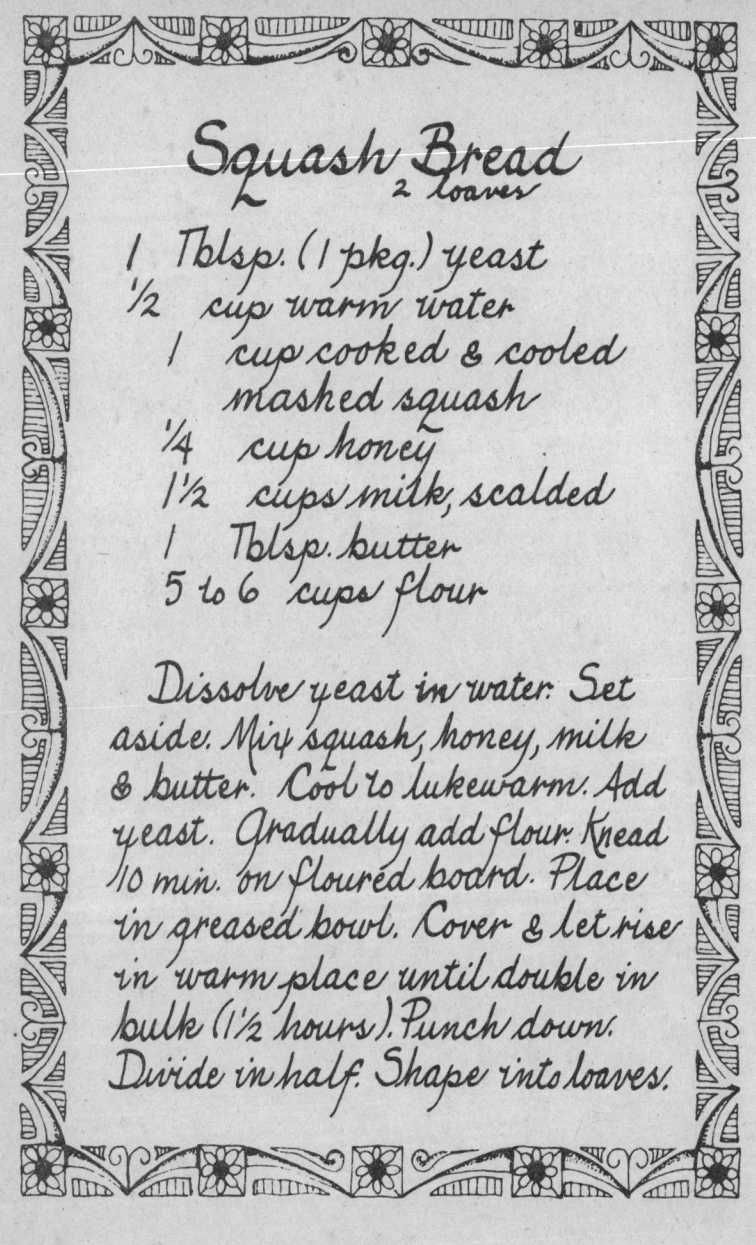

1 Tblsp. (1 pkg.) yeast
½ cup warm water
1 cup cooked & cooled mashed squash
¼ cup honey
1½ cups milk, scalded
1 Tblsp. butter
5 to 6 cups flour

Dissolve yeast in water. Set aside. Mix squash, honey, milk & butter. Cool to lukewarm. Add yeast. Gradually add flour. Knead 10 min. on floured board. Place in greased bowl. Cover & let rise in warm place until double in bulk (1½ hours). Punch down. Divide in half. Shape into loaves.

Place in well-greased bread pans. Cover & let rise in a warm place until light (about 1 hour). Bake at 400° for 10 min., then 375° about 25 min. more.

Silver-plated mustard jar
glass liner
wooden spoon

MERIDEN B. COMPANY

17 ← trademark on bottom

Swedish Rye Bread
2 loaves

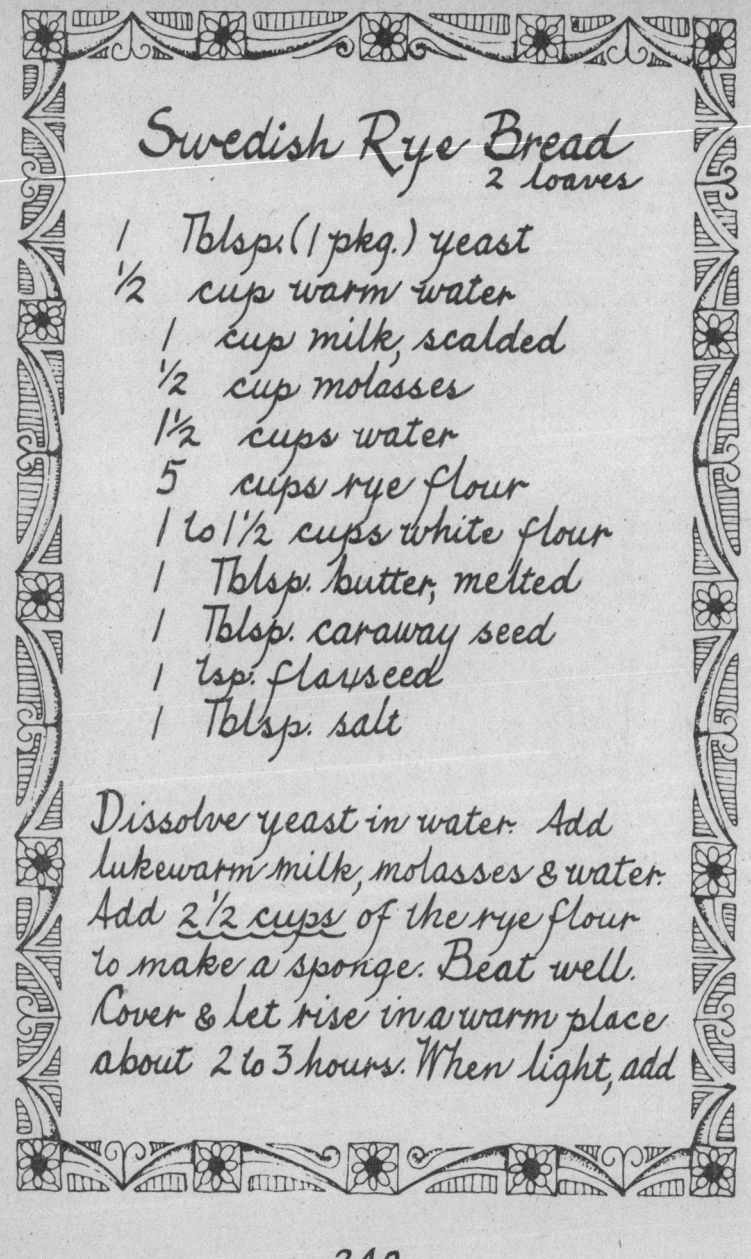

- 1 Tblsp. (1 pkg.) yeast
- ½ cup warm water
- 1 cup milk, scalded
- ½ cup molasses
- 1½ cups water
- 5 cups rye flour
- 1 to 1½ cups white flour
- 1 Tblsp. butter, melted
- 1 Tblsp. caraway seed
- 1 tsp. flaxseed
- 1 Tblsp. salt

Dissolve yeast in water. Add lukewarm milk, molasses & water. Add 2½ cups of the rye flour to make a sponge. Beat well. Cover & let rise in a warm place about 2 to 3 hours. When light, add

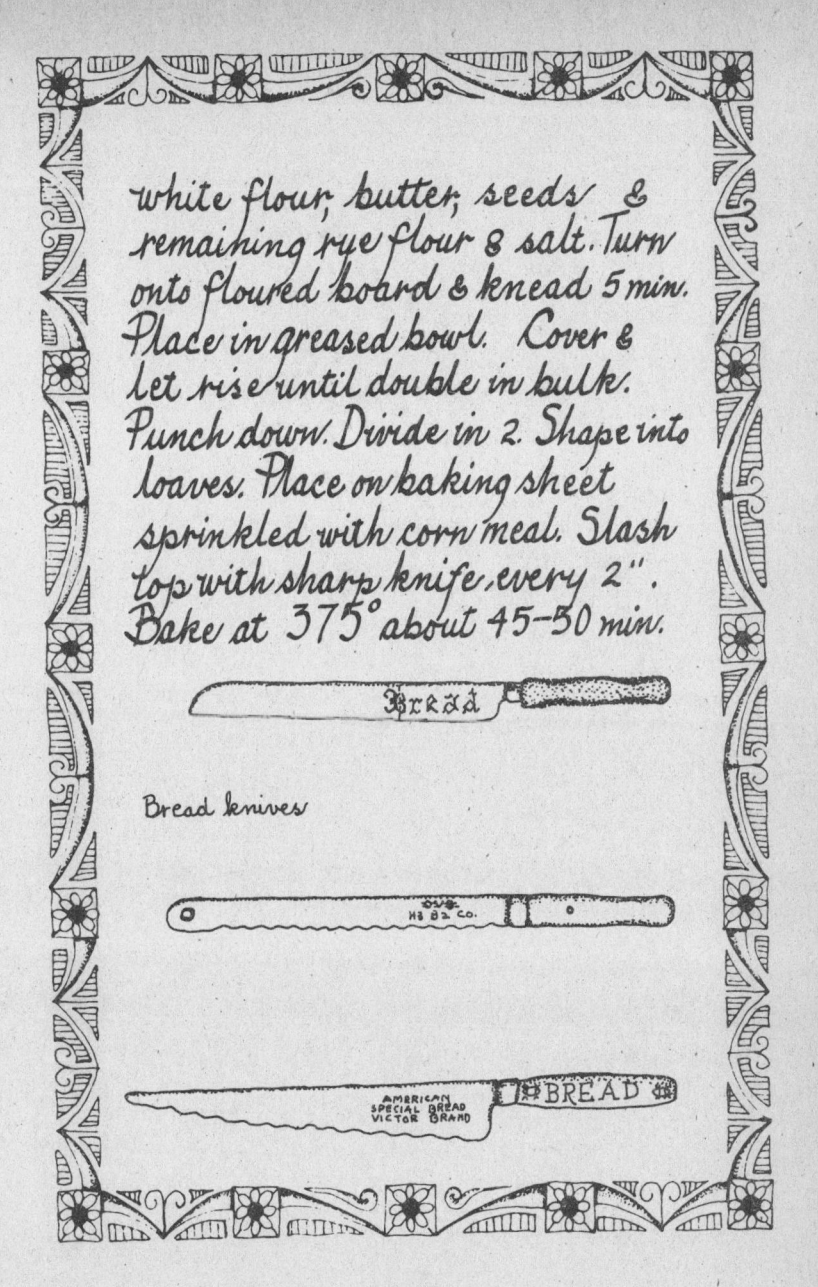

white flour, butter, seeds &
remaining rye flour & salt. Turn
onto floured board & knead 5 min.
Place in greased bowl. Cover &
let rise until double in bulk.
Punch down. Divide in 2. Shape into
loaves. Place on baking sheet
sprinkled with corn meal. Slash
top with sharp knife, every 2".
Bake at 375° about 45-50 min.

Bread knives

Wheat Germ Bread
2 loaves

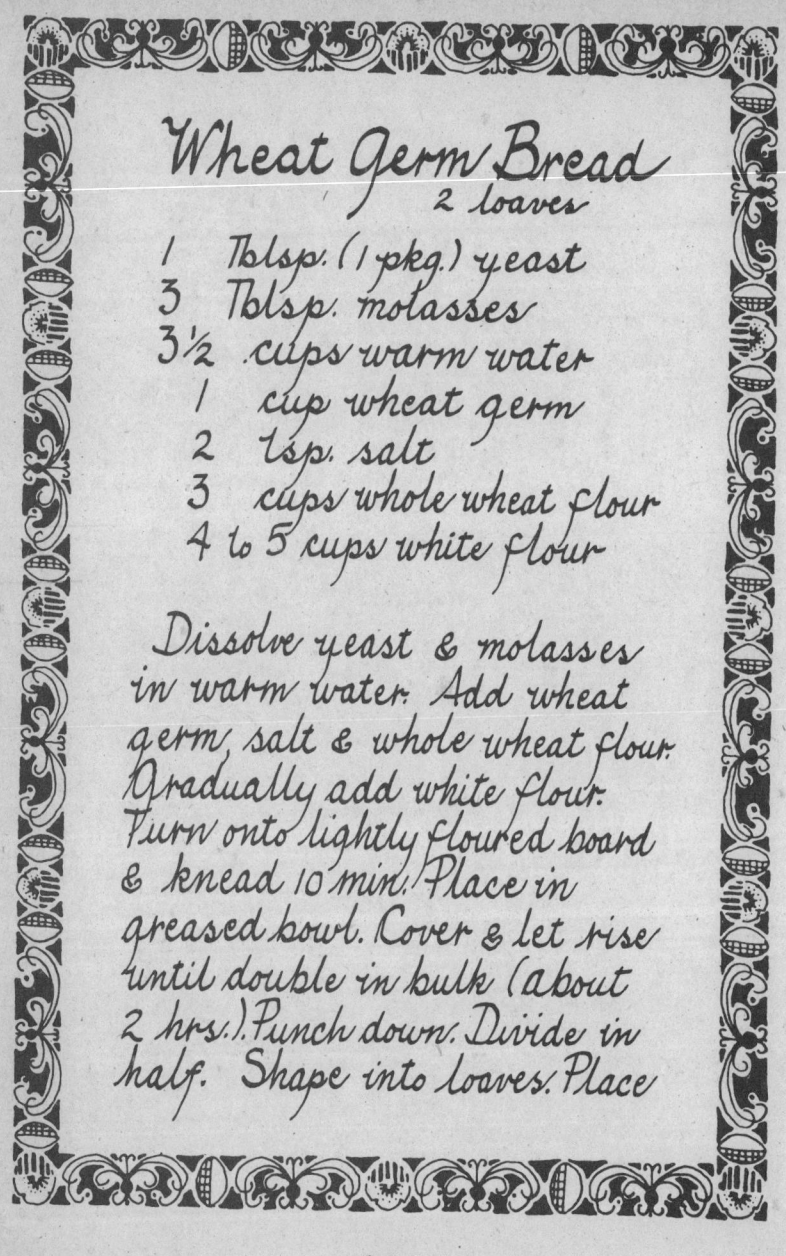

1 Tblsp. (1 pkg.) yeast
3 Tblsp. molasses
3½ cups warm water
1 cup wheat germ
2 tsp. salt
3 cups whole wheat flour
4 to 5 cups white flour

Dissolve yeast & molasses in warm water. Add wheat germ, salt & whole wheat flour. Gradually add white flour. Turn onto lightly floured board & knead 10 min. Place in greased bowl. Cover & let rise until double in bulk (about 2 hrs.). Punch down. Divide in half. Shape into loaves. Place

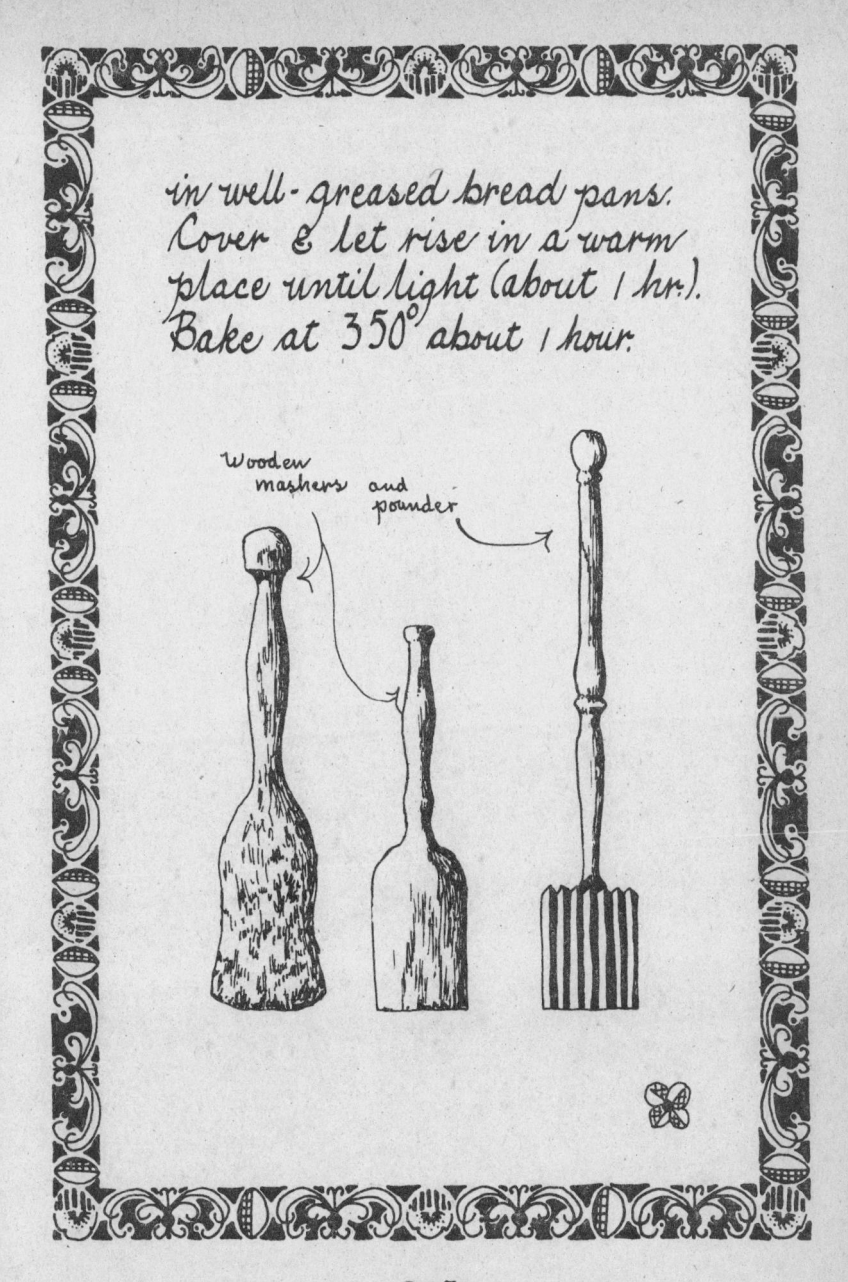

in well-greased bread pans.
Cover & let rise in a warm
place until light (about 1 hr.).
Bake at 350° about 1 hour.

Wooden mashers and pounder

Yogurt Bread
2 large loaves

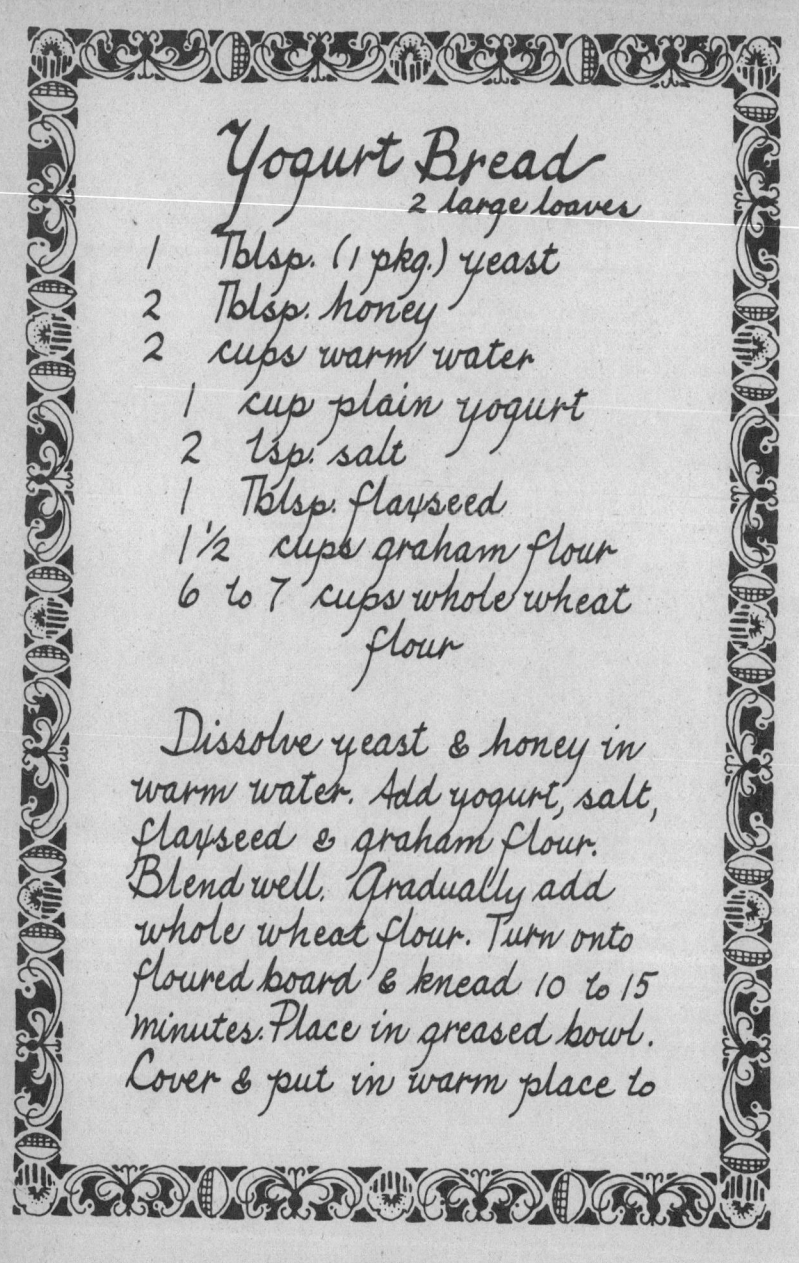

- 1 Tblsp. (1 pkg.) yeast
- 2 Tblsp. honey
- 2 cups warm water
- 1 cup plain yogurt
- 2 tsp. salt
- 1 Tblsp. flaxseed
- 1½ cups graham flour
- 6 to 7 cups whole wheat flour

Dissolve yeast & honey in warm water. Add yogurt, salt, flaxseed & graham flour. Blend well. Gradually add whole wheat flour. Turn onto floured board & knead 10 to 15 minutes. Place in greased bowl. Cover & put in warm place to rise until double in bulk (about 2-2½ hrs.). Punch down. Divide in half. Shape into loaves. Place in greased bread pans. Cover & let rise in warm place until light (about 1½ hrs.). Bake at 375° about 50-60 min.

U.S. Army World War II

Coffee pot tin-copper bottom

Quick Breads

Hints: Quick Breads

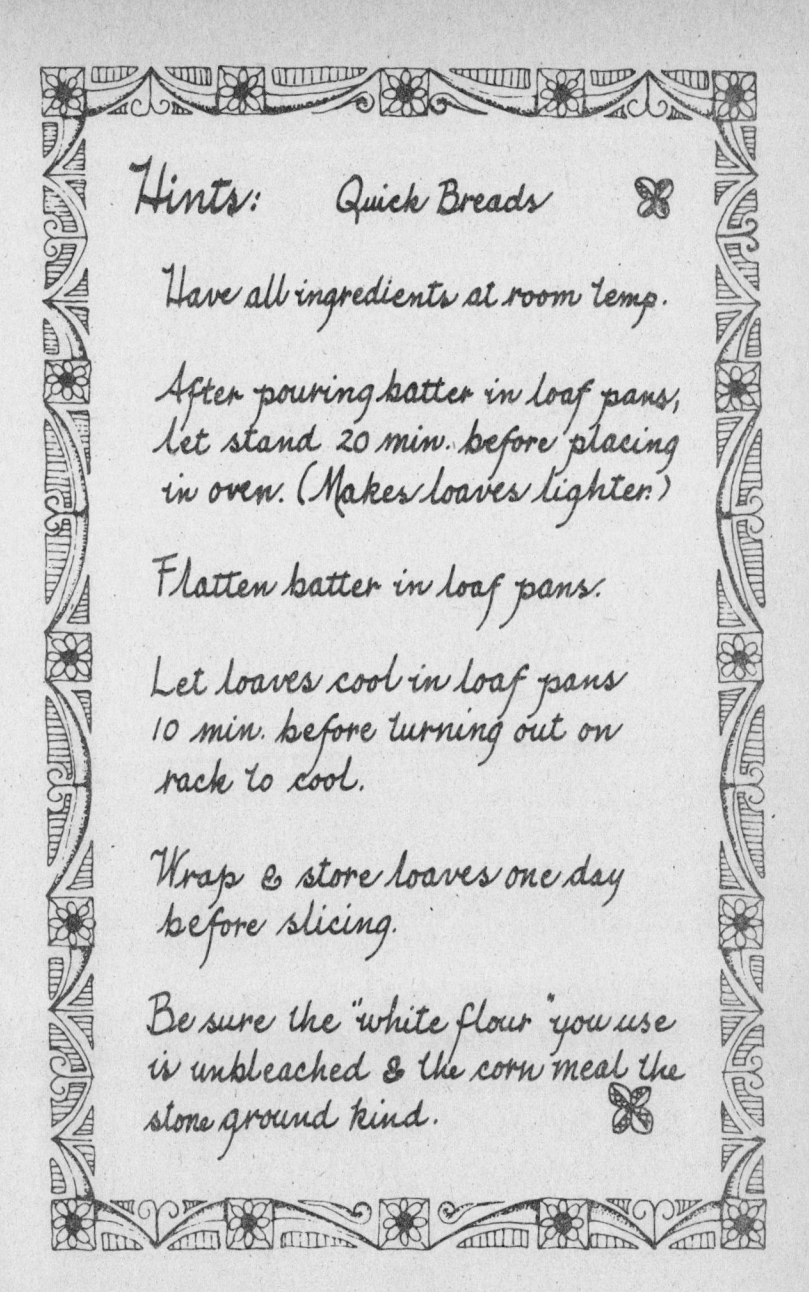

Have all ingredients at room temp.

After pouring batter in loaf pans, let stand 20 min. before placing in oven. (Makes loaves lighter.)

Flatten batter in loaf pans.

Let loaves cool in loaf pans 10 min. before turning out on rack to cool.

Wrap & store loaves one day before slicing.

Be sure the "white flour" you use is unbleached & the corn meal the stone ground kind.

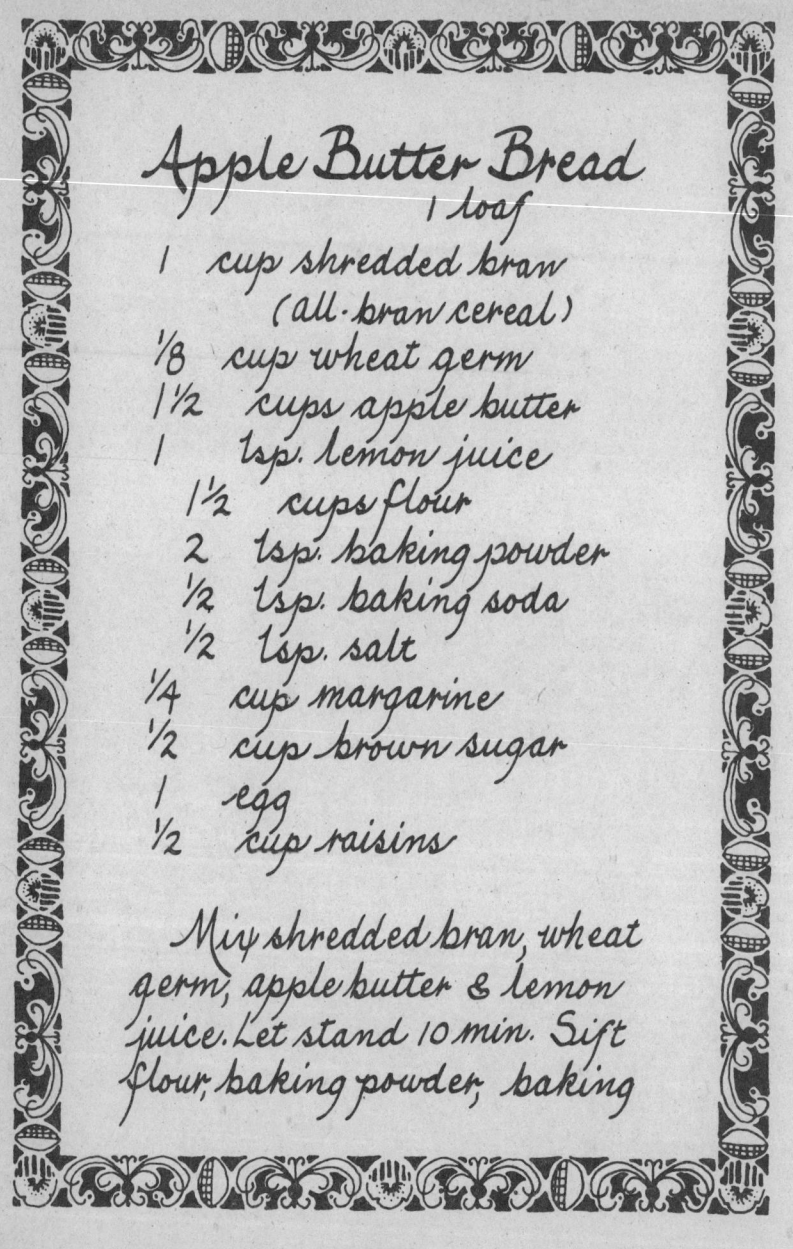

Apple Butter Bread
1 loaf

- 1 cup shredded bran (all-bran cereal)
- 1/8 cup wheat germ
- 1 1/2 cups apple butter
- 1 tsp. lemon juice
- 1 1/2 cups flour
- 2 tsp. baking powder
- 1/2 tsp. baking soda
- 1/2 tsp. salt
- 1/4 cup margarine
- 1/2 cup brown sugar
- 1 egg
- 1/2 cup raisins

Mix shredded bran, wheat germ, apple butter & lemon juice. Let stand 10 min. Sift flour, baking powder, baking soda & salt. Cream margarine & brown sugar. Beat in egg. Add bran mixture & raisins. Gradually add dry ingredients. Blend well. Pour into well-greased 9"x 5"x 3" loaf pan. Bake at 350° for one hour or until tested done.

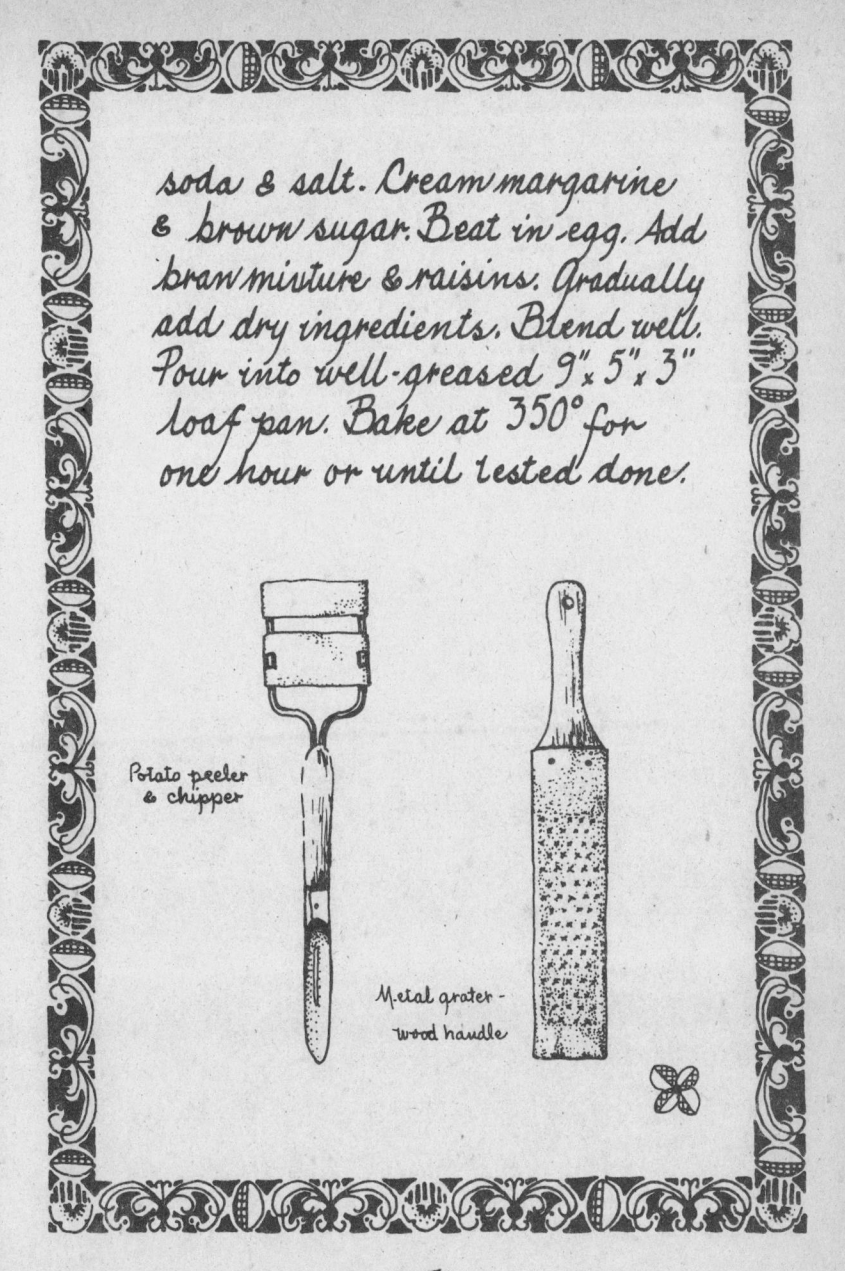

Potato peeler & chipper

Metal grater - wood handle

Baking Powder Bread
1 loaf

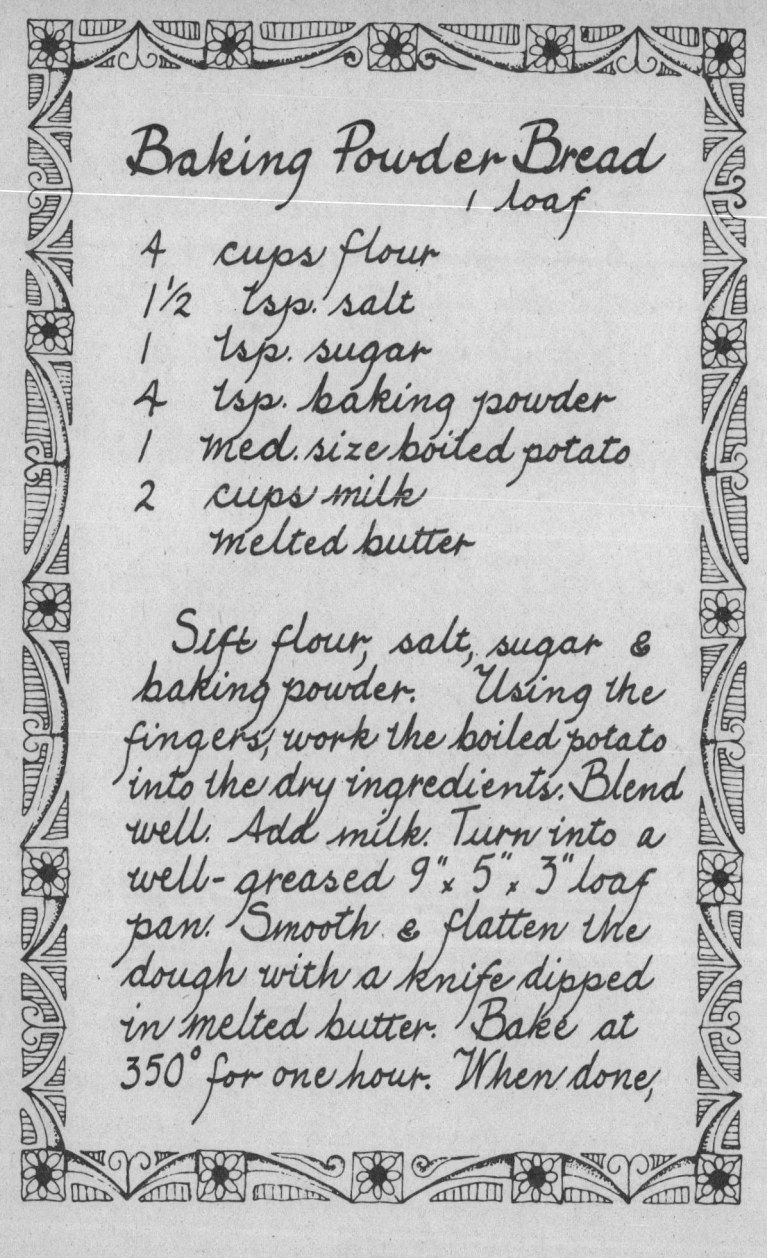

- 4 cups flour
- 1½ tsp. salt
- 1 tsp. sugar
- 4 tsp. baking powder
- 1 med. size boiled potato
- 2 cups milk
- melted butter

Sift flour, salt, sugar & baking powder. Using the fingers, work the boiled potato into the dry ingredients. Blend well. Add milk. Turn into a well-greased 9" x 5" x 3" loaf pan. Smooth & flatten the dough with a knife dipped in melted butter. Bake at 350° for one hour. When done, moisten crust a little with water & wrap in a clean cloth. Cool. Slices best the next day. (This bread is especially delicious toasted & spread with butter and/or orange marmalade.)

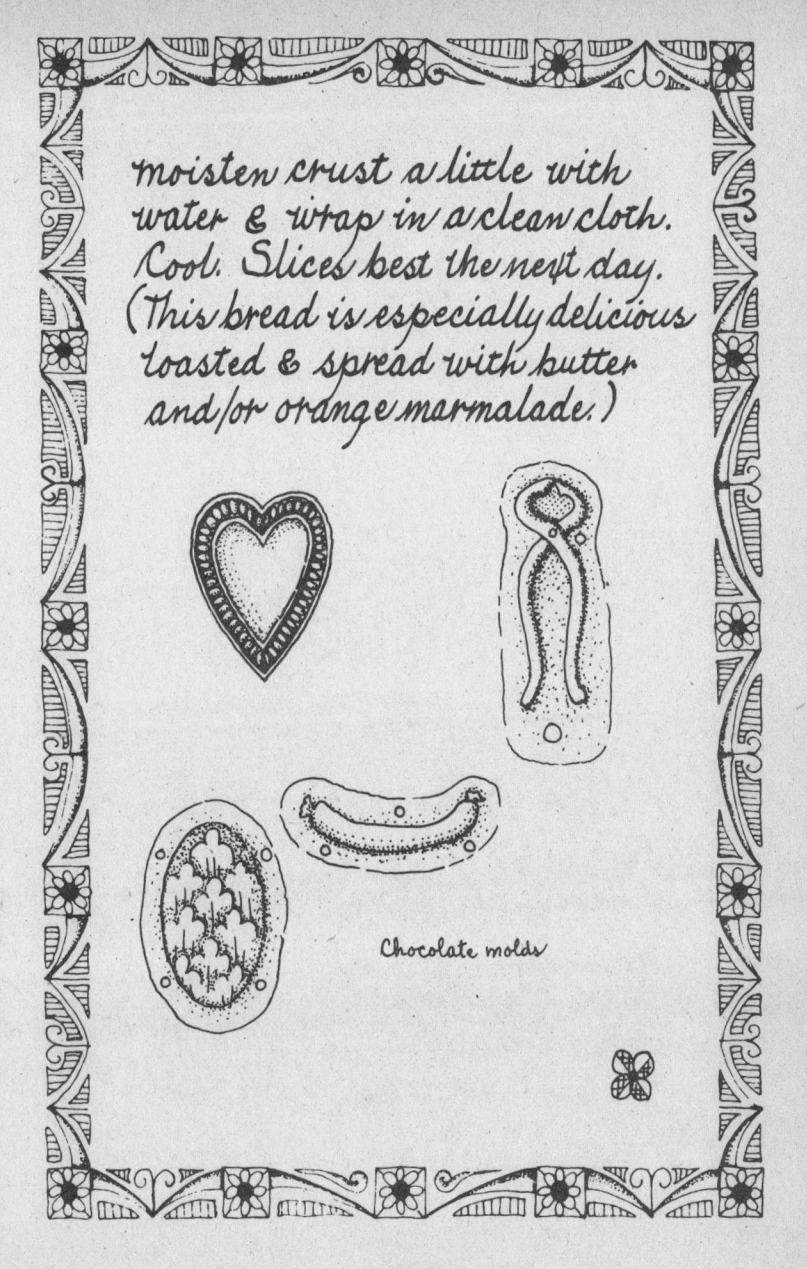

Chocolate molds

Banana Nut Bread
1 loaf

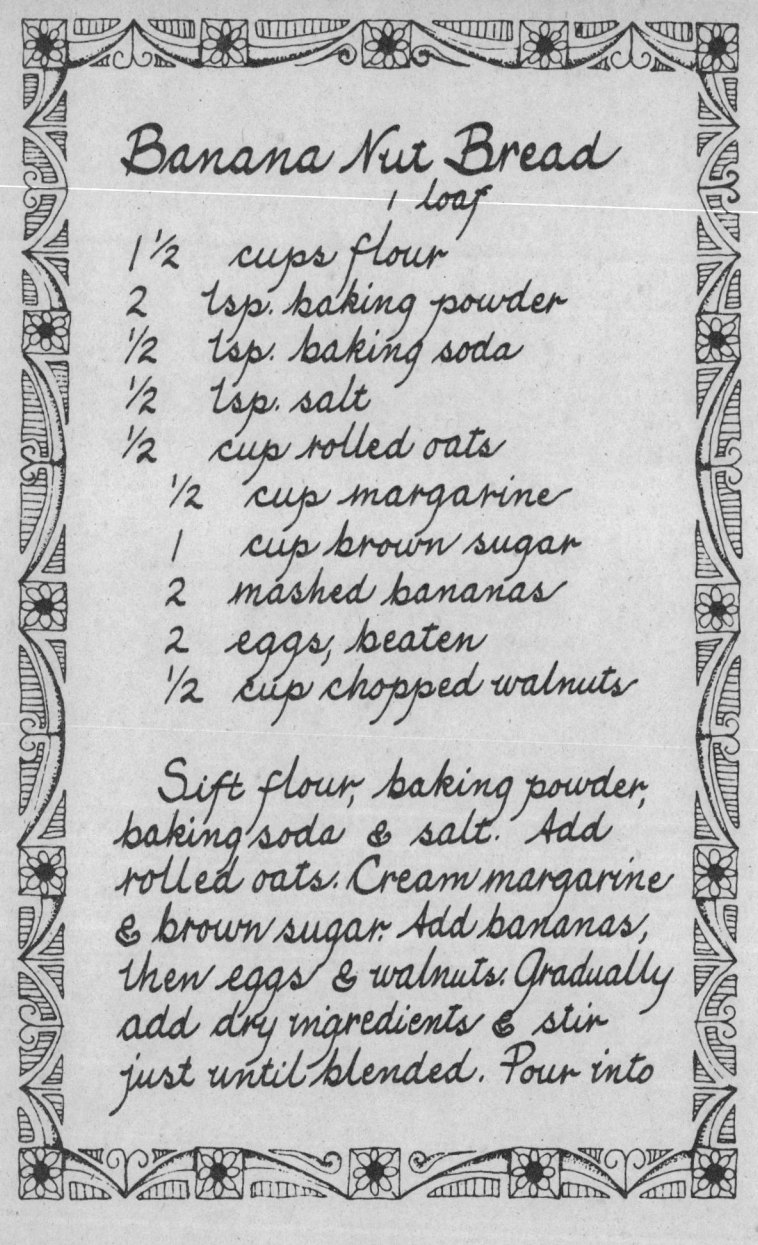

- 1½ cups flour
- 2 tsp. baking powder
- ½ tsp. baking soda
- ½ tsp. salt
- ½ cup rolled oats
- ½ cup margarine
- 1 cup brown sugar
- 2 mashed bananas
- 2 eggs, beaten
- ½ cup chopped walnuts

Sift flour, baking powder, baking soda & salt. Add rolled oats. Cream margarine & brown sugar. Add bananas, then eggs & walnuts. Gradually add dry ingredients & stir just until blended. Pour into well-greased 9"x 5"x 3" loaf pan. Bake at 350° one hour or until tested done.

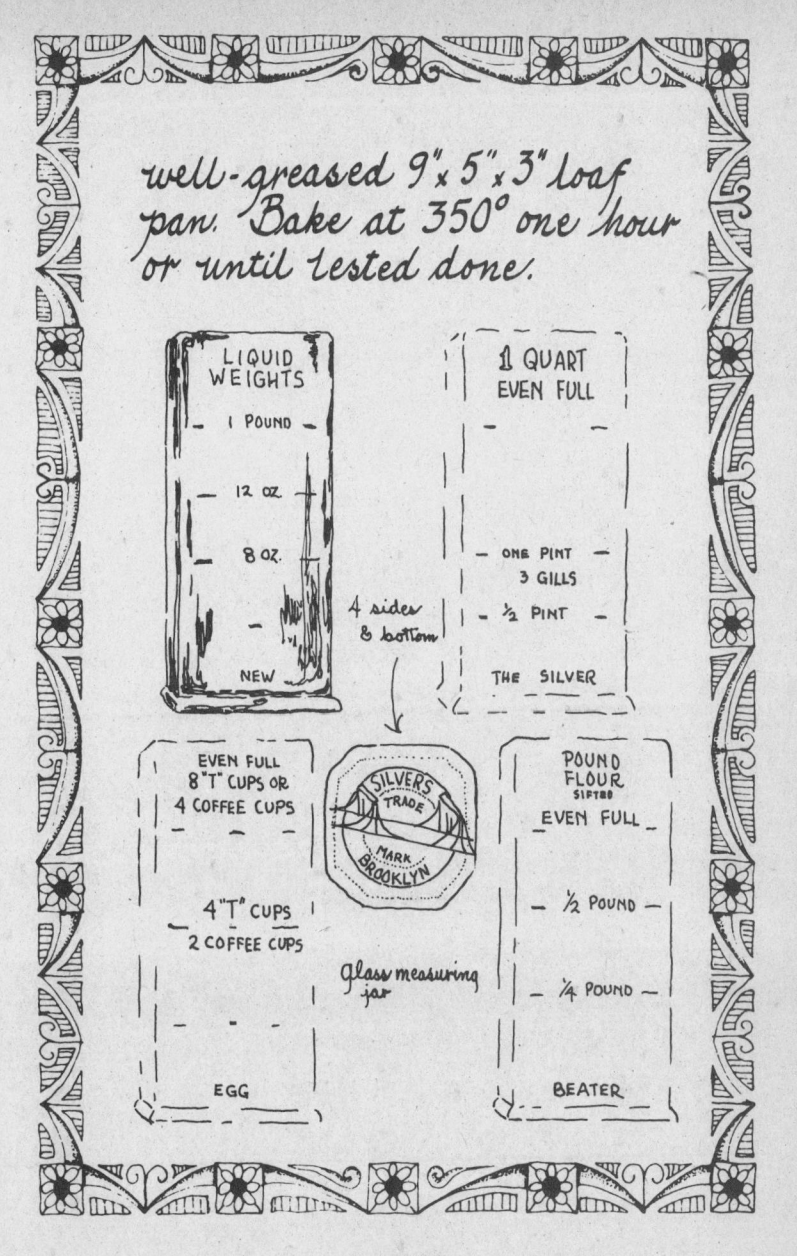

LIQUID WEIGHTS
- 1 POUND
- 12 OZ
- 8 OZ
NEW

4 sides & bottom

1 QUART EVEN FULL
- ONE PINT
- 3 GILLS
- ½ PINT

THE SILVER

EVEN FULL
8 "T" CUPS OR
4 COFFEE CUPS

4 "T" CUPS
2 COFFEE CUPS

EGG

SILVERS TRADE MARK BROOKLYN

glass measuring jar

POUND FLOUR SIFTED
EVEN FULL
- ½ POUND
- ¼ POUND

BEATER

Blackberry Jam Bread
1 loaf

2 cups flour
½ tsp. salt
1 tsp. baking powder
1 tsp. cinnamon
1 tsp. nutmeg
1 cup sugar
¾ cup shortening
3 eggs, separated
1 cup blackberry jam
½ cup sour milk
1 tsp. baking soda

Sift flour, salt, baking powder, cinnamon & nutmeg. Cream sugar & shortening. Beat in egg yolks, then blackberry jam. Mix sour milk with baking soda & add to batter

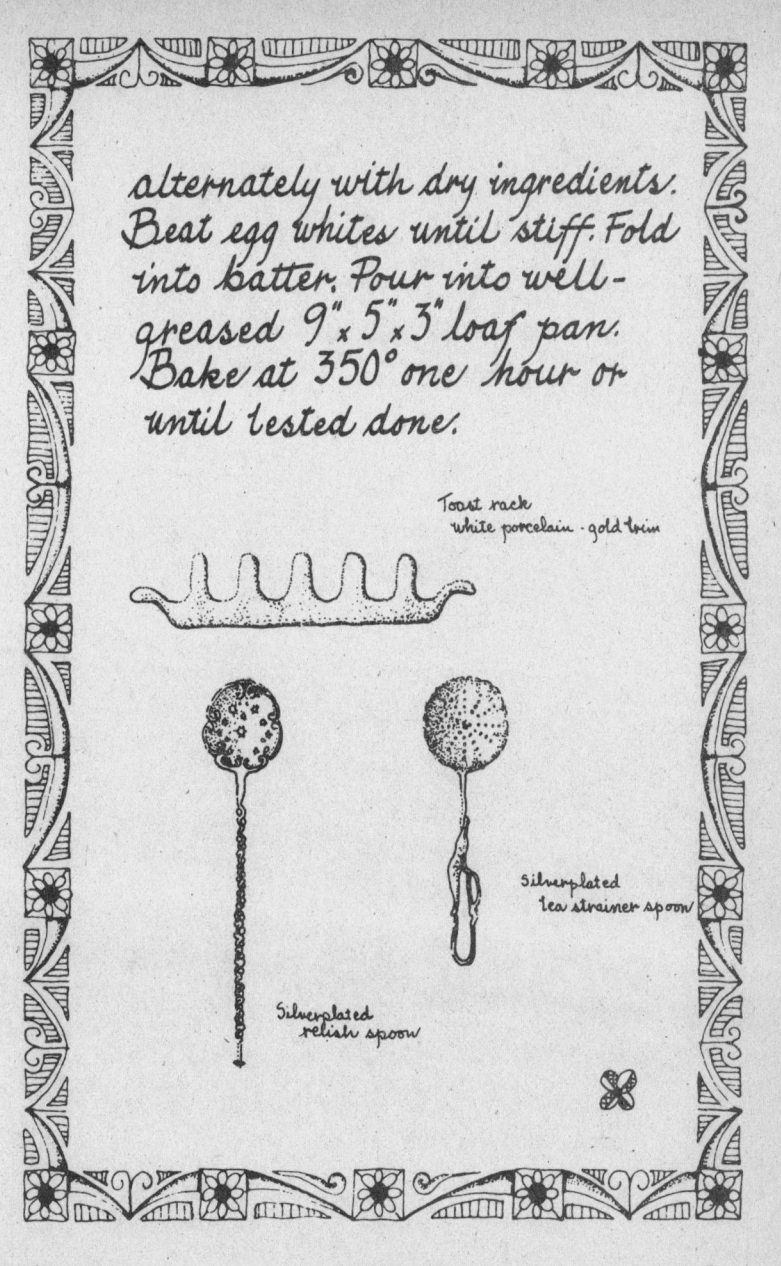

alternately with dry ingredients.
Beat egg whites until stiff. Fold
into batter. Pour into well-
greased 9" x 5" x 3" loaf pan.
Bake at 350° one hour or
until tested done.

Toast rack
white porcelain - gold trim

Silverplated
tea strainer spoon

Silverplated
relish spoon

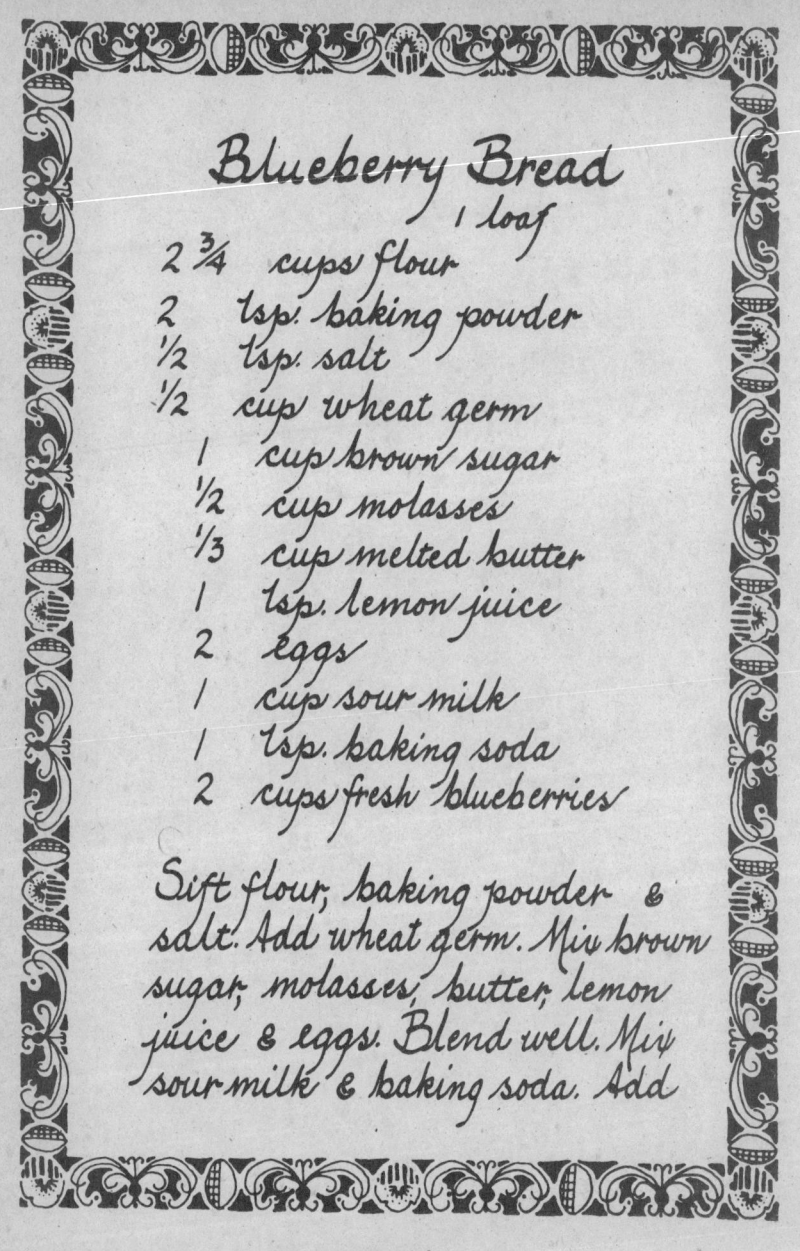

Blueberry Bread
1 loaf

- 2¾ cups flour
- 2 tsp. baking powder
- ½ tsp. salt
- ½ cup wheat germ
- 1 cup brown sugar
- ½ cup molasses
- ⅓ cup melted butter
- 1 tsp. lemon juice
- 2 eggs
- 1 cup sour milk
- 1 tsp. baking soda
- 2 cups fresh blueberries

Sift flour, baking powder & salt. Add wheat germ. Mix brown sugar, molasses, butter, lemon juice & eggs. Blend well. Mix sour milk & baking soda. Add to brown sugar mixture alternately with dry ingredients. Add blueberries, stirring only enough to blend. Pour into well-greased 9" x 5" x 3" loaf pan. Bake at 350° about one hour or until tested done.

Silver-plated cream pitcher

Bran Bread

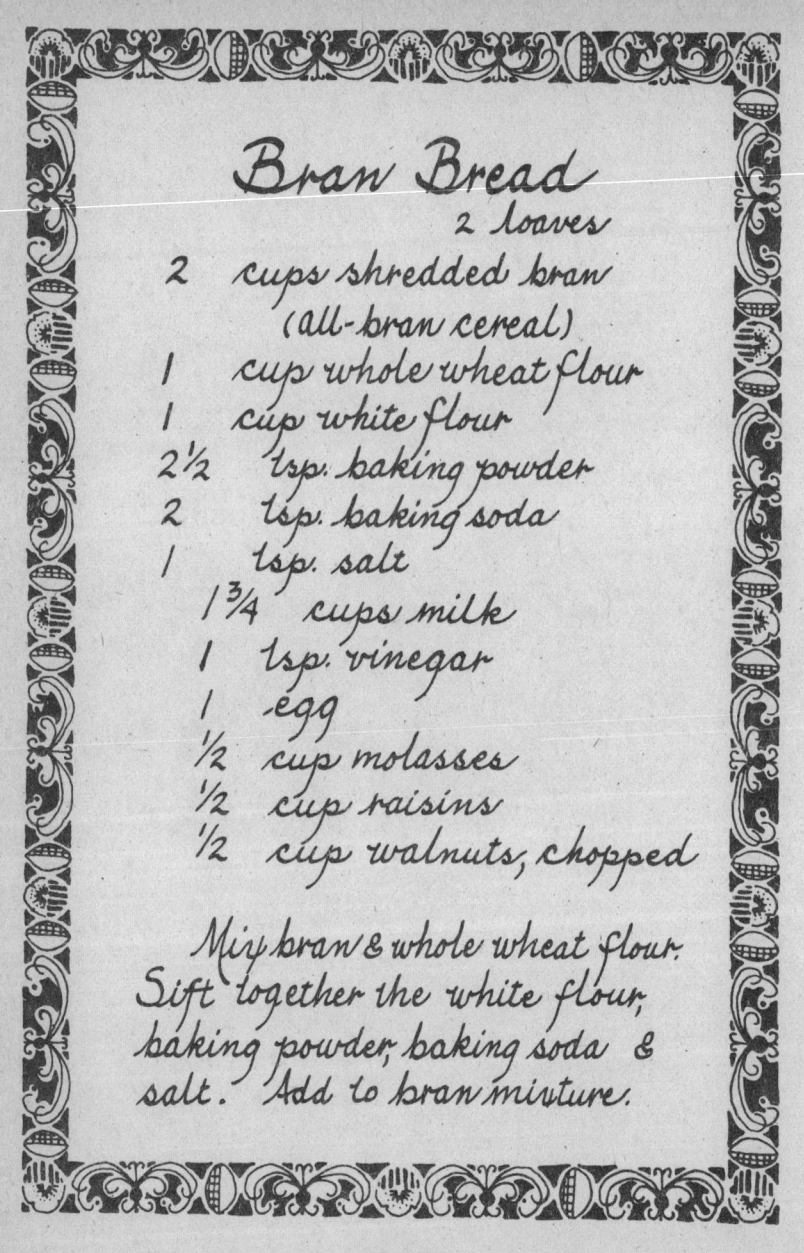

2 loaves

2	cups shredded bran (all-bran cereal)
1	cup whole wheat flour
1	cup white flour
2½	tsp. baking powder
2	tsp. baking soda
1	tsp. salt
1¾	cups milk
1	tsp. vinegar
1	egg
½	cup molasses
½	cup raisins
½	cup walnuts, chopped

Mix bran & whole wheat flour. Sift together the white flour, baking powder, baking soda & salt. Add to bran mixture.

Combine milk & vinegar. Add egg & molasses. Stir into flour mixture. Add raisins & walnuts. Mix only enough to blend. Pour into 2 well-greased loaf pans, 9" x 5" x 3". Bake at 350° for one hour or until done.

Silver-plated crumb tray

Candied Fruit Bread
1 loaf

- 2½ cups flour
- 1 tsp. ground ginger
- 1 tsp. cinnamon
- ½ tsp. baking powder
- ¾ cup molasses
- ½ cup brown sugar
- 1 tsp. baking soda
- 1 egg
- ⅓ cup milk
- ⅔ cup raisins
- ⅓ cup chopped candied fruit (fruit cake mix)

Sift together the flour, ginger, cinnamon & baking powder. Heat the molasses slightly. Add brown sugar, baking soda, egg & milk. Gradually add sifted dry ingredients, then raisins & chopped candied fruit. Blend well. Pour into well-greased 9"x 5"x 3" loaf pan. Bake at 300° for 1½ hours or until done.

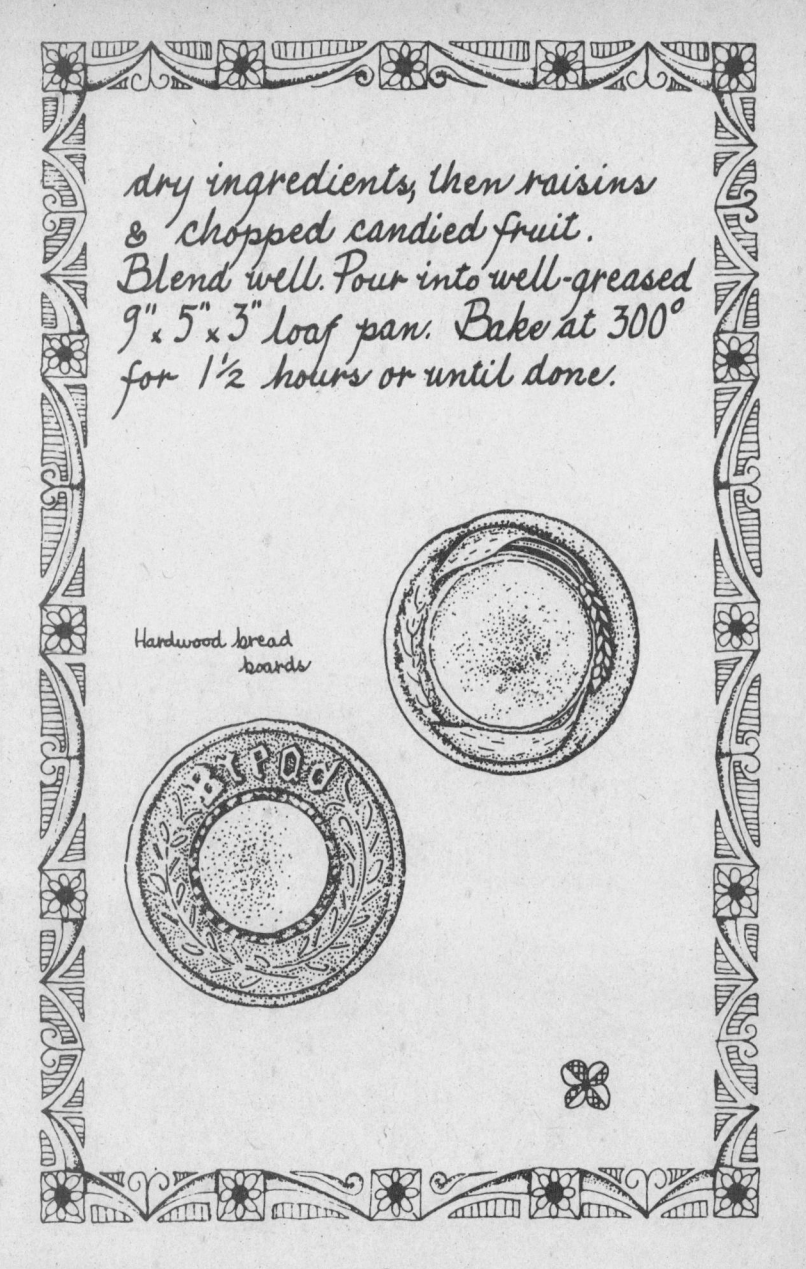

Hardwood bread boards

Carrot Bread
1 loaf

- 2 cups flour
- 3 tsp. baking powder
- ½ tsp. baking soda
- 1 tsp. salt
- ⅓ cup margarine
- ½ cup brown sugar
- 1 egg, beaten
- 1½ cups mashed cooked carrots
- ½ cup corn meal
- ¼ cup orange marmalade
- ½ cup raisins
- ½ cup orange juice
- 1 tsp. lemon juice

Sift together the flour, baking powder, baking soda & salt. Cream the margarine

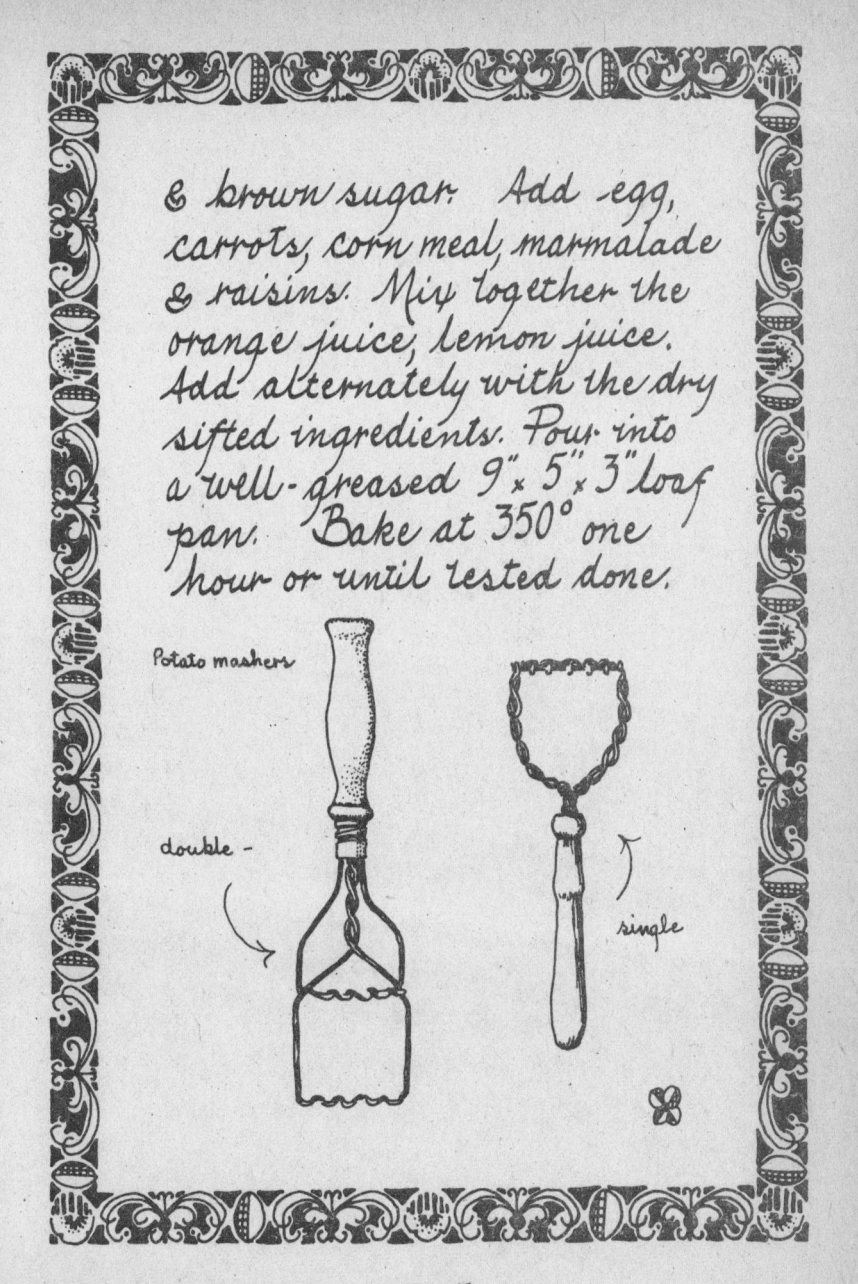

& brown sugar. Add egg, carrots, corn meal, marmalade & raisins. Mix together the orange juice, lemon juice. Add alternately with the dry sifted ingredients. Pour into a well-greased 9" x 5" x 3" loaf pan. Bake at 350° one hour or until tested done.

Potato mashers

double —

single

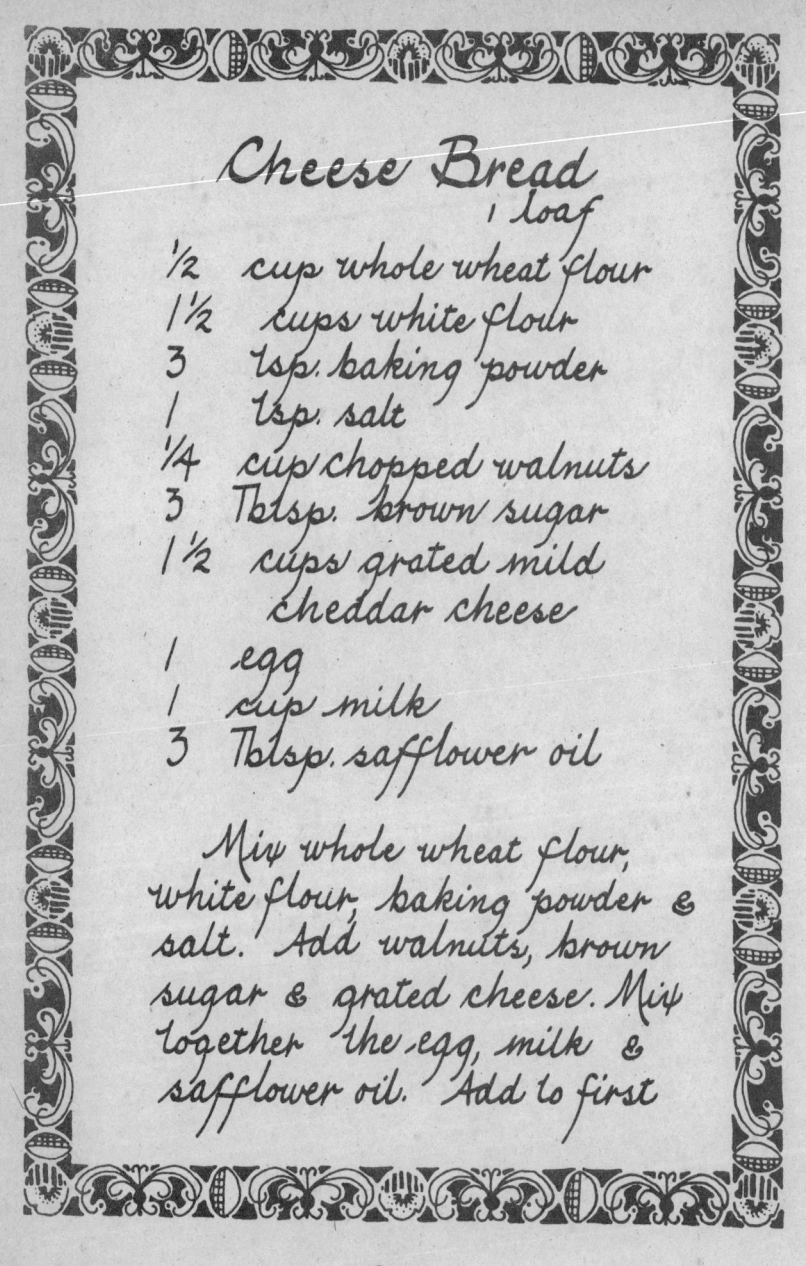

Cheese Bread
1 loaf

- ½ cup whole wheat flour
- 1½ cups white flour
- 3 tsp. baking powder
- 1 tsp. salt
- ¼ cup chopped walnuts
- 3 Tbsp. brown sugar
- 1½ cups grated mild cheddar cheese
- 1 egg
- 1 cup milk
- 3 Tbsp. safflower oil

Mix whole wheat flour, white flour, baking powder & salt. Add walnuts, brown sugar & grated cheese. Mix together the egg, milk & safflower oil. Add to first mixture. Stir until just blended. Pour into well-greased 9" x 5" x 3" loaf pan. Bake at 350° about one hour or until tested done.

grater - all metal

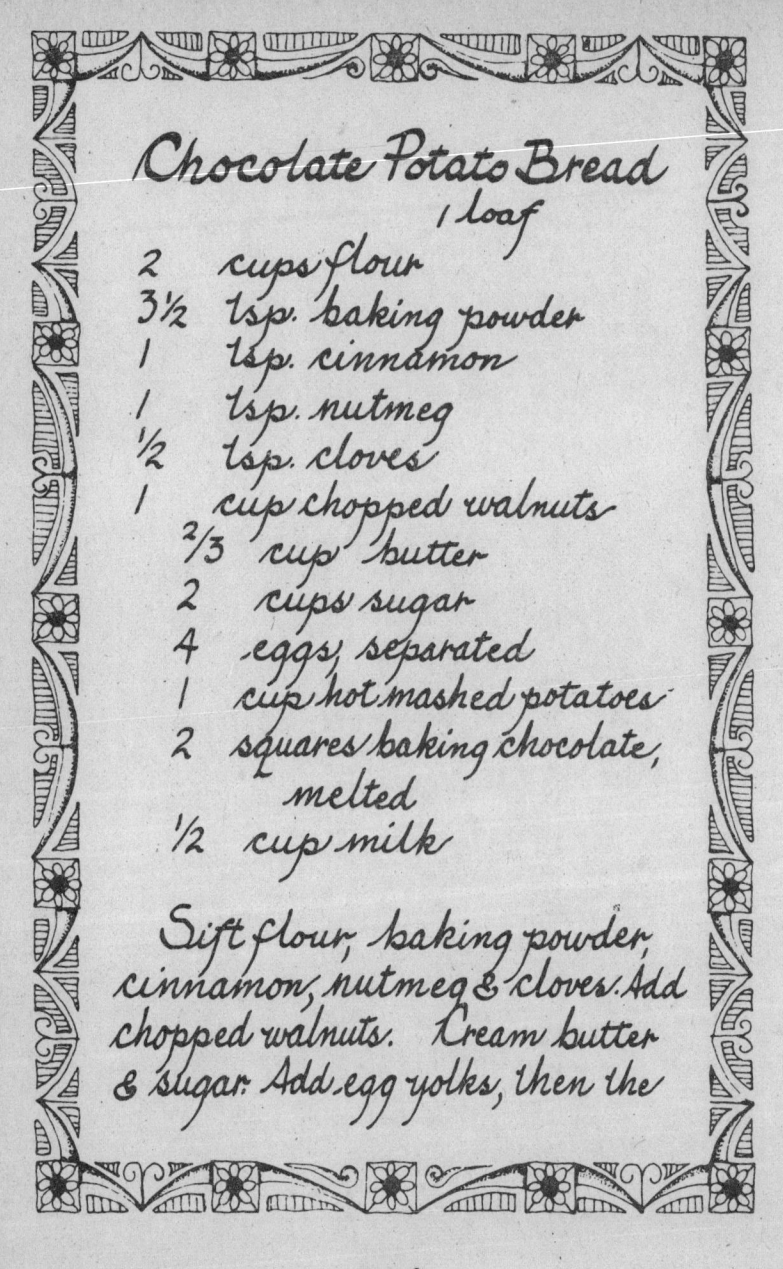

Chocolate Potato Bread
1 loaf

- 2 cups flour
- 3½ tsp. baking powder
- 1 tsp. cinnamon
- 1 tsp. nutmeg
- ½ tsp. cloves
- 1 cup chopped walnuts
- ⅔ cup butter
- 2 cups sugar
- 4 eggs, separated
- 1 cup hot mashed potatoes
- 2 squares baking chocolate, melted
- ½ cup milk

Sift flour, baking powder, cinnamon, nutmeg & cloves. Add chopped walnuts. Cream butter & sugar. Add egg yolks, then the mashed potatoes & melted chocolate. Beat well. Add milk alternately with dry ingredients. Whip egg whites until stiff. Fold into batter. Pour into well-greased 9"x 5"x 3" loaf pan. Bake at 350° about one hour, or until done.

Potato mashers - metal with wooden handles

Coarse Bread
2 loaves

- ½ cup corn meal
- 2 cups graham flour
- 1½ cups white flour
- 3 tsp. baking powder
- ½ tsp. salt
- 2 Tblsp. flaxseed
- 2 Tblsp. poppyseeds
- ¼ cup wheat germ
- ⅔ cup brown sugar
- ¼ cup walnuts, chopped
- ½ cup raisins
- 2 cups sour milk
- 2 tsp. baking soda
- 1 egg

Mix corn meal, graham flour, white flour, baking powder, salt, flaxseed, poppyseeds, wheat germ, brown sugar, walnuts & raisins. Combine the sour milk, baking soda & egg. Add to first mixture & stir just until blended. Pour into two well-greased 8½" x 4½" x 2½" loaf pans. Bake at 325° about 1¼ hours or until done. (This bread is especially good when sliced & spread with butter.)

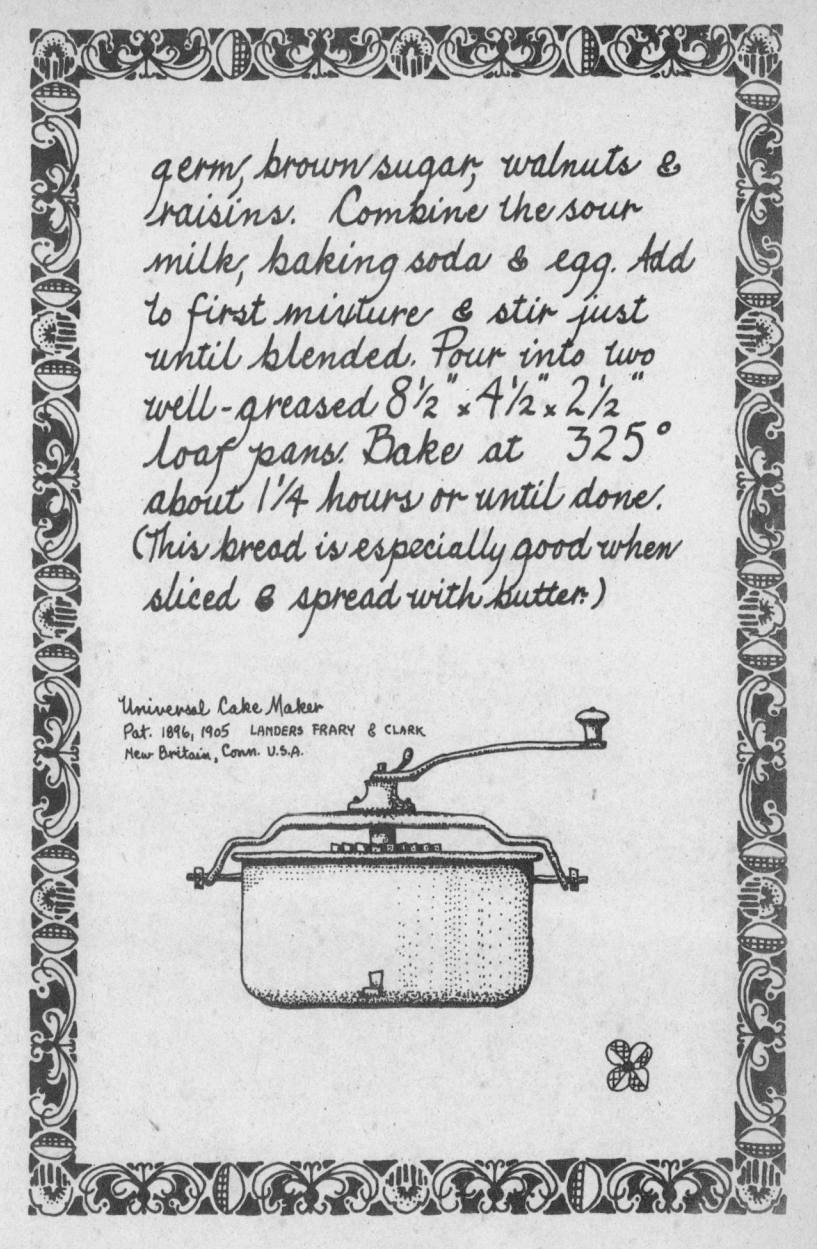

Universal Cake Maker
Pat. 1896, 1905 LANDERS FRARY & CLARK
New Britain, Conn. U.S.A.

Coffee Bread
1 loaf

- 2 cups flour
- 1 tsp. baking soda
- 1/3 cup butter
- 1/2 cup sugar
- 1 egg
- 1/2 cup molasses
- 1/2 cup strong coffee
- 1/2 cup raisins
- 1/2 cup pitted prunes, (uncooked) cut fine

Sift flour & baking soda together. Cream butter & sugar. Add egg. Beat well. Add molasses, coffee, raisins & prunes. Gradually add dry ingredients, stirring just until blended. Pour into well-greased

9" x 5" x 3" loaf pan. Bake at 350° one hour or until done.

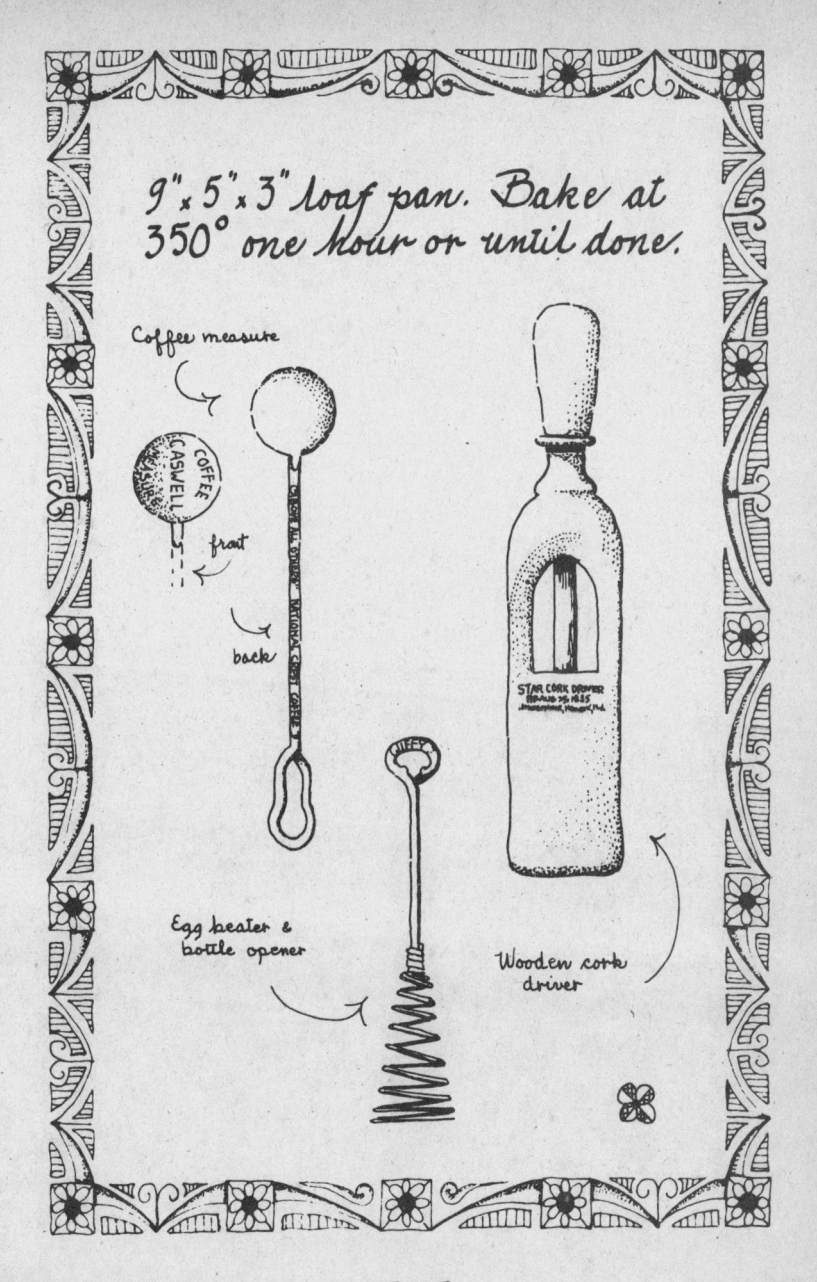

Coffee measure

front

back

Egg beater & bottle opener

Wooden cork driver

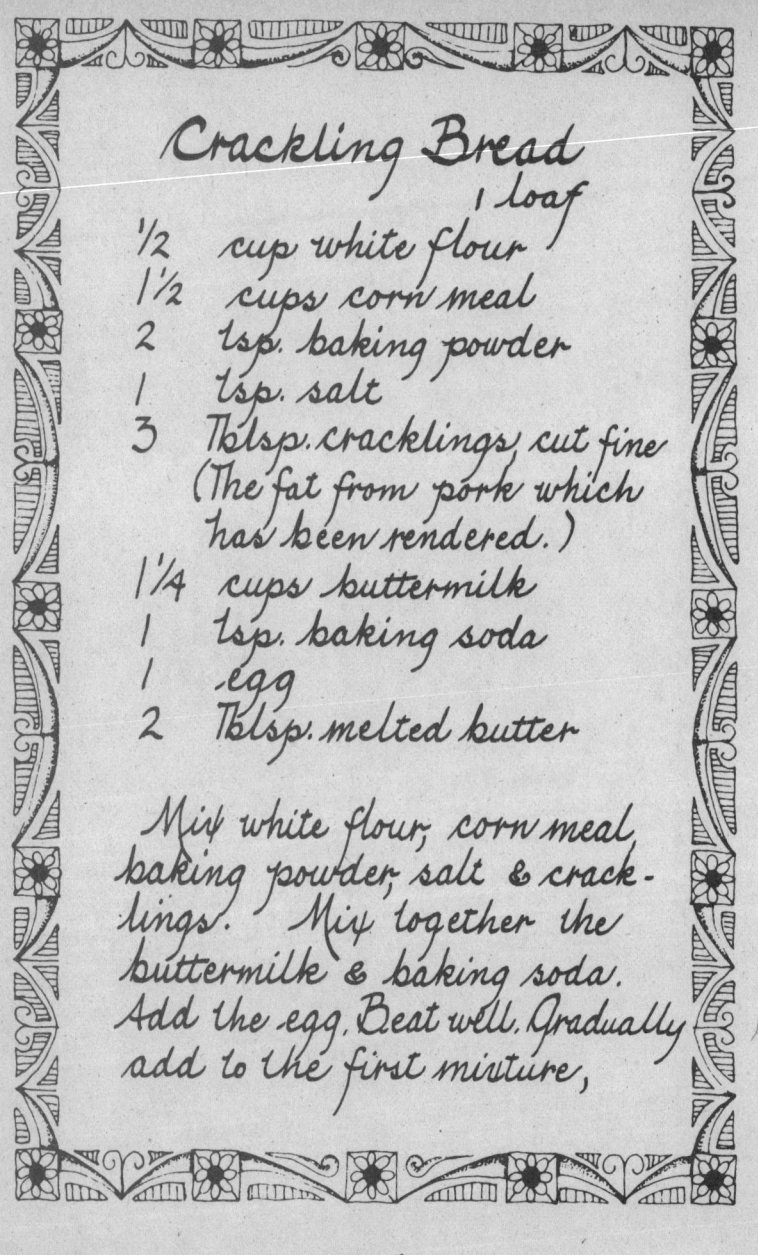

Crackling Bread
                    1 loaf

- 1/2 cup white flour
- 1 1/2 cups corn meal
- 2 tsp. baking powder
- 1 tsp. salt
- 3 Tblsp. cracklings, cut fine (The fat from pork which has been rendered.)
- 1 1/4 cups buttermilk
- 1 tsp. baking soda
- 1 egg
- 2 Tblsp. melted butter

Mix white flour, corn meal, baking powder, salt & cracklings. Mix together the buttermilk & baking soda. Add the egg. Beat well. Gradually add to the first mixture, stirring only until blended. Add the melted butter. Pour into a well-greased 8½" x 4½" x 2½" loaf pan. Bake at 400° about 30-40 minutes or until tested done.

Blue crockery pitcher

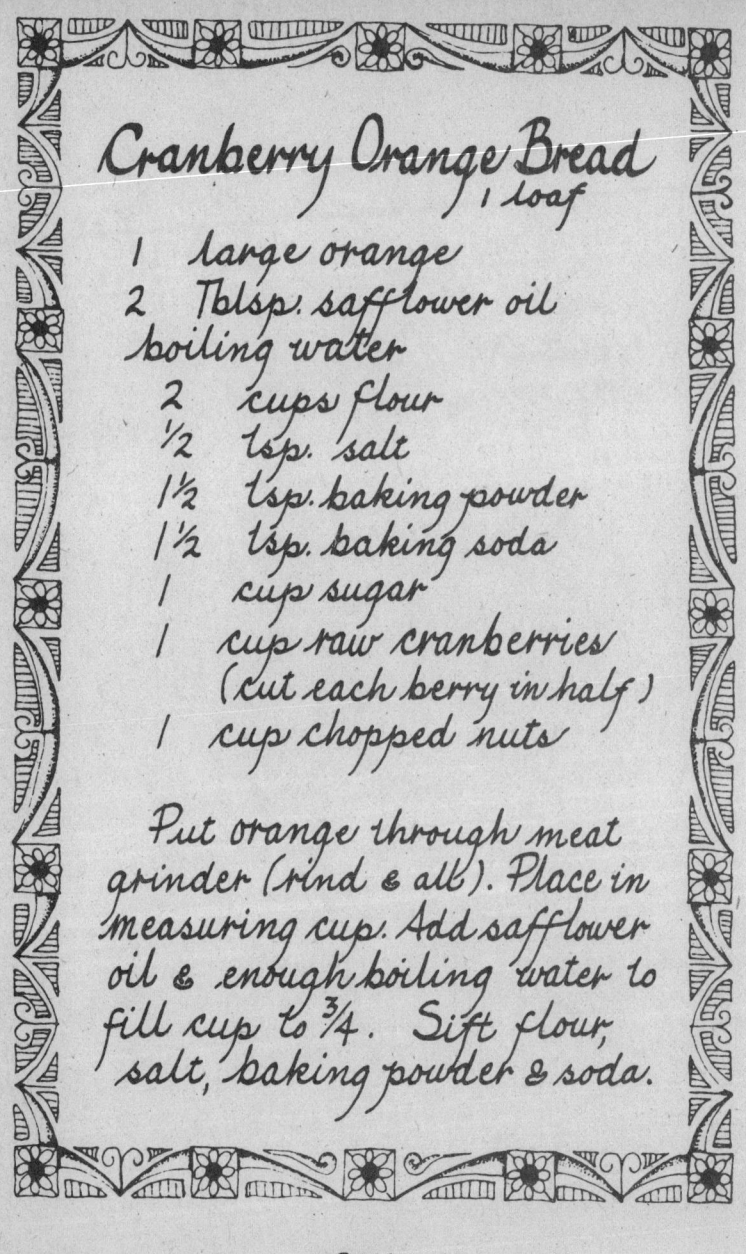

Cranberry Orange Bread
1 loaf

1 large orange
2 Tblsp. safflower oil
boiling water
2 cups flour
½ tsp. salt
1½ tsp. baking powder
1½ tsp. baking soda
1 cup sugar
1 cup raw cranberries
   (cut each berry in half)
1 cup chopped nuts

Put orange through meat grinder (rind & all). Place in measuring cup. Add safflower oil & enough boiling water to fill cup to ¾. Sift flour, salt, baking powder & soda.

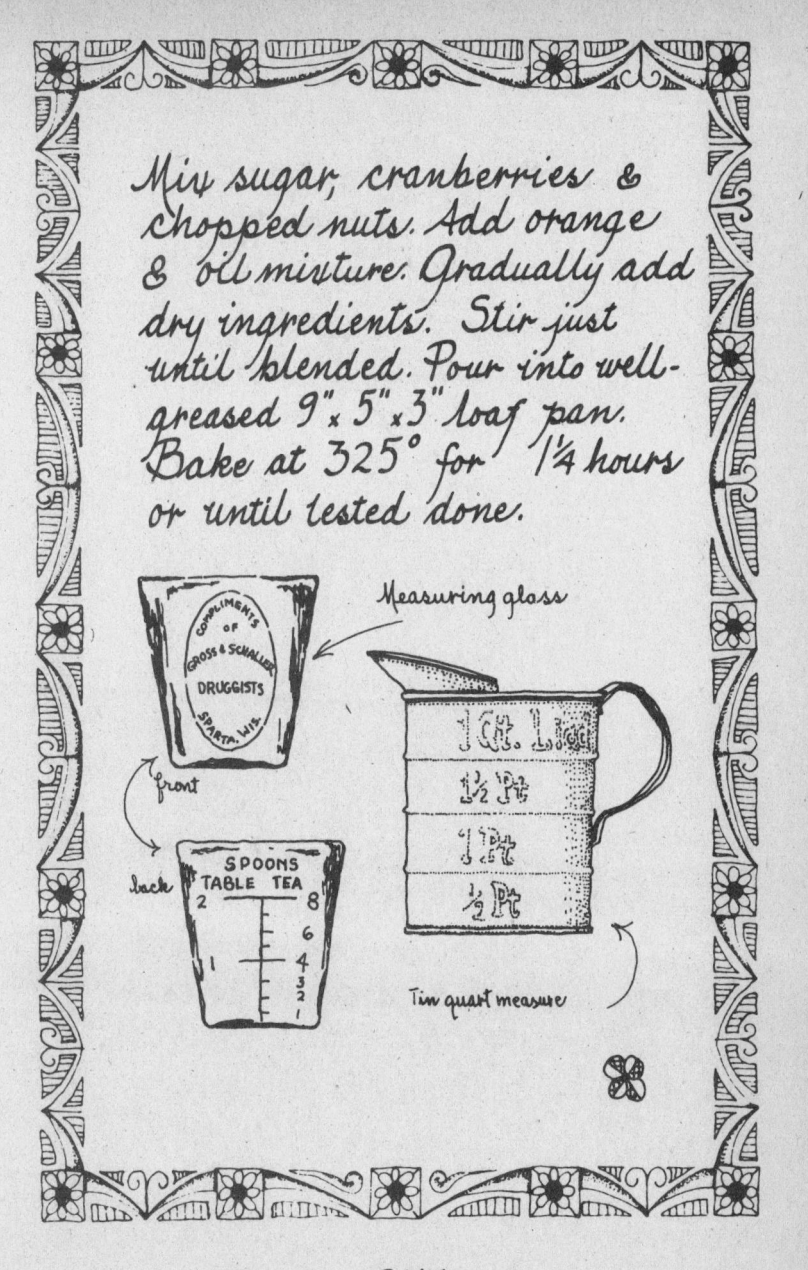

Mix sugar, cranberries & chopped nuts. Add orange & oil mixture. Gradually add dry ingredients. Stir just until blended. Pour into well-greased 9" x 5" x 3" loaf pan. Bake at 325° for 1¼ hours or until tested done.

Measuring glass

front / back

Tin quart measure

Fig Bread
2 loaves

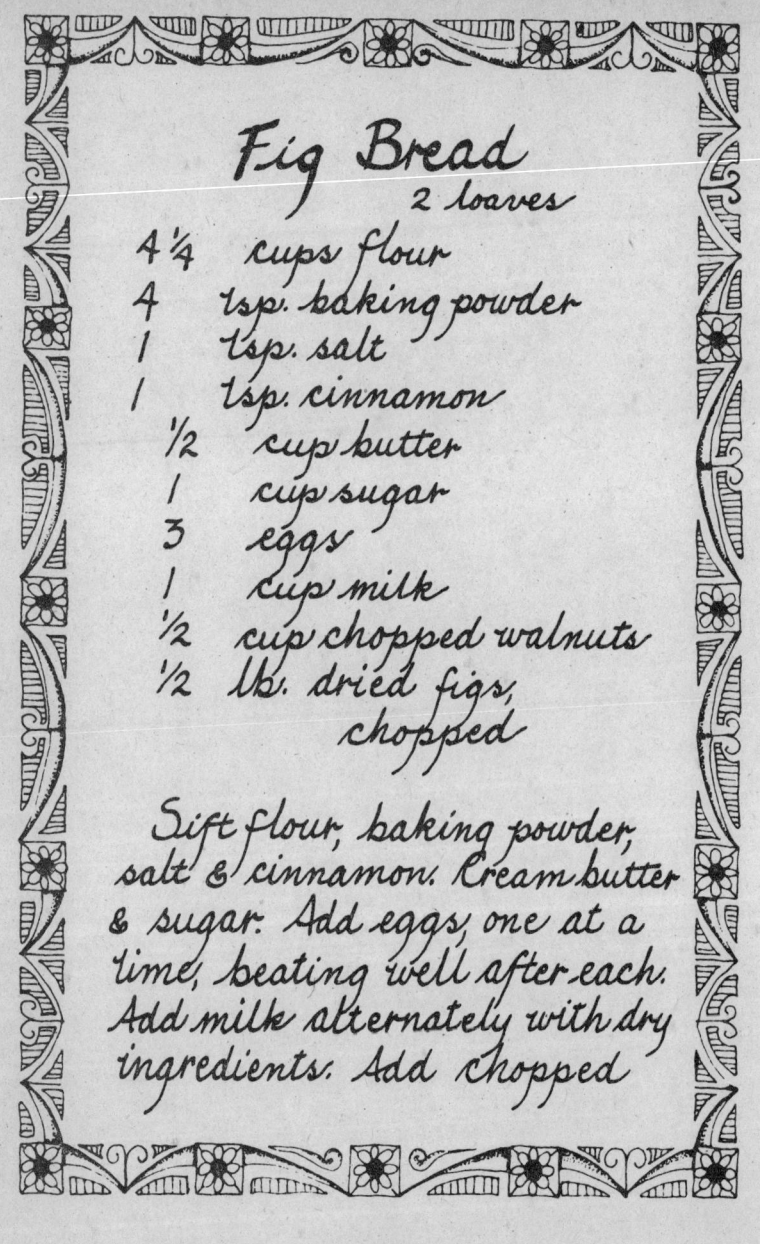

- 4 1/4 cups flour
- 4 tsp. baking powder
- 1 tsp. salt
- 1 tsp. cinnamon
- 1/2 cup butter
- 1 cup sugar
- 3 eggs
- 1 cup milk
- 1/2 cup chopped walnuts
- 1/2 lb. dried figs, chopped

Sift flour, baking powder, salt & cinnamon. Cream butter & sugar. Add eggs, one at a time, beating well after each. Add milk alternately with dry ingredients. Add chopped walnuts & figs. Stir only until blended. Pour into well-greased 9" x 5" x 3" loaf pans. Bake at 325° for 1¼ hours or until done.

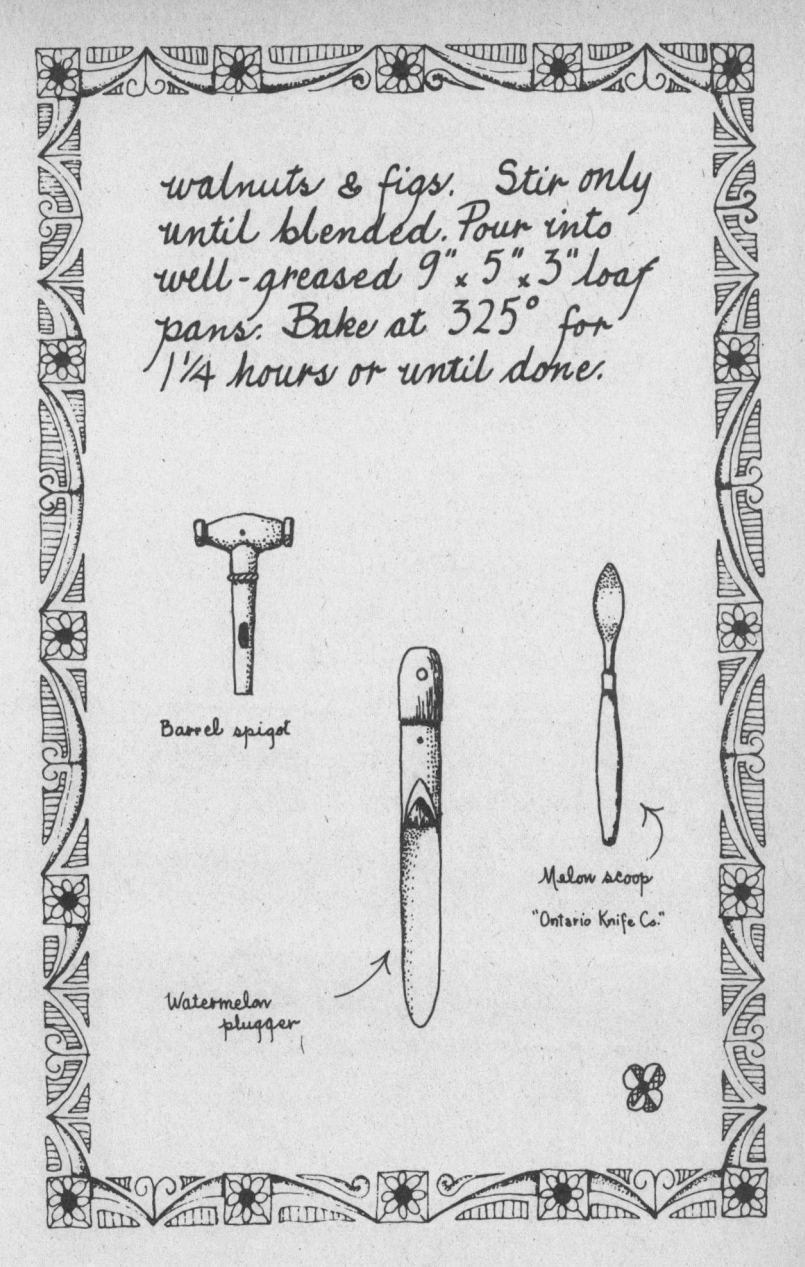

Barrel spigot

Watermelon plugger

Melon scoop
"Ontario Knife Co."

Grape-Nuts Bread
1 loaf

- 2 cups flour
- 2 tsp. baking powder
- 1 tsp. salt
- 1 cup Grape-Nuts cereal
- 1½ cups sour milk
- 1 tsp. baking soda
- ¾ cup brown sugar
- 1 egg, beaten
- 2 Tblsp. melted butter

Sift flour, baking powder & salt. Mix Grape-Nuts, sour milk & baking soda. Let stand 5 minutes. Add brown sugar & egg. Blend well. Gradually add sifted ingredients, then butter. Pour into well-greased 9" x 5" x 3" loaf pan. Bake at

350° one hour, or until done.

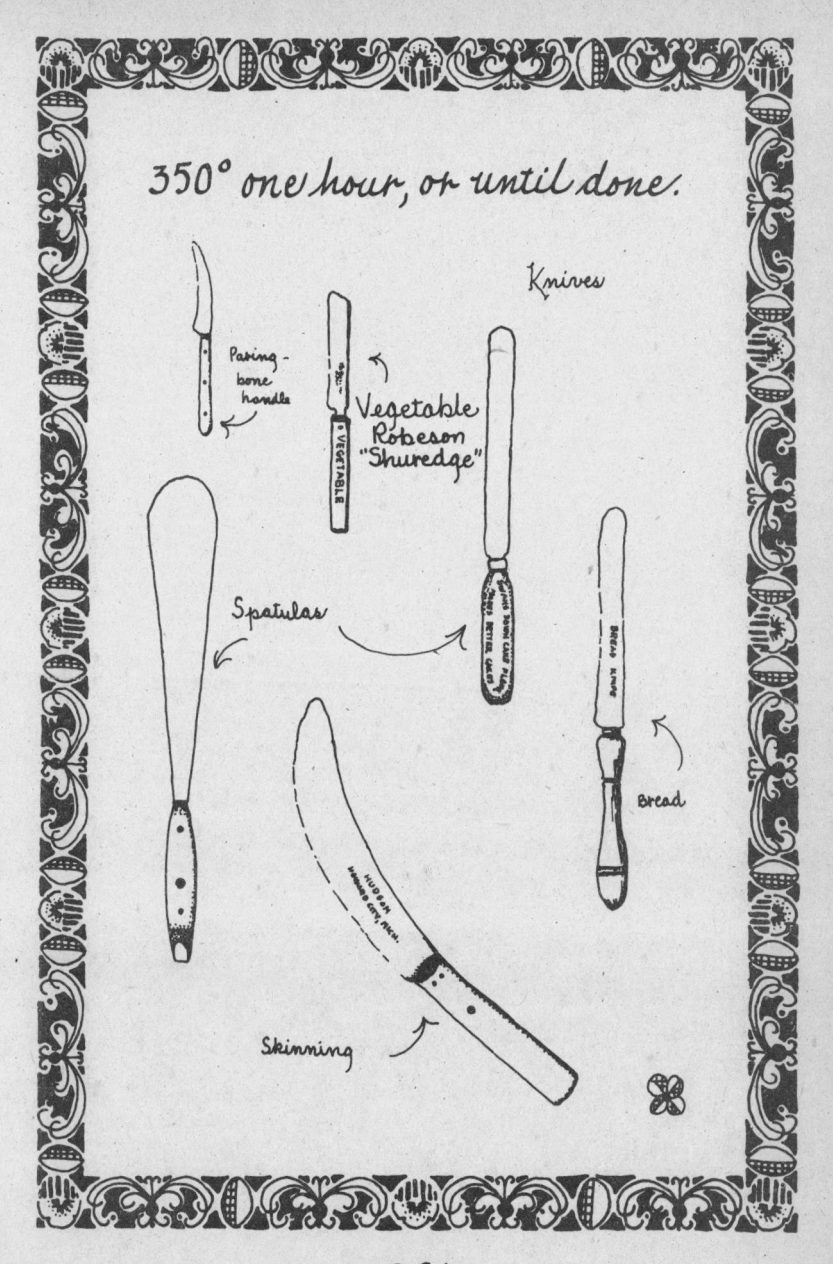

Knives

Paring – bone handle

Vegetable Robeson "Shuredge"

Spatulas

Bread

Skinning

281

Mincemeat Bread
1 loaf

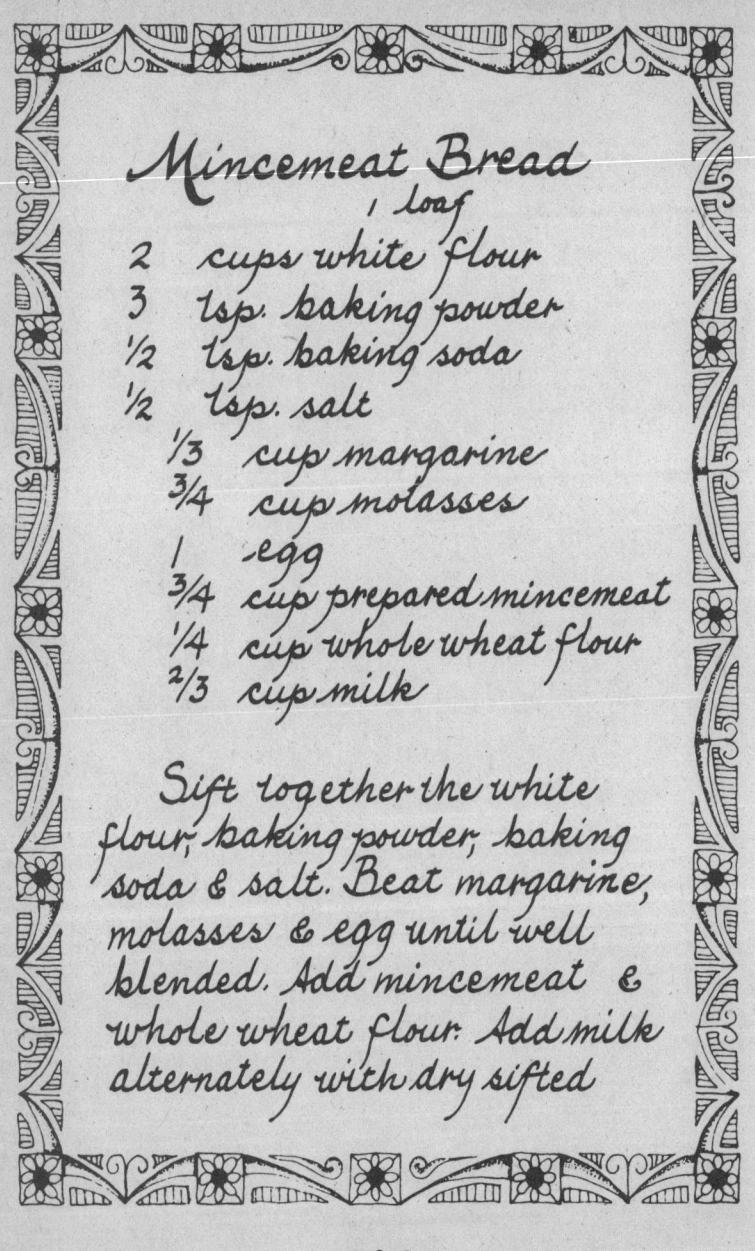

- 2 cups white flour
- 3 tsp. baking powder
- ½ tsp. baking soda
- ½ tsp. salt
- ⅓ cup margarine
- ¾ cup molasses
- 1 egg
- ¾ cup prepared mincemeat
- ¼ cup whole wheat flour
- ⅔ cup milk

Sift together the white flour, baking powder, baking soda & salt. Beat margarine, molasses & egg until well blended. Add mincemeat & whole wheat flour. Add milk alternately with dry sifted ingredients. Pour into well-greased 9" x 5" x 3" loaf pan. Bake at 375° for 30-35 minutes or until tested done.

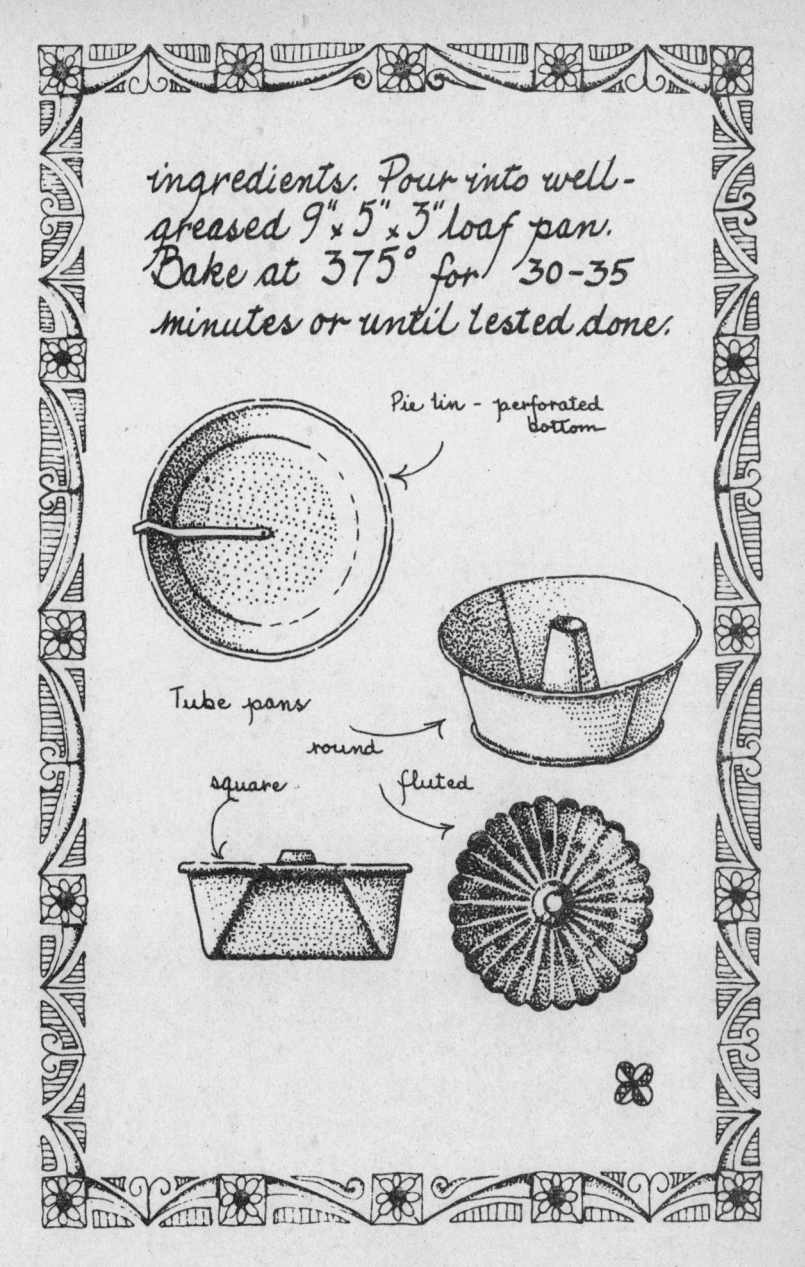

Pie tin - perforated bottom

Tube pans
round
square
fluted

Oatmeal Bread
1 loaf

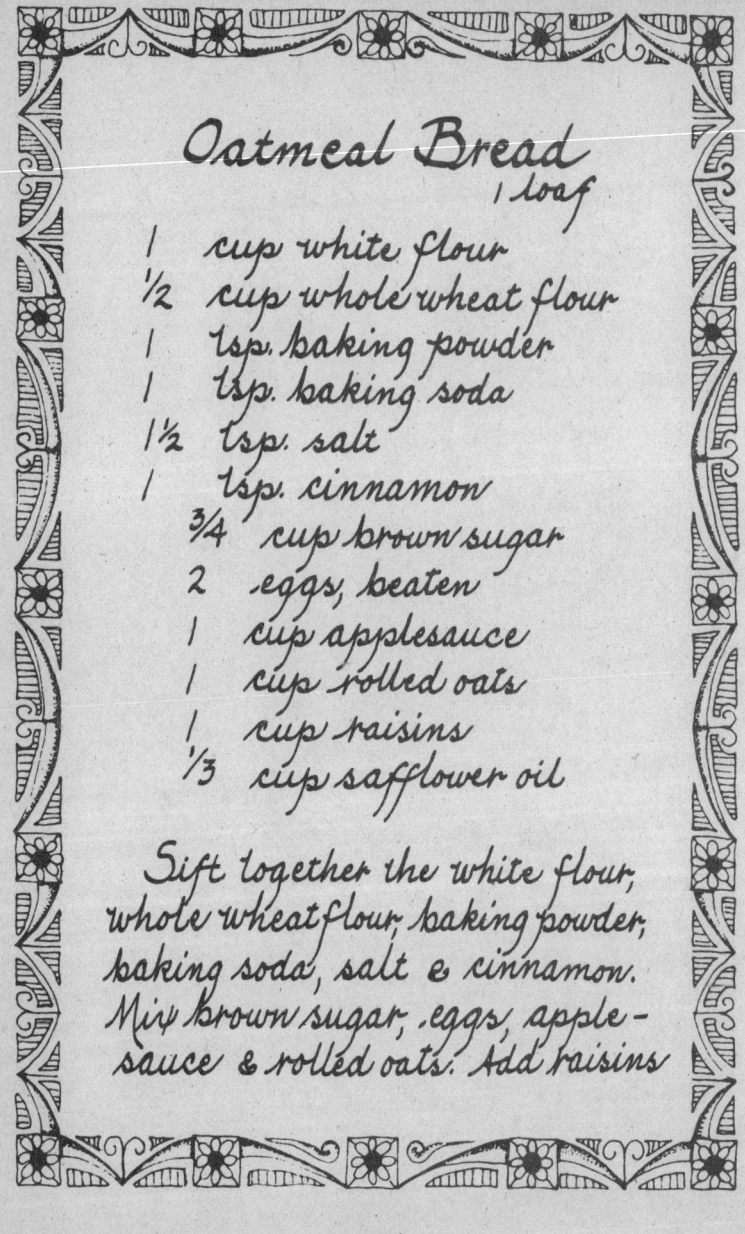

- 1 cup white flour
- ½ cup whole wheat flour
- 1 tsp. baking powder
- 1 tsp. baking soda
- 1½ tsp. salt
- 1 tsp. cinnamon
- ¾ cup brown sugar
- 2 eggs, beaten
- 1 cup applesauce
- 1 cup rolled oats
- 1 cup raisins
- ⅓ cup safflower oil

Sift together the white flour, whole wheat flour, baking powder, baking soda, salt & cinnamon. Mix brown sugar, eggs, applesauce & rolled oats. Add raisins

& safflower oil, then sifted ingredients. Mix only until blended. Pour into well-greased loaf pan 9" x 5" x 3". Bake at 350° one hour or until done.

Aluminum spice container

Cream pitcher
beige crockery,
blue stripes

Prune Bread
1 loaf

2 cups flour
1 tsp. baking soda
1 tsp. baking powder
1 tsp. cinnamon
1 tsp. allspice
1 tsp. nutmeg
1 tsp. salt
1½ cups brown sugar
3 eggs, beaten
1 cup safflower oil
1 cup buttermilk
1 tsp. vanilla
½ cup chopped nuts
1 cup cooked, chopped prunes

Sift flour, baking soda & powder, cinnamon, allspice, nutmeg & salt. Mix brown sugar, eggs, oil, buttermilk & vanilla. Blend well. Gradually add sifted ingredients. Add nuts & prunes. Pour into well-greased 9" x 5" x 3" loaf pan. Bake at 350° about 50-60 minutes.

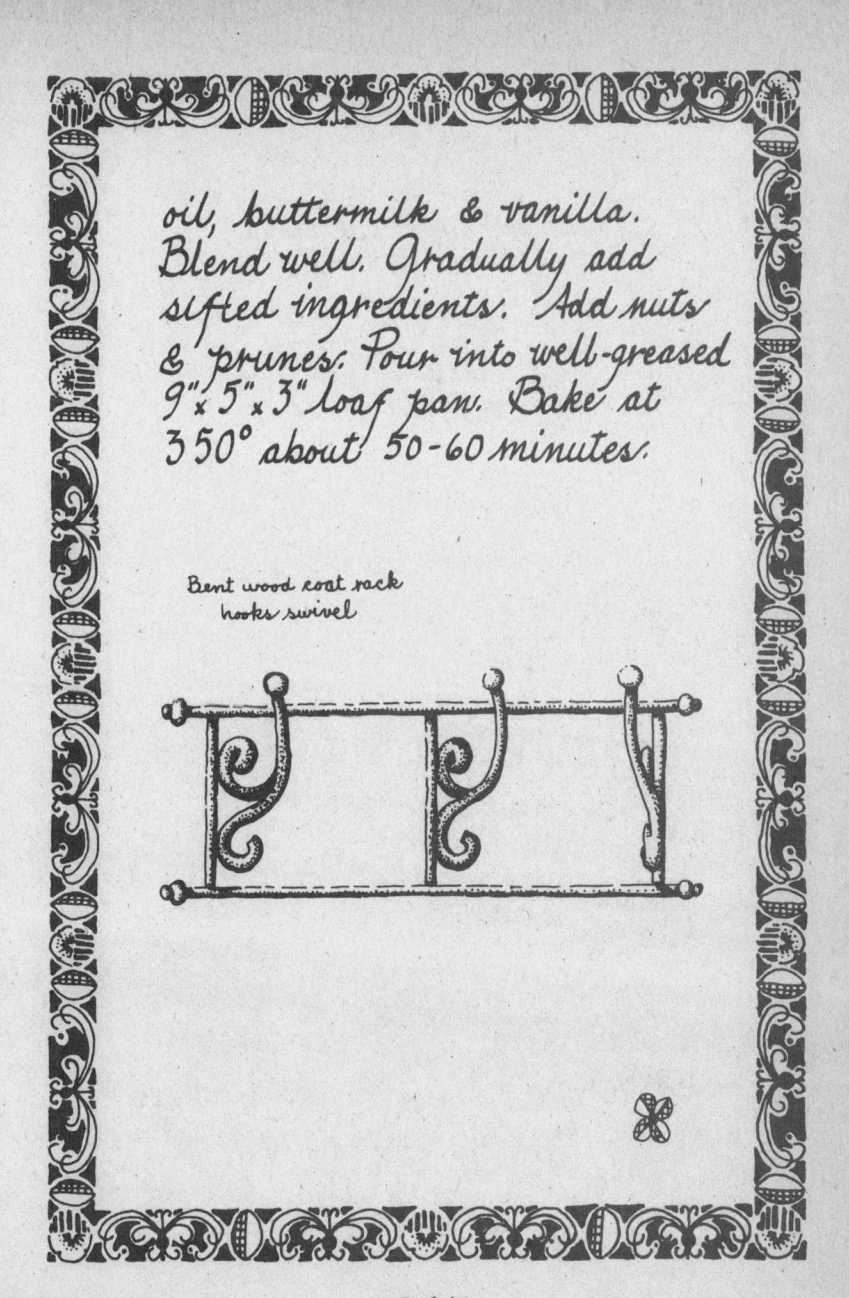

Bent wood coat rack hooks swivel

Pumpkin Bread
2 loaves

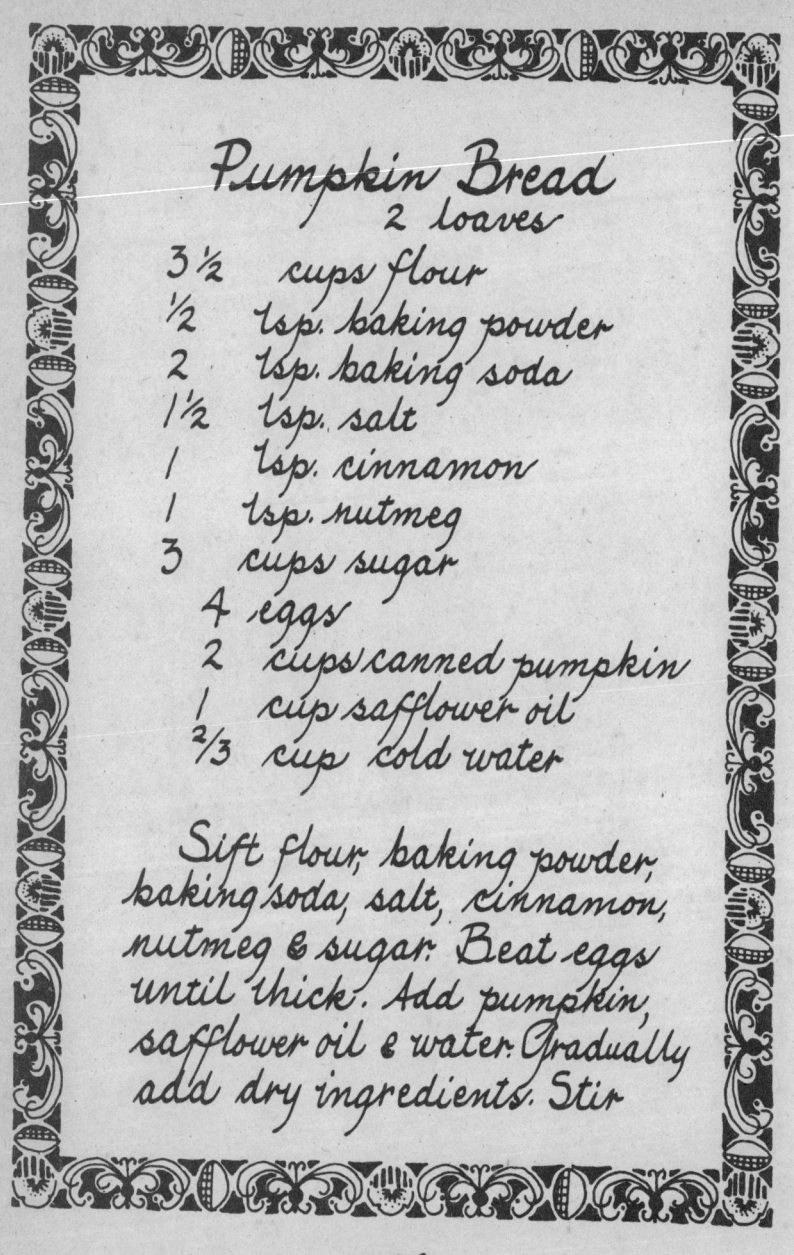

- 3½ cups flour
- ½ tsp. baking powder
- 2 tsp. baking soda
- 1½ tsp. salt
- 1 tsp. cinnamon
- 1 tsp. nutmeg
- 3 cups sugar
- 4 eggs
- 2 cups canned pumpkin
- 1 cup safflower oil
- ⅔ cup cold water

Sift flour, baking powder, baking soda, salt, cinnamon, nutmeg & sugar. Beat eggs until thick. Add pumpkin, safflower oil & water. Gradually add dry ingredients. Stir only until blended. Pour into 2 well-greased 9"x 5"x 3" loaf pans. Bake at 350° for one hour or until tested done.

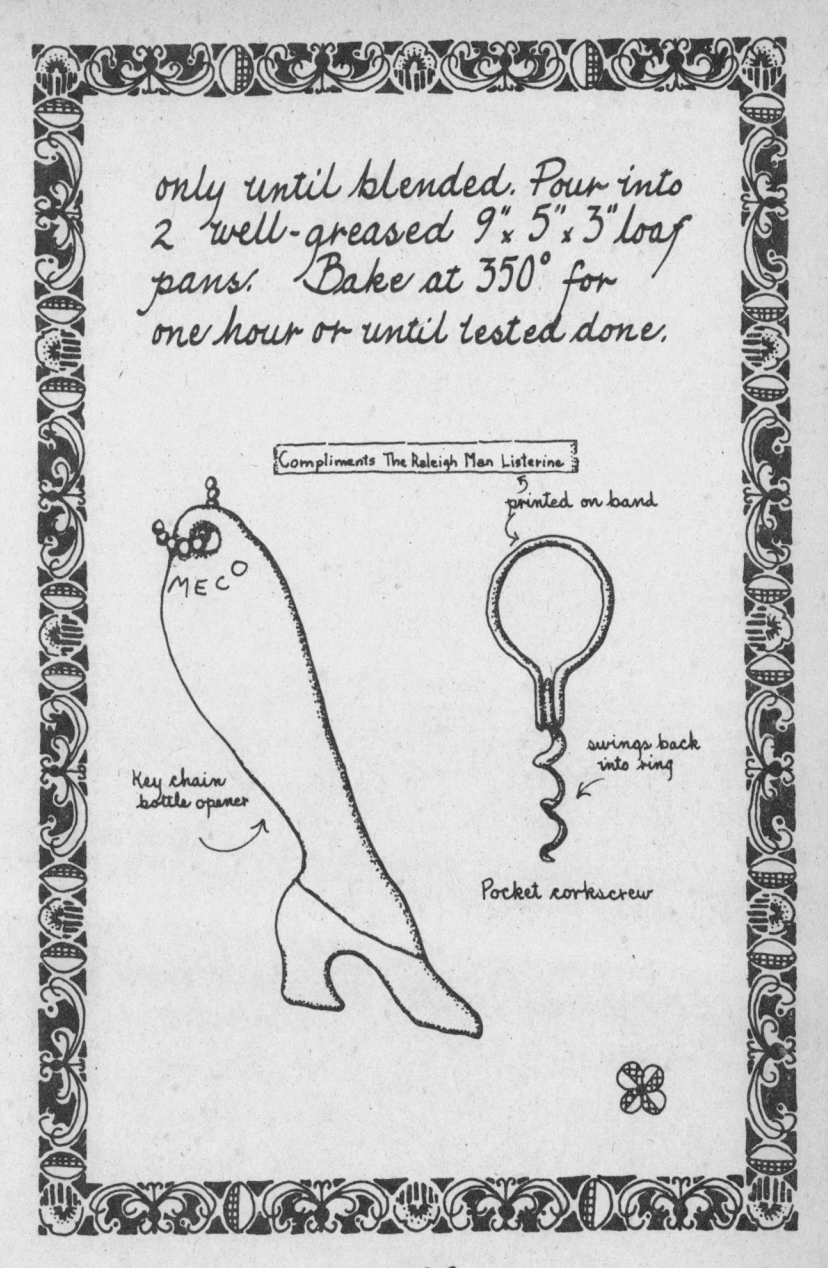

Compliments The Raleigh Man Listerine
printed on band

MECO

Key chain bottle opener

swings back into ring

Pocket corkscrew

Wheat Germ Bread
1 loaf

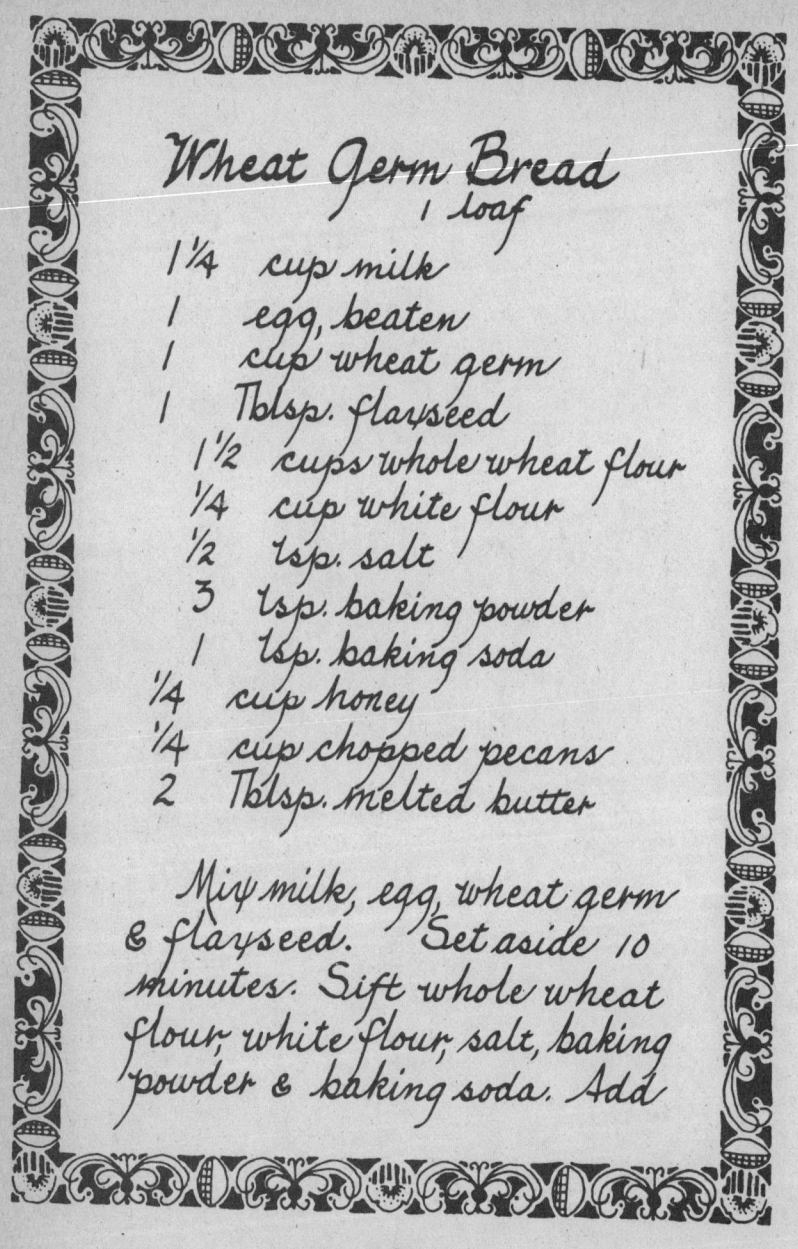

- 1¼ cup milk
- 1 egg, beaten
- 1 cup wheat germ
- 1 Tblsp. flaxseed
- 1½ cups whole wheat flour
- ¼ cup white flour
- ½ tsp. salt
- 3 tsp. baking powder
- 1 tsp. baking soda
- ¼ cup honey
- ¼ cup chopped pecans
- 2 Tblsp. melted butter

Mix milk, egg, wheat germ & flaxseed. Set aside 10 minutes. Sift whole wheat flour, white flour, salt, baking powder & baking soda. Add honey to the milk mixture, then add sifted ingredients. Add pecans & butter. Mix until just blended. Pour into well-greased 8½" x 4½" x 2½" loaf pan. Bake at 350° for 50-60 minutes or until done.

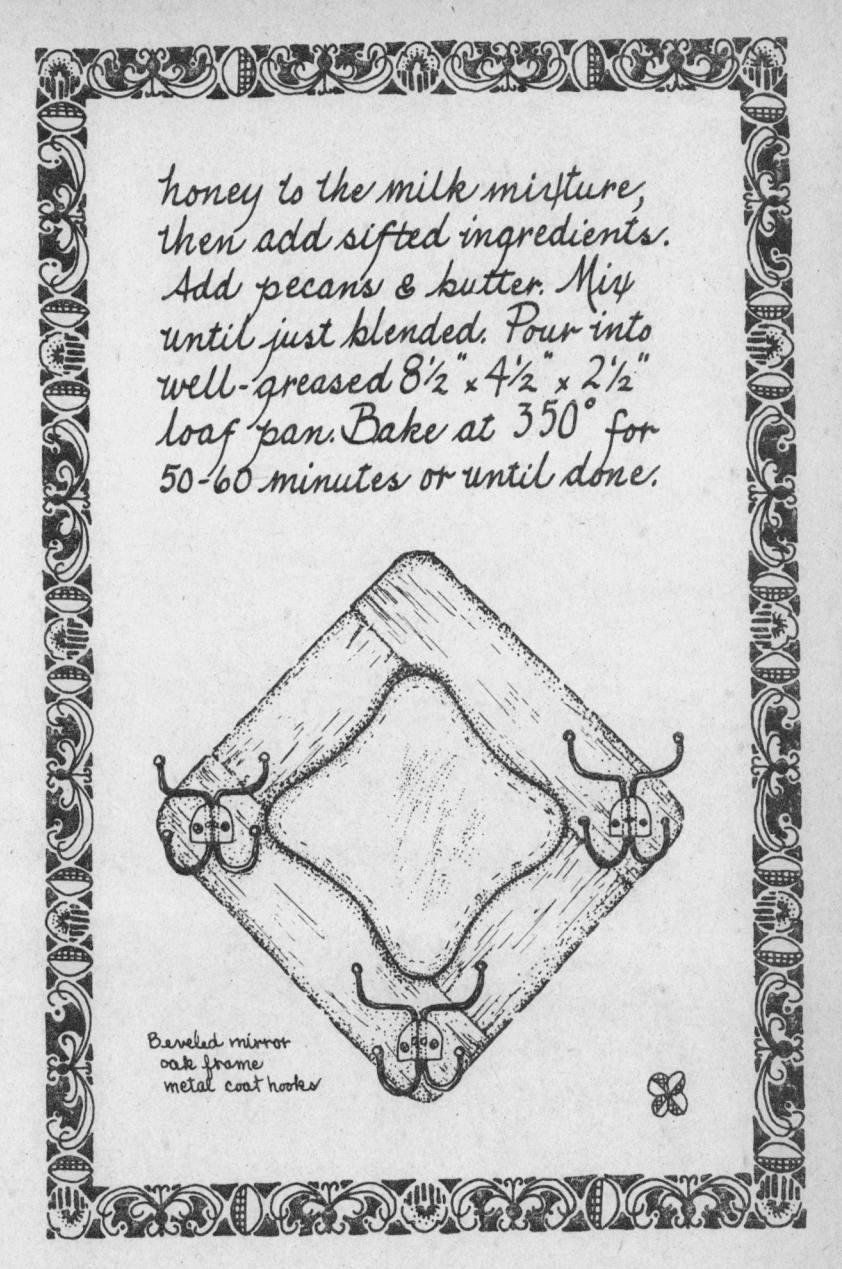

Beveled mirror
oak frame
metal coat hooks

Yogurt Bread
1 loaf

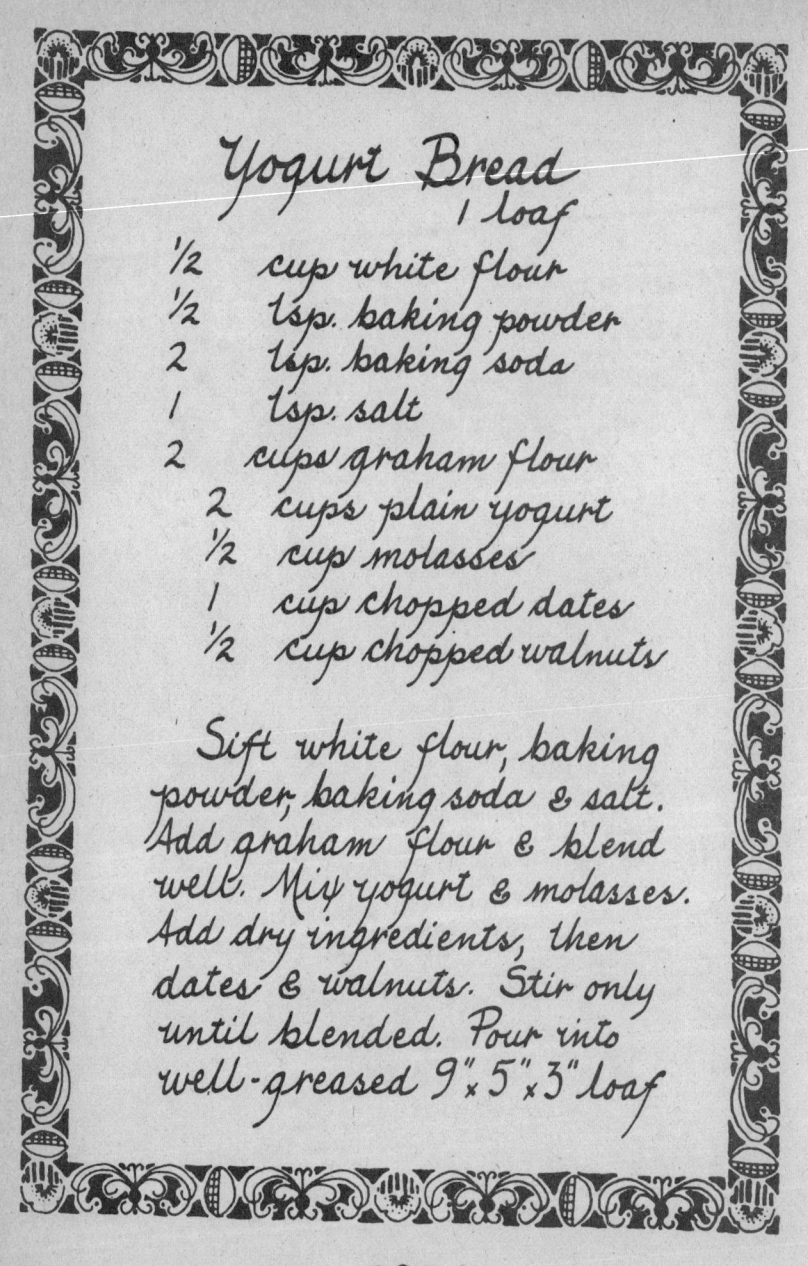

- ½ cup white flour
- ½ tsp. baking powder
- 2 tsp. baking soda
- 1 tsp. salt
- 2 cups graham flour
- 2 cups plain yogurt
- ½ cup molasses
- 1 cup chopped dates
- ½ cup chopped walnuts

Sift white flour, baking powder, baking soda & salt. Add graham flour & blend well. Mix yogurt & molasses. Add dry ingredients, then dates & walnuts. Stir only until blended. Pour into well-greased 9"x 5"x 3" loaf pan. Bake at 350° about one hour or until tested done.

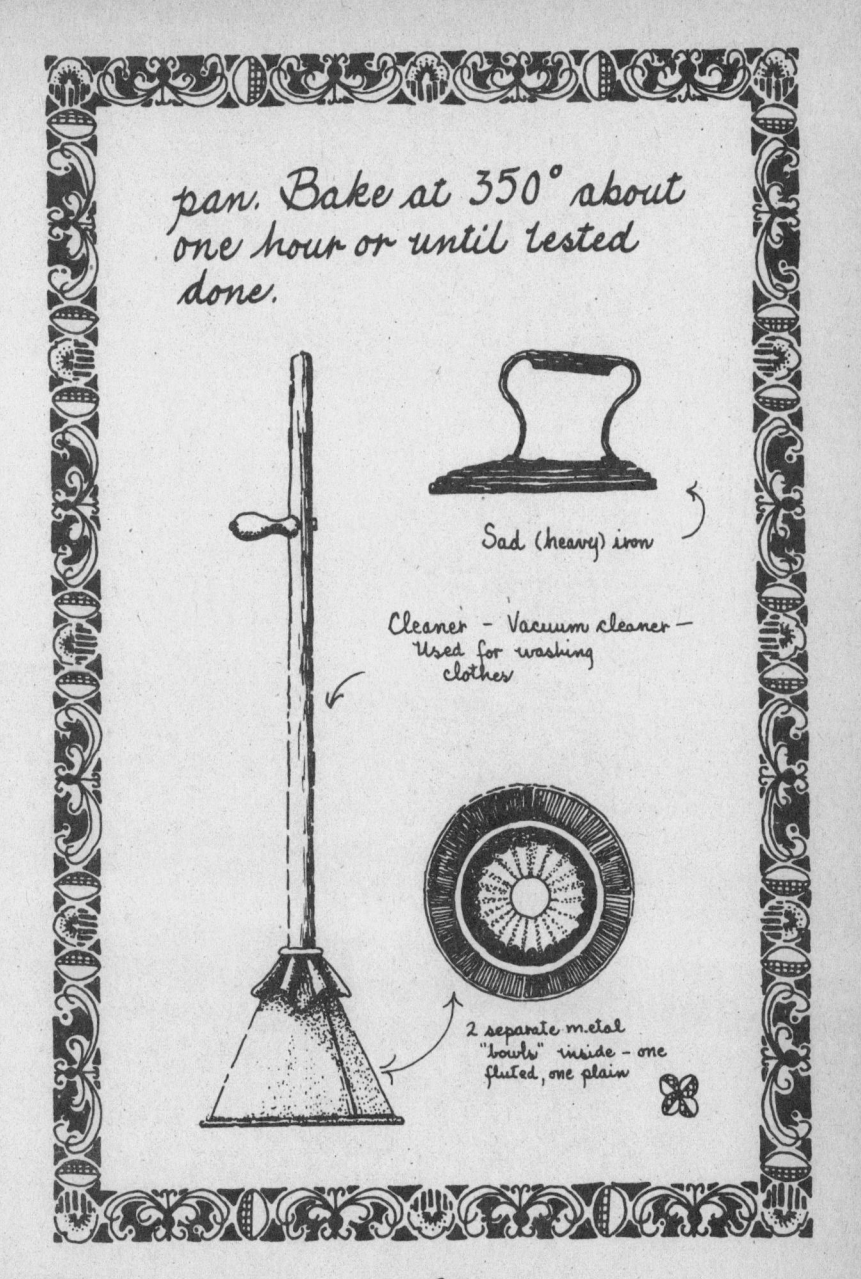

Sad (heavy) iron

Cleaner - Vacuum cleaner - Used for washing clothes

2 separate metal "bowls" inside - one fluted, one plain

Index

A

Almond
  Cracker Pie Crust, 111
  Squares, Honey, 88

Anise
  Bread, 200
  Drops, 8
  Pie, Pear, 124

Apple
  Pie, Dried, 120
  Pie, Fancy, 118
  Squares, 56

Apple Butter
  Bread, 250
  Pie, 122

Apricot
  Pie, Dried, 130
  Pie, Fresh, 132
  Squares, 58

B

Baked Alaska
  Pie, 162
Baking Crust
  Without Filling, 104
Baking Powder
  Bread, 252
Banana
  Cream Pie, 126
  Marshmallow
    Pie, 128
  Nut Bread, 254
Blackberry Jam
  Bread, 256
Blueberry
  Bread, 258
  Peach Pie, 134
  Pie, 136
Bran
  Bread (quick), 260
  Bread (yeast), 202
Breads, 197-293
Brownie Squares, 60
Buttermilk Pie, 178
Butter Nut
  Cookies, 10
Butterscotch
  Squares, 62

C

California
    Squares, 64
Candied Fruit
    Bread, 262
Caraway
    Cookies, 12
Carrot
    Bread, 264
    Cookies, 14
Cereal Squares, 66
Cheese
    Bread, 266
    Pie, 182
    Squares, 68
Cherry
    Cookies, 16
    Pie, 142
    Squares, 70
Chess Pie, 184
Chewer's
    Squares, 72
Chocolate
    Mint Pie, 188
    Mint Squares, 74
    Pie, Frozen, 186
    Potato Bread, 268
    Wafers, 18
Coarse Bread, 270
Coarse Rye
    Bread, 204

Cocoa Pie Crust, 114
Cocoanut
    Cream Pie, 180
    Squares, 76
Coffee Bread, 272
Concord Grape
    Pie, 144
Cookies, 7-53
Cracked Wheat
    Bread, 206
Crackling Bread, 274
Cranberry
    Orange Bread, 276
    Pie, 146
    Squares, 78
Creamy Peanut
    Squares, 80

D

Date
    Nut Pie, 164
    Rolls, 20
    Squares, 82
Decorating Pies, 105
Dried Apple Pie, 120
Dried Apricot
    Pie, 130

E

Easy Pie Crust, 108
Easy White Bread, 208
English Cookies, 22

F

Fancy Apple Pie, 118
Figaroons, 24
Fig Bread, 278
Filbert Squares, 84
French Bread, 210
Fresh Apricot Pie, 132
Fresh Berry Pie, 138
Fresh Lime Pie, 158
Fresh Peach Pie, 132
Frozen Chocolate Pie, 186

G

Ginger Snaps, 26

Gluten Bread, 212
Grape-Nuts Bread, 280
Gumdrop Cookies, 28

H

Hermits, 30
Hints
　Breads (quick), 249
　Breads (yeast), 199
　Pie Crusts, 102-105
Honey
　Almond Squares, 88
　Squares, 86

L

Lard Pie Crust, 108
Lattice Strips, How to Make, 105
Leftover Pie Crust, Using, 103
Licorice Cookies, 32

M

Meringue,
   Perfect, 116
Mincemeat
   Bread, 282
   Squares, 90
Mint
   Pie, Chocolate, 188
   Squares,
     Chocolate, 74
Mixed Fruit Pie, 140
Mock Macaroons, 34
Molasses Pie, 190

N

Nat's Bread, 214
Never Fail Pie
   Crust, 110
Not-So-Sweet
   Pecan Pie, 174
Nut Crust, 107

O

Oatmeal
   Bread (quick), 284
   Bread (yeast), 216
Orange
   Bread, Cranberry, 276
   Candy Squares, 92
   Pie Crust, 112

P

Peach
   Pie, Blueberry, 134
   Pie, Fresh, 132
Peanut
   Brittle Pie, 172
   Brittle Pie Crust, 113
   Butter Balls, 36
   Butter Dots, 38
   Butter Pie, 170
   Pie, 168

Squares, Creamy, 80
Pear Anise Pie, 124
Pecan
Pie, Not-So-Sweet, 174
Pie, Pumpkin, 166
Squares, 94
Perfect Meringue, 116
Persimmon Cookies, 40
Pie Crusts, 106-114
Pie Crust Hints, 102-105
Pies, 101-195
Pineapple
Cookies, 42
Pie, 160
Squares, 96
Plain Pie Crust, 106
Polish Easter Bread, 218
Potato
Bread, 220
Bread, Chocolate, 268
Pie, Sweet, 194
Prune
Bread, 286
Pie, 148
Pumpkin
Bread, 288
Cookies, 44
Pecan Pie, 166

Q . . .

Quick Breads, 247-293
Quick Breads Hints, 249

R . . .

Raisin Pie, 152
Rhubarb Custard Pie, 154
Rich Lemon Pie, 156
Ripe Currant Pie, 150
Rye
Bread, Coarse, 204
Bread, Sour, 236
Bread, Swedish, 240

S

Saffron Bread, 222
Salt-Rising Bread, 224
Sesame Seed Cookies, 46
Shoofly Pie, 192
Skillet Cookies, 48
Sourdough
　Bread, 228
　French Bread, 230
　Herb Bread, 232
　Pumpernickel Bread, 234
　Starter, 226
Sour Rye Bread, 236
Squares, 55-99
Squash Bread, 238
Swedish Rye Bread, 240
Sweet Potato Pie, 194

T

Toffee Squares, 98
Tropical Cookies, 50

W

Walnut Pie, 176
Wheat Germ
　Bread (quick), 290
　Bread (yeast), 242
　Cookies, 52
Whole Wheat Pie Crust, 114

Y

Yeast Breads, 197-245
Yogurt
　Bread (quick), 292
　Bread (yeast), 244

300